THE ESSENTIAL STEINER

RUDOLF STEINER

THE ESSENTIAL
STEINER

Basic Writings of Rudolf Steiner

Edited and Introduced by

ROBERT A. McDERMOTT

1817

Harper & Row, Publishers, San Francisco

Cambridge, Hagerstown, New York, Philadelphia
London, Mexico City, São Paulo, Sydney

FIRST EDITION

Designer: Jim Mennick

Library of Congress Cataloging in Publication Data

Steiner, Rudolf, 1861–1925.
THE ESSENTIAL STEINER.

Bibliography: p.
Includes index.
1. Anthroposophy—Addresses, essays, lectures. 2. Steiner, Rudolf, 1861–1925 —Addresses, essays, lectures. I. McDermott, Robert A. II. Title.
BP595.S85112 1984   299'.935   82-48943
ISBN 0-06-065345-0

---

84 85 86 87 88 10 9 8 7 6 5 4 3 2

for Anthroposophia

Contents

Preface

This book is intended as an introduction to the thought and writings of Rudolf Steiner, the Austrian-born philosopher, scientist, artist, and educator. The book consists of the editor's introduction to Steiner's life and work, twenty-five selections from Steiner's writings, a sixty-four page guide to further reading, and a bibliography of books by Steiner and authors influenced by him. Since the 250 pages of Steiner's writings reprinted in this anthology comprise less than one one-hundredth of his writings available in English, such a selection is necessarily somewhat subjective. There could be a dozen or more "essential Steiner" anthologies without duplication. In the editor's judgment, each selection in this so-called essential Steiner meets the following criteria: intelligible to a college-level reader; representative of an important segment of Steiner's thought; interesting or revealing in its own right. Each selection, whether a chapter or a lecture, is reprinted in its entirety without omission or abridgment.

The editor's introduction discusses the reasons why Steiner is not yet well known among academics and informed American readers, and attempts to introduce the broad range of Steiner's contributions to thought and culture. Since the reader's understanding of Steiner's life and thought will necessarily be influenced by the editor's introductions and choice of selections, a few words about his perspective and purpose might be useful. Unlike the editor's introduction and guide to further reading, the remainder of this section is written in the first person, in conformity with the personal nature of the topic.

With training in philosophy (Ph.D., Boston University), I have taught comparative philosophy and religion at Manhattanville College (1964–71) and Baruch College, The City University of

New York (1971–82), and am presently assistant provost at Baruch College. I have published scholarly articles and books on modern religious thought, including *The Essential Aurobindo* (Schocken Books, 1973). It was not until 1975, after I had taught comparative philosophy and religion for eleven years, had read widely and traveled around the world twice, that I came across the name of Rudolf Steiner for the first time.

During six years of daily walks between Grand Central Station and my office on 26th Street and Park Avenue South, I had managed not to visit the bookstore and national library of the Anthroposophical Society, then housed on the second floor of 211 Madison Avenue at 35th Street. In the spring of 1975, when I was sent by a friend to purchase Theodor Schwenk's *Sensitive Chaos,* I was astonished to find a bookstore featuring more than one hundred works on esoteric and spiritual subjects by a modern Western author whose name was entirely unknown to me. I was a bit suspicious to encounter an author of books on such diverse subjects as Goethe, education, sculpture, metals, bees, angels, art, western history, and farming. Since I regarded myself as an expert on the *Bhagavad Gita,* I accepted the sensible advice of the librarian, Fred Paddock, and returned home with Steiner's two books on the *Bhagavad Gita,* both of which proved to be fascinating and impressive.

I spent the next year (1975–76) as a senior Fulbright lecturer at the Open University in England, where I regularly attended lectures and discussions at Steiner House in London, took a course in Eurythmy, and began a serious study of Steiner's writings. Eight years and two hundred books later I can attest, with undiminished surprise and delight, that I have yet to find a work by Rudolf Steiner that I consider derivative or pedestrian.

In the summer of 1978 I attended the Rudolf Steiner Institute as a student, and had the good fortune of taking a course in the history of consciousness given by Stewart Easton. At the Rudolf Steiner Institute each summer since 1979, I have taught a course in history of Western philosophy from Steiner's perspective, and I have had the opportunity to discuss Steiner's teaching and spiritual significance with professors and others steeped in Anthroposophy.

There are hundreds of anthroposophists who know Steiner's writings and teachings far better than I. On the other hand, those whose lives are totally devoted to practical aspects of Steiner's teachings are simply too absorbed in the demands and rewards of their work in anthroposophical settings to bring this work to the attention of the academic and the larger reading public. Further, anthroposophists steeped in Steiner's teachings, particularly those who live in constant contact with fellow anthroposophists, tend to lose contact with nonanthroposophical thinking. Since Steiner's teachings are so broad and rich, with virtually unlimited scope for applications and expansions, groups dedicated to anthroposophical ideals seem to me generally less parochial and intolerant than similar spiritual movements. It can hardly be denied, however, that such communities develop their own language, frame of reference, shared assumptions, and limited contact with other modes of thought. This tendency toward a distinctinve set of assumptions and mode of discourse is further compounded by the fact that Steiner's writings are so vast, his thought so complex and deep, that most of his disciples are unwilling to venture into print without the benefit of a lifetime of study. Predictably, individuals who have been studying Steiner for a lifetime can scarcely believe that someone armed with only a few years of study would attempt to edit a book audaciously entitled *The Essential Steiner*. Yet, many of these same lifelong anthroposophists are the ones who recognize both the need for such a book and the improbability that it will be produced by one whose entire life has been spent in anthroposophical communities.

If some anthroposophists regard me as too new to Anthroposophy and too much in the academic world, academics and general readers may find me too enthusiastic about Steiner and Anthroposophy. Bridge-building, particularly between the academic world and a spiritual-esoteric thinker, is a risky venture. Although not everyone who reads this book will accept its claims by and about Steiner, everyone can benefit by an honest confrontation with these claims. Given the extent to which the contemporary intellectual climate militates against acceptance of a spiritual philosophy, it would seem to be justified to present Steiner's teachings in a positive light. A more compelling reason for my positive presentation is simply that Steiner's teachings seem to me well grounded and creatively applied.

R. A. McD.

Rye, New York
Novemeber 1983

Acknowledgments

While I cannot list all of the kindnesses extended to me while editing this volume, allow me to express my gratitude to those individuals who most significantly contributed either to my education or to the improvement of this edition:

Both for numerous conversations and for his important writings, I am most grateful to Stewart C. Easton.

I am especially grateful to Fred Paddock, Librarian of the Anthroposophical Society, and to David Adams, an art historian in Spring Valley, New York, both of whom made valuable suggestions on every page of the Guide to Further Reading and Bibliography.

Many faculty and board members of the Rudolf Steiner Institute, including Clopper Almon, Donald Bufano, Robert and Deborah Hill, Terry Neville, Herbert Koepf, Hans Gebert, John Hunter, J. Leonard Benson, and Georg Ungar offered valuable advice. James Hindes, Shirley Latessa and Werner Glas also made helpful suggestions.

Steven Usher, Managing Director of Anthroposophic Press, and Erdmutte Lloyd, Director of the Rudolf Steiner Press, facilitated arrangements concerning the use of copyrighted material. John Whalen and Jacob Needleman led me to John Loudon, editor at Harper & Row.

My research on Rudolf Steiner was greatly aided by my colleagues at Baruch College, including Martin Stevens, Dean of the School of Liberal Arts and Sciences, who directed a release-time program for faculty research; Philip E. Austin, Provost, who provided encouragement and a flexible schedule; Pauline Blacker and several typists in our Wang office, who transformed a steady stream of scribbled pages into manuscript.

All of my work is nourished by my wife, Ellen Dineen, and our children, Darren and Deirdre.

General Introduction:
Rudolf Steiner's Life and Work

Approaching Rudolf Steiner

If, as his followers claim, Rudolf Steiner is a genius in twelve fields, why do we not come across his name in colleges, in scholarly writings, and in the popular press? Experts in each of the fields in which he worked—including history, philosophy, science, art, social sciences, education, and Gospel commentary —seem equally unaware of his work. It is tempting to assume that the only possible reason for this neglect must be that Steiner's writings are either inferior or idiosyncratic. In fact, however, Steiner's contributions in these fields have not been rejected so much as ignored. Admittedly, readers of straight academic and mass-media materials have good reason to be wary of writings on such topics as karma and rebirth, etheric and astral bodies, and claims of knowledge of the cooperation between the Buddha and St. Francis in the spiritual world. Steiner's claims to privileged knowledge immediately, and rightly, render his writings suspect. It is neither surprising nor unfortunate that occult or esoteric thinkers are subject to special scrutiny.[1] Steiner himself wel-

---

1. In *Unfinished Animal: The Aquarian Frontier and the Evolution of Consciousness* (New York: Harper & Row, 1975), Theodore Roszak similarly observed:

   Conventional intellect continues to withhold its attentions from such gurus of the occult as Madame Blavatsky, Rudolf Steiner, and George Gurdjieff, for these are indeed eccentric minds that lack all the usual academic courtesies. Their philosophies draw with unrestricted license upon myth, legend, personal vision, and antique lore; and each claims access to privileged sources of knowledge available only to loyal initiates and disciples—hardly a style calculated to win the favor of skeptics or positivist critics.

   Yet, if we search the strange mythological extrapolations of these occult evolutionists to discover the vision they offer of human potentiality, we may,

comed such scrutiny, and in fact insisted that his claims ought not be accepted as a matter of belief. He referred to his teaching as spiritual science precisely because he practiced and advocated a phenomenological, or empirical, approach to the spiritual world.

Steiner would not object to an evaluation of his teachings on the basis of their practical applications in science, art, education, religion, and other areas where he has been influential. In the marketplace of truth and practical results, Steiner can afford to recommend his works and his followers with the same line as was used by Jesus concerning Christians: "By their fruits you shall know them." Steiner's followers worldwide number in the thousands, including many physicians, scientists, artists, teachers, and community workers. These individuals have created and maintain biodynamic farms, villages for people in need of special care, and thousands of schools including a recently founded German university with a doctoral program, law school, and medical school all approved by the Federal Republic of Germany. This list could be extended and elaborated. Suffice it to say that a quick survey of Steiner's writings and activities based on his thought (see Guide to Further Reading) will provide a convincing overview of the extent to which Steiner's Spiritual Science has proved productive of significant practical works.

The great religious figures, whether Buddha and Shankara or Jesus and St. Francis, did not seek primarily to found religious institutions and generate practical works, but to effect the kind of spiritual transformation for which practical works are the arena and the by-product. Similarly, Steiner's entire life may be seen as an attempt to solve the pressing problems of individual and social life, but his primary purpose was to show that long-range solutions require a spiritual foundation. It is primarily with respect to these foundations and secondarily their practical applications that Steiner wishes his followers to be empirical. In his lifelong at-

---

at the very least, find them among the most innovative psychologists of our time. In their work we see the evolutionary image being used for the first time in the modern West as a new standard of human sanity—or rather, as a newly discovered standard, for to a degree that far surpasses the work of Nietzsche or Bergson, they remain unabashedly loyal to the schools of the Hidden Wisdom, and so link contemporary thought on human potentiality with a rich basis in tradition (pp. 115–16).

tempt to establish a spiritual mode of knowledge, he sought neither admiration for his work nor belief in his teachings. Steiner was sufficiently sober concerning human nature, and particularly the limitations of disciples, to know that all but a few of those who come upon his teachings will focus on their practical results and neglect the disciplined source of these works. Steiner knew that disciples would focus more on his ideas than on practicing the discipline of his method for verifying and advancing his findings. During his own lifetime he witnessed the extent to which disciples would neglect his ideas and focus on Steiner himself as a spiritual phenomenon to be quoted and used as a defense against the ravages of confusion and chaos.

At every turn Steiner himself urged that his readers and others interested in his works look to the mode of spiritual perception that made both his knowledge and his work possible. He insisted that his distinctively contemporary Western spiritual teaching is committed to hard-earned spiritual and practical knowledge, not worshipful devotion, quiescent meditation, or traditional religious belief. On first view, it might appear that Steiner is simply repeating the spiritual teachings of the great world religions, but a closer look at Spiritual Science, or Anthroposophy, shows that its purpose is to bring to humanity an entirely new capability— knowledge of the spiritual world by conscious sense-free thinking.

Steiner regards his teaching as scientific because he maintains that anyone who conscientiously cultivates sense-free thinking will gradually attain knowledge of the higher or the spiritual world. At this point, we face the same apparent contradiction as is found in all spiritual teachings: because all but a tiny minority of humanity is capable of pursuing a spiritual discipline such as has been taught by the Buddha, Krishna, or Jesus, it is necessary to begin with more ordinary, frankly selfish, means and ends. Predictably, most of Steiner's followers bring to his spiritual teaching a variety of lower-level perspectives such as admiration for his practical achievements or belief in his teachings. Ultimately, however, followers and disciples will be limited to secondhand insights and experiences unless and until they pursue the disciplines such as the ones Steiner recommends. As Gotama the Buddha and Krishna of the Bhagavad Gita well knew, disciples want to emulate the spiritual power and wisdom of their masters, but they will not progress in this effort until they begin transforming ordinary motivations and activities. Similarly, followers of Rudolf Steiner will have to focus on the fact that his vast riches of knowledge and seemingly effortless power over diverse human activities are not the aim but the by-product of his painstaking spiritual discipline.

Anthroposophy may be thought of as a lofty spiritual disclosure and methodology which can be reached by any one of several paths. At the present time in America, the greatest number who come to Steiner's teachings do so through contact with Waldorf education. It is also possible to hear about Steiner through his contributions to farming, medicine, architecture, and eurythmy, or through the work of one of his interpreters such as Owen Barfield. Although Steiner recommended that the task of the present age is to replace faith or belief by spiritual knowledge, some amount of belief is necessary in order to take the initial step toward an inquiry concerning the basis of his myriad contributions. A reader of these pages who confidently rejects the possibility of spiritual knowledge—the kind of knowledge which Steiner apparently possessed and recommended to others—will presumably not read this book with profit, and will probably not read it at all. Even readers impressed by Steiner's productivity may prefer to ignore the possibility of a supersensible source for novel theories concerning the phenomenon of color, soil preparation, and the education of emotionally disturbed children. Close examination, however, will show the intimate relationship between Steiner's spiritual power, his original teachings, his richly varied contributions, and his increasingly effective successors.

Since the entire area of the esoteric or occult has been overpopulated by claims and counterclaims for which we have no satisfactory criteria and little or no verification, it is difficult to distinguish the genuine clairvoyant ("clear-seer"), or spiritual scientist, from the peddler of arrant nonsense. It is at this point that practical applications of Steiner's teachings can be helpful. If a person comes to respect a system of education which includes several hundred schools, with dedicated and competent faculty, with impressively educated graduates, it becomes reasonable to inquire about the basis of this educational system. Although most observers will no doubt settle for the educational results without regard to the theoretical basis of the curriculum and pedagogy, anyone who inquires further will gain some sense of how the same spiritual teacher who generated the Waldorf School Movement and dozens of volumes on the theory and practice of education, also generated hundreds of books on philosophy, psychology, science, art, and Christian exegesis.

The same phenomenon occurs in other areas as well: many farmers and gardeners have concluded that Steiner's method of soil preparation (for a compost heap) seems to be demonstrably more effective than fertilizer or any other method, but fewer are inclined to take up Steiner's teachings on the etheric or formative forces in the soil. In a more subtle way, it is also possible to read and marvel at Steiner's disclosures concerning great spiritual figures such as Buddha, Krishna, Moses, Jesus, John the Beloved Disciple, St. Paul, and many others without seriously investigating or attempting to imitate the method by which he was able to attain knowledge of past events recorded in the spiritual world.

As a knowledge of Steiner's contributions to practical tasks is an aid to the study and appreciation of his spiritual significance, so is the study of Steiner's life and teachings a helpful preparation for creative work in these practical areas. As interesting as the results of Steiner's trained clairvoyance may be, however, it is the clairvoyance itself which accounts for the significance and neglect of his teachings and works. For many observers, the idea of someone tracking souls, reporting on Atlantis and on the historical function of spiritual beings such as Lucifer, Ahriman, and the Archangel Michael, tends to cast a suspicious shadow over even the most effective systems of education and farming. The shadow of skepticism concerning knowledge of spiritual reality (a skepticism which Steiner refers to as "negative superstition") does not prevent the positive application of Steiner's teaching, but it does prevent a serious study of his spiritual experience and mission. In the hope of serving those receptive to Steiner's teachings and those who cast a skeptical shadow over all claims to esoteric knowledge, this book presents a selection of Steiner's writings accompanied by introductions to his work and an extended survey of his writings. In approaching each of these three phases—life, teachings, applications—the mystery of spiritual knowledge will surely press us for a response at each step. Exactly how we respond to the spiritual mystery attending all aspects of Steiner's life, teaching, and influence will tell us as much about ourselves as about the spiritual world—and that is a primary purpose of this book.

Life of an Initiate

It is characteristic of Rudolf Steiner that in the last year and a half of his life, while in failing health, he wrote his autobiography in response to the urgent appeal of his friends and followers. All the works of his mature life were undertaken in response to requests for some kind of help: his system of education was formulated in response to the workers at the Waldorf Astoria Tobacco factory in Stuttgart whose children were in need of a school, and to the owner, Emil Molt, who wanted to begin such a school out of enthusiasm for Steiner's threefold social principles; his lectures on Spiritual Science and medicine were given in response to questions brought to him by a group of medical doctors; in response to the appeal of German and Swiss theologians and students, he provided a liturgy and a spiritual basis for The Christian Community, a modern Christian church which draws on Steiner's esoteric interpretation of Christian revelation; in answer to similar requests, Steiner devised speech-and-movement-art therapies called eurythmy, an elaborate system of soil preparation called the biodynamic method, and a method for educating children with special spiritual and emotional needs.

As Steiner notes in his *Autobiography,* he tried to shape what he "had to say or felt obliged to do as demanded by the circumstances, rather than by anything personal" (p. 17). The following summary of Steiner's life follows the lead of his *Autobiography* in that it attempts to meet the demands of circumstance—specifically, our attempt to fathom a life capable of seeing into natural events and objects.

Although less richly blended than in the last twenty-five years of his life, the combination of esoteric and exoteric elements in Steiner's life and work are clearly evident in his early years. At the end of his life Steiner explained that the spiritual world was open to him from birth, but as a youth he had experienced some difficulty adjusting to the sense world. When he was eight, Steiner experienced the discarnate apparition of a recently deceased relative. This experience, and other direct contacts with the spiritual world, forced him to distinguish between those experiences which could be safely communicated and those about which he maintained a strict silence. It was not until he was forty that Steiner made public the nature, or results, of his supersensible (clairvoyant) powers of perception.

At age eight he borrowed a book on geometry from one of his teachers, and therein found a set of ideas, or experiences, which were both able to be shared and very close to his own sense-free way of knowledge. In his *Autobiography* Steiner describes his experience of geometry:

In this early relation to geometry I recognized the first beginning of the view of the world and of life that gradually took shape within me. In childhood it lived in me more or less unconsciously; by my twentieth year it had assumed a definite, fully conscious form.

I said to myself: The objects and events seen by means of the senses exist in space. This space is outside man, but within him exists a kind of soul-space, which is the setting for spiritual beings and events. It was impossible for me to regard thoughts as mere pictures we form of things. To me they were revelations of a spiritual world seen on the stage of the soul. To me, geometry was knowledge which man himself apparently produces, but its significance is completely independent of him. Of course, as a child I could not express this clearly to myself, but I felt that knowledge of the spiritual world must actually exist within the soul as an objective reality, just like geometry.

That the spiritual world is a reality was as certain to me as the reality of the physical. But I needed some kind of justification for this assumption. I wanted to prove to myself that it is no more an illusion to experience the spiritual world than it is to experience the physical. In regard to geometry I could say that one is privileged to know something which the soul experiences solely through its own power; this, I felt, justified me in speaking about the spiritual I experienced, just as I spoke about the physical. And I did speak of it that way. My mental pictures were of two kinds; I differentiated between things that were "seen" and things that were "not seen." This, though as yet undefined, played an important role in my inner life even before my eighth year (pp. 28–29).

Geometry came easily and spoke directly to Steiner because of its
independence from sense perception. By contrast, he had to work
diligently at those subjects which require an easy rapport with the
physical world. Presumably as a compensatory effort, Steiner attended a technical high school and college and worked primarily
on physical and natural sciences until he was in his late thirties.
His work as editor of Goethe's writings on natural science, for
example, which he began when he was twenty-two, offered a
blend of esoteric and exoteric thinking such as he found in geometry, but was even more significant because it brought his clairvoyant power to bear on the physical world. (Both the first chapter of
this book and the second section of the Guide to Further Readings indicate the importance of Goethe for Steiner's attempt to
gain knowledge of the world.)

When we view Steiner's early life from the hindsight of the
amazing powers made manifest in his later life, it is useful to focus
on those special events which foreshadow his later achievements.
Steiner's discovery of geometry at age eight is precisely the kind
of experience that enables us to glimpse the inner workings of an
Initiate in his formative years, prior to his initiation and the actual
performance of his work. Steiner was eight when he was visited,
in spirit form, by a relative who had died earlier that day, and
who sought his protection as she entered the spiritual world.
These and other secret spiritual experiences were apparently hidden even from Steiner's parents, his brother and sister, and others around him.

Most of what is known of the details of Steiner's early life, both
the externally observable and the inner spiritual, is due to the
disclosures which he made in his *An Autobiography*, which he
wrote during the last years of his life. Many of the details of life
are summarized in the Chronology (see below, pp. 25–33). By
way of summary, it may be said that he was born into a particular
spiritual-cultural environment which seems, admittedly in retro-
spect, entirely appropriate for his spiritual history and task: He
was born to loving and generous parents, was nourished by the
natural beauty of lower Austria, and was afforded the opportunity
to develop a fine blend of religious, scientific, and artistic sen-
sibilities. From an esoteric point of view, it is important to note

that the beginning of the Michaelic Age (or the age of the Arch-angel Michael, beginning in 1879) dawned as Steiner was ap-proaching adulthood, and the end of the Kali Yuga (or the begin-ning of the Age of Light in 1899), coincided with Steiner's experience, at age thirty-nine, of the "Mystery of Golgotha." Whatever relationship may exist between these momentous dates in the history of consciousness esoterically considered, such rela-tionships were not acknowledged by those around Steiner, and perhaps may not have been evident to Steiner himself.

The first clearly observable manifestation Steiner's supersensi-ble faculties occurred soon after he became a resident tutor with the Specht family. The youngest of the four Specht boys, Otto, suffered from an extreme autism (that is, a severe separation from reality). When Steiner accepted this "special pedagogical task," this ten year old boy "was considered so abnormal in his physical and mental development that the family doubted he could be educated at all" (*An Autobiography*, p. 96). Within two years Steiner brought the abilities of his pupil up to age level. Soon after, Steiner taught him Latin and Greek, thus enabling him to attend a regular high school and college, after which he attended medical school and became a doctor.

What Steiner learned while tutoring this boy became the basis of his entire philosophy of education for children in regular Stein-er schools and for children in need of special care:

This pedagogical task became a rich source of learning for me. The educational methods I had to adopt gave me insight into the way man's soul and spirit are connected with his bodily nature. It became my actual training in physiology and psychology. I came to realize that education and teaching must become an art, based upon knowledge of man (*An Autobiography*, p. 97).

During these same years, while Steiner was in his early twen-ties, he began to edit *Goethe's Natural Scientific Writings* for the Kuerschner edition. Throughout the 1880s, while Steiner was in his twenties, he continued to edit Goethe's work, wrote his own interpretation of Goethe, and finished his doctorate with a disser-tation concerned primarily with the philosophy of Fichte. (Stein-er's unnamed initiator to the spiritual world, the Master, had instructed him to build on Fichte and to gain an understanding of the materialism which it was Steiner's life task to transform.) As briefly chronicled in the Guide to Further Reading (Section 2: Early Writings), Steiner spent the last decade of the century, until he was forty, in Weimar, writing philosophy and lecturing. The major transformative experience of Steiner's life occurred in 1899, when he found himself "standing in the spiritual presence of the Mystery of Golgotha in a most profound and solemn festival of knowledge" *(An Autobiography,* p. 319).

With the exception of these remarkable spiritual experiences and an equally remarkable but generally unobservable spiritual capacity and destiny, Steiner apparently looked and acted very much like the son of a minor railway official and village peasant woman that he was. Although the usual conception of an Initiate probably connotes a life which is rarified and perhaps veiled in an obscure and distant past, Steiner's life was neither privileged nor unusual from an external point of view. As of every great spiritual figure, it should be said of Steiner that his life is observable on several levels, beginning with the most obvious biographical details and advancing to the most profound and mysterious spiritual mission. Both kinds of information are in *An Autobiography,* but a careful reading of this volume and others in which Steiner reveals his personal experience clearly indicates that the external details of his life may be important as background and props, but that the essential meaning of his life exists only on the spiritual level. With this in mind, it is worth reading carefully the following autobiographical sketch, which Steiner wrote in 1907 for his friend and occasional collaborator, Edouard Schuré.

In this sketch, which is also known as the Barr Document because Steiner wrote it at Barr at Alsace where he and Marie (von Sievers) Steiner were visiting with Schuré, Steiner offers some important revelations concerning his life and mission. In the first page of this document, Steiner refers to his meeting with a representative of the Master. Steiner was fifteen when he became acquainted with a herbalist whom he later recognized as a messenger from the Master who would be his initiator. As a precursor, the herbalist introduced young Steiner to the life of plants, and also to their secret virtues. Schuré suggests that this herbalist "had spent his life in conversing with the unconscious and fluid soul of herbs and flowers. He had the gift of seeing the vital principle of plants, their etheric body, and what occultism calls the elementals of the vegetable world."[2] Partly as a result of this introduction, the next step on the path to initiation, meeting with his Master, was not difficult for Steiner. According to Schuré, Steiner was nineteen when he accepted his spiritual life mission from the one whom he refers to as the Master. In keeping with esoteric tradition, Steiner did not disclose his identity.

During the time Rudolf Steiner spent with the Master, he came to understand that his task was to develop a new and deep synthesis of science and religion, or knowledge which is at once scientific and spiritual. Through this, as became evident after his experience of "The Mystery of Golgotha," Steiner more specifically understood his task to be the development of trained spiritually based thinking which showed the Christ, the Logos, to be the key to a new science of human and cosmic evolution.

Without the addition of special characteristics such as intuition, affect, and will, the term *knowledge* is not adequate to Steiner's mission and teaching. Although he is enormously knowledgeable, his task is not primarily the advancement of knowledge in the usual sense of the term. Rather, Steiner recommends the cultivation of knowledge based on individual spiritual effort in cooperation with the spiritual world. He exhibits and teaches a knowledge which presupposes disciplined surrender, dedication, and love.

The contents of this book—introductions, writings by Steiner, and Guide to Further Reading—present facets of Steiner's legacy in terms of his three-part achievement and teaching (thinking, feeling, and willing) and in terms of his teaching concerning karma and rebirth in the context of the Christian experience of human nature and cosmic evolution. As is evident in this inadequate attempt at summary, Steiner's vast spiritual legacy is not easily

---

2. Edouard Schuré, "The Personality of Rudolf Steiner and Its Development," *The Way of Initiation, or How to Attain Knowledge of the Higher World*, Foreword by Annie Besant (Chicago: The Occult Publishing Company, 1911), p. 26.

reduced to a few summary statements. Nor is this book an adequate summary. Rather, it should be regarded as one of many available essential first steps on the way to a study of Steiner's basic works.

Autobiographical Sketch
by Rudolf Steiner*

I

I was directed very early to Kant. In my fifteenth and sixteenth years I studied Kant intensively, and before entering the Vienna college *(Hochschule)* I occupied myself intensively with Kant's orthodox followers, belonging to the beginning of the nineteenth century, who are entirely forgotten by the official history of learning in Germany and are hardly mentioned anymore. Then was added a thorough study of Fichte and Schelling. Into this period fell—and this belongs already to the external occult influences—full clarity about the conception of time. This knowledge was in no way connected with my studies and was directed entirely from occult life. It was the knowledge that there is an evolution going in a backwards direction, interfering with that which goes forwards; the first is the occult, astral evolution. This knowledge is the condition for spiritual perception.

Then came the meeting with the representative of the M. [Master]

Then an intensive study of Hegel.

Then the study of more recent philosophy, as it had developed in Germany since the fifties, and in particular the so-called theory of knowledge in all its branches.

My boyhood passed, without this being intended externally by

---

* Written for Edouard Schuré at Barr in Alsace on September 9, 1907. *(Briefwechsel und Dokumente 1901–1925,* Dornach 1967. Bibl. Nr.262, pp. 7–18).

This essay is printed by permission of the holders of the author's rights. The English translation of Part I is reprinted by permission of *The Golden Blade,* where it appeared in 1966. Parts II and III have been translated by Fred Paddock.

anyone, in such a way that nobody brought to me any superstition; and if in my environment anyone spoke of superstitious matters, it was never otherwise than with an emphatic rejection. I came indeed to know the ritual of the Church, as I was brought into ritual acts as a so-called server; but there was nowhere real piety or religious feeling, even among the priests I met. On the contrary, I saw continually certain shadow-sides of the Catholic clergy.

I did not at once meet the M., but first someone sent by him who was completely initiated into the mysteries of the effects of all plants and their connection with the universe and with man's nature. For him, converse with the spirits of nature was a matter of course, which he described without enthusiasm, thereby awakening enthusiasm all the more.

My official studies were concerned with mathematics, chemistry, physics, zoology, botany, mineralogy, and geology. These studies offered a much surer basis for a spiritual conception of the world than I could have gained, for instance, from history or literature, which in the German academic world of that time had no definite method and no significant prospects.

During my first years at the college in Vienna I came to know Karl Julius Schröer. First I heard his lectures about German poetry from the time of Goethe's first publications onwards, about Goethe and Schiller, about the history of German poetry in the nineteenth century, and about Goethe's *Faust*. Then I took part in his "exercises in lecturing and composition." This was a special seminar, resembling that instituted by Uhland at Tübingen. Schröer had worked at German linguistics, and had made significant studies in the German dialects of Austria; his research was done in the style of the brothers Grimm, and in literary research he revered Gervinus. He had been, earlier, a director of the evangelical schools in Vienna. His father was the poet and outstanding educationalist, Christian Oeser. At the time when I came to know him, he was entirely concerned with Goethe. He wrote a widely read commentary on Goethe's *Faust* and also on Goethe's other plays. Before the decline of German Idealism he had studied at the universities of Leipzig, Halle, and Berlin. He was a living incorporation of the finest German culture. His *humanity* attracted people to him. Soon I grew into friendship with him and was often in his house. With him one found an idealistic oasis in the dry desert of German materialism. In external life this period was filled with the struggle of the nationalities in Austria. Schröer himself was remote from the sciences concerned with nature.

I worked from the beginning of 1880 onwards at Goethe's studies in natural science.

Then Joseph Kürschner founded the comprehensive collection, *German National Literature*, for which Schröer edited Goethe's dramas, with introductions and commentaries. Kürschner, on Schröer's recommendation, gave me the task of editing Goethe's scientific writings.

For this Schröer wrote a foreword, introducing me to the literary public.

For this collection I wrote introductions to Goethe's Botany, Zoology, Geology, and Theory of Color.

Anyone who reads these introductions can find in them theosophical ideas in the vesture of a philosophic Idealism.

A discussion of Haeckel's ideas is also in them.

My *Theory of Knowledge,* worked out in 1886, is a philosophic rounding off of these.

Then I was introduced, through my acquaintance with the Austrian poetess, M. E. delle Grazie, who had a fatherly friend in Professor Laurenz Müllner, into the circle of theological professors in Vienna. Marie Eugenie delle Grazie wrote an epic, *Robespierre,* and a drama, *Shadows*.

At the end of the eighties I became for a short time editor of the *German Weekly* in Vienna. This gave an opportunity for an intensive concern with the folk-souls of the different Austrian nationalities. A leading thread for a spiritual-cultural policy had to be found.

In all this there could be no question of the publication of occult ideas. The occult powers standing behind me gave only the counsel: "Everything in the clothing of Idealistic philosphy."

Simultaneously with all this my work as a teacher and private tutor went on, lasting for more than fifteen years.

The first contact at the end of the eighties with theosophical circles in Vienna had to remain without any external effect.

During my last months in Vienna I wrote my short essay, "Goethe as the Father of a New Aesthetics."

Then I was called to the Goethe and Schiller Archives in Weimar, which had then been founded in order to edit Goethe's scientific writings. I had no official position at the Archives; I was simply one of those working at the great Sophie edition of Goethe's works.

My next aim was to give out the foundation of my understanding of the world in a *purely philosophical* form. This was done in the two books, *Truth and Science,* and *The Philosophy of Spiritual Activity* [also translated as *Philosophy of Freedom*].

The Goethe and Schiller Archives were visited by a long series of learned, literary, and otherwise outstanding personalities of Germany and other countries. I came to know many of these personalities, because I soon became friendly with the director of the Goethe and Schiller Archives, Professor Bernhard Suphan, and was often in his house. When Suphan had visitors to the Archives, he often invited me. On one such occasion I met Treitschke.

A close friendship developed at that time with a German mythologist, Ludwig Laistner, author of *The Riddle of the Sphinx,* who died soon afterwards.

I had many conversations with Hermann Grimm, who spoke often to me of his work which was never carried out, a "History of the German Imagination."

Then came the *Nietzsche episode*. I had actually written, not long before, opposing Nietzsche.

My occult powers directed me to introduce into contemporary development in an inconspicuous way that which would lead towards the truly spiritual. One does not attain to knowledge by insisting absolutely on one's own point of view, but through willingness to immerse oneself in alien spiritual streams.

So I wrote my book about Nietzsche, entirely adopting Nietzsche's point of view. For this reason it is perhaps the most objective book about Nietzsche written inside Germany. Nietzsche's opposition to Wagner, and to Christianity, is given its due there.

For a time I was regarded as an unconditional "follower of Nietzsche."

At this time the "Society for Ethical Culture" was founded in Germany. This Society wished for a morality entirely unconcerned with any conception of the world. A complete cloud-castle, and a threat to education. I wrote *against* this foundation a critical article in the weekly journal, *The Future*.

Strongly critical replies followed. And my previous concern with Nietzsche brought the consequence that a pamphlet appeared against me: *Nietzschean Idiots*.

The occult point of view requires: "No unnecessary polemics," and "Where possible, do not defend yourself."

I wrote in peace my book, *Goethe's World Conception*, which formed the conclusion of my time at Wiemar.

Immediately after my article in *The Future*, Haeckel approached me. Two weeks later he contributed to *The Future* an article in which he publicly adopted my view that ethics can develop only on the ground of a conception of the world.

Not long afterwards was Haeckel's sixtieth birthday, which was celebrated as a great festivity in Jena. Haeckel's friends invited me. I then saw Haeckel for the first time. His personality is enchanting. He is personally the entire opposite of the tone of his writings. If Haeckel had ever studied philosophy, even a little (in this he is not only a dilettante, but a child), he would certainly have drawn the highest spiritual conclusions from his epoch-making phylogenetic studies.

In spite of all German philosophy, and in spite of all the rest of German culture, Haeckel's conception of phylogenesis is the most significant fact of German spiritual life in the second half of the nineteenth century. There is no better scientific foundation for occultism than Haeckel's teaching. The teaching of Haeckel is great, but Haeckel is the worst commentator upon it. One does not help civilization by pointing out Haeckel's weaknesses to his contemporaries, but by demonstrating to them the greatness of his ideas about phylogenesis. This I did in the two volumes of my *Conceptions of the World and of Life during the Nineteenth Century*, which are dedicated to Haeckel, and in my booklet, *Haeckel and His Opponents*.

In fact, the time of German spirituality lives on only in Haeckel's conception of phylogenesis. Philosophy is in a condition of the most miserable infertility; theology is a network of hypocrisy without the remotest conception of its own untruthfulness; and the sciences, in spite of their great empirical development, have fallen into the bleakest philosophical ignorance.

From 1890–1897 I was in Weimar.

In 1897 I went to Berlin to edit the *Magazine for Literature*. The writings, *Conceptions of the World and of Life in the Nineteenth Century* and *Haeckel and His Opponents*, belong to my time in Berlin. My next task was to be: to bring into being an effectual spiritual stream in the literature of the time. I put the *Magazine* in the service of this task. It was an old, respected organ, having existed since 1832 and passed through very different phases.

Gently and gradually I led over into esoteric paths. Carefully but definitely: while for Goethe's 150th birthday I wrote an essay, "Goethe's Secret Revelation," containing no more than I had already indicated in a public lecture in Vienna about Goethe's fairy story, "The Green Snake and the Beautiful Lily."

In the nature of the case, a readership gathered only slowly for the direction I was giving to the *Magazine*. It gathered indeed— but not quickly enough for the publisher to find the financial prospects satisfactory. I wanted to give spiritual foundations to the young writers' movement, and was indeed in the most lively contact with the most promising representatives of this movement. But on the one hand I was let down; on the other this movement soon sank into nothingness or naturalism.

Meanwhile a connection with working men had developed. I had become a teacher at the Berlin Workers' Educational Institute. I taught history and also natural sciences. My thoroughly idealistic historical method and my way of teaching soon became acceptable and well understood among the workmen. The number of students increased. I had to lecture almost every evening.

The time came when I could say to myself, in harmony with the occult powers which stood behind me:

You have provided a philosophical foundation for your conception of the world;

You have shown understanding for contemporary thought,

treating it as it could be treated only by someone who accepted it fully;

No one will be able to say: this occultist speaks about the spiritual world because he does not know the philosophical and scientific achievements of the age.

Now I had reached my fortieth year, before which no one should appear publicly as a teacher of occultism, according to the intention of the Masters. (Everywhere, when someone taught earlier, a mistake was made.)

Now I could devote myself publicly to Theosophy. The first consequence was that on the insistence of some leaders of German Socialism a general meeting of the Workers' Educational Institute was called, with the task of deciding between Marxism and me. But I was not ostracized. In the general meeting all the votes except four were in favor of retaining me as a teacher.

But the attacks of the leaders brought the consequence that after three months I had to resign. In order not to compromise themselves, they made the excuse that the Theosophical Movement claimed so much of my attention that I had not enough time for the Workers' Institute.

Almost from the beginning of my Theosophical activity, Fraülein von Sievers was at my side. She saw, too, the last phases of my relationship with working men in Berlin.

II

In the first half of the fifteenth century *Christian Rosenkreuz* went to the Orient, in order to find a balance between the initiation of the East and that of the West. After his return, one consequence of this was the definitive founding of the Rosicrucian direction in the West. In this form, Rosicrucianism was to be the strictly secret school for the preparation of what was to become the public task of esotericism at the turning of the 19th and 20th centuries, after external natural science would have reached a provisional solution of certain problems.

Christian Rosenkreuz marked these problems as follows:

1.) The discovery of spectral analysis, bringing to light the material constitution of the cosmos.

2.) The introduction of material evolution into the science of the organic world.

3.) The knowledge, gained through the recognition of hypnotism and suggestion, that there is a state of consciousness differing from the normal one.

Only after these material insights in the sphere of natural science had matured, were certain Rosicrucian principles to be brought out of the realm of the occult and made public.

Until that time the Christian-mystical initiation was given to the West in the form in which it flowed from the initiator, the "Unknown One from the Highlands," to St. Victor, Meister Eckhart, Tauler, etc.

Within this whole stream the initiation of Manes, into which Christian Rosenkreuz was also initiated in 1459, was considered as a "higher degree": it consists of a true knowledge of the function of evil. This initiation, with its background, must remain completely hidden from the masses for yet a long time to come. For where even the smallest ray of light escaped from it into literature, great harm resulted, as happened, for instance, in the case of the noble Guyau, whose pupil Friedrich Nietzsche became.

III

As information, it cannot be directly said as yet in this form.

The Theosophical Society was founded in 1875 in New York by H. P. Blavatsky and H. S. Olcott. This first founding had a pronounced Western character, as did the book *Isis Unveiled*, in which Blavatsky published a large number of occult truths. Concerning this writing, though, it must be said that the great truths revealed in it are rendered in a rather distorted, and often even caricatured, form. It is as if a well-proportioned face appeared completely distorted in a convex mirror. The things that are said in the *Isis* are true; but *the way* they are said is an uneven mirroring of the truth. The explanation for this is that the truths themselves are inspired by the great Initiates of the West, who are also the initiators of Rosicrucian wisdom. The distortion is caused by the discordant manner in which these truths were taken up by the soul of H. P. Blavatsky. Facts such as these should be proof to the educated world that these truths stem from a higher source of inspiration. For one who reproduced these truths in such a distorted way could never have come to them by herself. Because the initiators of the West now saw how little possibility they had of letting the stream of spiritual wisdom flow into mankind by this means, they decided to drop the whole project for the time being *in this form*. However, the gate was opened: Blavatsky's soul was already prepared in such a way that spiritual wisdom could flow into it. Eastern initiators could seize upon her. At first these Eastern initiators had nothing but the best of aims. They saw how, through Anglo-Americanism, mankind was steering towards the dreadful danger of a completely materialistic way of thinking. They—these Eastern initiators—wanted to implant in the Western world *their* form of spiritual knowledge, which they had preserved from ancient times. Under the influence of this stream the Theosophical Society took on an Eastern character, and it was this same influence that inspired Sinnett's *Esoteric Buddhism* and Blavatsky's *Secret Doctrine*. Both of these, however, became again distortions of the truth. Sinnett's work distorts the lofty revelations of the initiators by subjecting them to his philosophically inadequate intellectualism, and Blavatsky's *Secret Doctrine* distorts them through the sheer chaos of her own soul.

The consequence of this was that the initiators, including those of the East, gradually withdrew from the official Theosophical Society, leaving it to become the arena for all sorts of occult powers to distort its high purpose. There was a short period in which Annie Besant, through her pure and high-minded way of thinking and living, was open to the stream of the initiators. This brief episode came to an end when Annie Besant surrendered to the influences of certain Hindus who mainly under the influence of German philosophical doctrines, which they interpreted falsely, produced a grotesque intellectualism. Such was the situation when I found it necessary to join the Theosophical Society. At its cradle had stood true initiators, and *for this reason* the Society— even though subsequent events leave much to be desired—can serve *for the time being* as an instrument of the spiritual life of the present time. Continued successful development in the Western countries is dependent on how far it proves able to assimilate the principle of Western initiation. For Eastern initiations must, of necessity, leave untouched the Christ-principle as the central cosmic factor of evolution. Yet without this principle the Theosophical movement must remain without any decisive effect on Western culture, which has the life of Christ at its point of origin. In the West, the revelations of Oriental initiation would have to live as a mere sectarian alongside the living culture. Their only hope of affecting evolution would be if they could eradicate the Christ-principle from Western Culture. This, however, would be identical with extinguishing the essential meaning of the earth, which lies in the knowledge and realization of the intentions of the living Christ. To make these intentions known in their full wisdom, beauty, and deed-forms is, however, exactly the deepest aim of Rosicrucianism. As to the study of the Eastern wisdom, one can only be of the opinion that this study is of highest value, for the Western peoples have lost a sense for the esoteric, while the Eastern peoples have retained it. About the introduction of the appropriate esotericism for the West, there can again be but one view—that this can only be the Rosicrucian-Christian, for this has given birth to Western life and through its loss mankind would deny the earth its meaning and purpose. Only in this esotericism can blossom the harmony of science and religion, whereas any melding of Western knowledge with Eastern esotericism can only breed such infertile hybrids as Sinnett's *Esoteric Buddhism*. One can sketch the proper way thus:

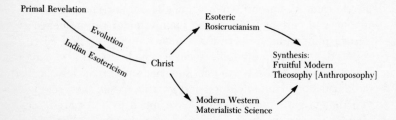

Primal Revelation

Evolution

Indian Esotericism

Christ

Esoteric Rosicrucianism

Modern Western Materialistic Science

Synthesis: Fruitful Modern Theosophy [Anthroposophy]

The wrong way, examples of which are Sinnett's *Esoteric Buddhism* and Blavatsky's *Secret Doctrine:*

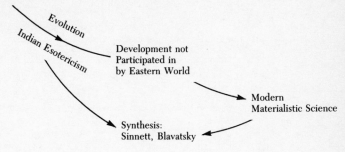

Primal Revelation

Evolution

Indian Esotericism

Development not
Participated in
by Eastern World

Modern
Materialistic Science

Synthesis:
Sinnett, Blavatsky

Chronology*

1861   Born on February 27, 1861, at Kraljevec on the Murr Island in Hungary (in present-day Yugoslavia). His father, Johann Steiner (1829–1910), was an employee of the Southern Austrian Railway; his mother was Franziska Steiner, Née Blie (1834–1918). Both parents came from Geras and Horn in Lower Austria.

1863–1868   Spent his childhood at Pottschach, a station on the Southern Austrian Railway.

1868–1878   Lived in Neudorfl, on the River Leitha in the Burgenland. Entered the Oberrealschule (technical high school) at Wiener-Neustadt in 1872; was graduated in 1879.

1879   Entered the Technische Hochschule (polytechnic college), Vienna, at 18; studied natural history, mathematics, chemistry. Did extensive philosophical reading; attended philosophy lectures at the University of Vienna by Karl Julius Schröer. Met Felix Kogutski, the herb gatherer.

1883   Through his professor Karl Julius Schröer began at 22 to edit *Goethe's Natural Scientific Writings* for Prof. Josef Kuerschner's edition.

1886   At age 25 wrote his *Theory of Knowledge Implicit in Goethe's World Conception*. Was tutor and friend of the Specht Family. Started foundations in relation to education and psychology.

1888   Read paper before the Goethe Society of Vienna:

* Based on "A Chronological Survey (1861–1925)," by Paul M. Allen (in Rudolf Steiner, *An Autobiography*, pp. 415–22), revised with the assistance of Dr. Stewart C. Easton.

"Goethe as the Father of a New Aesthetics" (November 8).

1889   Made first visit to Germany; visited the Goethe-Schiller Archives at Weimar to discuss work he was to undertake for the Weimar Edition. In Vienna entered into friendship with Rosa and Karl Mayreder, Marie Lang, and the Theosophists of the time, including Friedrich Eckstein.

1890   Moved to Weimar. Worked in the Goethe-Schiller Archives as a collaborating editor of the *Natural Scientific Writings of Goethe* for the Sophia Weimar Edition of Goethe's Works. Developed friendships with Herman Grimm, von Treitschke, Helmholtz, Haeckel, Suphan, Ludwig Laistner, Gabrielle Reuter, Otto E. Hartleben, and others.

1891   Received his PH.D. at University of Rostock. Thesis: *Die Grundfrage der Erkenntnistheorie (The Fundamentals of a Theory of Cognition)*.

1892   *Truth and Knowledge* published.

1893   Lectured to Vienna Science Club (February 20). Became a member of the Goethe Society, Weimar. Struggled with Monism.

1894   *The Philosophy of Spiritual Activity (The Philosophy of Freedom)* published. Visited Friedrich Nietzsche at his home.

1895   *Friedrich Nietzsche: Battler Against His Time* published (also published in English, as *Friedrich Nietzsche: Fighter for Freedom*).

1897   *Goethe's Conception of the World* published at Weimar. Began work as editor of the *Review of Literature*. Moved to Berlin as editor, critic, and writer.

1898   Inner life passed through "a severe test." Articles in the *Review* showed seed of future work in the art of speech. Experienced the darkness of the time.

1899   Article on "Goethe's Fairy Tale" published (August 1899). Married to Anna Eunicke (October 31). Began work as lecturer in the Workers' School, Berlin. Taught courses in public speaking, literature, and history. Spiritual struggle resolved when he found himself "standing in the spiritual presence of the Mystery of Golgotha in a most profound and solemn festival of knowledge" *(An Autobiography,* p. 319).

1900   *Conceptions of the World and of Life in the Nineteenth Century* published (later incorporated into first edition of *Riddles of Philosophy,* 1914). *Haeckel and His Opponents* published. Gave address at the five hundredth anniversary of Gutenberg. Gave memorial address for Friedrich Nietzsche in the circle of Die Kommenden (September 13). Gave first lecture in Brockdorff's Theosophical Library, Berlin, on Friedrich Nietzsche (September 22). Lectured on "Goethe's Secret Revelation in His Fairy Tale" (September 29). Gave lecture series in the Theosophical Library, published in 1901 as *Mysticism at the Dawn of the Modern Age.* Lectured in Giordano Bruno Bund.

1901   Gave series of lectures on "From Buddha to Christ," and "Christianity as Mystical Fact" (published in 1902) in the Theosophical Library.

1902   Founding of the German Section of the Theosophical Society, Berlin, October 19–20, 1902, with Rudolf Steiner as General Secretary and Marie von Sievers as Secretary, in the presence of Annie Besant. With Marie von Sievers, made his first visit to London in July to attend the Annual Meeting of the European Sections of the Theosophical Society. *Goethe's Standard of the Soul* published.

1903   Development of the Theosophical work in Berlin and other German cities. Establishment of Theosophical Headquarters at Motzstrasse 17. Attended the General Assembly of the Federation of the European Sections of the Theosophical Society, London, July 3–4. *Reincarnation and Karma* and *How Karma Works* published. The periodical *Luzifer* established (in 1904 renamed *Luzifer-Gnosis*).

1904   *Theosophy: An Introduction to the Supersensible*

Knowledge of the World and the Destination of Man
published. In June attended Theosophical Congress
at Amsterdam, lectured on mathematics and occultism. Made first large lecture tours through Germany. *From the Akashic Chronicle* appeared serially in
Luzifer-Gnosis (later to be published as *Atlantis and
Lemuria* and subsequently as *Cosmic Memory: Prehistory of Earth and Man*). *Schiller and Our Times*
appeared as first publication of the Philosophisch-
Anthroposophischer Verlag, Berlin (later Dornach,
Switzerland). Lectured throughout Germany and
Switzerland on Richard Wagner.

1906   *The Gates of Knowledge* published as a series of articles in *Luzifer-Gnosis* (and later published as *Stages
of Higher Knowledge*). Gave lecture series titled "At
the Gates of Theosophy" in Stuttgart. Met with *Edouard Schuré*.

1907   Gave lecture series in Munich on "The Theosophy of
the Rosicrucians." Lecture on "The Education of the
Child in the Light of Spiritual Science"(which contains fundamentals of Rudolf Steiner's approach to
education) published. Lecture tours continued in
Germany, Czechoslovakia, and Switzerland.

1908   First two lecture tours to Norway and Sweden; additional lectures in Germany, the Netherlands, Denmark, Switzerland, Hungary, Austria, and Czechoslovakia. Gave lecture series on "The Gospel of John"
(Hamburg); "The Apocalypse of John" (Nuremberg);
"Universe, Earth and Man" (Stuttgart); "Egyptian
Myths and Mysteries" (Leipzig). Additional single
lectures on "Kaspar Hauser," "Jakob Boehme," "The
Meaning of Fairy Tales," etc.

1909   *Occult Science, An Outline*, published. Gave lecture
series on "The Spiritual Hierarchies" (Duesseldorf);
"The Gospel of John in Relation to the Other Gospels" (Cassel); "The East in Light of the West" (Munich;) "The Gospel of St. Luke" (Basel); "Metamorphoses of the Soul" (Berlin); "Paths of Experience"

(Berlin); "The Christ Impulse and the Development of the Ego-Consciousness" (Berlin). Theosophical Congress at Budapest in May; last meeting between Rudolf Steiner and Annie Besant.

1910   The first Mystery Drama, *The Portal of Initiation*, performed at Munich (August). Lecture tours to Scandinavia, Austria, Italy, Denmark, and Switzerland. Gave lecture series on "Macrocosm and Microcosm" (Vienna); "The Manifestations of Karma"(Hamburg); "The Mission of Folk Souls" (Oslo); "Genesis: Secrets of the Biblical Story of Creation" (Munich); "Gospel of Matthew" (Bern); "Backgrounds of Gospel of Mark" (Berlin); lectured in several cities on "The Reappearance of the Christ in the Etheric." Lecture cycle on "Occult History" (Stuttgart).

1911   The Second Mystery Drama, *The Soul's Probation*. Gave first *Faust* lectures and lecture series in various cities on "Occult Physiology" (Prague); "Wonders of the World" (Munich); "From Jesus to Christ" (Karlsruhe); "The Inner Realities of Evolution" (Berlin); "The World of the Senses and the World of the Spirit" (Hannover). Lectured at the International Philosophical Congress (April 8) on "The Psychological Foundations of Anthroposophy," and on "The Spiritual Guidance of Man and Humanity" (Copenhagen). Anna Eunicke Steiner died on March 17th.

1912   The third Mystery Drama, *The Guardian of the Threshold*, published. Publication of *The Calendar 1912/13* with *The Calendar of the Soul* and *A Road to Self Knowledge*. Gave lecture cycles on "The Mission of Christian Rosenkreutz" (Vienna); "Spiritual Beings in the Heavenly Bodies and the Kingdoms of Nature" (Helsinki); "Earthly and Cosmic Man" (Berlin); "Anthroposophical Ethics" (Norrkoeping); "Man in Light of Occultism, Theosophy, Philosophy" (Oslo); "The Gospel of Mark" (Basel); "Between Death and Rebirth" (Berlin); "The Bhagavad Gita

and the Epistles of St. Paul" (Cologne). The first
beginnings of the art of Eurythmy. Initial preparations for founding the Anthroposophical Society.

1913   The fourth Mystery Drama, *The Souls' Awakening*,
published. Publication of *The Threshold of the Spir-
itual World*. Foundation of the Anthroposophical
Society at Berlin (February 2–3). Gave lecture series
on "The Mysteries of the East and of Christianity"
(Berlin); "The Effect of Occult Development" (The
Hague); "The Secrets of the Threshold" (Munich);
"The Fifth Gospel" (Oslo); "Christ and the Spiritual
World" (Leipzig). On September 20, laid the cor-
nerstone of the Goetheanum Building at Dornach,
Switzerland, as the world-wide center for the work
of Anthroposophy.

1914   Conducted the Second General Meeting of the Anthroposophical Society at Berlin in January and delivered a cycle of lectures on "Human and Cosmic
Thought." The first edition of *Riddles of Philosophy*
published, including *Conceptions of the World and
of Life in the Nineteenth Century*. Delivered lecture
series on "The Inner Nature of Man and Life between Death and Rebirth" (Vienna); "Ways to a
New Style of Architecture" (Dornach); "Christ and
the Human Soul" (Norrkoeping). Visited Paris and
Chartres with Edouard Schuré. When World War I
began, gave short course at Dornach on first aid.
Rudolf Steiner and Marie von Sievers were married
on December 24th.

1915   With the events of World War I, long lecture tours
curtailed. Spent considerable time at Dornach working on the construction of the Goetheanum building
which, despite the war, continued. Lecture tours on
"Eurythmy as Visible Speech" to Austria, parts of
Germany, and Switzerland.

1916   Lectured on subjects related to the war and to spiritual impulses in history, on Goethe's *Faust*, and on
the working of karma and reincarnation. Gave lec-

ture series on "The History of Art." *The Riddles of Man* published.

1917   *Von Seelenrätseln (Riddles of the Soul)* published, with the first statement on the fundamental principles of the threefold division of the human organism. Gave lecture series on "Cosmic and Human Metamorphoses" (Berlin); "Building Stones to a New Understanding of the Mystery of Golgotha" (Berlin); "The Karma of Materialism" (Berlin); "The Fall of the Spirits of Darkness" (Dornach).

1918   Work on the Goetheanum continued. Gave lecture series "Earthly Death and Cosmic Life" (Berlin); "Anthroposophic Life-Gifts" (Berlin); "Occult Psychology" (Dornach); "From Symptom to Reality" (Dornach); "The Social Needs of Our Time" (Dornach); "How Can Mankind Find the Christ Again?" (Dornach). Movement for the Threefold Social Order begun.

1919   *Threefold Commonwealth* published. First Rudolf Steiner (Waldorf) School for Boys and Girls opened in Stuttgart, inaugurating a worldwide educational movement. Taught courses on pedagogy to the faculty and took an active part in the initial stages of the school's operation. Gave many lecture courses on social questions. The first comprehensive scientific course for scientists given (Dornach). Development of the methods of speech, drama, and eurythmy continued. Lectured on Threefold Commonwealth ideas to workers in several of the large factories in Germany. Performances of Goethe's *Faust* given at the Goetheanum.

1920   The opening of the Goetheanum Building. Courses included second course for scientists, first course for physicians, lectures on Thomas Aquinas, Threefold Commonwealth, pedagogy, recitation and declamation, color for painters, etc.

1921   Course on astronomy and for lecturers given (Stuttgart). *Die Drei* published in Stuttgart. Courses included color for painters, medicine and therapy for physicians, curative Eurythmy for physicians and eurythmists, pedagogy for teachers, two courses for theologians; courses also given at the request of and especially for the workmen at the Goetheanum. Scientific Research Laboratory established (Dornach).

1922   Toured through Germany, speaking before large audiences on "The Nature of Anthroposophy," accompanied by Eurythmy performances. Lectures in Holland and England; lecture series on "New Ideals in Education." East-West Congress held in Vienna, June 1–12. Courses included "World Economy" (Dornach, July), "Man and the World of Stars," and one on natural science. Lectured on "The Spiritual Foundations of Education" (Oxford University) and on "Cosmology, Religion and Philosophy" (Dornach); delivered lecture series to theologians that led to the founding of The Christian Community. The Pedagogical Youth Course given; the beginnings of Biodynamic Agriculture and Gardening made at Dornach. On New Year's Eve, 1922, and New Year's Day, 1923, the Goetheanum building burned to the ground.

1923   Preparation made for reorganization of the Anthroposophical Society in many countries, including Germany, Switzerland, Austria, Norway, England, the Netherlands, and at Dornach. Courses on "Eurythmy as Visible Song," pedagogy, music and art, history of the Anthroposophical Movement, the Four Archangels, the Nature of Man, and Mystery Centers. At Ilkley, England, a course on "Education and Modern Spiritual Life." December 25–January 1, the Christmas Conference for the founding of the General Anthroposophical Society held, accompanied by a course on "World History in the Light of Anthroposophy."

1924   *An Autobiography* published in monthly installments. *Anthroposophical Leading Thoughts, Letters*

to the Members, and *The Michael Mystery* written
during this year and the first months of 1925.
Courses included medicine for physicians, curative
education, pedagogy, Eurythmy, Anthroposophy,
"Eurythmy as Visible Speech," "Biodynamic
Agriculture" (the Koberwitz Course), "Speech and
Drama," "The Apocalypse," as well as his *magnum
opus,* eight volumes of lectures on "Karmic Relationships." Lecture tours to Germany, Czechoslovakia, France, the Netherlands, and England. Final
lecture given at Michaelmas, on September 28,
1924.

1925   Rudolf Steiner died in his studio at Dornach on March
30, 1925.

I

KNOWLEDGE, NATURE, AND SPIRIT

Knowledge, Nature, and Spirit

INTRODUCTION

Goethe's Worldview

It is certainly appropriate that the first selection in a book of readings purporting to be "the essential Steiner" should be a chapter on Goethe, particularly one concerned with the role of the individual personality in the development of one's worldview. Steiner's entire lifework powerfully exemplifies Goethe's insistence that the self is the only proper standard of truth—scientific as well as artistic. Although their works are separated by a century—Goethe, 1749–1832; Steiner, 1861–1925—these two artist-philosophers of nature are at one in affirming the positive role of subjectivity, individuality, and volition in the process of attaining scientific knowledge. In light of this shared affirmation, Goethe and Steiner should be seen as an alternative, albeit an overwhelmingly neglected one, to the still prevalent view that excludes the subjective from the attempt to gain scientific knowledge.

Rudolf Steiner and the scientists influenced by his approach and contributions regard Goethe's natural science as a desperately needed corrective to the Cartesian paradigm. Essentially, Cartesianism stands for "the independence of mind and world," or, more precisely, "the *felt* alienation of mind from extended bodies." It is for this reason that the scientific observer separates, to the limit of his ability, "all mental elements from the observed world of material objects."[1] Since Steiner's chapter on Goethe's

---

1. Ronald Brady, "Goethe's Natural Science: Some Non-Cartesian Meditations," in Karl Schaefer et al., *Toward a Man-Centered Medical Science*, p. 139. This article is at once a brilliant exposition of Goethe's natural science and a plea for

natural science reprinted below is primarily concerned to establish a method of empirical science rooted in the knowing subject, it is worth pondering Ronald Brady's summary of Goethe's living, immediate empiricism:

In 1932 (the year of the centennial of Goethe's death), during a speech at the Saxon Academy of Science, Werner Heisenberg remarked that as science progresses, "the claim of the scientist to an understanding of the world in a certain sense diminishes." He meant, evidently, that the familiar world of experience is less and less the one studied by the scientist. The Cartesian paradigm has been, to be sure, the basis of extraordinary accomplishments, but these were increasingly bought at the cost of "renouncing the aim of bringing the phenomena of nature to our thinking in an immediate and living way." Heisenberg then spoke of the work of Goethe in this regard, claiming that "the renouncing of life and immediacy, which was the premise for the progress of all natural science since Newton, formed the real basis for the bitter struggle which Goethe waged against the physical optics of Newton."

Even a cursory reader of Newton's *Optics* and Goethe's *Farbenlehre* will quickly discover the difference between the two works. Newton had, by his premises, to reduce color to the relations of primary qualities in order to explain it. His text is not about the experience of color but of the other angles of refraction of paths of light. In Goethe's pages, however, we find considerations of color as given: felt polarities of tone, of brightness and darkness, of saturation. While Newton attempts to understand color in a reductionist manner, Goethe is performing that examination of immediate appearances that Husserl would term a "descriptive morphology." Some hundred years before Husserl formulated the epistemological principles of such a science, Goethe had already begun to practice it.[2]

Along with other aspects of Goethean natural science, Goethe's theory of color remains a neglected alternative to the Newtonian theory, except for the honored place it holds among scientists and artists influenced by the work of Rudolf Steiner. More important than the conclusions which they share, however, is their shared commitment to the unity of science and art in "life and immediacy."

---

the replacement of the Cartesian paradigm by the phenomenological approach exemplified by Goethe and Steiner.

2. Ibid., pp. 149–50.

For Goethe, the physical world and all of nature is potentially open to understanding through the willing discipline of imagination. He objects to the book by his friend Jacobi because its main thesis, "Nature conceals God," contradicts Goethe's conviction that he experiences the eternal or divine ideas in or through the study of nature. Scientists of the last three or four centuries, of course, agree with Jacobi against Goethe, and it must be admitted that an approach to science which requires even a modicum of supersensible perception is not likely to gain acceptance in the foreseeable future. It is no accident that Steiner, a clairvoyant from childhood, should be one of the few scientific thinkers of the present century who could take up Goethe's determined attempt to derive ideas from the direct experience of natural phenomena. Eschewing the spectator role characteristic of modern science, the Goethean approach to science, like the Goethean approach to art—for the same reason—emphasizes the indispensable role of the imagination in integrating scientific knowing. For Goethe and Steiner, scientific knowing, and indeed all knowing, consists in experiencing, or more precisely, seeing, ideas. Goethe himself reports an experience that exemplifies this kind of knowing. In his excellent article on Goethean science, Hans Gebert recounts the following story:

During his stay in Strasbourg, Goethe had been fascinated by the cathedral. He had examined it under all possible lighting conditions. Reflecting on the way in which its architecture combined the majestic with agreeable, he developed a view new to him about Gothic architecture in general and about its importance for Germany in particular. He not only observed and sketched the cathedral, but went so far as to use the tower to cure a predisposition to vertigo from which he suffered. Again and again he climbed to a small, unprotected platform just below the top of the tower, fighting the giddiness until it no longer occurred. He tried to experience the building in as many ways as he could. When he was about to leave Strasbourg he remarked to his friends that the tower was imcomplete. He also sketched what it would have looked like had it been finished. One of the friends confirmed from the original plans that Goethe was right in his projections. When asked who told him about the original design Goethe replied: "The tower itself. I observed it so long and so attentively and I bestowed on it so much affection that it decided at the end to reveal to me its manifest secret." Through observation, exercise, and mental effort he had penetrated to an imperceptible reality, to the idea of the architect.[3]

Superficially, Goethe's experience of the ideal, physically incomplete, steeple might be classified either as fantasy or mysticism, but both Goethe and Steiner maintain that such an experience is exactly the kind of knowing which is possible and necessary in the present age. It is precisely because Goethe had the power to see the ideal form in the physical world that Steiner regarded him as the most modern soul of the present age. In Goethe, and in Steiner to a far greater degree, we find a mystical knowing in and through, rather than separate from, the external world. Steiner agrees with, and extends into many diverse sciences, Goethe's insistence that the individual "is the most powerful and exact physical apparatus there can be" by which to observe the natural world. Goethe and Steiner agree that natural phenomena "reveal themselves fully to a person who approaches them with a free, unbiased spirit of observation and with a developed inner life in which the ideas of things manifest themselves." Another word for "developed inner life" is imagination—not fancy or fantasy, but the painstakingly trained process by which the sympathetic personal knower imaginatively gleans the ideal form of each physical object and natural process.

As a young man, an enormous effort in imaginative observation enabled Goethe to see the ideal form of the cathedral in Strasbourg; in later years, a most painstaking and exacting study of plant morphology revealed to him the *Urphlanze,* the ideal plant residing in each and every member of the plant kingdom. It is the combination or reunification of the material and spiritual which gives significance to the Goethe-Steiner approach to science and art.

As will become obvious in the second and third selections in this chapter, and even more dramatically in later chapters in this book, Steiner enormously advanced Goethe's elementary efforts at supersensible perception. We might say that Steiner begins

---

3. Hans Gebert, "About Goetheanistic Science," *Journal for Anthroposophy* (Spring 1979), pp. 45–46.

where Goethe leaves off. Steiner also makes this power systematic and shareable. Ever the scientist of spirit, Steiner sought to use Goethe as a powerful example of the method and results of the spiritual knowledge necessary for true progress in science and art. Goethe, however, did not study his own powers of intuition, and did not develop a systematic methodology by which others could attain his gift. In fact, Goethe seemed a bit surprised and confused by his ability. Standard biographies of Goethe note that after a severe illness, at age eighteen, he turned to introspection, religious mysticism, and alchemy. Typically, Steiner offers an explanation at a deeper level: he explained that during this illness Goethe's etheric body was loosened from his physical body, and thereby, in a physical-spiritual realignment appropriate for his destiny, Goethe was better able to penetrate to the etheric level of the physical world. The explanation of this capability, however, awaited the greater spiritual power and systematic rendering of Rudolf Steiner.

The Idea of Freedom

Steiner's approach to morality is analogous to the approach to science and art which he shared with Goethe, but it is not influenced by Goethe at all. Steiner's moral philosophy is based on a step which Goethe did not take. By making the act of free or imaginative thinking the object of thought, and thereby tracing the origin of free ideas to the "I," "inner self," or "spirit," Steiner went beyond Goethe in applying supersensible perception to the moral life. In this regard, he is more consistent than Goethe since his moral philosophy uses the same method and aims as his approach to science and art. As the ideal scientific and artistic experience realizes the universal in the particular, so, according to Steiner, does the free moral agent combine individual will with universal law. The universal is not "out there," but is the ideal realized by the deliberate, loving effort of the individual. In the chapter reprinted below, "The Idea of Freedom," Steiner explains that according to his moral point of view, which he terms *ethical individualism,* he acknowledges no external principles for moral action, but rather judges an action to be good which the individual intuitively loves. Contrary to popular linguistic fashion, one's love of an action or deed is rooted not in instinct or passion, but in that part of oneself that Steiner calls "I," or "ego," or "spirit":

An action is felt to be free insofar as the reasons for it spring from the ideal part of my individual being; every other part of an action, irrespective of whether it is carried out under the compulsion of nature or under the obligation of a moral standard, is felt to be *unfree*.

Man is free insofar as he is able to obey himself in every moment of his life. A moral deed is *my* deed only if it can be called a free one in this sense.*

Steiner's position, then, is opposed to both standard utilitarianism and Kant's categorical imperative. In opposition to utilitarianism, rightness or wrongness of an action is not determined primarily by its consequences (though consequences cannot be ignored), but rather by the source of the action—namely, that it arises in the part of my individuality, called "I" or "spirit," by which I am both free and capable of imaginatively expressing the universal morality realizable through the spiritual world. The instrument by which this process is attained is the imaginative creation of mental pictures of ideal concepts which are stimulated by conflicts in ordinary experience but rooted in spiritual experience. In opposition to Kant's categorical imperative—act so that the maxim of your act may serve as a universal law—Steiner insists that his principle is rooted in free individual choice rather than an external conception of duty.

Depending on one's reading of Kant's philosophical anthropology, however, it can be argued that Steiner's ethics is not as far from Kant's as he claims in this chapter. Both Kant and Steiner see the moral agent as capable of performing a free moral action by virtue of participation in what Kant calls the noumenal and Steiner calls the spiritual realm. But even if the similarity is granted, there is nevertheless an important difference between Kant's and Steiner's moral philosophy. Whereas freedom for Kant is an experience rooted in the experience of obligation ("I can

---

* Within the introductory sections, such unattributed quotations can be assumed to be taken directly from the Steiner material to follow.

because I ought"), freedom for Steiner is essentially a spiritual activity which can be verified, taught, and practiced as a way of life. For Steiner, acting in freedom is acting out of a pure love of the deed as one intuits the moral concept implicit in the deed. In his introduction to *The Philosophy of Freedom*, Michael Wilson offers the following helpful summary of this point:

> Man ultimately has his fate in his own hands, though the path to this condition of freedom is a long and a hard one, in the course of which he must develop merciless knowledge of himself and selfless understanding of others. He must, through his own labors, give birth to what St. Paul called "the second Adam that was made a quickening spirit." Indeed Steiner himself has referred to his philosophy of freedom as a Pauline theory of knowledge. (xii)

This connection between freedom and selfless, spiritual (Pauline) knowledge constitutes an essential background to the chapter, "The Idea of Freedom," reprinted below. This chapter occurs in the second half of *The Philosophy of Freedom*, which is concerned with metaphysics and morality; the first half is concerned entirely with developing an epistemology which would support the experience and reality of freedom which Steiner regards as essential for contemporary morality. In the first half of the book, entitled "Knowledge of Freedom," Steiner attempts to describe, and in the process to invite the reader to experience, the process of freethinking—thinking which can be experienced as originating in the free spiritual life. As imagination and intuition played an essential role in Steiner's approach to a new natural science and a new art, they are also essential for his work in epistemology and moral philosophy. Imagination is the faculty by which the individual creates mental pictures of an idea or concept and, in turn, uses such pictures as a motive for a moral deed. This ability is akin to the remarkable power by which Goethe was able to see the *Urpflanze* (ideal plant form), and by which Steiner was able to see creative ideas behind all kinds of phenomena, including plants, animals, and human beings. Intuition refers to the process of immediately grasping a thought or idea: "Intuition is for thinking what observation is for the percept." In later writings, the term intuition refers to a far more advanced apprehension of reality, including the apprehension of spiritual beings independent of their physical reality. In this chapter, he defines intuition as the conscious experience—in pure spirit—of a purely spiritual content. Only through an intuition can the essence of thinking be grasped. It is not too much to say that Steiner's moral philosophy, like his methodology for science and art, is essentially an attempt to link the polarities of human life—inner/outer, physical/spiritual, individual/universal, and determined/free. As with all Steiner's work and teaching, the preferred terms in these polarities can only be realized by diligent, willed action. And, as he argued persistently, such action is possible only when it is preceded by and based on a world-conception which allows for the possibility of knowing and realizing human freedom.

The Path of Higher Knowledge

Of the selections in this book, only the first two in this chapter, those from *Goethe's Conception of the World* (1897) and from *The Philosophy of Freedom* (1894), were written prior to his experience "around the turn of the century" whereby Steiner stood "in the spiritual presence of the Mystery of Golgotha in a most profound and solemn festival of knowledge" (*An Autobiography*, p. 319). In 1900 Steiner began to offer cycles of lectures in the Theosophical Library in Berlin, the first of which was later published as *Mysticism at the Dawn of the Modern Age*, and the second, in 1901, was *Christianity as Mystical Fact*. By 1904, when he published two of his major works, *Theosophy* and *Knowledge of the Higher Worlds and Its Attainment*, Steiner was beginning to reveal a genuinely esoteric capability and systematic approach to knowledge. As a treatise on higher knowledge, *Knowledge of the Higher Worlds* is a basic indispensable text, whereas *Theosophy* is concerned with higher knowledge only briefly and secondarily. *Knowledge of the Higher Worlds*, however, was written in serial form, and consequently is less systematic than *Theosophy*, which, like *Philosophy of Freedom* and *Occult Science*, is one of Steiner's most carefully constructed texts. The chapter from *Theosophy* reprinted below, "The Path of Knowledge," well serves as a systematic summary of descriptions, exercises, and rationales articulated in *Knowledge of the Higher Worlds*. Before turning to the summary account of supersensible knowledge in *Theosophy*, it would be helpful to ponder the opening passage of *Knowledge of the Higher Worlds:*

There slumber in every human being faculties by means of which he can acquire for himself a knowledge of higher worlds. Mystics, Gnostics, Theosophists—all speak of a world of soul and spirit which for them is just as real as the world we see with our physical eyes and touch with our physical hands. At every moment the listener may say to himself: that, of which they speak, I too can learn, if I develop within myself certain powers which today still slumber within me. There remains only one question—how to set to work to develop such faculties. For this purpose, they only can give advice who already possess such powers. As long as the human race has existed there has always been a method of training, in the course of which individuals possessing these higher faculties gave instruction to others who were in search of them. Such a training is called occult (esoteric) training, and the instruction received therefrom is called occult (esoteric) teaching, or spiritual science. This designation naturally awakens misunderstanding. The one who hears it may very easily be misled into the belief that this training is the concern of a special, privileged class, withholding its knowledge arbitrarily from its fellow creatures. He may even think that nothing of real importance lies behind such knowledge, for if it is true knowledge—he is tempted to think—there would be no need of making a secret of it; it might be publicly imparted and its advantages made accessible to all. Those who have been initiated into the nature of this higher knowledge are not in the least surprised that the uninitiated should so think, for the secret of initiation can only be understood by those who have to a certain degree experienced this initiation into the higher knowledge of existence. The question may be raised: how, then, under these circumstances, are the uninitiated to develop any human interest in this so-called esoteric knowledge? How and why are they to seek for something of whose nature they can form no idea? Such a question is based upon an entirely erroneous conception of the real nature of esoteric knowledge and proficiency. This esoteric knowledge is no more of a secret for the average human being than writing is a secret for those who have never learned it. And just as all who choose the correct method can learn to write, so, too, can all who seek the right way become esoteric students and even teachers. In one respect only do the conditions here differ from those that apply to external knowledge and proficiency. The possibility of acquiring the art of writing may be withheld from someone through poverty, or through the conditions of civilization into which he was born; but for the attainment of knowledge and proficiency in the higher worlds, there is no obstacle for those who earnestly seek them. (pp. 1–3)

Several important principles are contained in this frequently quoted passage. First, only one who has personally experienced higher knowledge or knowledge of the spiritual world can speak authoritatively concerning such knowledge. Second, Steiner recognizes that the knower-seeker relationship (whether it be a relationship to a living teacher or a body of spiritual teachings) and various difficulties on the path towards spiritual knowledge will lead seekers to collaborate in their efforts to implement a method such as his. Third, Steiner, says that a person who possesses a capacity for spiritual knowledge must be willing to advise others, to the extent of their capacities, independent of social or other external considerations. As a corollary to this principle, a spiritual teacher must not release spiritual knowledge to those who seem unable or unwilling to use such knowledge for spiritual purposes. Finally, Steiner touches on the difficult topic of the degree to which esoteric knowledge is accessible to the average person. Steiner suggests that esoteric knowledge is secret in roughly the same way that writing is secret for an illiterate; throughout *Knowledge of the Higher World*, *Theosophy*, and other writings, he also indicates that although the average person can attain the knowledge of higher worlds, it is more difficult to do so than to learn to write, and more difficult than the attainment of any other mode of knowledge. So while esoteric knowledge may be continuous with other kinds of knowledge, it is quite dissimilar with respect to the obstacles in the way of its attainment.

Turning now to "The Path of Knowledge," Steiner repeats his assurance that "knowledge of the spiritual science presented in this book can be acquired by every human being for himself." On the other hand, the requirements are such that not many will make a serious effort and even fewer will realize the level of attainment that Steiner recommends. To attain a vision of higher realities, one has to develop "the unprejudiced surrender to what is revealed by human life or by the world external." Again: "Complete inner selflessness is necessary for this surrender to the revelations of the new world." And again:

The seeker must be able to hold strict guard over both his thinking and his will. Thereby he becomes in all humility—without presumption—a messenger of the world of the True and Beautiful, and rises to be a participant in the Spirit-World. He rises from stage to stage of development. For one cannot reach the spiritual life by merely beholding it; it has to be attained through actual experience.

"The Path of Knowledge" concludes with an affirmation of personality and spiritual reality with which the chapter on Goethe's worldview was also concerned, but in *Theosophy* this concern is at a higher level of spiritual knowledge and discipline. Steiner assures us that the personality is not lost in the service of the spirit-world.

Goethe's Worldview*

Man learns to know the external side of Nature through perception; her more deeply lying forces are revealed in his own inner being as subjective experiences. In philosophical observation of the world, and in artistic feeling and production, the subjective experiences permeate the objective perceptions. What had to divide into two in order to penetrate into the human spirit becomes again one whole. Man satisfies his highest spiritual needs when he incorporates into the objectively perceived world what that world reveals to him in his inner being as its deeper mysteries. Knowledge and the productions of art are nothing else than perceptions filled with man's inner experiences. An inner union of a human soul-experience and an external perception can be discovered in the simplest judgment of an object or an event of the external world. When I say, "one body strikes the other," I have already carried over an inner experience to the external world. I see a body in motion; it comes into contact with another body, and as a result this second body is also set in motion. With these words the content of the perception is exhausted. This, however, does not satisfy me, for I feel that in the whole phenomenon there is more than what is yielded by mere perception. I seek for an inner experience that will explain the perception. I know that I myself can set a body in movement by the application of force, by pushing it. I carry this experience over into the phenomenon and say: the one body pushes the other. "Man never realizes how anthropomorphic he is." There are men who conclude from the presence of this subjective element in every judgment of the external world that the objective essence of

* From H. Collison, ed., "Personality and View of the World," *Goethe's Conception of the World* (London: Rudolf Steiner Press, 1928), pp. 47–61.

reality is inaccessible to man. They believe that man falsifies the immediate, objective facts of reality when he introduces his subjective experiences into it. They say: because man is only able to form a conception of the world through the spectacles of his subjective life, therefore all his knowledge is only a subjective, limited human knowledge. Those, however, who become conscious of what reveals itself in the inner being of man will not want to have anything to do with such unfruitful statements. They know that truth results from the interpretation of perception and idea in the cognitional process. They realize that in the subjective there lives the truest and deepest objectivity. "When the healthy nature of man works as one whole, when he feels himself to exist in the world as in a great and beautiful whole, when the harmonious sense of well-being imparts to him a pure, free delight, the Universe—if it could be conscious of itself—having attained its goal, would shout for joy and admire the summit of its own becoming and being." The reality accessible to mere perception is only the one-half of the whole reality; the content of the human spirit is the other half. If a man had never confronted the world, this second half would never come to living manifestation, to full existence. It would work, of course, as a hidden world of forces, but it would be deprived of the possibility of manifesting itself in its essential form. It may be said that without man the world would display a false countenance. It would exist as it does, by virtue of its deeper forces, but these deeper forces would remain veiled by what they themselves are bringing about. In the spirit of man they are released from their enchantment. Man is not only there in order to form for himself a picture of the finished world; nay, he himself cooperates in bringing the world into existence.

Subjective experiences assume different forms in different men. For those who do not believe in the objective nature of the inner world, this is another reason for denying that man has the capacity to penetrate to the true essence of things. For how can that be the essence of things which appears in one way to one man and in another way to another man? For those who penetrate to the true nature of the inner world the only consequence of the diversity of inner experiences is that Nature is able to express her abundant content in different ways. Truth appears to the individual man in an individual garb. It adapts itself to the particular nature of his personality. More especially is this the case with the highest truths, truths that are of the greatest significance for man.

In order to acquire these truths man carries over his most intimate spiritual experiences and with them at the same time the particular nature of his personality, to the world he has perceived. There are also truths of general validity which every man accepts without imparting to them any individual coloring. But these are the most superficial, the most trivial. They correspond to the common generic character of men, which is the same in them all. Certain attributes which are similar in all men give rise to similar judgments about objects. The way in which men view phenomena according to measure and number is the same in everyone—therefore all find the same mathematical truths. In the attributes, however, which distinguish the single personality from the common generic character, there also lies the foundation for the individual formulation of truth. The essential point is not that the truth appears in one man in a different form than in another, but that all the individual forms that make their appearances belong to one single whole, the uniform ideal world. In the inner being of individual men truth speaks in different tongues and dialects; in every great man it speaks a particular language communicated to this one personality alone. But it is always the one truth that is speaking. "If I know my relationship to myself and to the external world, I call it truth. And so each one can have his own truth, and it is nevertheless always the same."—This is Goethe's view. Truth is not a rigid, dead system of concepts that is only capable of assuming one single form: truth is a living ocean in which the spirit of man dwells, and it is able to display on its surface waves of the most diverse form. "Theory per se is useless except in so far as it makes us believe in the connection of phenomena," says Goethe. A theory that is supposed to be conclusive once and for all and purports in this form to represent an eternal truth, has no value for Goethe. He wants *living* concepts by means of which the spirit of the single man can connect the perceptions together in accordance with his individual nature. To know the truth means, to Goethe, to live in the truth. And to live in the truth means nothing else than that in the consideration of each single object man perceives what particular inner experience comes into play when he confronts this object. Such a view of human cognition cannot speak of boundaries to knowledge, nor of a limitation to knowledge consequential upon the nature of man. For the questions which, according to this view, man raises in knowledge, are not derived from the objects; neither are they imposed upon man by some other power outside his personality. They are derived from the nature of the personality itself. When man directs his gaze to an object there arises within him the urge to see more than confronts him in the perception. And so far as this urge extends, so far does he feel the need for knowledge. Whence does this urge originate? It can indeed only originate from the fact than an inner experience feels itself impelled within the soul to enter into union with the perception. As soon as the union is accomplished the need for knowledge is also satisfied.

The will-to-know is a demand of human nature and not of the objects. They can impart to man no more of their being than he demands from them. Those who speak of a limitation of the faculty of cognition do not know whence the need for knowledge is derived. They believe that the content of truth is lying preserved somewhere or other and that there lives in man nothing but the vague wish to discover the way to the place where it is preserved. But it is the being of the things itself that works itself out in the inner being of man and passes on to where it belongs: to the perception. Man does not strive in the cognitive process for some hidden element but for the equilibration of two forces that work upon him from two sides. One may well say that without man there would be no knowledge of the inner being of things, for without man there would exist nothing through which this inner being could express itself. But it cannot be said that there is something in the inner being of things that is inaccessible to man. Man only knows that there exists something more in the things than perception gives, because this other element lives in his own inner being. To speak of a further unknown element in objects is to spin words about something that does not exist.

Those natures who are not able to recognize that it is the speech of things that is uttered in the inner being of man hold the view that all truth must penetrate into man from without. Such natures either adhere to mere perception and believe that only through sight, hearing, and touch, through the gleaning of historical events and through comparing, reckoning, calculating, and weighing what is received from the realm of facts, is truth able to be cognized; or else they hold the view that truth can only come to man when it is revealed to him through means lying beyond the scope of his cognitional activity; or, finally, they endeavor through forces of a special character, through ecstasy or mystical vision, to attain to the highest insight—insight which, in their view, cannot be afforded them by the world of ideas accessible to thought. A special class of metaphysics also range themselves on the side of the Kantian School and of one-sided mystics. They, indeed, endeavor to form concepts of truth by means of thought, but they do not seek the content of these concepts in man's world of ideas; they seek it in a second reality lying behind the objects. They hold that by means of pure concepts they can either make out something definite about this content, or at least form conceptions of it through hypotheses. I am speaking here chiefly of the first-mentioned category of men, the "fact fanatics." We sometimes find it entering into their consciousness that in reckoning and calculation there already exists, with the help of thought, an elaboration of the content of perception. But then, so they say, thought-activity is only the means whereby man endeavors to cognize the connection between the facts. What flows out of thought as it elaborates the external world is held by these men to be merely subjective; only what approaches them from outside with the help of thinking do they regard as the objective content of truth, the valuable content of knowledge. They imprison the facts within their web of thoughts, but only what is so imprisoned do they admit to be objective. They overlook the fact that what thought imprisons in this way undergoes an exegesis, an adjustment, and an interpretation that is not there in mere perception. Mathematics is a product of pure thought-processes; its content is mental, subjective. And the technician who conceives of natural processes in terms of mathematical relations can only do this on the assumption that the relations have their foundation in the essential nature of these processes. This, however, means nothing else than that a mathematical order lies hidden within the perception and is only seen by one who elaborates the mathematical laws within his mind. There is, however, no difference of kind but only of degree between the mathematical and mechanical perceptions and the most intimate spiritual experiences. Man can carry over other inner experiences, other regions of his world of ideas into his perceptions with the same right as the results of mathematical research. The "fact fanatic" only apparently establishes purely external processes. He does not as a rule reflect upon the world of ideas and its character as subjective experience. And his inner experiences are poor in content, bloodless abstractions that are obscured by the powerful content of fact. The delusion to which he gives himself up can exist only so long as he remains stationary at the lowest stage of the interpretation of Nature, so long as he only counts, weighs, calculates. At the higher stages the true character of knowledge soon makes itself apparent. It can, however, be observed in "fact fanatics" that they prefer to remain at the lower stages. Because of this they are like an aesthete who wishes to judge a piece of music merely in accordance with what can be counted and calculated in it. They want to separate the phenomena of Nature off from man. No subjective element ought to flow into observation. Goethe condemns this mode by procedure in the words: "Man in himself, in so far as he uses his healthy senses, is the most powerful and exact physical apparatus there can be. The greatest mischief of modern physics is that the experiments have, as it were, been separated off from the human being. Man wishes to cognize Nature only by what artificial instruments show, and would thereby limit and prove what she can accomplish." It is fear of the subjective—fear emanating from a false idea of the true nature of the subjective—that leads to this mode of procedure. "But in this connection man stands so high that what otherwise defies portrayal is portrayed in him. What is a string and all mechanical subdivisions of it compared with the ear of the musician? Yes, indeed, what are the elemental phenomena of Nature herself in comparison with man, who must first master and modify them in order in some degree to assimilate them." In Goethe's view the investigator of Nature should not only pay attention to the immediate appearance of objects, but what apearance they would have if all the ideal, moving forces active within them were also to come to actual, external manifestation. The phenomena do not disclose their inner being and constitution until the bodily and spiritual organism of man is there to confront them. Goethe's view is that the phenomena reveal themselves fully to a man who approaches them with a free, unbiased spirit of observation and with a developed inner life in which the ideas of things manifest themselves. Hence a world-conception in opposition to that of Goethe is one that does not seek for the true being of things within the reality given by experience but within a second kind of reality lying behind this.

In F. H. Jacobi, Goethe encountered an adherent of such a world-conception. Goethe gives vent to his indignation in a remark in the *Tag- und Jahresheft* (1811): "Jacobi displeases me on the subject of divine things; how could I welcome the book of so cordially loved a friend in which I was to find this thesis worked out: Nature conceals God!—My pure, profound, inherent and practiced mode of conception has taught me to see God within Nature and Nature within God, inviolably; it has constituted the basis of my whole existence; how then could I fail to be forever spiritually estranged from a man of such excellence, whose heart I used to love and honor, when he makes such a strange—and to my mind—such an extraordinary, one-sided statement." Goethe's mode of conception affords him the certainty that he experiences Eternal Law in the penetration of Nature with ideas, and Eternal Law is to him identical with the Divine. If the Divine concealed itself behind the phenomena of Nature, although it is at the same time the creative element within them, it cuold not be perceived; man would have to *believe* in it. "God has afflicted you with the curse of metaphysics and has put a thorn in your flesh. He has blessed me with physics. I adhere to the atheist's (Spinoza) worship of the Godhead and relinquish to you all that you call—or would like to call—religion. You adhere to belief in God, I to vision." Where this vision ceases there is nothing for the human spirit to seek. In the *Prose Aphorisms* we read: "Man is in truth placed in the center of a real world and endowed with organs enabling him to know and to bring forth the actual as well as the possible. All healthy men have the conviction of their own existence and of a state of existence around them. There is, however, a hollow spot in the brain, that is to say, a place where no object is reflected, just as in the eye itself there is a minute spot which does not see. If a man pays special attention to this hollow place, if he sinks into it, he falls victim to a mental disease, and begins to divine things of another world, chimeras, without form or limit, but which as empty nocturnal spaces alarm and follow the man who does not tear himself free from them, like specters." From the same sentiment comes the utterance: "The highest would be to realize that all 'matters of fact' are really theory. The blue of the heavens reveals to us the fundamental law of chromatics. Let man seek nothing behind the phenomena, for they themselves are the doctrine."

Kant denies that man has the capacity to penetrate that region of Nature wherein her creative forces become directly perceptible. In his view concepts are abstract units into which human understanding groups the manifold particulars of Nature, but which have nothing to do with the *living* unity, with the creating whole of Nature out of which these perceptions actually proceed. In this grouping-together man experiences a subjective operation only. He can relate his general concepts to empirical perceptions, but these concepts are not in themselves living, productive, in such a way that it would ever be possible for man to perceive the emergence of the individual, the particular from them. A concept is to Kant a dead unit existing only in man. "Our understanding is a faculty of Concepts, i.e., a discursive understanding for which it obviously must be contingent on what kind and how very different the particular may be that can be given to it in Nature and brought under its concepts." (Kant's *Critique of Judgment*, para. 77). This is Kant's characterization of the Understanding. The following is the necessary consequence: "It is infinitely important for Reason not to let slip the mechanism of Nature in its products and in their explanation not to pass it by, because without it no insight into the nature of things can be attained. Suppose it be admitted that a supreme Architect immediately created the forms of Nature as they have been from the beginning, or that he predetermined those which in the course of Nature continually form themselves in the same model—our knowledge of Nature is not thus in the least furthered, because we cannot know the mode of action of that Being and the Ideas which are to contain the principles of the possibility of natural beings, and we cannot by them explain Nature as from above downwards.' (*Critique of Understanding*, para. 78). Goethe is convinced that in his world of ideas man has direct experience of the mode of action of the creative being of Nature. "When in the sphere of the moral, through belief in God, Virtue, and Immortality, we do indeed raise ourselves into a higher sphere where it is granted to us to approach the primordial Essence, so may it well be in the sphere of the Intellectual, that through the perception of an ever-lasting Nature we make ourselves worthy for a spiritual participation in her productions." Man's knowledge is, for Goethe, an actual "living into" the creative activity and sovereignty of Nature. Knowledge is able "to investigate, to experience how Nature lives in creative activity."

It is contrary to the spirit of Goethe's world-conception to speak of beings who lie outside the world of experience and the world of ideas accessible to the human mind, who, nevertheless, are supposed to contain the foundations of this world. Every kind of metaphysics is rejected by this world-conception. There are no questions of knowledge which, if rightly put, cannot also be answered. If science at any given time can make nothing of a certain region of phenomena, this is not due to the nature of the human spirit, but to the fortuitous circumstances that experience of this region is not yet complete. Hypotheses cannot be advanced in regard to things that lie outside the sphere of possible experience, but only in regard to such things as may at some time enter into this region. A hypothesis can never do more than assert: it is probable that within a region of phenomena this or that experience will be made. Objects and processes that do not lie within the range of man's sense-perception or spiritual perception cannot be spoken of by this mode of thinking. The assumption of a "thing-in-itself" that brings about perceptions in man, but that can never itself be perceived, is an inadmissible hypothesis. "Hypotheses are scaffoldings erected around the building and are taken away when the building is completed; they are indispensable to the workman, only he must not take the scaffolding for the building." In presence of a region of phenomena for which all the perceptions are given and which is permeated with ideas, the spirit of man declares itself satisfied. Man feels that a living harmony of idea and perception resounds within him.

The satisfying fundamental note which runs for Goethe through his world-conception is similar to that which may be observed in the mystics. Mysticism aims at finding the primordial principle of things, the Godhead within the human soul. Like Goethe, the mystic is convinced that the essential being of the world will be made manifest to him in inner experiences. But many mystics will not admit that penetration into the world of ideas constitutes the inner experience which is to them the essential thing. Many one-sided mystics have practically the same view as Kant of the clear Ideas of Reason. They consider that these clear Ideas of Reason lie outside the sphere of the creative whole of Nature and that they belong exclusively to the human intellect. Such mystics endeavor, therefore, to attain to the highest knowledge, to a higher kind of perception, by the development of abnormal conditions of perception, by the development of abnormal conditions, for example, by ecstacy. They deaden sense observation and rational thought within themselves and try to enhance their life of feeling. Then they think they directly feel active spirituality actually as the Godhead within themselves. When they achieve this they believe that God lives within them. The Goethean world-conception, however, does not derive its knowledge from experiences occurring when observation and thought have been deadened, but from these two functions themselves. It does not betake itself to abnormal conditions of man's mental life but is of the view that the normal, naive methods of procedure of the mind are capable of being perfected to such an extent that man may experience within himself the creative activity of Nature. "It seems to me that ultimately it is only a question of the practical, self-rectifying operations of the general human intellect that has the courage to exercise itself in a higher sphere." Many mystics plunge into a world of indefinite sensations and feelings; Goethe plunges into the crystal-clear world of ideas. One-sided mystics disdain clarity of ideas and think it superficial. They have no inkling of what is experienced by men who are endowed with the gift of entering profoundly into the living world of ideas. They are chilled when they give themselves up to the world of ideas. They seek a world-content that radiates warmth. But the world-content which they find does not explain the world. It consists only of subjective stimuli, of confused representations. A man who speaks of the coldness of the world of ideas can only *think* ideas, he cannot *experience* them. A man who lives the true life of the world of ideas feels within himself the being of the world working in a warmth that cannot be compared with anything else. He feels the fire of the World Mystery light up within him. This is what Goethe felt when the vision of weaving Nature dawned in him in Italy. He then realised how the yearning that in Frankfort he expressed in the words of Faust, can be appeased:

> Where shall I grasp thee, infinite Nature, where?
> Ye breasts, ye fountains of all life whereon
> Hang Heaven and Earth, from which the withered heart
> For solace yearns. . . .

For our cognition, the concept of the tree is conditioned by the percept of the tree. When faced with a particular percept, I can select only one particular concept from the general system of concepts. The connection of concept and percept is determined by thinking, indirectly and objectively, at the level of the percept. This connection of the percept with its concept is recognized *after* the act of perceiving; but that they do belong together lies in the very nature of things.

The process looks different when we examine *knowledge,* or rather the relation of man to the world which arises within knowledge. In the preceding chapters the attempt has been made to show that an unprejudiced observation of this relationship is able to throw light on its nature. A proper understanding of this observation leads to the insight that thinking can be *directly* discerned as a self-contained entity. Those who find it necessary for the explanation of thinking as such to invoke something else, such as physical brain processes or unconscious spiritual processes lying behind the conscious thinking which they observe, fail to recognize what an unprejudiced observation of thinking yields. When we observe our thinking, we live during this observation directly within a self-supporting, spiritual web of being. Indeed, we can even say that if we would grasp the essential nature of spirit in the form in which it presents itself *most immediately* to man, we need only look at the self-sustaining activity of thinking.

The Idea of Freedom*

When we are contemplating thinking itself, two things coincide which otherwise *must* always appear apart, namely, concept and percept. If we fail to see this, we shall be unable to regard the concepts which we have elaborated with respect to percepts as anything but shadowy copies of these percepts, and we shall take the percepts as presenting to us the true reality. We shall, further, build up for ourselves a metaphysical world after the pattern of the perceived world; we shall call this a world of atoms, a world of will, a world of unconscious spirit, or whatever, each according to his own kind of mental imagery. And we shall fail to notice that all the time we have been doing nothing but building up a metaphysical world hypothetically, after the pattern of *our own* world of percepts. But if we recognize what is present in thinking, we shall realize that in the percept we have only one part of the reality and that the other part which belongs to it, and which first allows the full reality to appear, is *experienced* by us in the permeation of the percept by thinking. We shall see in this element that appears in our consciousness as thinking, not a shadowy copy of some reality, but a self-sustaining spiritual essence. And of this we shall be able to say that it is brought into consciousness for us through *intuition*. Intuition is the conscious experience—in pure spirit—of a purely spiritual content. Only through an intuition can the essence of thinking be grasped.

Only if, by means of unprejudiced observation, one has wrestled through to the recognition of this truth of the intuitive essence of thinking will one succeed in clearing the way for an insight into the psychophysical organization of man. One will see

* From Michael Wilson, trans., "The Idea of Freedom," *The Philosophy of Freedom: The Basis for a Modern World Conception*, 7th English ed. (London: Rudolf Steiner Press, 1964), pp. 122–45.

that this organization can have no effect on the *essential nature* of thinking. At first sight this *seems* to be contradicted by patently obvious facts. For ordinary experience, human thinking makes its appearance only in connection with, and by means of, this organization. This form of its appearance comes so much to the fore that its real significance cannot be grasped unless we recognize that in the essence of thinking this organization plays no part whatever. Once we appreciate this, we can no longer fail to notice what a peculiar kind of relationship there is between the human organization and the thinking itself. For this organization contributes nothing to the essential nature of thinking, but recedes whenever the activity of thinking makes its appearance; it suspends its own activity, it yields ground; and on the ground thus left empty, the thinking appears. The essence which is active in thinking has a twofold function: first, it represses the activity of the human organization; secondly, it steps into its place. For even the former, the repression of the physical organization, is a consequence of the activity of thinking, and more particularly of that part of this activity which prepares the *manifestation* of thinking. From this one can see in what sense thinking finds its counterpart in the physical organization. When we see this, we can no longer misjudge the significance of this counterpart of the activity of thinking. When we walk over soft ground, our feet leave impressions in the soil. We shall not be tempted to say that these footprints have been formed from below by the forces of the ground. We shall not attribute to *these* forces any share in the production of the footprints. Just as little, if we observe the essential nature of thinking without prejudice, shall we attribute any share in that nature to the traces in the physical organism which arise through the fact that the thinking prepares its manifestation by means of the body.

An important question, however, emerges here. If the human organization has no part in the *essential nature* of thinking, what is the significance of this organization within the whole nature of man? Now, what happens in this organization through the thinking has indeed nothing to do with the essence of thinking, but it has a great deal to do with the arising of the ego-consciousness out of this thinking. Thinking, in its own essential nature, certainly contains the real I or ego, but it does not contain the ego-consciousness. To see this we have but to observe thinking with an open mind. The "I" is to be found within the thinking; the "ego-consciousness" arises through the traces which the activity of thinking engraves upon our general consciousness, in the sense explained above. (The ego-consciousness thus arises through the bodily organization. However, this must not be taken to imply that the ego-consciousness, once it has arisen, remains dependent on the bodily organization. Once arisen, it is taken up into thinking and shares henceforth in thinking's spiritual being.)

The "ego-consciousness" is built upon the human organization. Out of the latter flow our acts of will. Following the lines of the preceding argument, we can gain insight into the connections between thinking, conscious I, and act of will, only by observing first how an act of will issues from the human organization.

In any particular act of will we must take into account the motive and the driving force. The motive is a factor with the character of a concept or a mental picture; the driving force is the will-factor belonging to the human organization and directly conditioned by it. The conceptual factor, or motive, is the momentary determining factor of the will; the driving force is the permanent determining factor of the individual. A motive for the will may be a pure concept, or else a concept with a particular reference to a percept, that is, a mental picture. Both general concepts and individual ones (mental pictures) become motives of will by affecting the human individual and determining him to action in a particular direction. But one and the same concept, or one and the same mental picture, affects different individuals differently. They stimlate different men to different actions. An act of will is therefore not merely the outcome of the concept or the mental picture but also of the individual makeup of the person. Here we may well follow the example of Eduard von Hartmann and call this individual makeup the characterological disposition. The manner in which concept and mental picture affects the characterological disposition of a man gives to his life a definite moral or ethical stamp.

The characterological disposition is formed by the more or less permanent content of our subjective life, that is, by the content of our mental pictures and feelings. Whether a mental picture which enters my mind at this moment stimulates me to an act of will or not, depends on how it relates itself to the contents of all my other mental pictures and also to my idiosyncrasies of feeling. But after all, the general content of my mental pictures is itself conditioned by the sum total of those concepts which have, in the course of my individual life, come into contact with percepts, that is, have become mental pictures. This sum, again, depends on my greater or lesser capacity for intuition and on the range of my observations, that is, on the subjective and objective factors of experience, on my inner nature and situation in life. My characterological disposition is determined especially by my life of feeling. Whether I shall make a particular mental picture or concept into a motive of action or not, will depend on whether it gives me joy or pain.

These are the elements which we have to consider in an act of will. The immediately present mental picture or concept, which becomes the motive, determines the aim or the purpose of my will; my characterological disposition determines me to direct my activity towards this aim. The mental picture of taking a walk in the next half hour determines the aim of my action. But this mental picture is raised to the level of a motive for my will only if it meets with a suitable characterological disposition, that is, if during my past life I have formed the mental pictures of the sense and purpose of taking a walk, of the value of health, and further, if the mental picture of taking a walk is accompanied in me by a feeling of pleasure.

We must therefore distinguish (I) the possible subjective dispositions which are capable of turning certain mental pictures and concepts into motives, and (2) the possible mental pictures and concepts which are in a position to influence my characterological disposition so that an act of will results. For our moral life the former represent the *driving force,* and the latter, its *aims*.

The driving force in the moral life can be discovered by finding out the elements of which individual life is composed.

The first level of individual life is that of *perceiving*, more particularly perceiving through the senses. This is the region of our individual life in which perceiving translates itself directly into willing, without the intervention of either a feeling or a concept.

The driving force here involved is simply called *instinct*. The satisfaction of our lower, purely animal needs (hunger, sexual intercourse, etc.) comes about in this way. The main characteristic of instinctive life is the immediacy with which the single percept releases the act of will. This kind of determination of the will, which belongs originally only to the life of the lower senses, may, however, become extended also to the percepts of the higher senses. We may react to the percept of a certain event in the external world without reflecting on what we do, without any special feeling connecting itself with the percept, as in fact happens in our conventional social behaviour. The driving force of such action is called *tact* or *moral good taste*. The more often such immediate reactions to a percept occur, the more the person concerned will prove himself able to act purely under the guidance of tact; that is, *tact* becomes his characterological disposition.

The second level of human life is *feeling*. Definite feelings accompany the percepts of the external world. These feelings may become the driving force of an action. When I see a starving man, my pity for him may become the driving force of my action. Such feelings, for example, are shame, pride, sense of honor, humility, remorse, pity, revenge, gratitude, piety, loyalty, love, and duty.

The third level of life amounts to *thinking and forming mental pictures*. A mental picture or a concept may become the motive of an action through mere reflection. Mental pictures become motives because, in the course of life, we regularly connect certain aims of our will with percepts which recur again and again in more or less modified form. Hence with people not wholly devoid of experience it happens that the occurrence of certain percepts is always accompanied by the appearance in consciousness of mental pictures of actions that they themselves have carried out in a similar case or have seen others carry out. These mental pictures float before their minds as patterns which determine all subsequent decisions; they become parts of their characterological disposition. The driving force in the will, in this case, we can call *practical experience*. Practical experience merges gradually into purely tactful behavior. This happens when definite typical pictures of actions have become so firmly connected in our minds with mental pictures of certain situations in life that, in any given instance, we skip over all deliberation based on experience and go straight from the percept to the act of will.

The highest level of individual life is that of conceptual thinking without regard to any definite perceptual content. We determine the content of a concept through pure intuition from out of the ideal sphere. Such a concept contains, at first, no reference to any definite percepts. If we enter upon an act of will under the influence of a concept which refers to a percept, that is, under the influence of a mental picture, then it is this percept which determines our action indirectly by way of the conceptual thinking. But if we act under the influence of intuitions, the driving force of our action is *pure thinking*. As it is the custom in philosophy to call the faculty of pure thinking "reason," we may well be justified in giving the name of *practical reason* to the moral driving force characteristic of this level of life. The clearest account of this driving force in the will have been given by Kreyenbühl. In my opinion his article on this subject is one of the most important contributions to present-day philosophy, more especially to Ethics. Kreyenbühl calls the driving force we are here discussing, the *practical a priori*, that is, an impulse to action issuing directly from my intuition.

It is clear that such an impulse can no longer be counted in the strictest sense as belonging to the characterological disposition. For what is here effective as the driving force is no longer something merely individual in me, but the ideal and hence universal content of my intuition. As soon as I see the justification for taking this content as the basis and starting point of an origin, I enter upon the act of will irrespective of whether I have had the concept beforehand or whether it only enters my consciousness immediately before the action, that is, irrespective of whether it was already present as a disposition in me or not.

Since a real act of will results only when a momentary impulse to action, in the form of a concept or mental picture, acts on the characterological disposition, such an impulse then becomes the motive of the will.

The motives of moral conduct are mental pictures and concepts. There are moral philosophers who see a motive for moral behavior also in the feelings; they assert, for instance, that the aim of moral action is to promote the greatest possible quantity of pleasure for the acting individual. Pleasure itself, however, cannot become a motive; only an *imagined pleasure* can. The *mental picture* of a future feeling, but not the feeling itself, can act on my characterological disposition. For the feeling itself does not yet exist in the moment of action; it has first to be produced by the action.

The *mental picture* of one's own or another's welfare is, however, rightly regarded as a motive of the will. The principle of producing the greatest quantity of pleasure for oneself through one's action, that is, of attaining individual happiness, is called *egoism*. The attainment of this individual happiness is sought either by thinking ruthlessly only of one's own good and striving to attain it even at the cost of the happiness of other individuals (pure egoism), or by promoting the good of others, either because one anticipates a favorable influence on one's own person indirectly through the happiness of others, or because one fears to endanger one's own interest by injuring others (morality of prudence). The special content of the egoistical principles of morality will depend on the mental pictures which we form of what constitutes our own, or others', happiness. A man will determine the content of his egoistical striving in accordance with what he regards as the good things of life (luxury, hope of happiness, deliverance from various evils, and so on).

The purely conceptual content of an action is to be regarded as yet another kind of motive. This content refers not to the particular action only, as with the mental picture of one's own pleasures, but to the derivation of an action from a system of moral principles. These moral principles, in the form of abstract concepts, may regulate the individual's moral life without his worrying himself about the origin of the concepts. In that case, we simply feel that submitting to a moral concept in the form of a commandment overshadowing our actions, is a moral necessity. The establishment of this necessity we leave to those who demand moral subjection from us, that is, to the moral authority that we acknowledge (the head of the family, the state, social custom, the authority of the church, divine revelation). It is a special kind of these moral principles when the commandments is made known to us not through an external authority but through our own inner life (moral autonomy). In this case we hear the voice to which we have to submit ourselves, in our own souls. This voice expresses itself as *conscience*.

It is a moral advance when a man no longer simply accepts the commands of an outer or inner authority as the motive of his action, but tries to understand the reason why a particular maxim of behavior should act as a motive in him. This is the advance from morality based on authority to action out of moral insight. At this level of morality a man will try to find out the requirements of the moral life and will let his actions be determined by the knowledge of them. Such requirements are

(1) the greatest possible good of mankind purely for its own sake;

(2) the progress of civilization, or the moral *evolution* of mankind towards ever greater perfection;

(3) the realization of individual moral aims grasped by pure intuition.

The *greatest possible good of mankind* will naturally be understood in different ways by different people. This maxim refers not to any particular mental picture of this "good" but to the fact that everyone who acknowledges this principle strives to do whatever, in his opinion, most promotes the good of mankind.

The *progress of civilization,* for those to whom the blessings of civilization bring a feeling of pleasure, turns out to be a special case of the foregoing moral principle. Of course, they will have to take into the bargain the decline and destruction of a number of things that also contribute to the general good. It is also possible, however, that some people regard the progress of civilization as a moral necessity quite apart from the feeling of pleasure that it brings. For them, this becomes a special moral principle in addition to the previous one.

The principle of the progress of civilization, like that of the general good, is based on a mental picture, that is, on the way we relate the content of our moral ideas to particular experiences (percepts). The highest conceivable moral principle, however, is one that from the start contains no such reference to particular experiences, but springs from the source of pure intuition and only later seeks any reference to percepts, that is, to life. Here the decision as to what is to be willed proceeds from an authority very different from that of the foregoing cases. If a man holds to the principle of the general good, he will, in all his actions, first ask what his ideals will contribute to this general good. If a man upholds the principle of the progress of civilization, he will act similarly. But there is a still higher way which does not start from one and the same particular moral aim in each case, but sees a certain value in all moral principles and always ask whether in the given case this or that principle is the more important. It may happen that in some circumstances a man considers the right aim to be the progress of civilization, in others the promotion of the general good, and in yet another the promotion of his own welfare, and in each case makes that the motive of his aciton. But if no other ground for decision claims more than second place, then conceptual intuition itself comes first and foremost into consideration. All other motives now give way, and the idea behind an action alone becomes its motive.

Among the levels of characterological disposition, we have singled out as the highest the one that works as *pure thinking* or *practical reason*. Among the motives, we have just singled out *conceptual intuition* as the highest. On closer inspection it will at once be seen that at this level of morality *driving force* and *motive* coincide; that is, neither a predetermined characterological disposition nor the external authority of an accepted moral principle influences our conduct. The action is therefore neither a stereotyped one which merely follows certain rules, nor is it one which we automatically perform in response to an external impulse, but it is an action determined purely and simply by its own ideal content.

Such an action presupposes the capacity for moral intuitions. Whoever lacks the capacity to experience for himself the particular moral principle for each single situation, will never achieve truly individual willing.

Kant's principle of morality—Act so that the basis of your action may be valid for all men—is the exact opposite of ours. His principle means death to all individual impulses of action. For me, the standard can never be the way *all* men would act, but rather what, for me, is to be done in each individual case.

A superficial judgment might raise the following objection to these arguments: How can an action be individually made to fit the special case and the special situation, and yet at the same time be determined by intuition in a purely ideal way? This objection rests upon a confusion of the moral motive with the perceptible content of an action. The latter *may* be a motive, and actually *is* one in the case of the progress of civilization, or when we act from egoism, and so forth, but in an action based on pure moral intuition it is *not* the motive. Of course, my "I" takes notice of these perceptual contents, but it does not allow itself to be *determined* by them. The content is used only to construct a *cognitive concept*, but the corresponding *moral concept* is not derived by the "I" from the object. The cognitive concept of a given situation facing me is at the same time a moral concept only if I take the standpoint of a particular moral principle. If I were to base my conduct only on the general principle of the development of civilization, then my way through life would be tied down to a fixed route. From every occurrence which I perceive and which concerns me, there springs at the same time a moral duty: namely, to do my little bit towards seeing that this occurrence is made to serve the development of civilization. In addition to the concept which reveals to me the connections of events or objects according to the laws of nature, there is also a moral label attached to them which for me, as a moral person, gives ethical directions as to how I have to conduct myself. Such a moral label is justified on its own ground; at a higher level it coincides with the idea which reveals itself to me when I am faced with the concrete instance.

Men vary greatly in their capacity for intuition. In one, ideas just bubble up; another acquires them with much labor. The situations in which men live and which provide the scenes of their actions are no less varied. The conduct of a man will therefore depend on the manner in which his faculty of intuition works in a given situation. The sum of ideas which are effective in us, the concrete content of our intuitions, constitutes what is individual in each of us, notwithstanding the universality of the world of ideas. In so far as this intuitive content applies to action, it constitutes the moral content of the individual. To let this content express itself in life is both the highest moral driving force and the highest motive a man can have, who sees that in this content all other moral principles are in the end united. We may call this point of view *ethical individualism*.

The decisive factor of an intuitively determined action in any concrete instance is the discovery of the corresponding purely individual intuition. At this level of morality one can only speak of general concepts of morality (standards, laws) insofar as these result from the generalization of the individual impulses. General standards always presuppose concrete facts from which they can be derived. But the facts have first to be *created* by human action.

If we seek out the rules (conceptual principles) underlying the actions of individuals, peoples, and epochs, we obtain a system of ethics which is not so much a science of moral laws as a natural history of morality. It is only the laws obtained in this way that are related to human action as the laws of nature are related to a particular phenomenon. These laws, however, are by no means identical with the impulses on which we base our actions. If we want to understand how a man's action arises from his *moral* will, we must first study the relation of this will to the action. Above all, we must keep our eye on those actions in which this relation is the determining factor. If I, or someone else, reflect upon such an action afterwards, we can discover what moral principles come into question with regard to it. While I am performing the action I am influenced by a moral maxim insofar as it can live in me intuitively; it is bound up with my *love* for the objective that I want to realize through my action. I ask no man and no rule, "Shall I perform this action?"—but carry it out as soon as I have grasped the idea of it. This alone makes it *my* action. If a man acts only because he accepts certain moral standards, his action is the outcome of the principles which compose his moral code. He merely carries out orders. He is a superior automaton. Inject some stimulus to action into his mind, and at once the clockwork of his moral principles will set itself in motion and run its prescribed course, so as to result in an action which is Christian, or humane, or seemingly unselfish, or calculated to promote the progress of civilization. Only when I follow my love for my objective is it I myself who act. I act, at this level of morality, not because I acknowledge a lord over me, or an external authority, or a so-called inner voice; I acknowledge no external principle for my action, because I have found in myself the ground for my action, namely, my love of the action. I do not work out mentally whether my action is good or bad; I carry it out because I *love* it. My action will be "good" if my intuition, steeped in love, finds its right place within the intuitively experienceable world continuum; it will be "bad" if this is not the case. Again, I do not ask myself, "How would another man act in my position?"—but I act as I, this particular individuality, find I have occasion to do. No general usage, no common custom, no maxim applying to all men, no moral standard is my immediate guide, but my love for the deed. I feel no compulsion, neither the compulsion of nature which guides me by my instincts, nor the compulsion of the moral commandments, but I want simply to carry out what lies within me.

Those who defend general moral standards might reply to these arguments that if everyone strives to live his own life and do what he pleases, there can be no distinction between a good deed and a crime; every corrupt impulse that lies within me has as good a claim to express itself as has the intention of serving the general good. What determines me as a moral being cannot be the mere fact of my having conceived the idea of an action, but whether I judge it to be good or *evil*. Only in the former case should I carry it out.

My reply to this very obvious objection, which is nevertheless based on a misapprehension of my argument, is this: If we want to understand the nature of the human will, we must distinguish between the path which leads this will to a certain degree of development and the unique character which the will assumes as it approaches this goal. On the path towards this goal the standards play their rightful part. The goal consists of the realization of moral aims grasped by pure intuition. Man attains such aims to the extent that he is able to raise himself at all to the intuitive world of ideas. In any particular act of will such moral aims will generally have other elements mixed in with them, either as driv-

ing force or as motive. Nevertheless intuition may still be wholly
or partly the determining factor in the human will. What one
should do, that one does; one provides the stage upon which obligation becomes deed; one's own action is what one brings forth,
from oneself. Here the impulse can only be wholly individual.
And, in truth, only an act of will that springs from intuition can be
an individual one. To regard evil, the deed of a criminal, as an
expression of the human individuality in the same sense as one
regards the embodiment of pure intuition is only possible if blind
instincts are reckoned as part of the human individuality. But the
blind instinct that drives a man to crime does not spring from
intuition, and does not belong to what is individual in him, but
rather to what is most general in him, to what is equally present
in all individuals and out of which a man works his way by means
of what is individual in him. What is individual in me is not my
organism with its instincts and its feelings but rather the unified
world of ideas which lights up within this organism. My instincts,
urges, and passions establish no more than that I belong to the
general species *man;* it is the fact that something of the idea world
comes to expression in a particular way within these urges, passions, and feelings that establishes my individuality. Through my
instincts and cravings, I am the sort of man of whom there are
twelve to the dozen; through the particular form of the idea by
means of which I designate myself within the dozen as "I," I am
an individual. Only a being other than myself could distinguish
me from others by the difference in my animal nature; through
my thinking, that is, by actively grasping what expresses itself in
my organism as idea, I distinguish myself from others. Therefore
one cannot say of the action of a criminal that it proceeds from the
idea within him. Indeed, the characteristic feature of criminal
actions is precisely that they spring from the nonideal elements in
man.

An action is felt to be free insofar as the reasons for it spring
from the ideal part of my individual being; every other part of an
action, irrespective of whether it is carried out under the compulsion of nature or under the obligation of a moral standard, is felt
to be *unfree*.

Man is free insofar as he is able to obey himself in every moment of his life. A moral deed is *my* deed only if it can be called a free one in this sense. We have here considered what conditions are required for an intentional action to be felt as a free one; how this purely ethically understood idea of freedom comes to realization in the being of man will be shown in what follows.

Acting out of freedom does not exclude the moral laws; it includes them, but shows itself to be on a higher level than those actions which are merely dictated by such laws. Why should my action be of less service to the public good when I have done it out of love than when I have done it *only* because I consider serving the public good to be my duty? The mere concept of duty excludes *freedom* becaue it does not acknowledge the individual element but demands that this be subject to a general standard. Freedom of action is conceivable only from the standpoint of ethical individualism.

But how is a social life possible for man if each one is only striving to assert his own individuality? This objection is characteristic of a false understanding of moralism. Such a moralist believes that a social community is possible only if all men are united by a communally fixed moral order. What this kind of moralist does not understand is just the unity of the world of ideas. He does not see that the world of ideas working in *me* is no other than the one working in my fellow man. Admittedly, this unity is but an outcome of practical experience. But in fact it *cannot* be anything else. For if it could be known in any other way than by observation, then in its own sphere universal standards rather than individual experience would be the rule. Individuality is possible only if every individual being knows of others through individual observation alone. I differ from my fellow man, not at all because we are living in two entirely different spiritual worlds, but because from the world of ideas common to us both we receive different intuitions. He wants to live out *his* intuitions, I *mine*. If we both really conceive out of the idea, and do not obey any external impulses (physical or spiritual), then we cannot but meet one another in like striving, in common intent. A moral misunderstanding, a clash, is impossible between men who are morally *free*. Only the morally unfree who follow their natural instincts or the accepted commands of duty come into conflict with their neighbors if these do not obey the same instincts and the same commands as themselves. To *live* in love towards our actions, and to *let live* in the understanding of the other person's will, is the fundamental maxim of *free men*. They know no other *obligation* than what their will puts itself in unison with intuitively; how they will direct their *will* in a particular case, their faculty for ideas will decide.

Were the ability to get on with one another not a basic part of human nature, no external laws would be able to implant it in us. It is only because human individuals *are* one in spirit that they can live out their lives side by side. The free man lives in confidence that he and any other free man belong to one spiritual world, and that their intentions will harmonize. The free man does not demand agreement from his fellow man, but expects to find it because it is inherent in human nature. I am not here referring to the necessity for this or that external institution, but to the *disposition*, the *attitude of soul*, through which a man, aware of himself among his fellows, most clearly expresses the ideal of human dignity.

There are many who will say that the concept of the *free* man which I have here developed is a chimera nowhere to be found in practice; we have to do with actual human beings, from whom we can only hope for morality if they obey some moral law, that is, if they regard their moral task as a duty and do not freely follow their inclinations and loves. I do not doubt this at all. Only a blind man could do so. But if this is to be the *final* conclusion, then away with all this hypocrisy about morality! Let us then simply say that human nature must be *driven* to its actions as long as it is not *free*. Whether his unfreedom is forced on him by physical means or by moral laws, whether man is unfree because he follows his unlimited sexual desire or because he is bound by the fetters of unconventional morality, is quite immaterial from a certain point of view. Only let us not assert that such a man can rightly call his actions his *own*, seeing that he is driven to them by a force other than himself. But in the midst of all this framework of compulsion there arise men who establish themselves as *free spirits* in all the welter of customs, legal insofar as they obey only themselves, *unfree* insofar as they submit to control. Which of us can say that he is really free in all his actions? Yet in each of us there dwells a deeper being in which the free man finds expression.

Our life is made up of free and unfree actions. We cannot, however, think out the concept of man completely without coming upon the *free spirit* as the purest expression of human nature. Indeed, we are men in the true sense only insofar as we are free.

This is an ideal, many will say. Doubtless—but it is an ideal which is a real element in us working its way to the surface of our nature. It is no ideal just thought up or dreamed, but one which has life, and which announces itself clearly even in the least perfect form of its existence. If man were merely a natural creature, there would be no such thing as the search for ideals, that is, for ideas which for the moment are not effective but whose realization is required. With the things of the outer world, the idea is determined by the percept; we have done our share when we have recognized the connection between idea and percept. But with the human being it is not so. The sum total of his existence is not fully determined without his own self; his true concept as a *moral* being (free spirit) is not objectively united from the start with the percept-picture "man" needing only to be confirmed by knowledge afterwards. Man must unite his concept with the percept of man by his own activity. Concept and percept coincide in this case only if man himself makes them coincide. This he can do only if he has found the concept of the free spirit, that is, if he has found the concept of his own self. In the objective world a dividing line is drawn by our organization between percept and concept; knowledge overcomes this division. In our subjective nature this division is no less present; man overcomes it in the course of his development by bringing the concept of himself to expression in his outward existence. Hence not only man's intellectual but also his moral life leads to his twofold nature, perceiving (direct experience) and thinking. The intellectual life overcomes this twofold nature by means of knowledge, the moral life overcomes it through the actual realization of the free spirit. Every existing thing has its inborn concept (the law of its being and doing), but in external objects this concept is indivisibly bound up with the percept, and separated from it only within our spiritual organization. In man concept and percept are, at first, *actually* separated, to be just as *actually* united by him.

One might object: At every moment of a man's life there is a definite concept corresponding to our percept of him just as with everything else. I can form for myself the concept of a particular type of man, and I may even find such a man given to me as a percept; if I now add to this the concept of a free spirit, then I have two concepts for the same object.

Such an objection is one-sided. As object of perception I am subjected to continual change. As a child I was one thing, another as a youth, yet another as a man. Indeed, at every moment the percept-picture of myself is different from what it was the moment before. These changes may take place in such a way that it is always the same man (the type) who reveals himself in them, or that they represent the expression of a free spirit. To such changes my action, as object of perception, is subjected.

The perceptual object "man" has in it the possibility of transforming itself, just as the plant seed contains the possibility of becoming a complete plant. The plant transforms itself because of the objective law inherent in it; the human being remains in his incomplete state unless he takes hold of the material for transformation within him and transforms himself through his own power. Nature makes of man merely a natural being; society makes of him a law-abiding being; only *he himself* can make of himself a *free man*. Nature releases man from her fetters at a definite stage in his development; society carries this development a stage further; he alone can give himself the final polish.

The standpoint of free morality, then, does not declare the free spirit to be the only form in which a man can exist. It sees in the free spirit only the last stage of man's evolution. This is not to deny that conduct according to standards has its justification as one stage in evolution. Only we cannot acknowledge it as the absolute standpoint in morality. For the free spirit overcomes the standards in the sense that he does not just accept commandments as his motives but orders his action according to his own impulses (intuitions).

When Kant says of duty: "Duty! Thou exalted and mighty name, thou that dost comprise nothing lovable, nothing ingratiating, but demandest submission," thou that "settest up a law . . . before which all inclinations are silent, even though they secretly work against it (Kant's *Critique of Practical Reason,* chap. iii), then out of the consciousness of the free spirit, man replies: "Freedom! Thou kindly and human name, thou that dost comprise all that is morally most lovable, all that my manhood most prizes, and that makest me the servant of nobody, thou that settest up no mere law, but awaitest what my moral love itself will recognize as law because in the face of every merely imposed law it feels itself unfree."

This is the contrast between a morality based on mere law and a morality based on inner freedom.

The philistine, who sees the embodiment of morality in an external code, may see in the free spirit even a dangerous person. But that is only because his view is narrowed down to a limited period of time. If he were able to look beyond this, he would at once find that the free spirit just as seldom needs to go beyond the laws of his state as does the philistine himself, and certainly never needs to place himself in real opposition to them. For the laws of the state, one and all, just like all other objective laws of morality, have had their origin in the intuitions of free spirits. There is no rule enforced by family authority that was not at one time intuitively grasped and laid down as such by an ancestor; similarly the conventional laws of morality are first of all established by definite men, and the laws of the state always originate in the head of a statesman. These leading spirits have set up laws over other men, and the only person who feels unfree is the one who forgets this origin and either turns these laws into extrahuman commandments, objective moral concepts of duty independent of man, or else turns them into the commanding voice within himself which he supposes, in a falsely mystical way, to be compelling him. On the other hand, the person who does not overlook this origin, but seeks man within it, will count such laws as belonging to the same world of ideas from which he, too, draws his moral intuitions. If he believes he has better intuitions, he will try to put them into the place of the existing ones; if he finds the existing ones justified, he will act in accordance with them as if they were his own.

We must not coin the formula: Man exists only in order to realize a moral world order which is quite distinct from himself. Anyone who maintains that this is so, remains, in his knowledge of man, at the point where natural science stood when it believed that a bull has horns in order to butt. Scientists, happily, have thrown out the concept of purpose as a dead theory. Ethics finds it more difficult to get free of this concept. But just as horns do not exist *for the sake* of butting, but butting through the presence of horns, so man does not exist *for the sake* of morality, but morality through the presence of man. The free man acts morally because he has a moral idea; he does not act in order that morality may come into being. Human individuals, with the moral ideas belonging to their nature, are the prerequisites of a moral world order.

The human individual is the source of all morality and the center of earthly life. State and society exist only because they have arisen as a necessary consequence of the life of individuals. That state and society should in turn react upon individual life is no more difficult to comprehend than that the butting which is the result of the presence of the horns of the bull, which would become stunted through prolonged disuse. Similarly, the individual would become stunted if he led an isolated existence outside human society. Indeed, this is just why the social order arises, so that it may in turn react favorably upon the individual.

The Path of Knowledge*

Knowledge of the spiritual science presented in this book can be acquired by every human being for himself. Descriptions of the kind given here present a thought-picture of the higher worlds and they are in a certain respect the *first step* towards personal vision. For man is a thinking being. He can find his path to knowledge only when thinking is his starting-point. A picture of the higher worlds presented to his intellect is not fruitless for him, even if for the time being it is only like a narration of higher facts into which he has as yet no insight through his own vision. For the thoughts which are given him represent in themselves a force which works on further in his world of thought. This force will be active in him; it will awaken slumbering capacities. A man who is of the opinion that it is superfluous to occupy himself with such a thought-picture is mistaken; for he regards thought as something unreal and abstract. But thought is a living force. And just as in one who has knowledge thought is present as a direct expression of what is seen in the spirit, so the communication of this expression works in him to whom it is communicated as a seed, which brings forth from itself the fruit of knowledge.

Anyone disdaining the application of strenuous intellectual exertion in the effort to attain higher knowledge, and preferring to turn to other forces for that end, fails to take into account that thinking is the highest of the faculties possessed by man in the world of the senses.

To one who asks, "How can I gain personal knowledge of the higher truths of spiritual science?" the answer must be given, "Begin by making yourself acquainted with what is communicated

---

* From "The Path of Knowledge," *Theosophy: An Introduction to the Supersensible Knowledge of the World and the Destination of Man*, 4th ed. (London: Rudolf Steiner Press, 1973), pp. 130–47.

by others concerning such knowledge." And should he reply, "I want to see for myself; I do not want to know anything about what others have seen," the answer must be: "It is in the very assimilating of the communications of others that the first step towards personal knowledge consists." And if he should retort: "Then I am compelled first of all to have blind faith," one can only reply that in regard to some communications it is not a case of belief or disbelief, but merely of unprejudiced assimilation. The genuine spiritual investigator never speaks with the expectation of being met with blind credulity. He merely says, "I have experienced this in the spiritual regions of existence and I am narrating these experiences of mine." But he knows, too, that the assimilation of these experiences by another and the fact that the thoughts of that other person are permeated by the account are living forces making for spiritual development.

What is here to be considered will only be rightly viewed by one who takes into account the fact that all knowledge of the worlds of soul and spirit slumbers in the depths of the human soul. It can be brought to light through treading the "path of knowledge." But there can be insight not only into what one has oneself brought to light, but also into what someone else has brought up from the depths of the soul; and that, moreover, even when no actual preparation has yet been made for the treading of that path of knowlewdge. Genuine spiritual insight awakens the power of understanding in anyone whose inner nature is not clouded by preconceptions and prejudices. The unconscious knowledge rises to meet the spiritual facts discovered by another. This is not blind credulity but the right working of healthy human reason. This healthy comprehension should be considered a far better starting-point even for firsthand cognition of the spiritual world, than dubious mystical experiences and the like, which are often imagined to be more valuable than what healthy human understanding can recognize when confronted with the findings of genuine spiritual research.

It cannot be emphasized strongly enough how necessary it is for anyone who wishes to develop his faculties for higher knowledge to undertake strenuous efforts to cultivate his powers of thinking. This emphasis must be all the stronger because many people who would become seers place too little value on this earnest, self-denying labor of thinking. They say, "Thinking cannot help me to reach anything; what really matters is feeling or something similar." In reply it must be said that no one can in the higher sense (and that means in truth) become a seer who has not previously worked his way into the life of thought. In the case of many people a certain inner laziness plays an injurious role. They do not become conscious of this laziness because it clothes itself in contempt for abstract thought, idle speculations, and the like. But thinking is completely misunderstood if it is confused with a spinning of idle, abstract trains of thought. This abstract thinking can easily kill supersensible knowledge; live and vigorous thinking can become its foundation.

It would of course be more convenient if the power of higher seership could be acquired while shunning the labor of thinking. Many would like this to be possible. But in order to achieve higher seership an inner stability is necessary, an assurance of soul to which thinking alone can lead. Otherwise there merely results a meaningless flickering of pictures hither and thither, a distracting dislay of phenomena which indeed gives pleasure, but has nothing to do with a true penetration into higher worlds. Further, if we consider what purely spiritual experiences take place in a man who really enters the higher world, we shall realize that the matter has also another aspect. Absolute healthiness of the life of soul is essential in a seer. There is no better means of developing this healthiness than genuine thinking. In fact this health of soul may suffer seriously if the exercises for higher development are not based on thinking. Although it is true that the power of spiritual sight makes a healthy and rightly thinking man still healthier and more capable in life than he is without it, it is equally true that all attempts to develop while shirking the effort of thought, all vague dreamings in this domain, lend strength to fantasy-hunting and encourage a false attitude to life. No one who wishes to acquire higher knowledge has anything to fear if he pays heed to what is said here; but the attempt should only be made under the above premise. *This* premise has to do only with man's soul and spirit; to speak of any kind of injurious influence upon the bodily health is absurd.

Unfounded disbelief is indeed injurious. It works in the recipient as a repelling force. It hinders him from taking in the fruitful thoughts. Not blind faith, but the reception of the thought-world of spiritual science, is the prerequisite for the development of the higher senses. The spiritual investigator approaches his pupil with the injunction: "You are not to believe what I tell you but think it out yourself, make it part of the contents of your own thought-world; then my thoughts will themselves bring it about that you recognize them in their truth." This is the attitude of the spiritual investigator. He gives the stimulus; the power to accept it as true springs from within the recipient himself. And it is in this sense that the views of spiritual science should be studied. Anyone who steeps his thoughts in them may be sure that sooner or later they will lead him to vision of his own.

What has been said here already indicates one of the first qualities which everyone wishing to attain vision of higher realities has to develop in himself. It is the *unreserved, unprejudiced* surrender to what is revealed by human life or by the world external to man. If from the outset a man approaches a fact in the world bringing with him judgment originating in his life hitherto, he shuts himself off through this judgment from the calm, all-round effect which the fact can have on him. The learner must be able at each moment to make himself a perfectly empty vessel into which the new world flows. Knowledge arises only in those moments when every criticism coming from ourselves is silent. For example, when we meet a person, the question is not at all whether we are wiser than he. Even the most unintelligent child has something to reveal to the greatest sage. And if he approaches the child with his prejudgment, however wise it may be, his wisdom thrusts itself like a dulled glass in front of what the child ought to reveal to him.

Complete inner selflessness is necessary for this surrender to the revelations of the new world. And if a man test himself to find out in what degree he has this power of surrender, he will make astonishing discoveries. Anyone who wishes to tread the path of higher knowledge must train himself to be able to obliterate himself, together with all his preconceptions at any and every moment. As long as he obliterates himself the other flows into him.

Only a high degree of such selfless surrender enables a man to imbibe the higher spiritual realities which surround him on all sides. This faculty can be consciously developed. A man can try for example to refrain from any judgment on people around him. He should obliterate within himself the gauge of attraction and repulsion, of stupidity or cleverness, which he is accustomed to apply, and try without this gauge to understand people purely through themselves. The most effective exercises can be made in connection with people for whom he has an aversion. He should suppress this aversion with all his might and allow everything that they do to affect him without bias. Or, if he is in an environment that calls for this or that judgment, he should suppress the judgment and lay himself open to the impressions.

He should allow things and events to speak to him rather than speak about them. And this should also extend to his thought-world. He should suppress *in* himself whatever prompts this or that thought and allow only what is outside to give rise to the thoughts. Only when such exercises are carried out with the most solemn earnestness and perseverance do they lead to the goal of higher knowledge. He who undervalues such exercises knows nothing of their worth. And he who has experience in such things knows that selfless surrender and freedom from prejudice are true generators of power. Just as heat conducted to the steam boiler is transformed into the motive power of the locomotive, so do these exercises in selfless spiritual self-surrender transform themselves in man into the power of vision in the spiritual worlds.

By this exercise a man makes himself receptive to everything that surrounds him. But to this receptivity must be added the faculty of correct estimation. As long as a man is still inclined to value himself too highly at the expense of the world around him, he bars all access to higher knowledge. One who in face of each thing or event in the world yields himself up to the pleasure or pain which they cause *him*, is enmeshed in this overvaluation of himself. For through *his* pleasure and *his* pain he learns nothing about the things, but merely something about himself. If I feel sympathy with a human being, I feel, to begin with, nothing but *my* relation to him. If I make myself dependent on this feeling of pleasure, of sympathy, in my judgment and my conduct, I am placing my personality in the foreground: I am obtruding it upon the world. I want to thrust myself into the world just as I am, instead of accepting the world in an unbiased way and allowing it to play itself out in accordance with the forces working in it. In other words, I am tolerant only of what harmonizes with my personality. Towards everything else I exert a repelling force. As long as a man is enmeshed by the sense-world, he works in a particularly repelling way on all nonmaterial influences. The learner must develop in himself the capacity to conduct himself towards things and people in accordance with their peculiar natures and to recognize the due worth and significance of each one. Sympathy and antipathy, liking and disliking, must be made to play quite new roles. There is no question of man's eradicating these, of blunting himself to sympathy and antipathy. On the contrary, the more a man develops in himself the capacity to refrain from allowing every feeling of sympathy and antipathy to be followed immediately by a judgment, an action, the more delicate will be the sensitiveness he develops. He will find that sympathies and antipathies assume higher forms in him, if he curbs those already in him. Even something that is at first utterly unattractive has hidden qualities; it reveals them if a man does not in his conduct obey his selfish feelings. He who has developed in this respect has more delicate feelings, in every direction, than one who is undeveloped, because he does not allow his own personality to cause lack of receptivity. Each inclination that a man follows blindly blunts his power to see things in the environment in their true light. By obeying inclination we thrust ourselves through the environment, as it were, instead of laying ourselves open to it and feeling its true value.

A man becomes independent of the changing impressions of the outer world when every pleasure, every pain, every sympathy and antipathy, no longer evoke in him an egotistical response and egotistical conduct. The pleasure he feels in a thing makes him at once dependent on it. He loses himself in the thing. A man who loses himself in the pleasure or pain caused by constantly changing impressions cannot tread the path of higher knowledge. He must accept pleasure and pain with equanimity. Then he ceases to lose himself in them; he begins instead to understand them. A pleasure to which I surrender myself devours my being at the moment of surrender. I ought to use the pleasure only in order through it to reach an understanding of the thing that arouses pleasure in men. The important point ought not to be that the thing has aroused the pleasure in me; I ought to experience the pleasure and through it the essential nature of the thing in question. The pleasure should only be an intimation to me that there is in the thing a quality calculated to give pleasure. This quality I must learn to understand. If I go no further than the pleasure, if I allow myself to be entirely absorbed in it, then it only feeds my own pleasures; if the pleasure is to me only an opportunity to experience a quality or property of a thing, I enrich my inner being through this experience. To the seeker, pleasure and dis-pleasure, joy and pain, must be *opportunities* for learning about things. The seeker does not thereby become blunted to pleasure or pain, but he raises himself above them in order that they may reveal to him the nature of things. He who develops in this re-spect will learn to realize what good instructors pleasure and pain are. He will feel with every being and thereby receive the revela-tion of its inner nature. The seeker never says to himself merely, "Oh, how I suffer!" or "Oh, how glad I am!" but always "How suffering speaks!" "How joy speaks!" He eliminates the element of self in order that pleasure and joy from the outer world may work upon him. By this means he develops a completely new way of relating himself to things. Formerly he responded to this or that impression by this or that action, only because the impres-sions caused him joy or dislike. But now he lets pleasure and displeasure also become the organs by which things tell him what they themselves truly are in their own nature. In him, pleasure and pain change from being mere feelings to organs of sense by which the external world is perceived. Just as the eye does not itself act when it sees something, but causes the hand to act, so do pleasure and pain bring about nothing in the spiritual seeker, insofar as he employs them as means of knowledge, but they re-ceive impressions, and what is experienced through pleasure and displeasure is that which brings about the action. When a man uses pleasure and displeasure in such a way that they become organs of transmission, they build up within his soul the actual organs through which the soul-world reveals itself to him. The eye can serve the body only by being an organ for the transmission of sense-impressions; pleasure and pain become *eyes of the soul* when they cease merely to have value for themselves and begin to reveal to a man's own soul the soul outside it.

Through the qualities named, the student induces in himself the condition which allows the realities present in the world around him to work upon him without disturbing influences emanating from his own personality. But he has also to fit himself into the surrounding spiritual world in the right way. As a thinking being he is a citizen of the spiritual world. He can be this in a right way only if during mental activity he makes his thoughts move in accordance with the eternal laws of truth, the laws of the Spiritland. For only so can that realm work upon him and reveal its facts to him. A man does not reach the truth as long as he gives himself up only to the thoughts continually coursing through his Ego. For if he does, these thoughts take a course imposed on them by the fact that they come into existence within the bodily nature. The thought-world of a man who gives himself up to a mental activity determined primarily by his physical brain appears disorderly and confused. A thought enters it, breaks off, is driven out of the field by another. Anyone who tests this by listening to a conversation between two people, or who observes himself frankly, will gain an idea of this mass of will-o'-the-wisp thoughts. As long as a man devotes himself only to the calls of the life of the senses, the confused course of his thoughts will always be set right again by the facts of reality. I may think ever so confusedly; but in my actions everyday facts force upon me the laws corresponding to the reality. My mental picture of a town may be utterly confused; but if I wish to walk along a certain street in the town I must accommodate myself to existing facts. A mechanic may enter his workshop with a chaotic medley of ideas; but the laws of his machines compel him to adopt the correct procedure in his work. Within the world of the senses facts exercise their continuous corrective on thought. If I think out a false opinion about a physical phenomenon or the shape of a plant, the reality confronts me and sets my thinking right.

It is quite different when I consider my relations to the higher regions of existence. They reveal themselves to me only if I enter them with strictly controlled thinking. There my thinking must give me the right, the sure impulse; otherwise I cannot find the proper paths. For the spiritual laws prevailing in these worlds are not sensibly perceptible, and therefore they do not exert on me the compulsion described above. I am able to obey these laws only when they are allied to my own as those of a thinking being. Here I must be my own sure guide. The student's thinking must therefore be strictly regulated in itself. His thoughts must by degrees disaccustom themselves entirely from taking the ordinary daily course. They must in their whole sequence take on the inner character of the spiritual world. He must be able constantly to keep watch over himself in this respect and have himself in hand. With him one thought must not link itself arbitrarily with another, but only in the way that corresponds with the actual contents of the thought-world. The transition from one idea to another must correspond with the strict laws of thought. As thinker, the man must be to a certain extent a constant copy of these thought-laws. He must shut out from his train of thought everything that does not flow out of these laws. Should a favorite thought present itself to him, he must put it aside if the right sequence will be disturbed by it. If a personal feeling tries to force upon his thoughts a direction not proper to them, he must suppress it.

Plato required of those who wished to be admitted to his school that they should first have a mathematical training. And mathematics, with its strict laws which are independent of the course taken by sense-phenomena, forms a good preparation for the seeker. If he wishes to make progress in the study of mathematics he must get rid of all personal arbitrariness, all elements of disturbance. The student prepares himself for his task by overcoming through his own will all arbitrary thinking. He learns to follow purely the demands of thought. And so too he must learn to do this in all thinking intended to serve spiritual knowledge. This *thought-life* itself must be a reflection of undisturbed mathematical judgment and inference. He must strive, wherever he goes and where he is, to be able to think in this way. Then the laws of the spirit-world flow into him, laws which pass over and through

him, without a trace as long as his thinking has the usual, confused character. Regulated thinking leads him from reliable start-
ing-points to the most hidden truths. What has been said, however, must not be understood in a one-sided way. Although
mathematics acts as a good discipline, pure, healthy and vital
thinking can be achieved without mathematics.

The goal towards which the student must strive for his thinking
must also be the same for his actions. He must be able to obey the
laws of the nobly beautiful and the eternally true without any
disturbing influences from his personality. These laws must be
able to guide and direct him. If he begins to do something he has
recognized as right and his personal feelings are not satisfied by
the action, he must not *for that reason* abandon the path on
which he has entered. But on the other hand he must not persist
with it because it gives him joy, if he finds that it is not in harmony with the laws of the eternally Beautiful and True. In everyday life people allow their actions to be determined by what satisfies them personally, by what bears fruit for *themselves*. In so
doing they force their personality upon the world's events. They
do not bring to realization the true that is already traced in the
laws of the spirit-world, but simply the demands of their self-will.
We act in harmony with the spiritual world only when we follow
its laws alone. From what is done merely out of the personality,
there result no forces which can form a basis for spiritual knowledge. The seeker must not ask only, "What brings me advantages, what will bring me success?" He must also be able to ask:
"What have I recognized as the Good?" Renunciation of the fruits
of action for his personality, renunciation of all self-will; these are
the stern laws that he must prescribe for himself. Then he treads
the paths of the spiritual world, his whole being is penetrated by
these laws. He becomes free from all compulsion from the world
of the senses; his spirit-nature raises itself out of the material
sheath. Thus he makes actual progress on the path towards the
spiritual and spiritualizes his own nature. One cannot say, "Of
what use to me are the precepts to follow purely the laws of the
True when I am perhaps mistaken as to what is the True?" What
matters is the striving and the attitude to it. Even a man who is
mistaken has in his very striving after the True a force which

diverts him from the wrong path. If he is mistaken, this force guides him to the right paths. Even the objection, "But I may be mistaken," is harmful misgiving. It shows that the man has no confidence in the power of the True. For the important point is that he should not presume to decide on his aims and objects in life in accordance with his own egotistical views, but that he should selflessly yield himself up to the guidance of the spirit itself. It is not the self-seeking human will that can prescribe for the True; on the contrary, the True itself must become lord in the man, must penetrate his whole being, make him a mirror image of the eternal laws of the Spiritland. He must fill himself with these eternal laws in order to let them stream out into life.

The seeker must be able to hold strict guard over both his thinking and his will. Thereby he becomes in all humility—without presumption—a messenger of the world of the True and Beautiful, and rises to be a participant in the Spirit-World. He rises from stage to stage of development. For one cannot reach the spiritual life by merely beholding it; it has to be attained through actual experience.

If the seeker observes the laws here described, those of his soul-experiences that relate to the spiritual world will take on an entirely new form. He will no longer live merely *in them*. They will no longer have a significance merely for his personal life. They will develop into inner perceptions of the higher world. In his soul the feelings of pleasure and displeasure, of joy and pain, grow into organs of soul, just as in his body eyes and ears do not lead a life for themselves but selflessly allow external impressions to pass through them. And thereby the seeker gains the inner *calmness* and *assurance* that are necessary for investigation in the spirit-world. A great joy will no longer make him merely jubilant, but may be the messenger of qualities in the world which have hitherto escaped him. It will leave him calm; and through the calm, the characteristics of the joy-bringing beings will reveal themselves to him. Suffering will no longer merely oppress him, but will also be able to tell him about the qualities and attributes of the being which causes the suffering. Just as the eye does not desire anything for itself, but shows to man the direction of the path he has to take, so will joy and suffering guide the soul safely along its path. This is the state of balance of soul which the seeker must attain. The less joy and suffering exhaust themselves in the waves which they throw up in his inner life, the more will they form eyes for the supersensible world. As long as a man lives wholly in joy and pain he cannot gain *knowledge* through them. When he learns how to live through them, when he draws out of them his feeling of self, then they become his organs of perception; then he sees by means of them, cognizes by means of them. It is incorrect to think that the seeker becomes a dry, colorless being, incapable of joy or suffering. Joy and suffering are present in him, but—when he investigates in the spiritual world—in a different form; they have become "eyes and ears."

As long as we live in a personal relationship with the world, things reveal only what links them with our personality. But that is the transitory part of them. If we withdraw ourselves from the transitory nature and live with our feeling of self, with our "I," in our permanent nature, then the transitory parts of our nature become intermediaries; and what reveals itself through them is an imperishable reality, an eternal reality in the things. This relationship between his own eternal nature and the eternal in the things must be established by the seeker. Even before he begins other exercises of the kind described, and also during them, he should direct his thought to this imperishable aspect. When I observe a stone, a plant, an animal, a man, I should be able to remember that in each of them an eternal reality expresses itself. I should be able to ask myself what is the permanent reality that lives in the transitory stone, in the transitory human being? What will outlast the transitory, physical appearance? It must not be thought that such a directing of the spirit to the eternal destroys the power of devoted observation and our feeling for the qualities of everyday affairs, and estranges us from the immediate realities. On the contrary. Every leaf, every little insect, will unveil to us innumerable mysteries when not our eyes only, but *through* the eyes the spirit is directed upon them. Every sparkle, every shade of color, every cadence, will remain vividly perceptible to the senses; nothing will be lost; an infinitude of new life is gained in addition. Indeed a person who does not understand how to observe with the eye even the tiniest thing will achieve only pale, bloodless thoughts, not spiritual sight.

Everything depends upon our attitude of mind. How far we shall succeed will depend upon our capacities. We have only to do what is right and leave everything else to evolution. It must be enough for us at first to direct our minds to the permanent. If we do this, the knowledge of the permanent will thereby awaken in us. We must wait until it is given. And it is given at the right time to each one who waits with patience—and works. A man soon notices during such exercises what a mighty transformation takes place in him. He learns to consider each thing as important or unimportant only insofar as he recognizes it to be related to the permanent, to the eternal. His valuation and estimate of the world are different from those he has hitherto held. His feeling takes on a new relationship towards the whole surrounding world. The transitory no longer attracts him merely for its own sake, as formerly; it becomes for him a member, an image of the Eternal. And this eternal reality that lives in all things, he learns to love. It becomes familiar to him, just as the transitory was formerly familiar to him. Again this does not cause him to be estranged from life; he merely learns to value each thing according to its true significance. Even the trifles of life will not pass him by without trace; but, inasmuch as he is seeking the spiritual, he no longer loses himself in them but recognizes them at their worth. He sees them in their true light. Only an inferior seeker would go wandering in the clouds and lose sight of actual life; a genuine seeker will, from his high summit, with his power of clear survey and his just and healthy feeling for everything, know how to assign to each thing its proper place.

Thus there opens out to the seeker the possibility of ceasing to obey only the incalculable influences of the external world of the senses, which turn his will now here, now there. Through knowledge he has seen the eternal nature in things. Through the transformation of his inner world he has gained the capacity to perceive this eternal nature. For the seeker, the following thoughts have special importance. When he acts from out of himself, he is conscious that he is also acting out of the eternal nature of things.

For the things give utterance in *him* to this nature of theirs. He is therefore acting in harmony with the eternal World Order when he directs his action from out of the Eternal within him. He knows himself to be no longer merely impelled by the things; he knows that he impels them according to the laws implanted in them which have become the laws of his own being.

This ability to act out of his own inner being can only be an ideal towards which the seeker strives. The attainment of the goal lies in the far distance. But the seeker must have the will clearly to recognize this path. This is his will for freedom. For freedom is action out of one's own inner being. And only a man who draws his motives from the Eternal may act from out of his inner being. One who does not do this, acts according to motives other than those inherent in the things. Such a man opposes the World Order. And this must then prevail against him. That is to say, what he plans to carry through by his will can, in the last resort, not take place. He cannot become free. The arbitrary will of the individual annihilates itself through the effects of its deeds.

He who is able to work upon his inner life in such a way advances from stage to stage in spiritual knowledge. The fruit of his exercises will be that certain vistas of the supersensible world will unfold to his spiritual perception. He learns the meaning of the truths that are communicated about this world; and he will receive confirmation of them through his own experience. If this stage is attained, something approaches him which can become experience only through treading this path. In a manner whose significance now for the first time can become clear to him through the "great spiritual guiding Powers of the Human race" there is bestowed on him what is called consecration—Initiation. He becomes a "pupil of Wisdom." The less such an Initiation is thought to consist in any outer human relationship, the more correct will be the conception formed about it. What the seeker now experiences can only be indicated here. He receives a new home. He becomes thereby a conscious dweller in the supersensible world. The source of spiritual insight now flows to him from a higher sphere. The light of knowledge does not henceforward shine upon him from without but he is himself placed in the fountainhead of this light. The problems which the world presents receive new illumination. Henceforth he no longer holds converse with the things which are fashioned through the spirit, but with the forming Spirit itself. The separate life of the personality only exists now, in the moments of spiritual knowledge, in order to be a conscious image of the Eternal. Doubts concerning the spirit which could formerly have arisen in him vanish away; for only he can doubt who is deluded by things regarding the spirit that rules in them. And since the "pupil of Wisdom" is able to hold intercourse with the spirit itself, every false form in which he had previously imagined the spirit, vanishes. The false form under which the spirit is conceived is superstition. The initiate has passed beyond all superstition, for he knows what the true form of the spirit is. *Freedom* from the preconceptions of the personality, of doubt and of superstition—these are the hallmarks of one who has attained to discipleship on the path of higher knowledge. This state in which the personality becomes one with the all-embracing spirit of life, must not be confused with an absorption in the "All-Spirit" that annihilates the personality. No such annihilation takes place in a true development of the personality. Personality remains preserved as such in the relationship into which it enters with the spirit-world. It is not the subjection of the personality but its higher development that takes place. If we wish to have a simile for this coincidence or union of the individual spirit with the "All-Spirit," we cannot choose that of different circles which, coinciding, are lost in the one, but we must choose the picture of many circles of which each has a distinct shade of color. These differently colored circles coincide, but each separate shade preserves its existence within the whole. Not one loses the fullness of its individual power.

No further description of the path will be given here. It is contained, as far as is possible, in my *Occult Science—an Outline* which forms a continuance of this book.

What has been said here about the path of spiritual knowledge can only too easily, if it is not properly understood, mislead the reader into regarding it as a recommendation of moods of soul that ring with them the tendency to turn away from the immediate, joyous, active experience of life. As against this it must be emphasized that the particular mood of the soul which renders it fit for direct experience of the reality of the spirit cannot be extended over the whole of life. It is possible for the investigator of spiritual existence to bring his soul, for the purpose of that investigation, into the necessary condition of withdrawal from the realities of the senses, without being made in ordinary life into a man estranged from the world. On the other hand it must be recognized too that a knowledge of the spiritual world, not merely a knowledge gained by treading the path, but also a knowledge acquired through grasping the truths of spiritual science with ordinary, open-minded, healthy human understanding, leads to a higher moral status in life, to a knowledge of sensory existence that is in accord with the truth, to assurance in life and to inner health of the soul.

II
SPIRITUAL ANTHROPOLOGY

Spiritual Anthropology

INTRODUCTION

Theory of Human Nature

Most of Steiner's later work, particularly his research and teachings concerning the arts, sciences, and education, are based on his theory of human nature. Although it is complex, and perhaps confusing in places, Steiner's account of "the nature of man" in *Theosophy* (1904) remains his basic statement on this topic. All of his writings and lectures need to be thought through and contemplated to realize their full effect, and the foundation books—particularly *Theosophy* and *Occult Science*—present both an intellectual study and a spiritual challenge. Steiner urged that each sentence in these basic books be pondered meditatively. In addition to the inherent difficulty of the material, some readers may be confused by references from other sources relating to one or more of the following sets of organizational categories for human nature and behavior:

- Three powers or functions of the human being: thinking, feeling, and willing.
- Three parts of the individual corresponding to the threefold social order: economic, political-rights, and cultural-spiritual.
- Threefold (as well as four-/seven-/ninefold) constituent elements in the human being: physical, etheric and soul or astral, spirit or "I" (see below).

Before discussing the third of these organizational sets, we should briefly focus on the other two sets. Thinking (along with its lower counterpart, sensing), feeling, and willing are activities of psychological or soul life. The threefold social division—economic, political rights, and cultural-spiritual—do not directly correspond to thinking, feeling, and willing or to the threefold (or fourfold) constituents of the human being, but do correspond to the three-part system of the physical organism: the economic sphere corresponds to the head and senses system; the rights sphere corresponds to the rhythmic system; and the cultural-spiritual sphere corresponds to the metabolic system. The remainder of this discussion will concern the organization of the human being as set forth in "The Nature of Man," the first chapter in *Theosophy*.

Characteristically, Steiner introduces his description of human nature by inviting the reader to make a simple observation. He uses the text by Goethe to lead the reader to recognize the three ways in which each individual is connected with the world: A reader who follows the words of Goethe thoughtfully and imaginatively will be led to the conclusion that he perceives the world about him, he receives impressions from it, and he gains knowledge about it; or, observes objects, impressions, and knowledge. Again: objects brought to him by his senses he accepts as fact; his impressions give the world a meaning for himself; knowledge is a goal toward which he must strive. These three experiences correspond to the three sides of human nature: body, soul, and spirit. It is through the body that one's environment is revealed; it is through the soul that the indivdual experiences pleasure and displeasure, desire and aversion, and other emotions in relation to the world; it is through the spirit that the individual experiences the world, in Goethe's terms, as an objective "divine being."

In most contexts this threefold conception stands as Steiner's fundamental theory of human nature. It is an affirmation of, or return to, the conception of human nature held by the Christian Church until it was condemned as heresy by the Eighth Ecumenical Council held at Constantinople in 869.[1] It also stands in opposition to the two-principle, or body-soul, conception of human nature which has largely dominated both Christian and post-Christian thinking. To be accurate, however, and to gain the

1. See A. P. Shepherd, "The Battle for the Spirit: The Council of Constantinople, 869 A.D.," *The Golden Blade* (1963), pp. 22–36.

full benefit of Steiner's spiritual-scientific knowledge, we should recognize a fourth constituent of human nature, variously called life-body, ether-body, formative-force-body, or etheric-body. In itself, the physical body is lifeless and incapable of suporting the other two components of human nature, the soul or astral body, and spirit or Ego. The etheric-body provides life for the physical body and links it to soul and spirit.

These four concepts, corresponding to the four constituent parts of the human being, will be more understandable if considered in two other contexts: First, in relation to levels or modes of knowledge, and second, in relation to the experiences of sleep and death. The following discussion of the correspondence between levels of knowledge and levels of the human being concern the path of higher knowledge described in the previous chapter and anticipate some of the more important concepts developed in subsequent chapters. The discussion of the fourfold conception of human nature in relation to sleep and death will serve as an introduction to the two chapters on "Spirit and Destiny" and "Facing Karma," in the present chapter.

Human Nature and Higher Knowledge

Throughout Steiner's writings, and most systematically in *Theosophy, Occult Science*, and *Stages of Higher Knowledge*, Steiner describes four levels of apprehension corresponding to four levels of human nature. While the first level, sense perception, is not itself knowledge, the three remaining levels are progressively higher stages of knowledge, as follows:

- Sensory perception, made possible by the physical body;
- Imaginative knowledge, made possible by the etheric body;
- Inspirational knowledge, made possible by the astral or soul body;
- Intuitive knowledge, made possible by spirit, or the "I."

If we bring to an analysis of sense perception Steiner's theory of imagination as presented in the previous chapter, it should be clear that our relation to the external world must be more than the simple reception of sense impressions. Rather, sense impressions provide the opportunity for the formation of imaginative

pictures or images. These pictures are made possible simultaneously by the etheric forces of the object and knower, and signal
the development of a capacity for spiritual thinking. Steiner's indications for a new science of biodynamic farming, to take but one
of many possible examples, is due to his ability to see, or grasp
the image of, the etheric formative forces working in the mineral
and plant kingdoms. This ability to picture a spiritual form independent of the sensory level of perception is the first necessary
step toward the kind of free, spiritual thinking that leads gradually to a clairvoyant seeing into spiritual worlds. Seeing the etheric
formative forces in the world of nature both cultivates and reveals
the etheric body in the individual knower.

In the section subtitled "Preparation," in *Knowledge of the
Higher Worlds*, Steiner recommends that we take up the exercise
of fixing our attention on objects and events in the natural world,
paying attention particularly to all phenomena of growth and
decay. He explains that it is by such observations and spiritual
penetration of plant metamorphosis that we can begin to develop
the first stages of clairvoyance. He also explains that from the
ability to see images related to physical objects (such as the etheric body of a particular plant), it is a relatively short step to seeing
etheric forces as independent realities. Steiner calls this latter
seeing "Inspirational knowledge."

As imaginative knowledge is characterized by spiritual seeing,
specifically seeing the etheric bodies of plants, animals, and human beings, inspirational knowledge is characterized by a spiritual hearing. At the level of imagination, images are closely tied
to physical objects, but at the level of inspirational knowledge,
spiritual forces and beings can be perceived independently of
physical realities. In *Occult Science*, Steiner gives an exercise in
imagination: meditating on the process of coming-into-being and
dying-away of a plant. He continues:

If we want to go further and reach the corresponding Inspiration, we
shall have to do the exercise in another way. We shall have to concentrate our attention on the activity of soul that we are ourselves engaged
in, in order from the picture of the plant to arrive at the idea of the
coming-into-being and dying-away. The plant has now to disappear entirely from consciousness, and we are left meditating upon what we have

been doing in our soul. Only by means of such exercises is the ascent to Inspiration possible. (p.269)

This "ascent to Inspiration" is also an ascent to knowledge of one's soul-body or astral body. This body, which is entirely spiritual, and capable of existing independently of one's physical body and etheric body, is best understood as consciousness. It is the vehicle through which I consciously experience, remember, and gather to myself a personal identity which has an enduring significance. The astral body, and inspirational knowledge of which it is distinctively capable, relates the physical and etheric bodies to the Spirit or "I." As the physical and etheric worlds work on the astral body from below, forcing it to deal with the limits of these lower realms, the spiritual world works on the soul, or astral body, from above downwards into it.

The third level of knowledge, Intuition, corresponds to the fourth level or fourth constituent part of the human being. From our ordinary, commonsense vantage point, we might assume that the higher stages of knowledge are progressively more vague and obscure. Predictably, Steiner claims the reverse: Sensory knowledge (or sense perception, which is technically not knowledge at all) is only clear to the extent that we illumine the material world by the cognitive capacities of Imagination, Inspiration, and Intuition. More pointedly, we can truly understand our own self only if we ascend to the level of intuition. Or, in different terms which mean the same: we know our own self only if we see the physical body as an expression of the etheric, the etheric-body as an expression of the astral, and the astral as an expression of the "I."

In *Stages of Higher Knowledge* Steiner notes that the word "I" is peculiar in that it is the only term which no one outside myself can address to myself:

In ordinary life man has only one "intuition"—namely, of Ego itself, for the Ego can in no way be perceived from without; it can only be experienced in the inner life. There is one word that each can apply only to himself. This is the word "I." No other person can call me "I." To anyone else I am a "you." In the same way everyone is a "you" to me. Only I can say "I" to myself. This is because each man lives, not outside, but within the "I." In the same say, in intuitive cognition, one lives in all things.

The perception of the ego is the prototype of all intuitive cognition. Thus to enter into all things, one must first step outside oneself. One must become "selfless" in order to become blended with the "self," the 'Ego" of another being. (pp. 9–10)

By developing the ability to know intuitively, I can know my own self, the "I" on which my physical, etheric, and astral bodies are dependent: I can also know other beings who are entirely independent of the three lower parts of the person. Steiner does not prove the existence of the "I," nor of other spiritual beings which he claims are knowable by the practice of Spiritual Science, but he does describe what he sees through his own intuition, and insists that others can similarly work through imaginative and inspirational knowledge to intuitive knowledge of higher beings. The most dramatic examples and details of Steiner's spiritual knowledge are the examples of sleep and death.

Death, Rebirth, and Karma

In the concluding three paragraphs of the chapter on "Spirit and Destiny," Steiner explains that sleep is an apt image for death because while one sleeps events pursue their own course independently of one's conscious life. "Our personality actually incarnates anew every morning in our world of action. The activity of the soul after its earthly life parallels the activity of the soul during sleep. During the middle hours of daily sleep, the "I" and the astral body leave the physical and etheric bodies asleep on the bed, and themselves return to the spiritual world (see *Roots of Education,* below). Since waking consciousness consists in the interaction between the astral and etheric bodies, the departure of the astral body to a separate state of being allows the etheric body to repair the damage to the physical body incurred during its daytime activities.

But the biography of the sleeping self is important in another respect: after death, the sleep biography is relived in a striking reversal of our earthly life. Steiner's account of this phenomenon, which reads like a fascinating blend of Dante's *Purgatorio* and science fiction, can best be grasped by recounting the sequence of events which constitute death. The death of the physical body is immediate and irremediable, but the etheric, astral, and spirit bodies survive the death of the physical body for various periods. The etheric body, which has recorded all of the experiences of one's lifetime, remains attached to the astral body for approximately three days in order to present, in a vast, instantaneous panorama, the entire life which has just ended. Many individuals who have nearly died (as, for example, by drowning or from a heart attack), when restored to consciousness, recount similar experiences.

Having absorbed the panoramic "report" of the etheric body, the astral body remains in existence for approximately one-third the duration of a person's life-time. This is where sleep plays its significant and intriguing role. In this phase of the soul history, the "I" passes through a period called *kamaloca*. There are two major kamaloca experiences: during the first, the astral body, in which is embedded one's desires and emotions, continues to seek the kinds of satisfaction it enjoyed on earth, but to the extent that it clings to physical satisfaction, it can only be frustrated. By living through the frustration, the astral body is gradually purified of its attachment to the physical life and is eventually dissolved.

In the second kamaloca experience, the "I" relives its entire past life backwards—from death to birth. All of our past actions are now re-experienced, but with a painfully appropriate karmic twist: at this point, the soul or "I" receives the consequences of its earthly actions as they were experienced by the objects of those actions. Steiner describes this purgatorial experience in *Theosophy* and in one of his last and most profound works, *Anthroposophy—An Introduction:*

We now see that, after a few days, we must begin to experience what we have left un-experienced; and this holds for every single deed we have done to other human beings in the world. The last deeds done before death are the first to come before us, and so backwards through life. We first become aware of what our last evil or good deeds signify for the world. Our experience of them while on earth is now eliminated; what we now experience is their significance for the world.

And then we go farther back, experiencing our life again, but backwards. We know that while doing this we are still connected with the earth, for it is only the other side of our deeds that we experience now.

We feel as if our life from now onwards were being borne in the womb of the universe. What we now experience is a kind of embryonic stage for our further life between death and a new birth; only, it is not borne by a mother but by the world, by all that we did not experience in physical life. We live through our physical life again, backwards and in its cosmic significance. We experience it now with a very divided consciousness. Living here in the physical world and observing the creatures around him, man feels himself pretty well as the lord of creation; and even though he calls the lion the king of beasts, he still feels himself, as a human being, superior. Man feels the creatures of the other kingdoms as inferior; he can judge them, but does not ascribe to them the power to judge him. He is above the other kingdoms of Nature.

He has a very different feeling, however, when after death he undergoes the experience I have just described. He no longer feels himself confronting the inferior kingdoms of Nature, but kingdoms of the spiritual world that are superior to him. He feels himself as the lowest kingdom, the others standing above him.

Thus, in undergoing all he has previously left unexperienced, man feels all around him beings far higher than himself. They unfold their sympathies and antipathies towards all he now lives through as a consequence of his earthly life. In this experience immediately after death we are within a kind of "spiritual rain." We live through the spiritual counterpart of our deeds, and the lofty beings who stand above us rain down their sympathies and antipathies. We are flooded by these, and feel in our spiritual being that what is illuminated by the sympathies of these lofty beings of the higher hierarchies will be accepted by the universe as a good element for the future; whereas all that encounters their antipathies will be rejected, for we feel it would be an evil element in the universe if we did not keep it to ourselves. The antipathies of these lofty beings rain down on an evil deed done to another human being, and we feel that the result would be something exceedingly bad for the universe if we released it, if we did not retain it in ourselves. So we gather up all that encounters the antipathies of these lofty beings. In this way we lay the foundation of our destiny, of all that works on into our next earthly life in order that it may find compensation through other deeds. (pp. 116–18)

The content of the kamaloca experience is actually the history of our sleep life, with the important difference that it is fully conscious. During sleep we relive our waking life in summary form. These summaries are then relived on the astral plane after death.

Sleep time is also the occasion for the higher beings—whether angels, Buddhas, or avatars—to influence our unconscious life. The two phases of earthly life—waking and sleeping—interact with each other, as do the two phases of soul life—earthly and afterlife. Steiner teaches that if we do not take into account all four of these factors and the complex relations between them, our understanding of human nature and destiny, both individually and collectively considered, will necessarily be partial and, perhaps, counterproductive.

Rebirth and karma are the proverbial chicken and egg of human destiny: with the assistance of the Lords of Karma, the "I" chooses the personal and environmental conditions of its next life on the basis of attainments and limitations summarized by the astral life just prior to its dissolution. By keeping in mind Steiner's account of the four-part human nature, as well as his account of kamaloca, we can follow his fascinating description of the transition from the end of one life to the beginning of another. In one sense, this transition is the work of the "I," the spirit principle, but it could be understood equally well as the dynamic working of the law of karma. The "I" receives the impress of the astral body's summary and in turn presents it to its own spirit self. It is the karmic condition of the "I" at this point which largely determines the components of the next life—for example, one's parents, one's body, disposition, and capacities, as well as important intellectual and cultural influences. Steiner refers to the precise moment of transition from the end of one karmic life to the beginning of the next as the "cosmic midnight hour"; at this time the full effect of one's life has been finally gathered and sorted, and the "I" then begins the slow process of translating those credits and debits into the next earthly life.

The most mysterious aspect of the transition to the next life is the way in which karma uses the influence of higher beings and heavenly bodies. The various parts of our next body will be formed with the aid of planetary beings and forces. First, the astral body is formed as the soul travels past and absorbs the influence of the sun and stars. Second, the etheric body is formed under the influence of moon beings and forces. Finally, astral and etheric bodies join with the physical seed in the womb—chosen in advance with the aid of higher beings. In this threefold body the human being begins a life in union with its soul and spirit. When this life comes to an end, the entire process will begin again, but in the course of this life the "I" which reincarnates will have changed and, one hopes, improved its karmic capacities and destiny.

Theory of Human Nature*

The following words of Goethe point in a beautiful manner to the starting point of one of the ways by which the nature of man can be known. "As soon as a person becomes aware of the objects around him, he considers them in relation to himself, and rightly so, for his whole fate depends on whether they please or displease, attract or repel, help or harm him. This quite natural way of looking at or judging things appears to be as easy as it is necessary. Nevertheless, a person is exposed through it to a thousand errors which often make him ashamed and embitter his life. A far more difficult task is undertaken by those whose keen desire for knowledge urges them to observe the objects of nature in themselves and in their relations to each other; for they soon feel the lack of the test which helped them when they, as men, regarded the objects in reference to themselves personally. They lack the test of pleasure and displeasure, attraction and repulsion, usefulness and harmfulness. This they must renounce entirely: they ought as dispassionate and, so to speak, divine beings, to seek and examine what is, and not what gratifies. Thus the true botanist should not be moved either by the beauty or by the usefulness of the plants. He has to study their formation and their relation to the rest of the vegetable kingdom; and just as they are one and all enticed forth and shone upon by the sun, so should he with an equable, quiet glance look at and survey them all and obtain the test for this knowledge, the data for his deductions not out of himself, but from within the circle of the things which he observes."

The thought thus expressed by Goethe directs man's attention

* From "The Nature of Man," *Theosophy: An Introduction to the Supersensible Knowledge of the World and the Destination of Man*, 4th ed. (London: Rudolf Steiner Press, 1973), pp. 17–45.

to three kinds of things. First, the objects concerning which information continually flows to him through the portals of his senses, the objects which he touches, smells, tastes, hears, and sees. Second, the impressions which these make on him, characterizing themselves through the fact that he finds the one sympathetic, the other abhorrent; the one useful, the other harmful. Third, the knowledge which he, as a "so-to-speak, divine being," acquires concerning the objects—that is, the secrets of their activities and their being which unveil themselves to him.

These three regions are distinctly separate in human life. And man thereby becomes aware that he is interwoven with the world in a threefold way. The first way is something that he finds present, that he accepts as a given fact. Through the second way he makes the world into his own affair, into something that has a meaning for himself. The third way he regards as a goal towards which he has unceasingly to strive.

Why does the world appear to man in this threefold way? A simple consideration will explain it. I cross a meadow covered with flowers. The flowers make their colors known to me through my eyes. That is the fact which I accept as given. I rejoice in the splendor of the colors. Through this I turn the fact into an affair of my own. Through my feelings I connect the flowers with my own existence. A year later I go again over the same meadow. Other flowers are there. New joy arises in me through them. My joy of the former year will appear as a memory. It is in me; the object which aroused it in me is gone. But the flowers which I now see are of the same kind as those I saw the year before; they have grown in accordance with the same laws as did the others. If I have informed myself regarding this species and these laws, then I find them in the flowers of this year again just as I found them in those of last year. And I shall perhaps muse as follows: "The flowers of last year are gone; my joy in them remains only in my remembrance. It is bound up with my existence alone. That, however, which I recognized in the flowers of last year and recognize again this year, will remain as long as such flowers grow. That is something that has revealed itself to me, but is not dependent on my existence in the same way as my joy is. My feelings of joy remain *in me;* the laws, the *being* of the flowers remain outside me in the world."

Thus man continually links himself in this threefold way with the things of the world. One should not for the time being read anything into this fact, but merely take it as it stands. There follows from it that man has *three sides to his nature.* This and nothing else will for the present be indicated here by the three words *body, soul,* and *spirit.* Whoever connects any preconceived opinions, or even hypotheses with these three words will necessarily misunderstand the following explanations. By *body* is here meant that through which the things in man's environment reveal themselves to him; as in the above example, the flowers of the meadow. By the word *soul* is signified that by which he links the things to his own being, through which he experiences pleasure and displeasure, desire and aversion, joy and sorrow in connection with them. By *spirit* is meant that which becomes manifest in him when, as Goethe expressed it, he looks at things as a "so-to-speak, divine being." In this sense the human being consists of *body, soul,* and *spirit.*

Through his body man is able to place himself for the time being in connection with things; through his soul he retains in himself the impressions which they make on him; through his spirit there reveals itself to him what the things retain for themselves. Only when one observes man in these three aspects can one hope to be enlightened about his nature. For these three aspects show him to be related in a threefold way to the rest of the world.

Through his body he is related to the objects which present themselves to his senses from without. The materials from the outer world compose this body of his; and the forces of the outer world also work in it. And just as he observes the things of the outer world with his senses, so he can also observe his own bodily existence. But it is impossible to observe the soul-existence in the same way. Everything in me which is bodily process can be perceived with my bodily senses. My likes and dislikes, my joy and pain, neither I nor anyone else can perceive with bodily senses. The region of the soul is one which is inaccessible to bodily perception. The bodily existence of a man is manifest to all eyes; the soul-existence he carries within himself as his own world. Through the spirit, however, the outer world is revealed to him in a higher way. The mysteries of the outer world, indeed, unveil themselves in his inner being; but he steps in spirit out of himself and lets the things speak about themselves, about that which has significance not for him but for them. Man looks up at the starry heavens; the delight his soul experiences belongs to him; the eternal laws of the stars which he comprehends in thought, in spirit, belong not to him but to the stars themselves.

Thus man is citizen of three worlds. Through his body he belongs to the world which he also perceives through his body; through his soul he constructs for himself his own world; through his spirit a world reveals itself to him which is exalted above both the others.

It seems obvious that because of the essential differences of these three worlds, a clear understanding of them and of man's share in them can only be obtained by means of three different modes of observation.

1. The Corporeal Being of Man

We learn to know the body of man through bodily senses. And the way of observing it can differ in no way from that by which we learn to know other objects perceived by the senses. As we observe minerals, plants, animals, so can we observe man also. He is related to these three forms of existence. Like the minerals he builds his body out of the materials of Nature; like the plants he grows and propagates his species; like the animals, he perceives the objects around him and builds up his inner experiences on the basis of the impressions they make on him. We may therefore ascribe to man a mineral, a plant, and an animal existence.

The difference in structure of minerals, plants, and animals corresponds to the three forms of their existence. And it is this structure—the shape—which we perceive through the senses, and which alone we can call body. Now the human body is different from that of the animal. This difference everybody must recognize, whatever he may think in other respects regarding the relationship of man to animals. Even the most thoroughgoing materialist, who denies all soul, cannot but admit the truth of the following sentence which Carus utters in his *Organon der Natur und des Geistes:* "The finer, inner construction of the nervous system, and especially of the brain, still remains an unsolved problem for the physiologist and the anatomist; but that this concentration of the structures increases more and more in the animal, and in man reaches a stage unequaled in any other being, is a fully established fact; a fact which is of the deepest significance in regard to the mental evolution of man, of which, indeed, we may go so far as to say it is really in itself a sufficient explanation. Where, therefore, the structure of the brain has not developed properly, where smallness and poverty are revealed as in the case of microcephalics and idiots, it goes without saying that we can as little expect the apearance of original ideas and of knowledge, as one can expect propagation of the species from persons with completely stunted organs of generation. On the other hand, a strong and beautifully developed build of the whole man, and especially of the brain, will certainly not in itself take the place of genius, but it will at any rate supply the first and indispensable condition for higher knowledge."

Just as we ascribe to the human body the three forms of existence, mineral, plant, animal, so we must ascribe to it a fourth, the distinctively human form. Through his mineral existence man is related to everything visible; through his plantlike existence, to all beings that grow and propagate their species; through his animal existence, to all those that perceive their surroundings, and by means of external impressions have inner experiences; through his human form of existence he constitutes, even in regard to his body alone, a kingdom by himself.

2. The Soul-Being of Man

Man's soul-nature as his own inner world is different from his bodily nature. That which is his very own comes at once to the fore, when attention is turned to the simplest sensation. Thus no one can know whether another person perceives even such a simple sensation in exactly the same way as one does oneself. It is known that there are people who are color-blind. They see things only in different shades of grey. Others are partially color-blind.

They are unable, because of this, to perceive certain shades of colors. The picture of the world which their eyes give them is different from that the so-called normal persons. And the same holds good more or less in regard to the other senses. It will be seen, therefore, without further elaboration, that even simple sensations belong to the inner world. I can perceive with my bodily senses the red table which another person also perceives; but I cannot perceive his sensation of red. Sensation must therefore be described as belonging to the soul. If we grasp this fact alone quite clearly, we shall soon cease to regard inner experiences as mere brain processes or something similar. Feeling is closely allied to sensation. One sensation causes man pleasure, another displeasure. These are stirrings of his inner, his soul-life. In his feelings man creates a second world in addition to that which works on him from without. And a third is added to this— the will. Through the will man reacts on the outer world. And he thereby stamps the impress of his inner being on the outer world. The soul of man as it were flows outwards in the activities of his will. The actions of the human being differ from the occurrences of outer nature in that they bear the impress of his inner life. Thus the soul as that which is man's very own stands in contradistinction to the outer world. He receives from the outer world the incitements, but he creates in response to these incitements a world of his own. The body becomes the foundation of the soul-being of man.

3. The Spiritual Being of Man

The soul-being of man is not determined by the body alone. Man does not wander aimlessly and without a purpose from one sense impression to another; neither does he act under the influence of every casual incitement which plays upon him either from without or through the processes of his body. He reflects upon his perceptions and his acts. By reflecting upon his perceptions he gains knowledge of things: by reflecting upon his acts he introduces a reasonable coherence into his life. And he knows that he will fulfill his duty as a human being worthily only when he lets himself be guided by correct thoughts in knowing as well as in acting. The soul of man, therefore, is confronted by a twofold necessity. By the laws of the body it is governed by natural necessity; but it allows itself to be governed by the laws which guide it to exact thinking because it voluntarily acknowledges their necessity. Nature subjects man to the laws of metabolism, but he subjects himself to the laws of thought. By this means he makes himself a member of a higher order than that to which he belongs through his body. And this order is the *spiritual*. The spiritual is as different from the soul as the soul is different from the body. As long as we speak only of the particles of carbon, hydrogen, nitrogen, and oxygen which are in motion in the body, we have not got the soul in view. The soul-life begins only when within the motion of these particles, the feeling arises: "I taste sweetness" or "I feel pleasure." Just as little have we the spiritual in view as long as we consider merely those soul-experiences which course through a man who gives himself over entirely to the outer world and his bodily life. This soul-life is rather the basis of the spiritual just as the body is the basis of the soul-life. The scientist, or investigator of nature, is concerned with the body, the investigator of the soul (the psychologist) with the soul, and the investigator of the spirit with the spirit. To make clear to oneself through thought upon and observation of one's own self the difference between body, soul, and spirit, is a demand which must be made upon those who seek by thinking to enlighten themselves regarding the nature of man.

4. Body, Soul, and Spirit

Man can only come to a true understanding of himself when he grasps clearly the significance of thinking within his being. The brain is the bodily instrument for thinking. Just as man can only see colors with a properly constructed eye, so the suitably constructed brain serves him for thought. The whole body of man is so formed that it receives its crown in the organ of the spirit, the brain. The construction of the human brain can be understood only by considering it in relation to its task, which consists in being the bodily basis for the thinking spirit. This is borne out by a comparative survey of the animal world. Among the amphibians we find the brain small in comparison with the spinal cord; in mammals it is proportionately larger; in man it is largest in comparison with the rest of the body.

Many prejudices are prevalent regarding such statements about thinking as are brought forward here. Many persons are inclined to undervalue thinking, and to place higher the warm life of feeling or emotion. Some, indeed, say it is not by sober thinking, but by warmth of feeling, by the immediate power of the emotions, that one raises oneself to higher knowledge. People who talk thus fear to blunt the feelings by clear thinking. This certainly does result from the ordinary thinking that is concerned only with matters of utility; but in the case of thoughts that lead to higher regions of existence, the opposite happens. There is no feeling and no enthusiasm to be compared with the sentiments of warmth, beauty, and exaltation enkindled through the pure, crystal-clear thoughts which relate to higher worlds. For the highest feelings are as a matter of fact not those which come of themselves, but those which are achieved by energetic and persevering work in the realm of thought.

The human body is so built as to be adapted to thinking. The same materials and forces which are present in the mineral kingdom are so combined in the human body that by means of this combination thought can manifest itself. This mineral construction, built up in accordance with its task, will be called in the following pages the physical body of man.

This mineral structure, which is organized with reference to the brain as its central point, comes into existence through propagation and reaches its fully developed form through growth. Propagation and growth man shares in common with plants and animals. Through propagation and growth what is living differentiates itself from the lifeless mineral. Life gives rise to life by means of the germ. Descendant follows forefather from one living generation to another. The forces through which a mineral originates are directed upon the substances of which it is composed. A quartz crystal is formed through the forces inherent in the silicon and oxygen which are combined in the crystal. The forces which shape an oak tree must be sought for in an indirect way in the germ in the mother and father plants. The form of the oak is preserved through propagation from forefather to descendant. There are inner determining conditions innate in all that is living. It was a crude view of Nature which held that lower animals, even fishes, could evolve out of mud. The form of the living passes itself on by means of heredity. How a living being develops depends on what father or mother it has sprung from, or in other words, on the species to which it belongs. The materials of which it is composed are continually changing; the species remains constant during life, and is transmitted to the descendants. Therefore the species is that which determines the combination of the materials. This force which determines species will be here called *Life-force*. Just as the mineral forces express themselves in the crystals, so the formative life-force expresses itself in the species or forms of plant and animal life.

The mineral forces are perceived by man by means of his bodily senses and he can perceive only that for which he has such senses. Without the eye there is no perception of light, without the ear no perception of sound. The lowest organisms have only one of the senses belonging to man: a kind of sense of touch. Nothing can be perceived by such organisms, in the way a human being perceives, except those mineral forces which make themselves known through the sense of touch. In proportion as the other senses are developed in the higher animals does their surrounding world, which man also perceives, become richer and more varied. It depends, therefore, on the organs of a being whether that which exists in the outer world exists also for the being itself, as perception, as sensation. What is present in the air as a certain motion becomes in man the sensation of hearing. Man does not perceive the manifestations of the life-force through the ordinary senses. He sees the colors of the plants; he smells their perfume; the life-force remains hidden from this form of observation. But the ordinary senses have just as little right to deny that there is a life-force as has the man born blind to deny that colors exist. Colors are there for the person born blind as soon as he has been operated upon; in the same way, the objects, the various species of plants and animals created by the life-force (not merely the individual plants and animals) are present to man as objects of perception as soon as the necessary organ unfolds within him. An entirely new world opens out to man through the unfolding of this organ. He now perceives, not merely the colors, the odors, etc., of the living beings, but the life itself of these beings. In each plant, in each animal, he perceives, besides the physical form, the life-filled spirit-form. In order to have a name for this spirit-form let it be called the *ether-body*, or *life-body*.*

To the investigator of spiritual life, this matter presents itself in the following manner. The ether-body is for him not merely a product of the materials and forces of the physical body, but a real independent entity which first calls forth these physical materials and forces into life. It is in accordance with Spiritual Science to say: a purely physical body, a crystal for example, has its form through the action of the physical formative forces innate in that which is lifeless. A living body has its form not through the action of these forces, because the moment life has departed from it and it is given over to the physical forces only, it falls to pieces. The ether-body is an organism which preserves the physical body every moment during life from dissolution. In order to see this body, to perceive it in another being, one requires the awakened "spiritual eye." Without this, its existence can be accepted as a fact on logical grounds, but one can see it with the spiritual eye as one sees color with the physical eye. Offense should not be taken

---

* The author of this book, long after it was written, applied to what is here called etheric or life-body, the name *"formative-force-body"* (also cf. *Das Reich*, 4th book of the first year's issue). He felt moved to give it this name because he believes that one cannot do enough to prevent the misunderstanding due to confusing what is here meant by etheric body with the "vital force" of older natural science. In what concerns the rejection of this older concept of a vital force in the sense of modern natural science, the author shares in a certain respect the standpoint of those who are opposed to assuming such a vital force. For the purpose of assuming such a vital force was to explain the special mode of working in the organism of the inorganic forces. But that which works inorganically in the organism, does not work there in any other way than it does in the inorganic world. The laws of inorganic nature are in the organism no other than they are in the crystal, and so forth. But in the organism there is present something which is not inorganic: the formative life. The etheric body or formative-force-body lies at the base of this formative life. By assuming its existence, the rightful task of natural science is not interfered with: *viz.*, to observe the workings of forces in inorganic nature and to follow the workings into the organic world: and further, to refuse to think of these operations within the organism as being modified by a special vital force. The spiritual investigator speaks of the etheric body in so far as there manifests in the organism something other than what shows itself in the lifeless. In spite of all this the author does not here feel impelled to replace the term "etheric body" by the other "formative-force-body," since within the whole connected range of what is said here, any misunderstanding is excluded for everyone who really wants to see. Such a misunderstanding can only arise when the term is used in a development which cannot exhibit this connection.

at the expression "ether-body." Ether here designates something different from the hypothetical ether of the physicist. It should be regarded simply as a name for what is described here. And just as the physical body of man in its construction is a kind of reflection of its purpose, so is this also the case with man's etheric body. Moreover, it can be understood only when considered in relation to the thinking spirit. The etheric body of man differs from that of plants and animals, through being organized to serve the purposes of the thinking spirit. Just as man belongs to the mineral world through his physical body, he belongs through his etheric body to the life-world. After death the physical body dissolves into the mineral world, the ether-body into the life-world. By the word "body" is denoted that which gives any kind of being shape or form. The term "body" must not be confused with a bodily form perceptible to the physical senses. Used in the sense implied in this book the term "body' can also be applied to such forms as soul and spirit may assume.

In the life-body we still have something external to man. With the first stirrings of sensation the inner self responds to the stimuli of the outer world. You may trace ever so far what one is justified in calling the outer world, but you will not be able to find sensation. Rays of light stream into the eye, penetrating it till they reach the retina. There they call forth chemical processes (in the so-called visual-purple); the effect of these stimuli is passed on through the optic nerve to the brain where further physical processes arise. Could one observe these, one would simply see physical processes, just as elsewhere in the physical world. If I were able to observe the ether-body, I should see how the physical brain-process is at the same time a life-process. But the sensation of blue color, which the recipient of the rays of light has, I can find nowhere in this manner. It arises *only within the soul* of the recipient. If, therefore, the being of this recipient consisted only of the physical body and the ether-body, sensation could not exist. The activity by which sensation becomes a fact differs essentially from the operations of the formative life-force. It is an activity by which an inner experience is called forth from these operations. Without this activity there would be a mere life-process, such as is to be observed in plants. If one pictures a man receiving impressions from all sides, one must think of him at the same time as the *source* of the above-mentioned soul-activity which flows out from him to all the directions from which he is receiving the impressions. In all directions soul-sensations arise in response to the physical impacts. This fountain of activity shall be called the *sentient soul*. This sentient soul is just as real as the physical body. If a man stands before me, and I disregard his sentient soul by thinking of him as merely a physical body, it is exactly as if I were to call up in my mind, instead of a painting— merely the canvas.

A similar statement has to be made in regard to perceiving the sentient soul, as was previously made in reference to the ether-body. The bodily organs are blind to it. And blind to it also is the organ by which life can be perceived as life. But just as the ether-body is seen by means of this organ, so through a still higher organ can the inner world of sensation become a special kind of supersensible perception. A man would then not only sense the impressions of the physical and life-world, but would behold the sensations themselves. Before a man with such an organ, the sensation world of another being is spread out like an external reality.

One must distinguish between experiencing one's own world of sensation, and looking at that of another person. Every man of course can look into his own world of sensation; only the seer with the opened spiritual eye can see another person's world of sensation. Unless a man be a seer, he knows the world of sensation only as an inner one, only as the peculiar hidden experiences of his own soul; with the opened spiritual eye there shines out before the outward-turned spiritual gaze what otherwise lives only in the inner being of another person.

In order to prevent misunderstanding, it may be expressly stated here that the seer does not simply experience in himself what the other being has within him as content of his world of sensation. That being experiences the sensations in question from the point of view of his own inner being; the seer becomes aware of a manifestation of the world of sensation.

The sentient soul depends, as regards its activity, on the ether-body. For it draws from it that which it will cause to gleam forth as sensation. And since the ether-body is the life within the physical body, therefore the sentient soul is also indirectly dependent on the latter. Only with properly functioning and well-constructed eyes are correct color sensations possible. It is in this way that the nature of the body affects the sentient soul. The latter is thus determined and limited in its activity by the body. It lives within the limitations fixed for it by the nature of the body. The body accordingly is built up of mineral substances, is vitalized by the ether-body, and limits even the sentient soul. A man, therefore, who has the above-mentioned organ for seeing the sentient soul, knows it to be conditioned by the body. But the boundary of the sentient soul does not coincide with that of the physical body. It extends somewhat beyond the physical body. From this one sees that it proves itself to be greater than the physical body. Nevertheless the force through which its limits are set proceeds from the physical body. Thus between the physical body and the ether-body, on the one hand, and the sentient soul on the other, there inserts itself another distinct member of the human being. This is the *soul-body* or sentient body. One can express this in another way. One part of the ether-body forms a unity with the *sentient soul*, whereas the coarser part forms a kind of unity with the physical body. Nevertheless, the sentient soul extends, as has been said, beyond the soul-body.

What is here called sensation is only a part of the soul-being. (The expression sentient soul is chosen for the sake of simplicity.) Connected with sensations are the feelings of desire and aversion, impulses, instincts, passions. All these bear the same character of individual life as do the sensations, and are, like them, dependent on the bodily nature.

Just as the sentient soul enters into mutual action and reaction with the body, so does it also in thinking, with the spirit. In the first place thinking *serves* the sentient soul. Man forms thoughts about his sensations. He thus enlightens himself regarding the outside world. The child that has burnt itself thinks it over and reaches the thought "fire burns." Nor does man follow blindly his impulses, instincts, passions; his thinking about them brings about the opportunity through which he can gratify them. What is called material civilization moves entirely in this direction. It consists in the services which thinking renders to the sentient soul. An immeasurable amount of thought-power is directed to this end. It is thought-power that has built ships, railways, telegraphs, telephones; and by far the greatest proportion of all this serves only to satisfy the needs of sentient souls.

Thought-force permeates the sentient soul in a similar way to that in which the formative-life-force permeates the physical body. The formative-life-force connects the physical body with forefathers and descendants, and thus brings it under a system of laws with which the purely mineral body is in no way concerned. In the same way thought-force brings the soul under a system of laws to which it does not belong as mere sentient soul.

Through the sentient soul man is related to the animal. In animals, also, we observe the presence of sensations, impulses, instincts, and passions. But the animal obeys these immediately. They do not, in its case, become interwoven with independent thoughts, transcending the immediate experiences. This is also the case to a certain extent with undeveloped human beings. The mere sentient soul is therefore different from the evolved higher member of the soul which brings thinking into its service. This soul that is served by thought will be termed the *intellectual soul*. One could also call it the mind-soul.

The intellectual soul permeates the sentient soul. He who has the organ for "seeing" the soul sees, therefore, the intellectual soul as a separate entity, in relation to the mere sentient soul.

By thinking, man is led above and beyond his own personal life. He acquires something that extends beyond his soul. He comes to take for granted his conviction that the laws of thought are in conformity with the laws of the world. And he feels at home in the world because this conformity exists. This conformity is one of the weighty facts through which man learns to know his own nature. Man searches in his soul for truth, and through this truth it is not only the soul that speaks, but the things of the world. That which is recognized as truth by means of thought has an independent significance which refers to the things of the world, and not merely to one's own soul. In my delight at the starry heavens I live in my own inner being; the thoughts which I form for myself about the paths of heavenly bodies have the same significance for the thinking of every other person as they have for mine. It would be absurd to speak of my delight were I not in existence; but it is not in the same way absurd to speak of my thoughts, even without reference to myself. For the truth which I think today was true also yesterday, will be true tomorrow, although I concern myself with it only today. If a piece of knowledge gives me joy, the joy has significance just so long as it lives in me; the truth of the knowledge has its significance quite independently of this joy. By grasping the truth the soul connects itself with something that carries its value in itself. And this value does not vanish with the feeling in the soul any more than it arose with it. What is really truth neither arises nor passes away; it has a significance which cannot be destroyed. This is not contradicted by the fact that certain human truths have a value which is transitory, inasmuch as they are recognized after a certain period as partial or complete errors. A man must say to himself that truth exists in itself, and that his conceptions are only transient forms of eternal truths. Even he who says, like Lessing, that he contents himself with the eternal striving towards truth because the full, pure truth can, after all, exist only for a God, does not deny the eternity of truth but establishes it by such an utterance. For only that which has an eternal significance in itself can call forth an eternal striving after it. Were truth not it itself independent, if it acquired its value and significance through the feelings of the human soul, then it could not be the only unique goal for all mankind. One concedes its independent being by the very fact that one sets oneself to strive after it.

And as it is with the true, so it is with the truly good. Moral goodness is independent of inclinations and passions, inasmuch as it does not allow itself to be commanded by, but commands them. Likes and dislikes, desire and loathing belong to the personal soul of man; duty stands higher than likes and dislikes. Duty may stand so high in the eyes of a man that he will sacrifice his life for its sake. And a man stands the higher the more he has ennobled his inclinations, his likes and dislikes, so that without compulsion or subjection they themselves obey what is recognized as duty. Moral goodness has, like truth, its eternal value in itself, and does not receive it from the sentient soul.

By causing the self-existent true and good to come to life in his inner being, man raises himself about the mere sentient soul. The eternal spirit shines into it. A light is kindled in it which is imperishable. Insofar as the soul lives in this light, it is a participant of the eternal. It unites therewith its own existence. What the soul carries within itself of the true and the good is immortal in it. Let us call that which shines forth in the soul as eternal the *consciousness-soul*.* We can speak of consciousness even in connection with the lower soul-stirrings. The most ordinary everyday sensation is a matter of consciousness. To this extent animals also have consciousness. By consciousness-soul is meant the kernel of human consciousness, the *soul within the soul*. The consciousness-soul is thus distinguished as a distinct member of the soul from the intellectual soul. This latter is still entangled in the sensations, the impulses, the passions, etc. Everyone knows how at first he counts as true that which he prefers in his feelings, and so on. Only that truth, however, is permanent which has freed itself from all flavor of such sympathy and antipathy of feeling. The truth is true, even if all personal feelings revolt against it. The part of the soul in which this truth lives will be called consciousness-soul.

Thus three members have to be distinguished in the soul as in the body: *sentient soul, intellectual soul, consciousness-soul*. And just as the body works from below upwards with a limiting effect on the soul, so the spiritual works from above downwards into it, expanding it. For the more the soul fills itself with the true and the good, the wider and the more comprehensive becomes the eternal in it. To him who is able to "see" the soul, the radiance which proceeds from a human being because his eternal element is expanding, is just as much a reality as the light which streams out from a flame is real to the physical eye. For the seer the corporeal man counts as only part of the whole man. The physical body, as the coarsest structure, lies within outers, which mutually

---

* *Bewusstein-Seele* (consciousness-soul) may also, as indicated by Dr. Steiner, be translated "spiritual soul." —TRANS.

interpenetrate both it and each other. The ether-body fills the physical body as a life-form; extending beyond this on all sides is to be perceived the soul-body (astral form). And beyond this, again, extends the sentient soul, then the intellectual soul which grows the larger the more it receives into itself of the true and the good. For this true and good cause the expansion of the intellectual soul. A man living only and entirely according to his inclinations, his likes and dislikes, would have an intellectual soul whose limits coincide with those of his sentient soul. These formations, in the midst of which the physical body appears as if in a cloud, may be called the *human aura*. The aura is that in regard to which the being of man becomes enriched, when it is seen as this book endeavors to present it.

In the course of his development as a child, there comes the moment in the life of a man in which, for the first time, he feels himself to be an independent being distinct from the whole of the rest of the world. For finely strung natures it is a significant experience. The poet Jean Paul says in his autobiography: "I shall never forget the event which took place within me, hitherto narrated to no one, and of which I can give place and time, when I stood present at the birth of my self-consciousness. As a very small child I stood at the door of the house one morning, looking towards the woodpile on my left, when suddenly the inner vision, 'I am an I' came upon me like a flash of lightning from heaven and has remained shining ever since. In that moment my ego had seen itself for the first time and forever. Any deception of memory is hardly to be conceived as possible here, for no narrations by outsiders could have introduced additions to an occurrence which took place in the holy of holies of a human being, and of which the novelty alone gave permanence to such everyday surroundings." It is well known that little children say of themselves, "Charles is good," "Mary wants to have this." One feels it to be right that they speak of themselves as if of others, because they have not yet become conscious of their independent existence, because the consciousness of the self is not yet born in them. Through self-consciousness, man describes himself as an independent being, separate from all others, as "I." In "I" man includes all that he experiences as a being with body and soul. Body and soul are the carriers of the ego or "I"; in them it acts. Just as the physical body has its center in the brain, so has the soul its center in the ego. Man is aroused to sensations by impacts from without; feelings manifest themselves as effects of the outer world; the will relates itself to the outside world in that it realizes itself in external actions. The "I" as the essential being of man remains quite invisible. Excellently, therefore, does Jean Paul call a man's recognition of his ego an occurrence taking place only in his veiled holy of holies; for with his "I" man is quite alone. And this "I" is the man himself. That justifies him in regarding his ego as his true being. He may, therefore, describe his body and his soul as the sheaths or veils within which he lives; and he may describe them as bodily conditions through which he acts. In the course of his evolution he learns to regard these instruments ever more and more as servants of his ego. The little word "I" is a name which differs from all other names. Anyone who reflects in an appropriate manner on the nature of this name, will find that in so doing an avenue to the understanding of the human being in the deeper sense is revealed. Every other name can be applied to its corresponding object by all men in the same way. Everybody can call a table "table" or a chair "chair." This is not so with the name "I." No one can use it in referring to another person; each one can call only himself "I." Never can the name "I" reach my ears from outside when it refers to me. Only from within, only through itself, can the human being refer to himself as "I." When the human being therefore says "I" to himself, something begins to speak in him that has nothing to do with any one of the worlds from which the sheaths so far mentioned are taken. The "I" becomes ever more and more ruler of body and soul. This also expresses itself in the aura. The more the "I" is lord over body and soul, the more definitely organized, the more varied and the more richly colored is the aura.

The effect of the "I" on the aura can be seen by the "seeing" person. The "I" itself is invisible even to him; this remains truly within the veiled "holy of holies." But the "I" absorbs into itself the rays of the light which flashes up in a man as eternal light. As he gathers together the experiences of body and soul in the "I," so too he causes the thoughts of truth and goodness to stream into the "I." The phenomena of the senses reveal themselves to the "I" from the one side, the spirit reveals itself from the other. Body and soul yield themselves up to the "I" in order to serve it; but the "I" yields itself up to the spirit in order that the spirit may fill it to overflowing. The "I" lives in body and soul; but the spirit lives in the "I." And what there is of spirit in the "I" is eternal. For the "I" receives its nature and significance from that with which it is bound up. In so far as it experiences itself in the physical body, it is subject to the laws of the mineral world; through its ether-body to the laws of propagation and growth; by virtue of the sentient and intellectual souls to the laws of the soul-world; insofar as it receives the spiritual into itself it is subject to the laws of the spirit. That which the laws of mineral and of life construct, comes into being and vanishes; but the spirit has nothing to do with becoming and perishing.

The "I" lives in the soul. Although the highest manifestation of the "I" belongs to the consciousness-soul, one must nevertheless say that this "I," raying out from it, fills the whole of the soul, and through the soul exerts its action upon the body. And in the "I" the spirit is alive. The spirit sends its rays into the "I" and lives in it as in a sheath or veil, just as the "I" lives in its sheaths, the body and soul. The spirit develops the "I" from within, outwards; the mineral world develops it from without, inwards. The spirit forming an "I" and living as the "I" will be called *Spirit-self*, because it manifests as the "I," or ego, or self of man. The difference between the Spirit-self and the consciousness-soul can be made clear in the following way. The consciousness-soul is in touch with the self-existent truth which is independent of all antipathy and sympathy; the Spirit-self bears within it the same truth, but taken up into and enclosed by the "I," individualized by the latter and absorbed into the independent being of the man. It is through the eternal truth becoming thus individualized and bound up into one being with the "I," that the "I" itself attains to eternity.

The Spirit-self is a revelation of the spiritual world within the "I," just as from the other side sensations are a revelation of the physical world within the "I." In what is red, green, light, dark, hard, soft, warm, cold, one recognizes the revelations of the corporeal world; in what is true and good, the revelations of the spiritual world. In the same sense in which the revelation of the corporeal world is called sensation, let the revelation of the spiritual be called *intuition*. Even the most simple thought contains intuitions, for one cannot touch it with the hands or see it with the eyes; its revelation must be received from the spirit through the "I." If an undeveloped and a developed man look at a plant, there lives in the "I" of the one something quite different from that which is in the "I" of the other. And yet the sensations of both are called forth by the same object. The difference lies in this, that the one can form far more perfect thoughts about the object than can the other. If objects revealed themselves through sensation alone, there could be no progress in spiritual development. Even the savage is affected by Nature; but the laws of Nature reveal themselves only to the thoughts, fructified by intuition, of the more highly developed man. The stimuli from the outer world are felt even by the child as incentives to the will; but the commandments of the morally good disclose themselves to him only in the course of his development, in proportion as he learns to live in the spirit and understand its revelations.

Just as there could be no color sensations without physical eyes, so there could be no intuitions without the higher thinking of the Spirit-self. And as little as sensation creates the plant on which the color appears, does intuition create the spiritual realities about which it is merely giving information.

The "I" of a man, which comes to life in the soul, draws into itself messages from above, from the spirit-world, through intuitions, just as through sensations it draws in messages from the physical world. And in so doing it fashions the spirit-world into the individualized life of its own soul, even as it does the physical world by means of the senses. The soul, or rather the "I" lighting up in it, opens its portals on two sides: towards the corporeal and towards the spiritual.

Now just as the physical world can only give information about itself to the ego by building out of physical materials and forces a body in which the conscious soul can live and possess organs to perceive the corporeal world outside itself, so does the spirit-world build, with its spirit-substances and spirit-forces, a spirit-body in which the "I" can live and, through intuitions, perceive the spiritual. (It is evident that the expressions *spirit-substance*, *spirit-body* contain a contradiction, according to the literal meaning of the words. They are used only in order to direct attention to what, in the spiritual, corresponds to the physical body of man.)

Just as within the physical world each human body is built up as a separate physical being, so is the spirit-body within the spirit-world. In the spirit-world there is an "inner" and an "outer" for man just as there is in the physical world. As man takes in the materials of the physical world around him and assimilates them in his physical body, so does he take up the spiritual from the spiritual environment and make it into his own. The spiritual is the eternal nourishment of man. And as man is born out of the physical world, so is he born out of the spirit through the eternal laws of the true and the good. He is separated from the spirit-world outside him, as he is separated from the whole physical world, as an independent being. This independent spiritual being will be called the *Spirit-man*.

If we investigate the human physical body, we find the same materials and forces in it as are to be found outside it in the rest of the physical world. It is the same with the Spirit-man. In it pulsate the elements of the external spirit-world; in it the forces of the rest of the spirit-world are active. As within the physical skin a being is enclosed and limited which is alive and feels, so also is it in the spirit-world. The spiritual skin, which separates the Spirit-man from the homogeneous spirit-world, makes him an independent being within it, living a life within himself and perceiving intuitively the spiritual content of the world—let us call this spiritual skin (auric sheath) the *spirit-sheath*. Only it must be kept clearly in mind that the spiritual skin expands continually with advancing human evolution, so that the spiritual individuality of man (his auric sheath) is capable of enlargement to an unlimited extent.

The Spirit-man lives within this spirit-sheath. It is built up by the spiritual life-force. In a similar way to that in which one speaks of an ether-body, one must therefore speak of an ether-spirit in reference to the Spirit-man. Let this ether-spirit be called *Life-spirit*. The spiritual being of man therefore is composed of three parts, *Spirit-man, Life-spirit,* and *Spirit-self*.

For one who is a seer in the spiritual regions, this spiritual being of man is a perceptible reality as the higher, truly spiritual part of the aura. He sees the Spirit-man as Life-spirit within the spirit-sheath, and he sees how this Life-spirit grows continually larger, by taking in spiritual nourishment from the spiritual external world. Further, he sees how the spirit-sheath continually increases, widens out through what is brought into it, and how the Spirit-man becomes ever larger and larger. Insofar as this becoming larger is seen spatially, it is, of course, only a picture of the reality. In spite of this, man's soul is directed towards the corresponding spiritual reality in conceiving this picture. For the difference between the spiritual and the physical being of man is that the latter has a limited size while the former can grow to an unlimited extent. Whatever of spiritual nourishment is absorbed has an eternal value. The human aura is accordingly composed of two interpenetrating parts. Color and form are given to the one by the physical existence of man, and to the other by his spiritual existence. The ego marks the separation between them in such wise that the physical, after its own manner, yields itself and builds up a body that allows a soul to live within it; and the "I" yields itself and allows to develop in it the spirit, which now, for its part, permeates the soul and gives it the goal in the spirit-world. Through the body the soul is enclosed in the physical; through the Spirit-man there grow wings for its movement in the spiritual world.

In order to comprehend the whole man, one must think of him as put together out of the components mentioned above. The body builds itself up out of the world of physical matter in such wise that its construction is adapted to the requirements of the thinking ego. It is penetrated with life-force, and thereby becomes the etheric or life-body. As such it opens itself through the sense-organs towards the outer world and becomes the soul-body. This the sentient soul permeates and becomes a unity with. The sentient soul does not merely receive the impact of the outer world as sensations; it has its own inner life which it fertilizes through thinking, on the one hand, as it does through sensations on the other. It thus becomes the intellectual soul. It is able to do this by opening itself to intuitions from above, as it does to sensations from below. Thus it becomes the consciousness-soul. This is possible for it because the spirit-world builds into it the organ of intuition, just as the physical body builds for it the sense-organs. As the senses transmit to the human organism sensations by means of the soul-body, so does the spirit transmit to it intuitions through the organ of intuition. The Spirit-self is thereby linked into a unity with the consciousness-soul, just as the physical body is with the sentient soul in the soul-body. Consciousness-soul and Spirit-self form a unity. In this unity the Spirit-man lives as Life-spirit, just as the etheric body forms the bodily basis for the soul-body. And as the physical body is enclosed in the physical skin, so is the Spirit-man in the spirit-sheath. The members of the whole man are therefore as follows:

A. Physical body
B. Ether-body or life-body
C. Soul-body
D. Sentient soul
E. Intellectual soul
F. Consciousness-soul
G. Spirit-self
H. Life-spirit
I. Spirit-man

Soul-body (C) and sentient soul (D) are a unity in the earthly man; in the same way are consciousness-soul (F) and Spirit-self (G) a unity. Thus there come to be seven parts in the earthly man:

1. Physical body
2. Etheric or life-body
3. Sentient soul-body
4. Intellectual soul
5. Spirit-filled Consciousness-soul
6. Life-spirit
7. Spirit-man

In the soul the "I" flashes forth, receives the impetus from the spirit and thereby becomes the bearer of the Spirit-man. Thus man participates in the three worlds, the physical, the soul, and the spiritual. He is rooted in the physical world through his physical body, ether-body, and soul-body and blossoms through the Spirit-self, Life-spirit, and Spirit-man up into the spiritual world. The stalk, however, which takes root in the one and blossoms in the other, is the soul itself.

This arrangement of the members of man can be expressed in a simplified way, but one entirely consistent with the above. Although the human "I" lights up in the consciousness-soul it nevertheless penetrates the whole soul-being. The parts of this soul-being are not at all as distinctly separate as are the limbs of the body: they interpenetrate each other in a higher sense. If then one regards the intellectual soul and the consciousness-soul as the two sheaths of the "I" that belong together, with the "I" itself as their kernel, then one can divide man into physical body, life-body, astral body, and "I." The expression astral body designates here what is formed by soul-body and sentient soul together. This expression is found in the older literature, and may be applied here in a somewhat broad sense to that in the constitution of man which lies beyond the sensibly perceptible. Although the sentient soul is in certain respects energized by the "I," it is still so intimately connected with the soul-body that, in thinking of both as united, a single expression is justified. When, now, the "I" saturates itself with the Spirit-self, then this Spirit-self makes its appearance in such wise that the astral body is worked over from within the soul. In the astral body there are primarily active the impulses, desires, and passions of man, insofar as they are felt by him; sense-perceptions are also active in it. Sense-perceptions arise through the soul-body as a member in man which comes to him from the external world. Impulses, desires, and passions, etc., arise in the sentient soul, insofar as it is energized from within, before this "inner" has yielded itself to the Spirit-self. If the "I" saturates itself with the Spirit-self, then the soul energizes the astral body with this Spirit-self. This expresses itself in the illumination of the impulses, desires, and passions by what the "I" has received from the spirit. The "I" has then, through its participation in the spiritual world, become ruler in the world of impulses, desires, etc., To the extent to which it has become this, the Spirit-self manifests in the astral body. And the astral body is thereby transmuted. The astral body itself then appears as a two-fold body—in part untransmuted and in part transmuted. Therefore, the Spirit-self, as manifested in man, can be designated as the trasmuted astral body.

A similar process takes place in a man when he receives the Life-spirit into his "I." The life-body then becomes transmuted. It becomes penetrated with the Life-spirit. This manifests itself in such wise that the life-body becomes quite other than it was. For this reason one can also say that Life-spirit is the transmuted life-body. And if the "I" receives the Spirit-man, it thereby receives the necessary force with which to permeate the physical body. Naturally, that part of the physical body, thus transmuted, is not perceptible to the physical senses. For it is just that part of the physical body which has been spiritualized that has become the Spirit-man. The physical body is then present to the physical sesnses as physical, but in so far as this physical is spiritualized, it must be perceived by spiritual faculties of perception. To the external senses the physical, even when permeated by the spiritual, appears to be merely sensible.

Taking all this as basis, the following arrangement of the members of man may also be given:

1. Physical body
2. Life-body
3. Astral body
4. "I" as soul-kernel
5. Spirit-self as transmuted astral body
6. Life-spirit as transmuted life-body
7. Spirit-man as transmuted physical body

Spirit and Destiny*

Midway between body and spirit lives the *soul*. The impressions which come to it through the body are transitory. They are present only as long as the body opens its organs to the things of the outer world. My eye perceives the color of the rose only as long as the rose is in front of it and my eye is itself open. The presence of the things of the outer world as well as of the bodily organs is necessary in order that an impression, a sensation, or a perception can occur. But what I have recognized in my intellect as truth concerning the rose does not pass with the present moment. And as regards its truth, it is not in the least dependent on me. It would be true even though I had never stood before the rose. What I know through the spirit is rooted in an element of the soul-life through which the soul is linked with a world-content that manifests itself in the soul independently of its bodily basis. The point is not whether what manifests itself is essentially imperishable, but whether its manifestation for the soul takes place in such a way that the soul's perishable bodily basis takes no part, but only that which is independent of the perishable element. The enduring element in the soul comes under observation at the moment one becomes aware that the soul has experiences which are not bounded by its perishable factor. Again the important point is not whether these experiences come to consciousness primarily through perishable processes of the bodily organization, but the fact that they contain something which does indeed dwell in the soul, but yet in its truth is independent of the transient process of the perception. The soul is placed between the present and duration in that it holds the

* From "Re-embodiment of the Spirit and Destiny," *Theosophy: An Introduction to the Supersensible Knowledge of the World and the Destination of Man*, 4th ed. (London: Rudolf Steiner Press, 1973), pp. 46–67.

middle place between body and spirit. But it also mediates between the present and duration. It preserves the present for remembrance. It thereby rescues the present from the impermanence, and takes it up into the duration of its own spiritual being. It also stamps that which endures upon the temporal and impermanent by not merely yielding itself up in its own life to the transitory incitements, but by determining things from out of its own initiative, and embodying its own nature in them in the shape of the actions it performs. By remembrance the soul preserves the yesterday; by action it prepares the tomorrow.

My soul would always have to preceive afresh the red of the rose, in order to have it in consciousness, if it could not retain it through remembrance. What remains after an external impression, what can be retained by the soul, can again become a conception, independently of the external impression. Through this power of forming conceptions, the soul makes the outer world so into its own inner world that it can then retain the latter in the memory—for remembrance—and, independent of the impressions acquired, lead therewith a life of its own. The soul-life thus becomes the enduring result of the transitory impressions of the external world.

But action also receives permanence when once it is stamped on the outer world. If I cut a twig from a tree, something has taken place through my being, which completely changes the course of events in the outer world. Something quite different would have happened to the branch of the tree if I had not interfered by my action. I have called into life a series of effects which, without my existence, would not have been present. What I have done today endures for tomorrow; it becomes lasting through the deed, as my impressions of yesterday have become permanent for my soul through memory.

For this fact of becoming permanent through action we do not, in our ordinary consciousness, form a definite conception like that which we have for memory for the becoming permanent of an experience which has occurred as the result of a perception. But will not the "I" of a man be just as much linked to the alteration in the world resulting from his deed as it is to a memory resulting from an impression? The "I" judges new impressions differently, according as it has or has not this or that other recollection. But as "I" it has also entered into a different relation to the world according as it has performed one deed or another. Whether in the relation between the world and my "I" a certain something new is present or not, depends upon whether or not I have made an impression on another person through an action. I am a different man in relation to the world after having made an impression on my surroundings.

The fact that what is here indicated is not so generally noticed as is the change in the "I" through the acquiring of a recollection, is solely due to the circumstance that the recollection unites itself, immediately on being formed, with the soul-life, which man always feels to be his own; but the external effects of the deed are independent of soul-life and work out in consequences which again are something different from what is retained in the recollection. But apart from this it must be admitted that, after a deed has been accomplished, there is something in the world which the ego has sealed with its own character. If one really thinks out what is here being considered, the question must arise as to whether the results of a deed on which the "I" has stamped its own nature might not retain a tendency to return to the "I," just as an impression preserved in the memory revives in response to some external inducement. What is preserved in the memory waits for such an inducement. Could not that which has retained the imprint of the "I" in the external world wait also, so as to approach the human soul from *without,* just as memory, in response to a given inducement, approaches it from *within?* This matter is put forward here only as a question, for certainly it might happen that the opportunity would never occur, through which the results of a deed, bearing the impress of the ego, could meet the human soul. But that these results do exist, as such, and that, through their presence, they determine the relation of the world to the "I," is seen at once to be a possible conception when one really follows out in thought the matter before us. In the following considerations, we shall inquire whether there is anything in human life which, starting from this possibility, points to a reality.

Let us first consider memory. How does it originate? Evidently in quite a different way from sensation or perception. Without the eye I cannot have the sensation "blue." But through the eye I in no way have the remembrance of blue. If the eye is to give me this sensation now, a blue thing must come before it. The body would allow all impressions to sink back again into nothing were it not that whilst the present image is being formed through the act of perception, something is also taking place in the relationship between the outer world and the soul, as a result of which the man is able, subsequently, to form, through his own inner processes, a fresh image of that which he received in the first place as an image from outside himself. (Anyone who has acquired practice in observing the life of the soul will be able to realize how erroneous it is to say that a man has a perception today, and tomorrow, through memory, the same perception appears again, having meanwhile remained somewhere or other within him. No; the perception which I *now* have is a phenomenon which passes away with the "now." When recollection takes place, a process occurs in me which is the result of something that happened, *in addition* to the calling forth of the actual present image, in the relation between the external world and me. The image called forth through remembrance is a new one, and not the old one preserved. Recollection consists in the fact that one can make a fresh mental image to oneself, and not that a former image can revive. What appears again in recollection is something different from the original image itself. These remarks are made here because in the domain of Spiritual Science it is necessary that more accurate conceptions should be framed than is the case in ordinary life (and indeed in ordinary science). I remember; that is, I experience something which is itself no longer present. I unite a past experience with my present life. This is the case with every remembrance. Let us say for instance, that I meet a man and recognize him again because I met him yesterday. He would be a complete stranger to me were I not able to unite the picture which I made yesterday by perception with my impression of him today. The picture of today is given me by the sense-perception, that is to say, by my sense-organization. But who conjures yesterday's picture into my soul? It is the same being in me that was present during my experience yesterday, and is also present in that of today. In the previous explanations it has been called *soul*. Were it not for this faithful preserver of the past, each external impression would be always new to a man. Clearly the process by which perception becomes a recollection is that the soul imprints it upon the body, as though it were stamped upon it. But the soul must both make the impression and also itself perceive the impression it has made, just as it perceives any object outside itself. It is in this way that the soul is the preserver of memory.

As preserver of the past, the soul continually gathers treasures for the human spirit. That I can distinguish what is correct from what is incorrect depends on the fact that I, as a human being, am a thinking being, able to grasp the truth in my spirit. Truth is eternal, and it could always reveal itself to me again in things, even if I were always to lose sight of the past and each impression were to be a new one to me. But the spirit within me is not restricted to the impressions of the present alone; the soul extends its horizon over the past. And the more it is able to bring to the spirit out of the past, the richer does it make the spirit. Thus the soul hands on to the spirit what it has received from the body. The spirit of man therefore carries at each moment of its life a twofold possession within itself: first, the eternal laws of the good and the true; second, the remembrance of the experiences of the past. What it does, it accomplishes under the influence of these two factors. If we want to understand a human spirit we must therefore know two different things about it: first, how much of the eternal has revealed itself to it; second, how much treasure from the past lies stored up within it.

These treasures by no means remain in the spirit in an unchanged form. The impressions man acquires from his experiences fade gradually from the memory. Not so their fruits. One does not remember all the experiences one lived through during childhood while acquiring the faculties of reading and writing. But one could not read or write if one had not had the experiences, and if their fruits had not been preserved in the form of abilities. And that is the transmutation which the spirit effects on the treasures of memory. It consigns whatever can merely lead to pictures of the separate experiences to their fate and extracts from them only the force necessary for enhancing its own abilities. Thus not one experience passes by unutilized; the soul preserves each one as memory, and from each the spirit draws forth all that can enrich its abilities and the whole content of its life. The human spirit grows through assimilated experiences. And although one cannot find the past experiences in the spirit as it were in a store-room, one nevertheless finds their effects in the abilities which the man has acquired.

Spirit and soul have thus far been considered only within the period lying between birth and death. One cannot stop there. Anyone wishing to do so would be like a man who observes the human body also within the same limits. Much can certainly be discovered within these limits, but the human form can never be explained by what lies between birth and death. It cannot build itself up directly out of mere physical substances and forces. It can descend only from a form like its own, which arises as the result of what has been handed on by heredity. The physical materials and forces build up the body during life; the forces of propagation enable another body, a body which can have the same form, to proceed from it; that is to say, one which is able to be the bearer of a similar life-body. Each life-body is a repetition of its forefather. Only because it is such a repetition does it appear, not in any chance form, but in that passed on to it by heredity. The forces which make possible my human form lay in my forefathers. But the *spirit* of a man appears also in a definite form (the word "form" is naturally used in a spiritual sense). And the forms of the spirit are the most varied imaginable in different persons. No two men have the same spiritual form. Investigations in this region should be made in just as quiet and matter-of-fact a manner as in the physical world. It cannot be said that the differences in human beings in a spiritual respect arise only from the differences in their environment, their upbringing, etc. This is by no means the case; for two people under similar influences as regards environment, upbringing, etc., develop in quite different ways. One must therefore admit that they have entered on their path of life with quite different qualities. Here one is brought face-to-face with an important fact which, when its full bearing is recognized, sheds light on the being of man. A person who is set upon directing his outlook exclusively towards material happenings could indeed assert that the individual differences of human personalities arise from differences in the constitution of the material germs. (In view of the laws of heredity discovered by Gregor Mendel and further developed by others, such a view can say much that gives it the appearance of justification, even to a scientific judgment.) One who judges in this way only shows, however, that he has no insight into the real relation of man to his experience. For it is obvious to careful observation that external circumstances affect different persons in different ways, because of something which is not the direct result of their material development. To the really accurate investigator in this domain it becomes apparent that what proceeds from the material basis can be distinguished from that which, it is true, arises through the mutual interaction of the man with his experiences, but which can only take shape and form in that the soul itself enters into this mutual interaction. It is clear that the soul stands here in relation to something within the external world, which, by virtue of its very nature, cannot be connected with the material, germinal basis.

Human beings differ from their animal fellow-creatures on the earth through their physical form. But in respect of this form they are, within certain limits, like one another. There is only one human species. However great may be the differences between races, tribes, peoples, and personalities, as regards the physical body, the resemblance between man and man is greater than between man and any animal species. Everything that finds expression in the human species is conditioned through inheritance from forefathers to descendants. And the human form is bound to this heredity. As the lion can inherit its physical form only through lion forefathers, so can the human being inherit his physical body only through human forefathers.

Just as the physical similarity of men is clear to the eye, so does the difference of their spiritual forms reveal itself to the unprejudiced spiritual gaze. There is one very evident fact through which this is expressed. It consists in the existence of the life history of a human being. Were a human being merely a member of a species, no life history could exist. A lion, a dove, lay claim to interest insofar as they belong to the lion or the dove species. The single being in all its essentials has been understood when one has described the species. It matters little whether one has to do with father, son, or grandson. What is of interest in them, father, son, and grandson have in common. But what a human being signifies begins, not where he is merely a member of a species, but where he is a single individual being. I have not in the least understood the nature of Mr. Smith if I have described his son or his father. I must know his own life history. Anyone who reflects on the nature of biography becomes aware that in respect of the spiritual *each man is a species for himself*. Those people, to be sure, who regard a biography merely as a collection of external incidents in the life of a person, may claim they can write the biography of a dog in the same way as that of a man. But anyone who depicts in a biography the real individuality of a man grasps the fact that he has in the biography of one human being something that corresponds to the description of a whole species in the animal kingdom. The point is not—and this is quite obvious—that one can relate something in the nature of a biography about an animal, especially clever ones, but the point is that the human biography does not correspond to life history of the individual animal but to the description of the animal species. Of course there will always be people who will seek to refute what has been said here by urging that owners of menageries, for instance, know how single animals of the same species differ from one another. The man who judges thus shows, however, that he is unable to distinguish the difference between individuals from a difference which reveals itself as acquired *only* through individuality.

Now if genus or species in the physical sense becomes intelligible only when one understands it as conditioned by heredity, so too the spiritual being can be understood only through a similar *spiritual heredity*. I have received my physical human form because of my descent from human forefathers. Whence have I that which finds expression in my life history? As physical man, I repeat the shape of my forefathers. What do I repeat as spiritual man? Anyone claiming that what is comprised in my life history required no further explanation, but has just to be accepted as such, must be regarded as being also bound to maintain that he has seen, somewhere, an earthmound on which the lumps of matter have, quite by themselves, conglomerated into a living man.

As physical man I spring from other physical men, for I have the same shape as the whole human species. The qualities of the species, accordingly, could thus be acquired within the species through heredity. As spiritual man I have my own form as I have my own life history. I can therefore have obtained this form from no one but myself. And since I entered the world not with undefined but with defined soul-predispositions, and since the course of my life, as it comes to expression in my life-history, is determined by these predispositions, my work upon myself cannot have begun with my birth. I must, as spiritual man, have existed before my birth. In my forefathers I certainly did not exist, for they, as spiritual human begins, are different from me. My life history is not explainable through theirs. On the contrary, I must, as spiritual being, be the repetition of someone through whose life history mine can be explained. The only thinkable alternative would be this: that I owe the form of the content of my life history to a spiritual life only, prior to birth (or more correctly to conception). But one would only be entitled to hold this idea if one were willing to assume that what acts upon the human soul from its physical surroundings is of the same nature as what the soul receives from a purely spiritual world. Such an assumption contradicts really accurate observation. For what affects the human soul out of its physical environment works in the same way as a later experience works on a similar earlier experience in the same life. In order to observe these relations correctly, one must acquire a perception of how there are operating in human life impressions whose influence upon the aptitudes of the soul is like standing before a deed that has to be done, in contrast to what has already been practiced in physical life. But the soul does not bring faculties gained in this immediate life to meet these impressions, but aptitudes which receive the impressions in the same way as do the faculties acquired through practice. Anyone who penetrates into these matters arrives at the conception of earth-lives which must have preceded this present one. He cannot in his thinking stop at purely spiritual experiences preceding this present earth-life. The physical form which Schiller bore, he inherited from his forefathers. But just as little as Schiller's physical form can have grown directly out of the earth can his spiritual being have arisen directly out of a spiritual environment. He must himself be the reembodiment of a spiritual being through whose life history his own will be explicable, just as his physical human form is explicable through human propagation. In the same way, therefore, as the physical human form is again and again a repetition, a reembodiment, of the distinctively human species, so too the spiritual human being must be a reembodiment of the same spiritual human being. For, as spiritual human being, each one is in fact his own species.

It might be objected to what has been stated here that it is a mere spinning of thoughts, and such external proofs might be demanded as one is accustomed to demand in ordinary natural science. The reply to this is that the reembodiment of the spiritual human being is, naturally, a process which does not belong to the domain of external physical facts, but is one that takes place entirely in the spiritual region. And to this region no other of our ordinary powers of intelligence has entrance, save that of *thinking*. He who will not trust to the power of thinking, cannot in fact enlighten himself regarding higher spiritual facts. For him whose spiritual eye is opened, the above trains of thought act with exactly the same force as does an event that takes place before his physical eyes. Anyone who ascribes to a so-called proof, constructed according to methods of natural science, greater power to convince than the above observations concerning the significance of life history may be in the ordinary sense of the word a great scientist; but from the paths of true spiritual investigation he is very far distant.

One of the most dangerous assumptions consists in claiming to explain the spiritual qualities of a man by inheritance from father, mother, or other ancestors. Anyone who is guilty of the assumption, for example, that Goethe inherited what constituted his essential being from father or mother will at first be hardly accessile to argument, for there lies within him a deep antipathy to unprejudiced observation. A materialistic spell prevents him from seeing the mutual connections of phenomena in the true light.

In such observations as the above, the antecedents are provided for following the human being beyond birth and death. Within the boundaries formed by birth and death, the human being belongs to the three worlds—of the bodily element, of soul, and of spirit. The soul forms the intermediate link between body and spirit, inasmuch as it endows the third member of the body, the soul-body, with the capacity for sensation, and inasmuch as it permeates the first member of the spirit, the Spirit-self, as consciousness-soul. Thus it takes part and lot during life with the body as well as with the spirit. This comes to expression in its whole existence. It will depend on the organization of the soul-body, how the sentient soul can unfold its capabilities. And on the other hand, it will depend on the life of the consciousness-soul to what extent the Spirit-self can develop within it. The more highly organized the soul-body is, the more complete is the intercourse which the sentient soul will be able to develop with the outer world. And the Spirit-self will become so much the richer and more powerful, the more the consciousness-soul brings nourishment to it. It has been shown that during life this nourishment is supplied to the Spirit-self through assimilated experiences and the fruits of those experiences. For the interaction of soul and spirit described above can, of course, only take place where soul and spirit are within each other, penetrating each other, that is, within the union of Spirit-self with consciousness-soul.

Let us consider first the interaction of the soul-body and the sentient soul. The soul-body, as has become evident, is the most finely elaborated part of the body; but it nevertheless belongs to the body and is dependent on it. Physical body, ether-body, and soul-body compose, in a certain sense, one whole. Hence the soul-body is also involved in the laws of physical heredity through which the body receives its shape. And since it is the most mobile and, so to speak, the most volatile form of body, it must also exhibit the most mobile, volatile manifestations of heredity. While, therefore, the difference in the physical body corresponding to races, peoples, and tribes is the smallest, and while the ether-body shows, on the whole, a preponderating likeness, although a greater divergence as between single individuals, in the soul-body the difference is already a very considerable one. In it is expressed what is felt to be the *external, personal* peculiarity of a man. It is therefore also the bearer of that part of this personal peculiarity which is passed on from parents, grandparents, etc., to their descendants. True, the soul as such leads a complete life of its own; it shuts itself up with its inclinations and disinclinations, its feelings and passions. But as a whole it is nevertheless active, and therefore this whole comes to expression also in the sentient soul. And because the sentient soul interpenetrates and, as it were, fills the soul-body, the latter forms itself according to the nature of the soul and can in this way, as the bearer of heredity, pass on inclinations, passions, etc., from forefathers to children. On this fact rests what Goethe says: "From my father I have stature and the serious manner of life, from my mother a joyous disposition and the love of telling stories." Genius, of course, he did not receive from either.

In this way we are shown what part of a man's soul-qualities he hands over, as it were, to the line of physical heredity. The substances and forces of the physical body are in like manner present in the whole circle of external, physical Nature. They are continually being taken up from it and given back to it. In the space of a few years the substance which composes our physical body is entirely renewed. That this substance takes the form of the human body, and that it is perpetually renewed within this body, depends upon the fact that it is held together by the ether-body. And the form of the latter is not determined by events between birth—or conception—and death alone, but is dependent on the laws of heredity which extend beyond birth and death. That soul-qualities also can be transmitted by heredity, that is, that the progress of physical heredity receives an impulse from the soul, is due to the fact that the soul-body can be influenced by the sentient soul.

Now how does the interaction between soul and spirit proceed? During life, the spirit is bound up with the soul in the way shown above. The soul receives from it the gift of living in the good and true and of thereby bringing, in its own life, in its tendencies, impulses, and passions, the spirit itself to expression. The Spirit-self brings to the "I," from the world of the spirit, the eternal laws of the true and good. These link themselves through the consciousness-soul with the experiences of the soul's own life. These experiences themselves pass away but their fruits remain. The Spirit-self receives an abiding impression by having been linked with them. When the human spirit meets with an experience similar to one to which it has already been linked, it sees in it something familiar and is able to adopt a different attitude towards it from the one it would adopt if it were facing it for the first time. This is the basis of all learning. And the fruits of learning are acquired capacities. The fruits of the transitory life are in this way graven on the eternal spirit. And do we not see these fruits? Whence spring the innate predispositions and talents described above as characteristic of the spiritual man? Surely only from capacities of one kind or another which the human being brings with him when he begins his earthly life. These capacities, in certain respects, exactly resemble those which we can also acquire for ourselves during our earthly life. Take the case of a genius. It is known that Mozart, when a boy, could write out from memory a long musical work after hearing it only once. He was able to do this only because he could survey the whole at once. Within certain limits, a man is also able during life to increase his capacity of rapid survey, of grasping connections, so that he then possesses new faculties. Lessing has said of himself that through a talent for critical observation he had acquired for himself something that came near to genius. One has either to regard such abilities founded on innate capacities as a miracle or to consider them as fruits of experiences which the Spirit-self has had through a soul. They have been graven on this Spirit-self, and since they have not been implanted in this life, they must have been in a former one. The human spirit is its own species. And just as man, as a physical being belonging to a species, transmits his qualities within the species, so does the *spirit* within *its* species, that is, within itself. *In each life the human spirit appears as a repetition of itself with the fruits of its former experiences in previous lives.* This life is consequently the repetition of others, and brings with it what the Spirit-self has, by work, acquired for itself in the previous life. When the Spirit-self absorbs something that can develop into fruit, it saturates itself with the Life-spirit. Just as the life-body reproduces the form, from species to species, so does the Life-spirit reproduce the soul from personal existence to personal existence.

The preceding considerations give validity to that conception which seeks the reason for certain life processes of man in repeated earth-lives. That conception can really only receive its full significance by means of observations which spring from spiritual insight such as can be acquired by following the path of knowledge described at the close of this book. Here the only intention was to show that ordinary observation, rightly orientated by thinking, already leads to this conception. But observation of this kind, it is true, will at first leave the conception to become something like a silhouette. And it will not be possile to defend the conception entirely against the objections advanced by observation which is neither accurate nor rightly guided by thinking. But on the other hand it is true that anyone who acquires such a conception through ordinary thoughtful observation makes himself ready for supersensible observation. To a certain extent he develops something that one needs must have *prior* to this supersensible observation, just as one must have eyes *prior* to observing through the senses. Anyone who objects that through the formation of such a conception one can readily suggest to oneself the supersensible observation proves only that he is incapable of entering into the reality and that it is he himself who is thereby suggesting his objections.

Thus the experiences of the soul become enduring not only within the boundaries of birth and death, but beyond death. The soul does not stamp its experiences, however, only on the spirit which flashes up in it; it stamps them on the outer world also, through its action. What a man did yesterday is today still present in its effects. The relationship between cause and effect in this connection is illustrated by the parallel relation between death and sleep. Sleep has often been called the younger brother of death. I get up in the morning. My consecutive activity has been interrupted by the night. Now under ordinary circumstances, it is not possible for me to begin my activity again just as I like. I must connect it with my doings of yesterday, if there is to be order and coherence in my life. My actions of yesterday are the conditions predetermining those actions which fall to me today. I have created my fate of today by what I did yesterday. I have separated myself for a while from my activity; but this activity belongs to me and draws me again to itself, after I have withdrawn myself from it for a while. My past remains bound up within me; it lives on in my present, and will follow me into my future. If the effects of my yesterday were not to be my fate today, I should have had, not to wake this morning, but to be newly created out of nothing. It would be absurd if under ordinary circumstances I were not to occupy a house that I have had built for me.

The human spirit is as little newly created when it begins its earthly life as a man is newly created every morning; let us try to make clear to ourselves what happens when entrance into this life takes place. A physical body, receiving its form through the laws of heredity, comes upon the scene. This body becomes the bearer of a spirit which repeats a previous life in a new form. Between the two stands the soul, which leads a self-contained life of its own. Its inclinations and disinclinations, its wishes and desires, minister to it; it presses thought into its service. As sentient soul, it receives the impressions of the outer world and carries them to the spirit, in order that the spirit may extract from them the fruits that are to endure. It plays, as it were, the part of intermediary; and its task is fulfilled when it is adequate to this part. The body forms impressions for the sentient soul which transforms them into sensations, retains them in the memory as conceptions, and hands them over to the spirit to hold permanently. The soul is really that through which man belongs to his whole earthly life. Through his body he belongs to the physical human species. Through it he is a member of this species. With his spirit he lives in a higher world. The soul binds the two worlds together for a time.

But the physical world into which the human spirit enters is no strange field of action to it. On that world the traces of its own former actions are imprinted. Something in this field of action belongs to this spirit. It bears the impress of its being. It is related to it. As the soul in the first place transmitted impressions from the outer world to the human spirit in order that they might remain enduringly within it, so later the soul, as the organ of the human spirit, converted the faculties bestowed on it by the spirit into deeds which in their effects are also enduring. Thus the soul has actually immersed itself in these actions. In the effects of his deeds a man's soul lives further a second life of its own. Now this provides us with a motive for examining life from this angle in order to perceive how the processes of fate enter into it. Something happens to a man. He is probably at first inclined to regard such a happening as something coming into his life by chance.

But he can become aware of how he himself is the outcome of such chances. Anyone who studies himself in his fortieth year and in the search after his soul-nature refuses to be content with an unreal abstract conception of the "I," may well say to himself: "I am indeed nothing else whatever than what I have become through what has happened to me according to fate up to the present. Should I not be a different man, if, for example, I had had a certain series of experiences when twenty years old instead of those that I did have?" The man will then seek his "I," not only in those educative impulses which came to him from within outwards, but also in what has formatively thrust itself into his life from without. He will recognize his own "I" in that which happens to him. If one gives oneself up unreservedly to such a perception, then only a further step of really intimate observation of life is needed in order to see, in what comes to one through certain experiences of destiny, something which lays hold upon the "I" from without, just as memory works from within in order to make a past experience flash up again. Thus one can make oneself able to perceive in the experiences of fate how a former action of the soul finds its way to the ego, just as in memory an earlier experience finds its way into the mind as a conception, if called forth by an external cause. It has already been alluded to as a possible conception, that the *consequences of a deed* may meet the human soul again. A meeting of this kind in regard to certain consequences of action is out of the question in the course of one earth-life, because that earth-life was particularly arranged for the carrying out of the deed. Experience is derived from its accomplishment. A definite *consequence* of that action can as little react upon the soul in that case as one can remember an experience while one is still in the midst of it. It can only be a question here of the experience of the results of actions which do not confront the ego while it has the same soul-content which it had during the earth-life in which the deed was committed. One's gaze can only be directed to the consequences of action from another earth-life. As soon as one realizes that what happens to one seemingly as a destined experience is bound up with the "I," just as much as what shapes itself from out of the inner being of that "I"—then one is forced to the conclusion that in such a destined experience one is concerned with the consequences of action from previous earth-lives. One sees that one is thus led, through an intimate grasp of life, guided by thinking, to what for the ordinary consciousness is the paradoxical assumption—namely, that the destined experiences of one earth-life are linked with the actions of preceding earth-lives. This conception again can only receive its full content through supersensible knowledge; lacking this it remains a mere silhouette. But once more, this conception, derived from the ordinary consciousness, prepares the soul so that it is enabled to *behold* its truth in actual supersensible observation.

Only the one part of my deed is in the outer world: the other is in myself. Let us make clear by a simple example taken from natural science this relation of "I" to deed. Creatures that once could see, migrated to the caves of Kentucky, and through their life in them have lost their power of sight. Existence in darkness has put the eyes out of action. Consequently the physical and chemical activity that is present when seeing takes place is no longer carried on in these eyes. The stream of nourishment, which was formerly expended on this activity, now flows to other organs. These creatures can now live only in these caves. They have by their act, by the immigration, created the conditions of their later lives. The immigration has become a part of their fate. A being that once acted has united itself with the results of the action. It is so also with the human spirit. The soul could only mediate and make over certain capacities to the spirit through being active itself. And these capacities correspond to the actions. Through an action which the soul has performed, there lives in the soul the predisposition, full of energy, to perform another action, which is the fruit of that first action. The soul carries this as a necessity within itself, until the latter action has come to pass. One might also say: through an action, the necessity has been imprinted upon the soul to carry out the consequences of that action.

By means of its actions, the human spirit has really brought about its own fate. In a new life it finds itself linked to what it did in a former one. One may ask, "How can that be, when the human spirit on reincarnating finds itself in an entirely different world from that which it left at some earlier time?" This question is based on a very superficial conception of the linkings of fate. If I change my scene of action from Europe to America I also find myself in new surroundings. Nevertheless, my life in America depends entirely on my previous life in Europe. If I have been a mechanic in Europe, my life in America will shape itself quite differently from the way in which it would had I been a bank clerk. In the one case I should probably be surrounded in America by machinery, in the other by banking arrangements. In each case my previous life decided my environment; it attracts to itself, as it were, out of the whole surrounding world, those things that are related to it. So it is with the Spirit-self. It inevitably surrounds itself in a new life with that to which it is related from previous lives. And on that account sleep is an apt image for death, because the man during sleep is withdrawn from the field of action in which his fate awaits him. While one sleeps, events in this field of action pursue their course. One has for a time no influence on this course of events. Nevertheless, our life in a new day depends on the effects of the deeds of the previous one. Our personality actually incarnates anew every morning in our world of action. What was separated from us during the night is spread out, as it were, around us during the day. So it is with the actions of the former embodiments of man. They are bound up with him as his destiny, as life in the dark caves remains bound up with the creatures who, through migration into them, have lost their power of sight. Just as these creatures can only live in the surroundings in which they have placed themselves, so the human spirit can live only in the surroundings which by its acts it has created for itself. That I find in the morning a state of affairs which I created on the previous day is brought about by the direct progress of the events themselves. That I, when I reincarnate, find surroundings which correspond with the results of my deeds in a previous life, is brought about by the relationship of my reincarnated spirit with the things in the world around. From this one can form a conception of how the soul is set into the constitution of man. The physical body is subject to the laws of heredity. The human spirit, on the contrary, has to incarnate over and over again; and its law consists in its bringing over the fruits of the former lives into the following ones. The soul lives in the present. But this life in the present is not independent of the previous lives. For the incarnating spirit brings its destiny with it from its previous incarnations. And this destiny determines its life. What impressions the soul will be able to have, what wishes it will be able to have gratified, what sorrows and joys shall grow up for it, with what individuals it shall come into contact—all this depends on the nature of the actions in the past incarnations of the spirit. Those people with whom the soul was bound up in one life, the soul must meet again in a subsequent one, because the actions which have taken place between them must have their consequences. When this soul seeks reembodiment, those others, who are bound up with it, will also strive towards their incarnation at the same time. The life of the soul is therefore the result of the self-created destiny of the human spirit. The course of man's life between birth and death is therefore determined in a threefold way. And thereby he is dependent in a threefold way on factors which lie on the other side of birth and death. The body is subject to the law of heredity; the soul is subject to its self-created fate. Using an ancient expression, one calls this fate, created by the man himself, his *karma*. And the spirit is under the law of reembodiment, repeated earth-lives. One can accordingly express the relationship between spirit, soul, and body in the following way as well: the spirit is immortal; birth and death reign over the body according to the laws of the physical world; the soul-life, which is subject to destiny, mediates the connection of both during an earthly life. All further knowledge about the being of man presupposes acquaintance with the three worlds to which he belongs. These three worlds are dealt with in the following pages.

A thinking which frankly faces the phenomena of life, and is not afraid to follow out to their final consequences the thoughts resulting from a living, vivid contemplation of life, can, by pure logic, arrive at the conception of the law of destiny and repeated incarnations. Just as it is true that for the seer with the opened spiritual eye, past lives, like an opened book, lie before him as *experience*, so it is true that the truth of all this can become obvious to the unbiased reason which reflects upon it.

Facing Karma*

At the end of the two public lectures I have given in this city,** I emphasized that Anthroposopy should not be considered a theory or mere science, nor as knowledge in the ordinary sense. It is rather something that grows in our souls from mere knowledge and theory into immediate life, into an elixir of life. In this way, Anthroposophy not only provides us with knowledge, but we receive forces that help us in our ordinary lives during physical existence as well as in the total life that we spend during physical existence and the nonphysical existence between death and a new birth. The more we experience Anthroposophy as bringing to us strength, support, and life-renewing energies, the more do we understand it.

Upon hearing this, some may ask, "If Anthroposophy is to bring us a strengthening of life, why do we have to acquire so much of what appears to be theoretical knowledge? Why are we virtually pestered at our branch meetings with descriptions about the preceding planetary evolutions of our earth? Why do we have to learn about things that took place long ago? Why do we have to acquaint ourselves with the intimate and subtle laws of reincarnation, karma, and so on?"

Some people may believe that they are being offered just another science. This problem, which forces itself upon us, demands that we eliminate all easy and simplistic approaches toward answering it. We must carefully ask ourselves whether, in raising this question, we are not introducing into it some of the easygoing ways of life that become manifest when we are reluctant to learn and to acquire something in a spiritual way. This is an uncomfort-

* From Dietrich von Asten, trans., *Facing Karma* (New York: Anthroposophical Press, 1975), pp. 1–20.
** Vienna, 1912. —ED.

able experience for us and we are forced to wonder whether something of this attitude of discomfort does not find expression in the question that is being asked. As it is, we are led to believe that the highest goal that anthroposophy may offer us can be attained on easier roads than on that taken by us through our own literature.

It is often said, almost nonchalantly, that man has only to know himself, that all he has to do in order to be an anthroposophist is to be good. Yes, it is profound wisdom to know that to be a good person is one of the most difficult tasks, and that nothing in life demands more in the way of preparation than the realization of this ideal to be good. The problem of self-knowledge, however, cannot be solved with a quick answer (as many are inclined to believe). Therefore, today, we will shed light on some of these questions that have been raised. We then will come to see how Anthroposophy meets us, even if only by appearance, as a teaching or as a science, but that it also offers in an eminent sense a path toward self-knowledge and what may be called the pilgrimage toward becoming a good person. To accomplish this we must consider from different points of view how Anthroposophy can be fruitful in life.

Let us take a specific question that does not concern scientific research, but everyday life—a question known to all of us. How can we find comfort in life when we have to suffer in one way or another, when we fail to find satisfaction in life? In other words, let us ask ourselves how Anthroposophy can offer comfort and consolation when it is really needed. Obviously, what can be said here only in general terms must always be applied to one's own individual case. If one lectures to many people, one can only speak in generalities.

Why do we need comfort, consolation in life? Because we may be sad about a number of events, or because we suffer as a result of pains that afflict us. It is natural that, at first, man reacts to pain as though he is rebelling inwardly against it. He wonders why he has to stand pain. "Why am I afflicted by this pain? Why is life not arranged for me in such a way that I don't suffer pain, that I am content?" These questions can be answered satisfactorily only on the basis of true knowledge concerning the nature of human karma, of human destiny. Why do we suffer in the world? We refer here to outer as well as to inner sufferings that arise in our psychic organization and leave us unfulfilled. Why are we met by such experiences that leave us unsatisfied?

In pursuing the laws of karma, we shall discover that the underlying resons for suffering are similar to what can be described by the following example relating to the ordinary life between birth and death. Let us assume that a youngster has lived until his eighteenth year at the expense of his father. Then the father loses all his wealth and goes into bankruptcy. The young man must now learn something worthwhile and make an effort to support himself. As a result, life hits him with pain and privation. It is quite understandable that he does not react sympathetically to the pain that he has to go through.

Let us now turn to the period when he has reached the age of fifty. Since, by the necessity of events, he had to educate himself at an early age, he has become a decent person. He has found a real foothold in life. He realizes why he reacted negatively to pain and suffering when it first hit him, but now he must think differently about it. He must say to himself that the suffering would not have come to him if he had already acquired a sense of maturity—at least, to the limited degree that an eighteen-year-old can attain one. If he had not been afflicted by pain, he would have remained a good-for-nothing. It was the pain that transformed his shortcomings into positive abilities. He must owe it to the pain that he has become a different man in the course of forty years. What was really brought together at that time? His shortcomings and his pain were brought together. His shortcomings actually sought pain in order that his immaturity might be removed by being transformed into maturity.

Even a simple consideration of life between birth and death can lead to this view. If we look at the totality of life, however, and if we face our karma as it has been explained in the lecture two days ago, we will come to the conclusion that all pain that hits us, that all suffering that comes our way, are of such a nature that they are being sought by our shortcomings. By far the greater part of our pain and suffering is sought by imperfections that we have brought over from previous incarnations. Since we have these imperfections within ourselves, there is a wiser man in us than we ourselves are who chooses the road to pain and suffering. It is, indeed, one of the golden rules of life that we all carry in us a wiser man than we ourselves are, a much wiser man. The one to whom we say, "I," in ordinary life is less wise. If it was left to this less wise person in us to make a choice between pain and joy, he would undoubtedly choose the road toward joy. But the wiser man is the one who reigns in the depth of our unconscious and who remains inaccessile to ordinary consciousness. He directs our gaze away from easy enjoyment and kindles in us a magic power that seeks the road of pain without our really knowing it. But what is meant by the words: Without really knowing it? They mean that the wiser man in us prevails over the less wise one. He always acts in such a way that our shortcomings are guided to our pains and he makes us suffer because with every inner and outer suffering we eliminate one of our faults and become transformed into something better.

Little is accomplished if one tries to understand these words theoretically. Much more can be gained when one creates sacred moments in life during which one is willing to use all one's energy in an effort to fill one's soul with the living content of such words. Ordinary life, with all its work, pressure, commotion, and duties provides little chance to do so. In this setting, it is not always possible to silence the less wise man in us. But when we create a sacred moment in life, short as it may be, then we can say, "I will put aside the transitory effect of life; I will view my sufferings in such a way that I feel how the wise man in me has been attracted by them with a magic power. I realize that I have imposed upon myself certain experiences of pain without which I would not have overcome some of my shortcomings." A feeling of blissful wisdom will overcome us that makes us feel that even if the world appears to be filled with suffering, it is, nevertheless, radiating pure wisdom. Such an attitude is one of the fruits of Anthroposophy for the benefit of life. What has been said may, of course, be forgotten, but if we do not forget it, but practice such thoughts regularly, we will become aware of the fact that we have planted a seed in our soul. What we used to experience as feelings of sadness and attitudes of depression will be transformed into positive attitudes toward life, into strength and energy. Out of these sacred moments in life will be born more harmonious souls and stronger personalities.

We may now move on to another step in our experience. The anthroposophist should be determined to take this other step only after he has comforted himself many times with regard to his sufferings in the way just described. The experience that may now be added consists of looking at one's joys and at everything that has occurred in life in the way of happiness. He who can face destiny without bias and as though he had himself wanted his sufferings, will find himself confronted by a strange reaction when he looks at his joy and happiness. He cannot face them in the same way that he faced his sufferings. It is easy to see how one can find comfort in suffering. He who does not believe this only has to expose himself to the experience.

It is difficult, however, to come to terms with joy and happiness. Much as we may accept the attitude that we have wanted our suffering, when we apply the same attitude to joy and happiness, we cannot but feel ashamed of ourselves. A deep feeling of shame will be experienced. The only way to overcome this feeling is to realize that we were not the ones who gave ourselves our joys and happiness through the law of karma. This is the only cure, as otherwise the feeling of shame can become so intense that it virtually destroys us in our souls. Relief can only be found by not making the wiser man in us responsible for having driven us toward our joys. With this thought, one will feel that one hits the truth, because the feeling of shame will disappear. It is a fact that our joy and happiness come to us in life as something that is bestowed upon us, without our participation, by a wise divine guidance, as something we must accept as grace, as something that is to unite us with the universe. Happiness and joy shall have such an effect upon us in the sacred moments in our lives and in our intimate hours of introspection that we shall experience them as grace, as grace from the divine powers of the world who want to receive us and who, as it were, embed us in their being.

While our pain and suffering lead us to ourselves and make us more genuinely ourselves, we develop through joy and happiness, provided that we consider them as grace, a feeling that one

can only describe as being blissfully embedded in the divine
forces and powers of the world. Here the only justified attitude
toward happiness and joy is one of gratitude. Nobody will understand joy and happiness in the intimate hours of self-knowledge
when he ascribes them to his karma. If he involves karma, he
commits an error that is liable to weaken and paralyze the spiritual in him. Every thought to the effect that joy and happiness are
deserved actually weakens and paralyzes us. This may be a hard
fact to understand because everyone who admits that his pain is
inflicted upon himself by his own individuality would obviously
expect to be his own master also with regard to joy and happiness.
But a simple look at life can teach us that joy and happiness have
an extinguishing power. Nowhere is this extinguishing effect of
joy and happiness better described than in Goethe's *Faust* in the
words, "And thus I stagger from desire to pleasure. And in pleasure I am parched with desire." Simple reflection upon the influence of personal enjoyment shows that inherent in it is something
that makes us stagger and blots out our true being.

No sermon is here being delivered against enjoyment, nor is an
invitation extended to practice self-torture, or to pinch ourselves
with red-hot pliers, or the like. If one recognizes a situation in the
right way, it does not mean that one should escape from it. No
escape, therefore, is suggested, but a silent acceptance of joy and
happiness whenever they appear. We must develop the inner
attitude that we experience them as grace—and the more the
better. Thus do we immerse ourselves the more in the divine.
Therefore, these words are said not in order to preach asceticism,
but in order to awaken the right mood toward joy and happiness.

If it is thought that joy and happiness have a paralyzing and
extinguishing effect, and that therefore man should flee from
them, then one would promote the ideal of false asceticism and
self-torture. In this event, man, in reality, would be escaping
from the grace that is given to him by the gods. Self-torture practiced by ascetics, monks, and nuns is nothing but a continuous
rebellion against the gods. It behooves us to feel pain as something that comes to us through our karma. In joy and happiness,
we can feel that the divine is descending to us.

May joy and happiness be for us a sign as to how close the gods have attracted us, and may our pain and suffering be a sign as to how far removed we are from what we are to become as good human beings. This is the fundamental attitude toward karma without which we cannot really move ahead in life. In what the world bestows upon us as goodness and beauty, we must conceive the world powers of which it is said in the Bible, "And he looked at the world and he saw that it was good." But inasmuch as we experience pain and suffering, we must recognize what man has made of the world during its evolution, which originally was a good world, and what he must contribute toward its betterment by educating himself to bear pain with purpose and energy.

What has now been described are two ways to confront karma. To a certain extent, our karma consists of suffering and joys. We relate ourselves to our karma with the right attitude when we can consider it as something we really wanted and when we can confront our sufferings and joys with the proper understanding. But a review of karma can be extended further, which we shall do today and tomorrow.

Karma not only shows us what is related to our lives in a joyful and painful manner. But as the result of the working of karma, we meet many people during the course of our lives with whom we only become slightly acquainted, and people with whom we are connected in various ways during long periods of our lives as relatives and friends. We meet people who either cause us pain directly, or as a result of some joint undertaking that runs into obstructions. We meet people who are helpful, or to whom we can be helpful. In short, many relationships are possible. If the effects of karma, as described the day before yesterday, are to become fruitful, then we must accept the fact that the wiser man in us wants certain experiences. He seeks a person who seems accidentally to cross our paths. He is the one who leads us to other people with whom we get engaged in this or that way. What is really guiding this wiser man in us when he wants to meet this or that person? What is he basing himself on? In answer, we have to say to ourselves that we want to meet him because we have met him previously. It may not have happened in the last life; it could have happened much earlier. The wiser man in us leads us to this person because we had dealings with him in a previous life, or because we may have incurred a debt in one way or another. We are led to this person as though by magic.

We are now reaching a manifold and intricate realm that can be covered only by generalities. The indications here stem from clairvoyant investigation. They can be useful to anybody since they can be applied to many special situations.

A strange observation can be made. We all have experienced or observed how, toward the middle of our lives, the ascending growth-line gradually tilts over to become a descending line, and our youthful energies begin to decline. We move past a climax and from there on we move downward. This point of change is somewhere in our thirties. It is also the time in our lives when we are living most intensively on the physical plane. In this connection, we can fall prey to a delusion. The events that from childhood precede this climax were brought with us into this incarnation. They were, so to speak, drawn out of a previous existence. The forces that we have brought along with us from the spiritual world are now placed outside ourselves and used to fashion our lives. These forces are used up when we reach this middle point.

In considering the descending curve of our lives, we perceive the lessons that we have learned in the school of life, that we have accumulated and have worked over. They will be taken along into the next incarnation. This is something we carry into the spiritual world; previously, we took something out of it. This is the time when we are fully engaged on the physical plane. We are thoroughly enmeshed with everything that comes to us from the outside world. We have passed our training period; we are fully committed to life and we have to come to terms with it. We are involved with ourselves, but we are primarily occupied with arranging our environments for ourselves, and in finding a proper relationship to the world in which we live. The human capacities that are seeking a relationship to the world are our power of reasoning and that part of our volitional life that is controlled by reason. What is thus active in us is alien to the spiritual world, which withdraws from us and closes up. It is true that in the middle of our lives we are the farthest removed from the reality of the spirit.

Here occult investigation reveals a significant fact. The people with whom we meet, and the acquaintances we make in the middle period of our lives are, curiously enough, the very people with whom we were engaged during the period of early childhood in one of our previous incarnations. It is an established fact that, as a general rule, although not always, we meet in the middle period of our lives, as a result of karmic guidance, the very people who were once our parents. It is unlikely that we meet in early childhood the persons who were once our parents. This happens during the middle of life. This may appear as a strange fact, but this is the way it is. When we attempt to apply such rules to the experience of life, and when we direct our thoughts accordingly, then we can learn a great deal. When a person at about the age of thirty establishes a relationship to another, either through the bonds of love or of friendship, or when they get involved in conflict, or in any other experience, we will understand a great deal more about these relationships if we consider hypothetically that the person may have once been related to the other as a child is to his parents.

In reversing this relationship, we discover another remarkable fact. The very people with whom we have been associated in our early childhood, such as parents, sisters and brothers, playmates and other companions, as a rule are the very people whom we have met in the previous or one of our previous incarnations around our thirtieth year. These people frequently appear as our parents, sisters, or brothers in the present incarnation.

Curious as this may appear to us at first, let us try to apply it to life. The experience of life becomes enlightened if we look at it in this way. We may, of course, err in our speculation. But if, in solitary hours, we look at life so that it is filled with meaning, we can gain a great deal. Obviously, we must not arrange karma to our liking; we must not choose the people we like and assume that they may have been our parents. Prejudices must not falsify the real facts. You realize the danger that we are exposed to and the many misconceptions that may creep in. We must educate ourselves to remain open-minded and unbiased.

You may now ask what the relation is to the people we meet during the declining curve of our lives. We have discovered that at the beginning of our lives, we meet people with whom we were acquainted during the middle period of a previous life, while now, during the middle of our lives, we recognize those with whom we were involved at the beginning of previous existences. But how about the period of our descending life? The answer is that we may be led to people with whom we were involved in a previous life, or we may not yet have been involved with them. They will have been connecnted with us in a previous life if we are meeting under special circumstances that occur at decisive junctures of a life span, when, for example, a bitter disappointment confronts us with a serious probation. In such a situation, it is likely that we are meeting during the second period of our lives people with whom we were previously connected. Thereby conditions are dislodged and experiences that were caused in the past can be resolved.

Karma works in many ways and one cannot force it into definite patterns. But as a general rule, it can be stated that during the second half of our lives we encounter people with whom the karmic connections that are beginning to be woven cannot be resolved in one life. Let us assume that we have caused suffering to someone in a previous life. It is easy to assume that the wiser man in us will lead us back to this person in a subsequent life in order that we may equalize the harm that we have done. But life conditions cannot always permit that we can equalize everything, but perhaps only a part of it. Thereby matters are complicated, and it becomes possible that such a remainder of karma may be corrected in the second half of life. Looking at it this way, we are placing our connections and communications with other people in the light of this karma.

But there is something else that we can consider in the course of karma. This is what I have called in my two recent public lectures the process of maturing and the acquisition of life experiences. These terms may be used with utter modesty. We may take into account the process by which we become wiser. Our errors may render us wiser and it is really best for us when this happens because during one lifetime we do not often have the opportunity to practice wisdom. For this reason, we retain the

lessons that we have learned from our errors as strength for a
future life. But what really is the wisdom and the life experience
that we can acquire?

Yesterday I referred to the fact that our ideas cannot be taken
immediately from one life to another. I pointed to the fact that
even a genius like Plato could not carry the ideas of his mind into
a new incarnation. We carry with us our volitional and soul powers, but our ideas are given us anew in every life, just as is the
faculty of speech. The greater part of our ideas live in speech.
Most of our ideas are derived from our faculty to express ourselves in a language. The ideas we conceive during the time between birth and death are always related to this particular earthly
existence. This being so, it is true that our ideas will always depend on the where and how of our incarnations, no matter how
many we have to live through. Our wealth of ideas is always
derived from the outer world, and depends on the way karma has
placed us into race, family, and speech relationships.

In our ideas and concepts we really know nothing of the world
except what is dependent on karma. A great deal is said with this
statement. This means that everything we can know in life and
acquire in the form of knowledge is something quite personal. We
never can transcend the personal level with regard to everything
we may acquire in life. We never come quite as far as the wiser
man in us, but we always remain with the less wise man. If someone believes that he can, by himself, know more about his higher
self from observations in the outer world, he is being led by his
laziness into an unreal world. Thereby we are saying nothing less
than that we know nothing of our higher self as a result of what we
acquire in life.

How can we gain an understanding of our higher self; how do
we come to such knowledge? To find an answer, we must ask
ourselves the simple question, "What do we really know?" First
of all, we know what we have learned from experience. We know
this and nothing else. Anyone who wants to know himself and
does not realize that he carries in his soul nothing but a mirror of
the outer world may delude himself into believing that he can
find his higher self by introspection. What he finds within, however, is nothing else than what has come in from outside. Lazi-

ness of thinking has no place in this quest. So we must inquire about the other worlds into which our higher self is embedded, and thereby we learn about the various incarnations of the earth and the world picture described by spiritual science.

Just as we try to understand a child's soul with regard to its outer life conditions by examining the child's surroundings, so must we ask what the environment of the higher self is. Spiritual science gives us insight into the worlds in which our higher self lives by its accounts of the evolution of Saturn and all its secrets, of the Moon and Earth evolution, of reincarnation and karma, of *devachan** and *kamaloka*, and so on. This is the only way we can learn about our higher self, about that self that extends beyond the physical plane. He who refuses to accept these secrets is as playful as a little kitten in regard to himself. It is not by petting and caressing oneself that one can discover the divine man in oneself. Only what is experienced in the outer world is stored inside, but the divine man in us can be found only when we search in our soul for the mirrored world beyond the physical.

The very things that are uncomfortable to learn make up knowledge of self. In reality, true Anthroposophy is true knowledge of self. Properly received, the science of the spirit enlightens us about our own self. Where is this self? Is it within our skin? No, it is poured into the entire world, and what is in the world is linked to the self; also, what once was in the world is connected with this self. Only if we get to know the world can we also get to know the self.

Anthroposophical knowledge, although it may appear first as mere theory, points to nothing less than a path to self-knowledge. He who wants to find himself by staring into his inner being may be motivated by the noble desire to be good and unselfish. But in reality, he becomes more and more selfish. In contrast to this, the struggle with the great secrets of existence, the attempt to emancipate oneself from the complacent personal self, the acceptance of the reality of the higher worlds and the knowledge that can be obtained from them, all lead to true self-knowledge.

---

* In his early lectures, Steiner used sanskrit terms: *devachan* for spirit-land or spiritual world, and *kamaloca*, the period equaling approximately one-third of a person's life on earth in which the soul relives the experience of its nights spent in sleep. —ED.

While contemplating Saturn, Sun, and Moon, we lose ourselves in cosmic thoughts. Thus, a soul thinking in Anthroposophy exclaims, "In thy thinking cosmic thoughts are living." He
then adds to these words, "Lose thyself in cosmic thoughts."

A soul creating out of Anthroposophy says, "In thy feeling cosmic forces are weaving," and adds in the same breath, "Feel thyself through cosmic forces." These universal powers will not reveal themselves when we expect them to be flattering or when we
close our eyes and pledge to be a good human being. Only when
we open our spiritual eye and perceive how "cosmic forces" work
and create, and when we realize that we are embedded in these
forces, will we have an experience of our own self.

Thus, a soul that draws strength from Anthroposophy will say,
"In thy willing cosmic beings are working," and he will quickly
add, "Create thyself through beings of will."

The meaning of these words can be realized if self-knowledge is
practiced in the right way. If this is done, one recreates oneself
out of the cosmic forces.

These thoughts may appear to be dry and abstract, but they are
not mere theory. They have the inherent power of a seed planted
in the earth. It sprouts and grows; life shoots in all directions and
the plant becomes a tree. Thus it is with the experiences we
receive through the science of the spirit that we become capable
of transforming ourselves. "Create thyself through beings of will."
Thus, Anthroposophy becomes an elixir of life. Our view of spirit
worlds opens up, we draw strength from these worlds and once we
can fully absorb them, they will help us to know ourselves in all
our depth. Only when we imbue ourselves with world knowledge
can we take hold of ourselves and gradually move from the less
wise man in us, who is split off by the guardian of the threshold,
to the wise man in us. This, which remains hidden to the weak,
can be gained by the strong through Anthroposophy.

> In thy thinking cosmic thoughts are living;
> Lose thyself in cosmic thoughts.
> In thy feeling cosmic forces are weaving;
> Feel thyself through cosmic forces.
> In thy willing cosmic beings are working;
> Create thyself through beings of will.

III

HISTORICAL VISION

Historical Vision

INTRODUCTION

Consciousness Determines Events

As the previous chapter presents Steiner's claims for a super-sensible knowledge of natural phenomena, or knowledge of spirit in nature, this chapter presents Steiner's claims for a knowledge of spirit in (or behind, or beneath) history. Both his attempt to see the inner form or force of natural phenomena and his attempt to see the consciousness at the source of historical events are specific examples of Steiner's spiritual science. According to his esoteric or supersensible reading of planetary and human evolution, the observable, or external, events chronicled by historians are the expression of a mode of consciousness characteristic of each age. This view of history, based on consciousness rather than observable and largely environmental factors, has not been in favor among Western historians since the philosophy of Hegel was largely eclipsed by historians of a more empiricist bent—Marxists, Freudians, pragmatists, and other social historians who shun the highly speculative, idealistic philosophies of history such as those of Hegel or Steiner. For most academic historians, Steiner's philosophy of history is even less acceptable than Hegel's: whereas Hegel interprets the content of world history according to the logic of thought, Steiner claims to present and interpret historical processes by a kind of spiritual seeing. The first selection in this chapter, "The Akashic Record," establishes the distinctive basis of Steiner's approach to history. Steiner claims to see spiritually, or read supersensibly, an eternal summation of all historical events called the Akashic Record or the Akasha Chronicle. *Cosmic Memory* (1904), perhaps the most vivid example of

Steiner's radically ambitious and generally suspect claims to historical knowledge, begins with a discussion of the Atlantean civilization which purportedly lasted a million years before it ended
approximately in the tenth millenium B.C. Readers who are new
to spiritual science and to esoteric thought may well find Steiner's
writings on such topics either unfounded, or ludicrous, or both.
Happily, Steiner recognizes the difficulty which some readers will
experience on encountering his claims for knowledge of events in
remote prehistory:

The author of this present book in no way claims that he should be
believed blindly. He merely wishes to report what his best efforts have
enabled him to discover. He will welcome any correction based on
competent knowledge. He feels obliged to communicate these events
concerning the development of mankind because the signs of the times
urge it. Moreover, a long period of time had to be described in outline
here in order to afford a general view. Further details on much that is
only indicated now will follow later.

 Only with difficulty can the writings in the Akasha Chronicle be translated into our colloquial language. They are more easily communicated in
the symbolical sign language used in mystery schools, but as yet the
communication of this language is not permitted. Therefore the reader is
requested to bear with much that is dark and difficult to comprehend,
and to struggle toward a generally understandable manner of presentation. Many a difficulty in reading will be rewarded when one looks upon
the deep mysteries, the important human enigmas which are indicated.
A true self-knowledge of man is, after all, the result of these "Akashic
Records," which for the scientist of the spirit are realities as certain as are
mountain ranges and rivers for the eye of sense. An error of perception
is, of course, possible here and there. (pp.112–113)

 Most readers of Steiner's *Cosmic Memory*, particularly those of
us trained academically, will indeed experience what Steiner here
refers to as "many a difficulty in reading." He also suggests, however, that the rewards of this effort will be a deeper understanding of the mysterious process by which human nature and human
history have been formed and continue to evolve. One of the
more difficult and persistent enigmas which is illumined by Steiner's reading of history concerns the particular changes in awareness from age to age and culture to culture. Specifically, anyone

studying history will want to know, at some point, why modern Western science developed when it did, and why it did not develop in the Middle Ages or in Asia. There are, of course, tentative beginnings of science, or what appears to be science, in Greece, during the sixth century B.C., in the medieval Arabic world, and in medieval China (for example as chronicled and brilliantly analyzed by Joseph Needham in his multivolume study, *Science and Civilization in China*). Anyone who studies the notebooks of Leonardo da Vinci must wonder, why were these sketches and plans for remarkable inventions not implemented sooner? Stewart Easton gives the example of Hero of Alexandria, who probably lived in the second century of the Christian era, and who invented a steam engine of a primitive kind *(Man and World*, p. 21). The usual explanation for this phenomenon is simply that the cultural environment of Hero's or Leonardo's inventions was unfavorable for application at that time. Steiner and historians who accept his reading of the evolution of consciousness, by contrast, argue that the cultural environment is itself a by-product of a soul configuration of a particular epoch.

When Steiner describes transformative events in history, he is essentially describing transformations of consciousness. He reads particular social, physical, and artistic developments as expressions of particular states of consciousness. On first hearing, Steiner's terms (or the English translations of the terms)—such as intellectual soul or consciousness-soul—are not altogether compelling, but with the help of examples such as are included in the following pages, these terms can take on vivid meaning and can be very instructive. All of the readings in the following chapter relate back to the consciousness manifested in the Fourth Post-Atlantean epoch, which Steiner dates from the middle of the eighth century B.C. to the early fifteenth century A.D. This period, which Steiner refers to as the age of the Intellectual Soul, includes the convergence of the Greco-Roman tradition, Hebraic tradition, early Christian experience, and the synthesis of these three traditions in European Christianity.

Steiner expects that like the other Post-Atlantean epochs, the present epoch, called the age of the Consciousness Soul, will also last for approximately 2,160 years, from early fifteenth century to mid thirty-sixth century. The focus of the first, second, and fifth parts of this book are concerned with modern and contemporary modes of consciousness, and consequently are examples of Fifth Post-Atlantean consciousness; the present part and the one following, on esoteric Christianity, focus entirely on the Fourth Post-Atlantean epoch. Steiner's reading of the evolution of consciousness throughout the Fourth Post-Atlantean epoch, particularly the radical transformation of consciousness wrought by the intervention of the Christ Being in the first century, is revealing for an understanding of our present situation.

According to Steiner, the present age will be more intelligible, more humane and creative, to the extent that humanity recognizes its tasks and possibilities in light of the evolution of consciousness. Specifically, he identifies the task of the present age as the reunification of scientific knowledge with spiritual wisdom. He argues that a spiritual mode of knowing is not only compatible with contemporary science, but necessary for the next phase of scientific advancement. It is important to keep in mind what Steiner is *not* saying: he is not recommending a two-truth theory, whereby science and religious, or spiritual, knowledge will cohabitate. Nor is he recommending a return to medieval Christian faith. Rather, he sees the present age as a unique opportunity for the cultivating of a single capacity, called imagination or intuition, which will generate both scientific and spiritual knowledge —or, scientific-spiritual knowledge of both the material and the spiritual worlds. Further, he sees this possibility as the appropriate and logical achievement within the evolution of consciousness. In fact, according to Steiner, the task of the present age is only fully intelligible when seen in the light of the steady decrease in the ancient, atavistic clairvoyance and proportionate increase in rational, intellectual thinking which has characterized the evolution of consciousness at least from Atlantis through the Four Post-Atlantean epochs to the present. Beginning in the present century, and presumably for centuries and epochs to come, Steiner foresees the development of a distinctively modern clairvoyant capability. Steiner recommends that we contemplate this thought-picture and recognize the present need to deepen and purify the scientific impulse by applying the kind of spiritual seeing of which the ancient world was capable, but which has not yet been applied to the external or natural world studied by contemporary scientific consciousness.

Ancient Wisdom

As historians of civilization tend to view the two examples cited above, Hero of Alexandria and Leonardo, as having the same capabilities and mode of consciousness as contemporary humanity, historians of philosophy do not ordinarily consider the possibility that ancient Greek philosophers possessed a different kind of intellectual or psychic capability. Steiner maintains, however, that by virtue of exhibiting the fourth-century-B.C. mode of consciousness, and as a result of having been a remarkable genius who was also initiated in Greek mystery wisdom, Plato represents an extraordinary combination in the evolution of human thought. In the academic study of philosophy, Plato is regarded as the first great thinker to attempt systematic answers to fundamental questions by the method of reason alone. Steiner does not deny Plato's importance in this respect, but says it is equally important to understand that Plato was also the heir to the Greek mystery tradition, and as such experienced, or saw, ideas in a way that is entirely foreign to our sense-bound mode of perception. Whereas modern scholarship tends to regard Plato's references to the "Ideas" as either metaphoric or simply mistaken, Steiner contends that Plato lived at a time when ideas could be grasped by intellectual vision. At the same time, Plato did not see ideas with the ease or strength that had been possible during the Third Post-Atlantean epoch, prior to the eighth century B.C. For an initiate such as Homer, in the ninth century B.C., the Olympian gods, though nonphysical, were objects of a kind of sight which had largely been lost by the time of Plato, and which was entirely impossible in the early centuries of the Christian era. Similarly, the vision of the ideal forms had become increasingly difficult during the three centuries from Pythagoras to Plato—and for each successive century thereafter. During the Middle Ages, a direct perception of the spiritual world became less and less possible, and was replaced by faith, an assent which is rooted in neither direct vision nor understanding. Steiner's writings on the evolution of consciousness, of which the present chapter is but a minute sample, traces the steady loss of clairvoyance from the Indian and Egyptian epochs through the crucial transition period, beginning with Plato when clairvoyance was gradually replaced by a rationality so powerfully intellectual as to be incapable of spiritual insight. As important as Plato is for understanding the transtion from clairvoyance and mystery wisdom to rational thought, Steiner maintains that this transition would not have been realized without the consciousness of individuality made possible by the Christ Being. According to Steiner, the Christ and early Christianity continued the mystery tradition of the Greeks, but with the significant difference that the Christ became the new initiator of secret knowledge and power. By entering and transforming the human body, the Christ Being created the possibility of experiencing the divine in individual terms. In this sense, the descent of the cosmic Christ Being, according to Steiner, reversed the descent into matter by bringing into human consciousness the spiritual Ego or "I," which is the source of free-thinking and free moral action (as described in the previous chapter). This entire historical drama can be diagramed, albeit crudely, as shown on the following page.

This entire cycle, covering 10,800 years, has had as its primary task the perfection of the physical, rational, and ego powers of humanity in combination with the spiritual powers possessed by the Atlanteans and those born in the early epochs of the present cycle. The kind of consciousness described in Steiner's *Philosophy of Freedom, Knowledge of Higher Worlds,* and *Theosophy* is possible in this century because human freedom can at last be realized both in the physical and the spiritual realm. Without an adequate understanding of the evolution of the spiritual and material components of human nature and consciousness, however, the task of the present age will be neither understood nor realizable. Consequently, Steiner spends as much time explaining the period from Plato to early Christianity as he does explaining the present age. It is also the reason that this chapter, which concerns Steiner's historical vision, or his understanding of the evolution of consciousness, focuses almost exclusively on that astonishing period in human history.

Evolution of Human Consciousness Through Seven Post-Atlantean Epochs

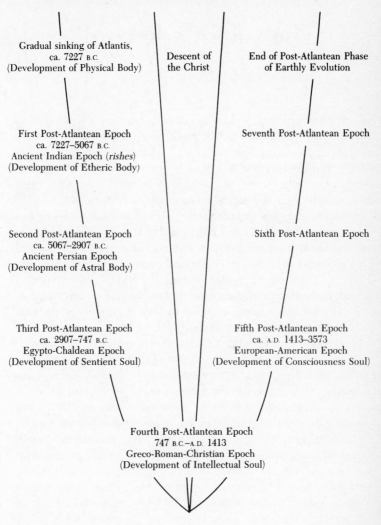

Gradual sinking of Atlantis,
ca. 7227 B.C.
(Development of Physical Body)

Descent of
the Christ

End of Post-Atlantean Phase
of Earthly Evolution

First Post-Atlantean Epoch
ca. 7227–5067 B.C.
Ancient Indian Epoch (*rishes*)
(Development of Etheric Body)

Seventh Post-Atlantean Epoch

Second Post-Atlantean Epoch
ca. 5067–2907 B.C.
Ancient Persian Epoch
(Development of Astral Body)

Sixth Post-Atlantean Epoch

Third Post-Atlantean Epoch
ca. 2907–747 B.C.
Egypto-Chaldean Epoch
(Development of Sentient Soul)

Fifth Post-Atlantean Epoch
ca. A.D. 1413–3573
European-American Epoch
(Development of Consciousness Soul)

Fourth Post-Atlantean Epoch
747 B.C.–A.D. 1413
Greco-Roman-Christian Epoch
(Development of Intellectual Soul)

The Akashic Record*

By means of ordinary history man can learn only a small part of what humanity experienced in prehistory. Historical documents shed light on but a few millennia. What archaeology, paleontology, and geology can teach us is very limited. Furthermore, everything built on external evidence is unreliable. One need only consider how the picture of an event or people, not so much remote from us, has changed when new historical evidence has been discovered. One need but compare the descriptions of one and the same thing as given by different historians, and he will soon realize on what uncertain ground he stands in these matters. Everything belonging to the external world of the senses is subject to time. In addition, time destroys what has originated in time. On the other hand, external history is dependent on what has been preserved in time. Nobody can say that the essential has been preserved, if he remains content with external evidence.

Everything which comes into being in time has its origin in the eternal. But the eternal is not accessible to sensory perception. Nevertheless, the ways to the perception of the eternal are open for man. He can develop forces dormant in him so that he can recognize the eternal. In *Knowledge of the Higher Worlds and Its Attainment*, I refer to this development. These present essays will also show that at a certain high level of his cognitive power, man can penetrate to the eternal origins of the things which vanish with time. A man broadens his power of cognition in this way if he is no longer limited to external evidence where knowledge of the past is concerned. Then he can *see* in events what is not peceptible to the senses, that part which time cannot destroy. He

* From Karl E. Zimmer, trans., "From the Akasha Record," *Cosmic Memory: Prehistory of Earth and Man* (New York: Harper & Row, 1981), pp. 38–42.

penetrates from transitory to nontransitory history. It is a fact that this history is written in other characters than is ordinary history. In gnosis and in theosophy it is called the "Akasha Chronicle." Only a faint conception of this chronicle can be given in our language. For our language corresponds to the world of the senses. That which is described by our language at once receives the character of this sense world. To the uninitiated, who cannot yet convince himself of the reality of a separate spiritual world through his own experience, the initiate easily appears to be a visionary, if not something worse.

The one who has acquired the ability to perceive in the spiritual world comes to know past events in their eternal character. They do not stand before him like the dead testimony of history, but appear in full *life*. In a certain sense, what has happened takes place before him.

Those initiated into the reading of such a living script can look back into a much more remote past than is represented by external history; and—on the basis of direct spiritual perception—they can also describe much more dependably the things of which history tells. In order to avoid possible misunderstanding, it should be said that spiritual perception is not infallible. This perception also can err, can see in an inexact, oblique, wrong manner. No man is free from error in this field, no matter how high he stands. Therefore one should not object when communications emanating from such spiritual sources do not always entirely correspond. But the dependability of observation is much greater here than in the external world of the senses. What various initiates can relate about history and prehistory will be in *essential* agreement. Such a history and prehistory does in fact exist in all mystery schools. Here for millennia the agreement has been so complete that the conformity existing among external historians of even a single century cannot be compared with it. The initiates describe *essentially* the same things at all times and in all places.

Following this introduction, several chapters from the Alasha Chronicle will be given. First, those events will be described which took place when the so-called *Atlantean* Continent still existed between America and Europe. This part of our earth's surface was once land. Today this forms the floor of the Atlantic

Ocean. Plato tells of the last remnant of this land, the island Poseidon, which lay westward of Europe and Africa. In *The Story of Atlantis and Lost Lemuria*, by W. Scott-Elliott, the reader can find that the floor of the Atlantic Ocean was once a continent, that for about a million years it was the scene of a civilization which, to be sure, was quite different from our modern ones, and the fact that the last remnants of this continent sank in the tenth millennium B.C. In this present book the intention is to give information which will supplement what is said by Scott-Elliott. While he describes more the outer, the external events among our Atlantean ancestors, the aim here is to record some details concerning their spiritual character and the inner nature of the conditions under which they lived. Therefore the reader must go back in imagination to a period which lies almost ten thousand years behind us, and which lasted for many millennia. What is described here, however, did not take place only on the continent now covered by the waters of the Atlantic Ocean, but also in the neighboring regions of what today is Asia, Africa, Europe, and America. What took place in these regions later developed from this earlier civilization.

Today I am still obliged to remain silent about the sources of the information given here. One who knows anything at all about such sources will understand why this has to be so. But events can occur which will make a breaking of this silence possible very soon. How much of the knowledge hidden within the theosophical movement may gradually be communicated, depends entirely on the attitude of our contemporaries.

Osiris, Buddha, and Christ*

*"When, set free from the body, you rise up into the free aether,
you become an immortal god, having escaped from death."*

In these words Empedocles epitomizes what the ancient Egyptians thought about the eternal element in man and its connection with the divine. A proof of this can be found in the so-called *Book of the Dead*, which has been deciphered by the diligence of nineteenth-century scholars. It is "the greatest coherent literary work which has come down to us from ancient Egypt." It embraces all kinds of instructions and prayers which were placed in the tomb of a deceased person to serve as a guide when he was released from his mortal tenement. The most intimate ideas of the Egyptians about the Eternal and the origin of the world are contained in this work. They point to conceptions of the gods similar to those held by Greek mysticism.

Osiris gradually became the favorite and most widely recognized of the various deities worshipped in different parts of Egypt. The ideas about the other divinities were brought together in him. Whatever the majority of the Egyptian people may have thought about Osiris, the *Book of the Dead* indicates that priestly wisdom saw in him a being who might be found in the human soul itself. Everything said about death and the dead shows this plainly. While the body is given to earth and preserved there, the eternal part of man enters upon the path to the eternal Primality. It comes to judgment before Osiris, who is surrounded by forty-two judges of the dead. The fate of the eternal part of man depends upon the verdict of these judges. If the soul has

---

* Editor's title. From Charles Davy and Adam Biddleston, trans., "Egyptian Mystery Wisdom," *Christianity as Mystical Fact and the Mysteries of Antiquity*, 2nd ed. (London: Rudolf Steiner Press, 1972) pp. 83–93.

confessed its sins and is deemed reconciled to eternal justice, invisible powers approach it and say: "The Osiris N. has been purified in the pool which lies south of the field of Hotep and north of the field of Locusts, where the gods of verdure purify themselves at the fourth hour of the night and the eighth hour of the day with the image of the heart of the gods, passing from night to day." Thus, within the eternal cosmic order, the eternal part of man is addressed as an Osiris. After the name Osiris comes the deceased person's own name. And the person who is being united with the eternal cosmic order also calls himself "Osiris." "I am the Osiris N. Growing under the blossoms of the fig-tree is the name Osiris N."

So man becomes an Osiris. Being Osiris is only a perfected stage of human development. It seems obvious that even the Osiris who is a judge within the eternal cosmic order is no more than a perfected man. Between human existence and divine existence there is a difference in degree and in number. At the root of this is the view of the Mysteries concerning the secret of "number." Osiris as a cosmic being is One; therefore he is present undivided in each human soul. Each person is an Osiris, yet the One Osiris must be represented as a separate being. Man is engaged in development; his evolutionary course will culminate in his existence as a god. In this context we must speak of *divinity*, rather than of a separate divine being, complete in himself.

There can be no doubt, according to this view, that a person can really enter upon the Osiris existence only if he has already reached the portals of the eternal cosmic order as an Osiris. Hence the highest life a man can lead must consist in changing himself into Osiris. Even during mortal life, a true man will live as a perfect Osiris as far as he can. He becomes perfect when he lives as an Osiris, when he passes through the experiences of Osiris. Thus we see the deeper significance of the Osiris myth. It becomes the ideal of the man who wishes to awaken the eternal within him.

Osiris had been torn to pieces, killed by Typhon. The fragments of his body were cherished and cared for by his consort, Isis. After his death he caused a ray of his own light to fall upon her, and she bore him Horus. Horus took up the earthly tasks of

Osiris. He is the second Osiris, still imperfect, but progressing towards the true Osiris.

The true Osiris is in the human soul, which is at first of a transitory nature but is destined to give birth to the eternal. Man may therefore regard himself as the tomb of Osiris. The lower nature (Typhon) has killed the higher nature in him. The love in his soul (Isis) must cherish the dead fragments of his body, and then the higher nature, the eternal soul (Horus) will be born, which can progress to Osiris life. A man who is aspiring to the highest form of existence must repeat in himself, as a microcosm, the macrocosmic Osiris process. That is the meaning of Egyptian initiation. What Plato describes as a cosmic process—that the Creator has stretched the soul of the world on the body of the world in the form of a cross, and that the cosmic process is the release of this crucified soul—this process had to be enacted in man on a smaller scale if he was to be qualified for the Osiris existence. The candidate for initiation had to develop himself in such a way that his soul-experience, his becoming an Osiris, blended into one with the cosmic Osiris process.

If we could look into the temples of initiation where persons underwent the transformation into Osiris, we should see that what took place represented in microcosm a process of world-evolution. Man, who is descended from the "Father," was to give birth in himself to the Son. The divinity he bears within him, hidden under a spell, was to become manifest in him. This divinity is suppressed by the power of his earthly nature; this lower nature must first be buried in order that the higher nature may arise.

Thus we are able to interpret what we are told about the incidents of initiation. The candidate was subjected to secret processes, by means of which his earthly nature was killed and his higher part awakened. It is not necessary to study these processes in detail, so long as we understand their meaning. This is conveyed in the confession that every one who went through initiation could make. He could say: "Before me hovered the endless perspective, at the end of which is the perfection of the divine. I felt that the power of the divine is within me, I buried all that holds down this power. I died to earthly things. I was dead. I had died as a lower man; I was in the underworld. I had intercourse with the dead: that is, with those who had already become part of the eternal cosmic order. After my sojourn in the underworld, I rose from the dead. I overcame death, but now I have become a different person. I have nothing more to do with perishable nature: in me it has become permeated with the Logos. I now belong to those who live eternally, and who will sit at the right hand of Osiris. I myself shall be a true Osiris, part of the eternal cosmic order, and judgment of life and death will be placed in my hands." The candidate for initiation had to submit to the experience which made such a confession possible for him. It was thus an experience of the highest order.

Let us now imagine that a noninitiate hears of such experiences. He cannot know what has really taken place in the initiate's soul. In his eyes, the initiate died physically, lay in the grave, and rose again. Something which is a spiritual reality at a higher stage of existence appears in the realm of sense-reality as an event which breaks through the order of nature. It is a "miracle." Initiation was a "miracle" in this sense. Anyone who really wished to understand it must have awakened inner powers to enable him to stand on a higher plane of existence. He must have approached these higher experiences through a course of life specially adapted for the purpose. In whatever way these prepared experiences were enacted in individual cases, they are always found to be of a quite definite type. And so an initiate's life is a typical one. It may be described independently of any single personality. Or rather, an individual could be described as being on the way to the divine only if he had passed through these typical experiences.

Such a personality was Buddha, living in the midst of his disciples. As such a one did Jesus appear at first to his circle of followers. Nowadays we know of the parallelism between the biographies of Buddha and of Jesus. Rudolf Seydel has shown it convincingly in his book, *Buddha und Christus*. (Compare also the excellent essay by Dr. Hübbe-Schleiden, *Jesus ein Buddhist*.) We have only to follow out the two lives in detail in order to see that all objections to the parallelism are invalid.

The birth of Buddha is announced by a white elephant, which overshadows the queen, Maya, and tells her that she will bring

forth a divine man, who "will attune all beings to love and friendship, and will unite them in a close inward bond". We read in St.
Luke's Gospel: ". . . to a virgin betrothed to a man whose name
was Joseph, of the house of David; and the virgin's name was
Mary. And the angel came to her, and said, 'Hail, thou that are
highly favored. . . . Behold, thou shalt conceive in thy womb, and
bring forth a son, and shalt call his name Jesus. He will be great,
and will be called the Son of the Most High'."

The Brahmins, or Indian priests, who know what the birth of a
Buddha means, interpret Maya's dream. They have a definite,
typical idea of a Buddha, to which the life of the personality about
to be born will have to correspond. Similarly we read in Matthew
2:4, that when Herod "had gathered all the chief priests and
scribes of the people together, he inquired of them where the
Christ was to be born." The Brahmin Asita says of Buddha: "This
is the child who will become Buddha, the redeemer, the leader to
immortality, freedom, and light." Compare with this Luke 2:25:
"And behold, there was a man in Jerusalem, whose name was
Simeon; and this man was just as devout, looking for the consolation of Israel: and the Holy Spirit was upon him. . . . And when
the parents brought in the child Jesus, to do for him after the
custom of the law, he took up the child in his arms, and blessed
God, and said, Lord, now lettest thou thy servant depart in
peace, according to thy word: for mine eyes have seen thy salvation, which thou hast prepared before the face of all people; a
light to lighten the Gentiles, and for glory to thy people Israel."

It is related of Buddha that at the age of twelve he was lost, and
found again under a tree, surrounded by poets and sages of that
ancient time, whom he was teaching. With this incident the following passage in St. Luke corresponds: "Now his parents went to
Jerusalem every year at the feast of the Passover. And when he
was twelve years old, they went up to Jerusalem according to the
custom of the feast. And when the feast was over and they were
returning, the boy Jesus stayed behind in Jerusalem; and Joseph
and his mother knew not of it. But they, supposing him to have
been in the company, went a day's journey; and they sought him
among their kinsfolk and acquaintance. And when they found him
not, they turned back to Jerusalem, seeking him. And it came to

pass that after three days they found him in the temple, sitting among the teachers, listening to them and asking them questions. And all who heard him were astonished at his understanding and answers" (Luke 2:41–47).

After Buddha had lived in solitude, and returned, he was received by the benediction of a virgin; "Blessed is thy mother, blessed is thy father, blessed is the wife to whom thou belongest." But he replied, "Only they are blessed who are in Nirvana"—i.e., those who have entered the eternal cosmic order. In St. Luke's gospel (11:27), we read: "And it came to pass, as he spoke these words, a certain woman in the crowd lifted up her voice and said to him, 'Blessed is the womb that bare thee, and the paps which thou hast sucked.' But he said, 'Blessed rather are those who hear the word of God, and keep it'."

In the course of Buddha's life, the tempter comes to him and promises him all the kingdoms of the earth. Buddha refuses everything with the words: "I know well that I am destined to have a kingdom, but I do not desire an earthly one. I shall become Buddha and make all the world exult with joy." The tempter has to admit, "My reign is over." Jesus answers the same temptation with the words: "Get thee hence, Satan, for it is written, Thou shalt worship the Lord they God, and him only shalt thou serve. Then the devil left him" (Matthew 4:10, 11). This account of the parallelisms might be extended to many other points, with the same results.

The life of Buddha ended sublimely. During a journey he felt ill; he came to the river Hiranja, near Kuschinagara. There he lay down on a carpet spread for him by his favorite disciple, Ananda. His body began to shine from within. He died transfigured, as a body of light, saying, "Nothing endures."

The death of Buddha corresponds with the transfiguration of Jesus. "And it came to pass about eight days after these sayings, he took Peter and John and James, and went up on to a mountain to pray. And as he prayed, the fashion of his countenance was altered, and his raiment became dazzling white."

Buddha's earthly life ends at this point, but it is here that the most important part of the life of Jesus begins—His suffering, death, and resurrection. The difference between Buddha and

Christ lies in the necessity that required the life of Christ to continue beyond that of Buddha. Buddha and Christ will not be understood simply by mixing them together. (Later chapters will make this clear.) Other accounts of Buddha's death will not be considered here, although they reveal profound aspects of the subject.

The agreement in these two redemptive lives leads to an unequivocal conclusion, indicated by the narratives themselves. When the priest-sages hear what kind of birth is to take place, they know what is involved. They know they have to do with a divine man; they know beforehand what kind of personality is appearing. And therefore the course of his life must correspond with what they know about the life of a divine man. In the wisdom of their Mysteries such a life is traced out for all eternity. It *can* be only as it *must* be; it comes into manifestation like an eternal law of nature. Just as a chemical substance can behave only in a quite definite way, so a Buddha or a Christ can live only in a quite definite way. The true course of his life is not described by writing an episodic biography, but far better by relating the typical features which are contained for all time in the wisdom of the Mysteries. The Buddha legend is no more a biography in the ordinary sense than the Gospels are meant to be a biography in the ordinary sense of Christ Jesus. In neither is the merely accidental given; both relate the course of life marked out for a world-redeemer. The source of the two accounts is to be found in the Mystery traditions, not in external history. For those who have recognized their divine nature, Buddha and Jesus are initiates in the most eminent sense. (Jesus is an initiate through the indwelling of the Christ Being in him.) Hence their lives are lifted out of transitory things, and what is known about initiates applies to them. The casual incidents in their lives are not narrated. Of such it might be announced "In the beginning was the Word, and the Word was with God, and the Word was a God and the Word was made flesh and dwelt among us."

But the life of Jesus contains more than that of Buddha. Buddha's life ends with the Transfiguration; the most momentous part of the life of Jesus begins after the Transfiguration. In the language of initiates this means that Buddha reached the point at which divine light begins to shine in men. He is on the verge of earthly death. He becomes the cosmic light. Jesus goes farther. He does not die physically at the moment when the cosmic light shines through him. At that moment he is a Buddha. But at that same moment he enters upon a stage which finds expression in a higher degree of initiation. He suffers and dies. The earthly element disappears. But the spiritual element, the cosmic light, does not. His resurrection follows. He is revealed to his followers as Christ. Buddha, at the moment of his Transfiguration, flows into the blissful life of the Universal Spirit. Christ Jesus awakens the Universal Spirit once more, but in a human form, in present existence. Such an event had formerly taken place in a pictorial sense during the higher stages of initiation. Those initiated in the spirit of the Osiris myth attained to such a resurrection in their consciousness as a pictorial experience. In the life of Jesus, this "great" initiation was added to the Buddha initiation, not as an imaginal experience but as a reality. Buddha showed by his life that man is the Logos, and that he returns to the Logos, to the light, when his earthly part dies. In Jesus, the Logos itself became a person. In him the Word was made flesh.

The ritual enacted in the inner recesses of the ancient Mystery temples was therefore transmuted, through Christianity, into a fact of world history. His community recognized Christ Jesus as an initiate who had been initiated in a uniquely great way. He proved to them that the world is divine. For the community of Christians, the wisdom of the Mysteries was indissolubly bound up with the personality of Christ Jesus. That which man had previously sought to attain through the Mysteries was now replaced by the belief that Christ had lived in earth, and that the faithful belonged to Him.

Henceforth, part of what had formerly been attainable only through mystical methods could be replaced, for Christian adherents, by the conviction that the divine had been manifested in the Word present among them. The sole decisive factor now was not something for which each individual soul had to undergo a long preparation, but what had been seen and heard, and was handed down by those who were with Jesus. "That which was from the beginning, which we have heard, which . . . our hands have touched, concerning the Word of life . . . that which we have seen and heard we declare to you, so that you may have fellowship with us." Thus do we read in the first Epistle of St. John. And this immediate reality is to embrace all future generations in a living bond of union, and as a church is to extend mystically from race to race. It is in this sense that the words of St. Augustine are to be understood: "I should not believe the Gospels if I were not moved thereto by the authority of the Catholic Church." Thus the Gospels do not contain within themselves evidence for their truth, but they are to be believed because they are founded on the personality of Jesus, and because the Church mysteriously draws from that personality the power to make the truth of the Gospels manifest.

The Mysteries handed down traditionally the means of arriving at truth; the Christian community itself propagates the truth. To the confidence in the mystical forces which light up in the inner being of man during initiation, was to be added confidence in the One, primal Initiator.

The mystics sought to become divine; they wished to experience divinity. Jesus was made divine; we must hold fast to Him, and then we shall become partakers of His divinity, in the community founded by Him—that became the Christian conviction. That which became divine in Jesus was made so for all His followers. "Lo, I am with you always, even unto the end of the world" (Matt. 28:20). He who was born in Bethlehem has an *eternal* character. Thus the Christmas antiphon speaks of the birth of Jesus as if it took place each Christmas: "Christ is born today; the Savior has come into the world today; today the angels are singing on earth."

In the Christ-experience is to be seen a definite stage of initiation. When the mystic of pre-Christian times passed through this Christ-experience, he was, through his initiation, in a state which enabled him to perceive spiritually, in the higher worlds, something to which no fact in the world of sense corresponded. He experienced that which comprises the Mystery of Golgotha in the higher world. If the Christian mystic goes through this experience by initiation, he beholds the historical event which took place on Golgotha, and at the same time he knows that this event, enacted

in the physical world, has the spiritual content that could formerly be found only in the supersensible facts of the Mysteries. Thus
there was poured out on the Christian community, through the
Mystery of Golgotha, that which had formerly been poured out
on the mystics within the temples. And initiation gives Christian
mystics the possibility of becoming conscious of what is contained
in the Mystery of Golgotha, whereas faith makes man an unconscious partaker of the mystical stream which flowed from the
events depicted in the New Testament and has ever since permeated the spiritual life of humanity.

Greek Mystery Wisdom*

Numerous facts combine to show that the philosophical wisdom of the Greeks rested on the same convictions as mystical knowledge does. We understand the great philosophers only when we approach them with feelings gained through study of the Mysteries. With what veneration does Plato speak in the *Phaedo* of the "secret teachings." "It appears," he says, "that those who established the Mysteries for us were not unenlightened; for a long time they have been enjoining upon us that anyone who reaches the underworld without having been initiated and sanctioned falls into the mire; but that he who arrives there purified and consecrated will dwell with the gods. For those who have to do with the Mysteries say that there are many thyrsusbearers, but few truly inspired. These latter are, in my opinion, none other than those who have devoted themselves in the right way of wisdom. I myself have not neglected the task of becoming one of them, as far as I was able, but have striven after this in every way."

It is only a man who places his search for wisdom entirely at the service of the condition of soul created by initiation who could speak thus of the Mysteries. And there is no doubt that a flood of light is shed on the words of the great Greek philosophers when they are illuminated from the Mysteries.

The relation of Heraclitus of Ephesus (535–475 B.C.) to the Mysteries is plainly indicated in a traditional saying about him— that his thoughts "were an impassable road": anyone coming upon them without being initiated found only "disease and darkness," but they were "brighter than the sun" for anyone introduced to them by a mystic. And when it is said of his book that he depos-

* From Charles Davy and Adam Biddleston, trans., "The Greek Sages Before Plato in the Light of Mystery Wisdom," *Christianity as Mystical Fact and the Mysteries of Antiquity*, 2nd ed. (London: Rudolf Steiner Press, 1972) pp. 33–45.

ited it in the temple of Artemis, this means that initiates alone could understand him. Heraclitus was called "The Obscure," because it was only through the Mysteries that light could be thrown on his views.

Heraclitus comes before us as a man who took life with the utmost earnestness. We see plainly from his characteristics, if we know how to reconstruct them, that he bore within him intimate knowledge which he knew that words could only indicate, not express. Out of such temper of mind arose his celebrated utterance, "All things flow away," which Plutarch explains thus: "No one can dip twice in the same stream, or touch twice the same mortal being. For they are all in flow, dispersed and gathered together, suddenly and swiftly, and not so much at different times as simultaneously, a perpetual gathering and releasing, coming and going."

A man who thinks in this way has seen through the nature of transitory things, for he has felt compelled to characterize the essence of transitoriness itself in the clearest terms. Such a description could not be given unless the transitory were being measured by the eternal, and in particular it could not be extended to man without having seen into his inner nature. Heraclitus has indeed extended his characterization to men. "Life and death, waking and sleeping, youth and age are the same; this changes into that, and that again into this." These words show full knowledge of the illusory nature of the lower personality. He says still more forcibly, "Life and death are found in our living, even as in our dying." What does this mean but that if we value life more than death, we are under the spell of the transitory? Dying is to perish, in order to make way for new life, but the eternal is living in the new life as in the old. The same eternal appears in transitory life as in death. When we grasp this eternal, we look upon life and death with the same feeling. Life has a special value only when we have not been able to awaken the eternal within us. The saying, "All things flow away," might be repeated a thousand times, but unless said with this feeling it is an empty sound. The knowledge of eternal becoming is valueless if it fails to lift us out of our attachment to the transitory.

A turning away from that thirst for life which binds us to the transistory is indicated by Heraclitus when he says, "How can we say about our daily life, 'we are,' when from the standpoint of the eternal we know that 'we are and are not'?" (cf. *Fragments of Heraclitus*, No. 81). "Hades and Dionysus are one and the same," another *Fragment* says. Dionysus, the god of joy in life, of germination and growth, to whom the Dionysiac festivals were dedicated, is, for Heraclitus, the same as Hades, the god of destruction and annihilation. Only one who sees death in life and life in death, and in both the eternal, high above life and death, can view the merits and demerits of existence in the right light. Then even imperfections become justified, for in them too lives the eternal. What they are from the standpoint of the limited lower life, they are only in appearance: "It is not always best for men to have their wishes gratified. Illness makes health sweet and good; hunger makes food appreciated, and toil, rest. . . . The sea contains the purest and impurest water. Drinkable and wholesome for fishes, it is undrinkable and injurious for human beings." Here Heraclitus is not drawing attention primarily to the transitoriness of earthly things, but to the splendor and majesty of the eternal.

Heraclitus speaks vehemently against Homer and Hesiod, and the learned men of his day. He wished to show up their way of thinking, which remains bound to the transistory only. He did not want gods endowed with qualities taken from a perishable world, and he could not regard as the highest form of science one that investigates the becoming and passing away of things. For him, the eternal speaks out of the perishable, and for this eternal he has a profound symbol. "The harmony of the world arises from opposites held in tension, as in the lyre and the bow." What depths are hidden in this image! By the harmonizing of divergent forces, unity is attained. One tone contradicts another, yet together they produce harmony. If we apply this to the spiritual world, we have the thought of Heraclitus: "The immortal is mortal; the mortal, immortal; death is immortal life for mortals; for immortals, mortal life is death."

A primal fault for man is to fix his cognition on the transitory. Thereby he turns away from the eternal, and life becomes a danger for him. Whatever happens to him comes through life, but these happenings lose their sting if he ceases to set absolute value on life. His innocence is then restored. It is as though he were able to return from the so-called seriousness of life to his childhood. An adult takes seriously much that for a child is merely play, but anyone who attains to real knowledge becomes like a child. "Serious" values lose their value, looked at from the standpoint of eternity. Life then seems like play. On this account Heraclitus says: "Eternity is a child at play; it is the reign of a child." Where does the original fault lie? In taking with the utmost seriousness much that does not deserve to be so taken. God has poured Himself into the universe of things. If we make use of these things with no reference to God, we are treating them quite seriously as "the tombs of God." We should play with them like a child, and should devote our earnestness to awakening the Divine element which sleeps spellbound within them.

Contemplation of the eternal acts like a destroying fire on ordinary assumptions about the nature of things. The spirit dissolves thoughts of sensuality; it consumes them. That is the higher meaning of the Heraclitean thought, that fire is the primary element of all things. This thought is certainly to be taken first as an ordinary physical explanation of the phenomena of the universe. But no one understands Heraclitus who does not think of him in the same way that Philo, living in the early days of Christianity, thought of the laws of the Bible. "There are people,' he says, "who take the written laws *merely* as symbols of spiritual teaching; they diligently search for the latter, but despise the laws themselves. I can only blame such people, for they should pay heed both to discerning the hidden meaning and to observing the obvious one." If we argue whether Heraclitus meant by "fire" physical fire, or whether fire for him was only a symbol of eternal spirit which dissolves and reconstitutes all things, that is putting a wrong construction upon his thought. He meant both, and yet neither. For spirit was also alive, for him, in ordinary fire, and the force which is physically active in fire lives on a higher plane in the human soul, which melts in its crucible mere sense-knowledge, so that out of this the contemplation of the eternal may arise.

It is very easy to misunderstand Heraclitus. He makes strife the "Father of things," but only of "things," not of the eternal. If there were no contradictions in the world, if the most multifarious interests were not in conflict with one another, the world of becoming, of transitory things, would not exist. But what is revealed in this antagonism, what is diffused in it, is not strife but harmony. Just because there is strife in all things, the spirit of the wise should pass over them like a breath of fire, and change them into harmony.

At this point there shines forth one of the great thoughts of Heraclitean wisdom. What is man as a personal being? From the above point of view Heraclitus derives the answer. Man is composed of the conflicting elements into which divinity has poured itself. In this state he finds himself, and beyond it he becomes aware of the spirit within him—the spirit which is rooted in the eternal. But the spirit is born, for man, out of the conflict of elements, and it has itself to calm them. In man, nature surpasses herself. The same universal force which created antagonism and the mixture of elements has afterwards to do away with the conflict through its wisdom.

Here we arrive at the eternal dualism which lives in man, the perpetual antagonism between the temporal and the eternal. Through the eternal he has become something quite particular, and out of this he has to create something higher. he is both dependent and independent. He can participate in the eternal Spirit he contemplates only in proportion to the compound of elements which the eternal Spirit has brought about within him. And it is just on this account that he is called upon to fashion the eternal out of the temporal. The spirit works within him, but in a special way. It works out of the temporal. It is the peculiarity of the human soul that something temporal should be able to work and gain strength like something eternal. That is why the soul is akin both to a god and to a worm. Man, because of this, stands between God and animals. The dynamic force within him is his daimonic element; the element which strives out beyond himself. In a striking phrase—"Man's daimon is his destiny"—Heraclitus refers to this fact. "Daimon" is here meant in the Greek sense. In modern language one would say "spirit." The personality is the vehicle of the daimonic element. This element is not confined within the limits of the personality, and for it the birth and death of the personality are of no significance. What is the relation of the daimonic element to the personality which comes and goes? The personality is only a form of appearance for the daimon.

Anyone who has arrived at this knowledge looks beyond himself, backwards and forwards. His experience of the daimonic within himself testifies to his own immortality. And he can no longer limit his daimon to the one function of filling out his personality, for his personality can be no more than one of the forms in which the daimon is manifest. The daimon cannot limit himself to one personality; he has power to animate many. He is able to move from one personality into another. The great thought of reincarnation springs as a matter of course from the Heraclitean premises, and not only the thought but the experience of the fact. The thought only paves the way for the experience. Anyone who becomes conscious of the daimonic element in himself does not find it to be a newborn innocent. He finds that it has characteristics. Whence do they come? Why have I certain natural aptitudes? Because other personalities have already worked upon my daimon. And what becomes of the work which I accomplish in the daimon if I am not to assume that its task ends with my own personality? I am working for a future personality. Between me and the cosmic unity something interposes which reaches beyond me, but is yet not the same as divinity. This something is my daimon. My today is only the outcome of yesterday, my tomorrow will be the outcome of today; in the same way my life is the outcome of a former life and will be the foundation of a future one. Just as mortal man looks back to innumerable yesterdays and forward to many tomorrows, so does the soul of the sage look upon many lives in his past and many in the future. The thoughts and aptitudes I acquired yesterday I am using today. Is it not the same with life? Do not people come to the horizon of existence with the most diverse capacities? Whence this difference? Does it proceed from nothing?

Natural science takes much credit for having banished miracle from our view of organic life. David Frederick Strauss, in his *Die alte und die neue Glaube [The Old and New Faith]* considers it a great achievement that we no longer think of a complete organic being as a miracle created from nothing. We understand its perfection when we are able to explain it as a development from imperfection. The structure of an ape is no longer a miracle if we assume its ancestors to have been primitive fishes which have been gradually transformed. Let us at least agree to accept as reasonable in the domain of spirit what seems to us to be right in the domain of nature. Is the perfected spirit to have the same preconditions as the imperfect one? Does a Goethe have the same antecedents as any Hottentot? The antecedents of an ape are as unlike those of a fish as the antecedents of Goethe's mind are unlike those of a savage. The spiritual ancestry of Goethe's soul is different from that of the savage soul. The soul has grown as well as the body. The spiritual ancestry of Goethe is richer than that of a savage. Let us take the doctrine of reincarnation in this sense, and we shall no longer find it unscientific. We shall be able to explain in the right way what we find in our souls, and we shall not take what we find as if created by a miracle. If I can write, it is because I learned to write. No one who has a pen in his hand for the first time can sit down and write. But if someone has come into the world with "the stamp of genius," must he owe it to a miracle? No, even the "stamp of genius" must be acquired. It must have been learned. And when it appears in a person, we call it a spiritual element. But this element had first to learn; it will have acquired in a former life the talent it shows in a later one.

In this form, and in this form only, did the thought of eternity pass before the mind of Heraclitus and other Greek sages. They never spoke of a continuance of the immediate personality after death. Compare some verses of Empedocles (490–430 B.C.). He says of those who accept the data of experience as miracles:

Foolish and ignorant they, and do not reach far with their thinking,
Who suppose that what has not existed can come into being,
Or that something may die away wholly and vanish completely;
Impossible that any beginning can come from Not-Being,
Impossible also that being can fade into nothing;
For wherever a being is driven, it will there continue to be,
Never will any believe, who have been in these matters instructed,
That spirits of men live only as long as so-called life endures,
That only so long do they live, receiving their joys and their sorrows,
Or that ere they were born and when they are dead, they are nothing.

The Greek sage did not even raise the question whether there was an eternal part in man, but asked only in what this eternal element consisted and how man can nourish and cherish it in himself. For it was clear to him from the outset that man is an intermediate creation between the earthly and the divine. It was not a question of the divine outside and beyond the world. The divine lives in man, but in a human way. It is the force urging man to make himself ever more and more divine. Only one who thinks in this way can say with Empedocles:

> When, set free from the body, you rise up into the free aether,
> You became an immortal God, having escaped from death.

What may be done for a human life from this point of view? It may be initiated into the encircling order of the eternal. For in man there must be forces which merely natural life does not develop. And his life might pass away unused if the forces remained idle. To unlock them, and so to make man akin to the divine— that was the task of the Mysteries. And this was also the mission which the Greek sages set before themselves. In this way we can understand Plato's saying, that "he who passes unsanctified and uninitiated into the underworld will lie in the mire, but he who arrives there after initiation and purification will dwell with the gods." We have to do here with a conception which treats the significance of immortality as being closely bound up with the Universe. Everything man undertakes in order to awaken the eternal within him, he does in order to enhance the value of the world's existence. The knowledge he gains does not make him an idle spectator of the universe, forming images for himself of what would be there just as much if he did not exist. The force of his cognition is a higher, creative force of nature. What flashes up within him spiritually is something divine which was previously under a spell; without his cognition it would have lain idle, waiting for another deliverance. Thus a human personality does not live in and for itself, but for the world. Life when looked at in this way extends far beyond individual existence. In this light we can understand utterances such as that of Pindar, giving a vista of the eternal: "Happy is he who has seen the Mysteries before descending under the hollow earth. He knows the end of life, and he knows the beginning promised by Zeus."

We can understand also the proud traits and solitary nature of sages such as Heraclitus. They were able to say of themselves that much had been revealed to them, for they did not attribute their knowledge to their transitory personality, but to the eternal daimon within them. Their pride was of necessity stamped with humility and modesty, expressed in the words, "All knowledge of perishable things is in perpetual flux, like the things themselves." Heraclitus calls the eternal universe a game; he could also call it the most serious of realities. But the word "serious" has been worn out by being applied to earthly experiences. On the other hand, a realization of "the play of the eternal" gives man a security in life which he cannot have if he takes transitory things too seriously.

A conception of the universe different from that of Heraclitus grew up, on the ground of the Mysteries, in the community founded by Pythagoras during the sixth century B.C. in Southern Italy. The Pythagoreans saw the basis of things in the numbers and geometrical figures whose laws they investigated by means of mathematics. Aristotle says of them: "They were the first to advance the study of mathematics and were so engrossed in it that they took the elements of mathematics to be the elements of all things. Now as numbers are naturally the first thing in mathematics, and they thought they saw many resemblances in numbers to things and processes, and certainly more in numbers than in fire, earth, and water, so, for them, one type of number came to mean justice; another, the soul and spirit; another, time, and so on with all the rest. Moreover they found in numbers the characteristics and relations of harmony; and so everything else, in accordance with its whole nature, seemed to be a reflection of numbers, and numbers seemed to be the first thing in nature."

The mathematical and scientific study of natural phenomena must always lead to a certain Pythagorean habit of thought. When a string of a certain length is struck, a particular note is produced. If the string is shortened in certain numerical proportions, other notes will be produced. The pitch of the notes can be expressed in numbers. Physics also expresses color-relations in figures. When two bodies combine into one substance, it always happens that a certain definite quantity of one of them, expressible in numbers, combines with a certain definite quantity of the other. The Pythagoreans studied these orderings of measures and numbers in nature. Geometrical figures play a similar role. Astronomy, for instance, is mathematics applied to the heavenly bodies.

One fact, above all, impressed the Pythagoreans. This was that man, quite alone and purely through his mental activity, discovers the laws of numbers and figures, and yet, when he looks abroad into nature, he finds that things are obeying the same laws which he has ascertained for himself in his own mind. Man forms the idea of an ellipse and ascertains the laws of ellipses; and the heavenly bodies move according to the laws he has established. (It is not, of course, a question here of the astronomical views of the Pythagoreans. Anything that may be said of these can equally be said of Copernican views in our present context.) Hence it follows directly that the achievements of the human soul are not an activity apart from the rest of the world, but that in them cosmic laws are expressed. The Pythagoreans said: The senses show us physical phenomena, but not the harmonious order they obey. The human mind must first find these rules of harmony within itself, if it wishes to behold them in the outer world. The deeper meaning of the world, that which bears sway within it as an eternal, law-abiding necessity—this makes its appearance in the human soul and becomes a present reality there.

The meaning of the world is revealed in the soul. This meaning is not to be found in what we see, hear, and touch, but in what the soul brings to light from its own depths. The eternal laws are thus hidden in the depths of the soul. If we descend there, we shall find the Eternal. God, the eternal harmony of the Cosmos, is in the human soul. The soul-element is not confined to the bodily substance enclosed within the skin, for in the soul are born the laws by which worlds circle in celestial space. The soul is not in the personality. The personality serves only as the organ through which the order which pervades cosmic space may express itself. There is something of the spirit of Pythagoras in a saying by one of the Fathers, Gregory of Nyssa: "We are told that

human nature is small and limited, and that God is infinite, and it
is asked how the finite can embrace the infinite. But who dares to
say that the infinity of the Godhead is limited by the boundary of
the flesh, as though by a vessel? For not even during our lifetime
is the spiritual nature confined within the boundaries of the flesh.
The material body, it is true, is limited by neighboring parts, but
the soul reaches out freely into the whole of creation through the
activities of thought."

The soul is not the personality; the soul belongs to infinity.
From such a point of view the Pythagoreans must have considered that only fools could imagine the soul-force to be all used
up in the personality.

For them too, as for Heraclitus, the essential point was the
awakening of the eternal in the personal. Knowledge for them
meant intercourse with the eternal. The more a man brought the
eternal element within him into existence, the more highly were
they bound to value him. Life in their community consisted in
cultivating intercourse with the eternal. The object of Pythagorean education was to lead the members of the community
to this intercourse. The education was therefore a philosophical
initiation, and the Pythagoreans might well say that by their manner of life they were aiming at a goal similar to that of the Mysteries.

Plato as Mystic*

The importance of the Mysteries for the spiritual life of the Greeks can be seen in Plato's conception of the universe. There is only one way of understanding him thoroughly: he must be placed in the light which streams forth from the Mysteries.

Plato's later disciples, the Neoplatonists, credit him with a secret doctrine which he imparted only to those who were worthy, and then under the "seal of secrecy." His teaching was looked upon as secret in the same sense as the wisdom of the Mysteries. Even if Plato's seventh letter was not the work of Plato himself, as has been claimed, this makes no difference for our present purpose. It need not concern us whether Plato or someone else expressed the attitude of mind set forth in this letter, for this attitude was inherent in Plato's conception of the world. In the letter we read as follows: "This much I may say about all those who have written or may hereafter write as if they knew the aim of my endeavor—no credence is to be attached to their words, whether they obtained their information from me or from others, or invented it themselves. I have written nothing on this subject, nor would it be allowable to do so. A teaching of this kind cannot be expressed in words, as other teachings can be; it needs a long study of the subject and a making oneself with it. Then it is as though a spark leaps forth and kindles a light in the soul; a light which thereafter is able to sustain itself." This utterance might indicate only the writer's powerlessness to express his meaning in words—a mere personal weakness—if the idea of the Mysteries were not to be found in them. The subject on which Plato had not written, and would never write, must be something about which

* From Charles Davy and Adam Biddleston, trans., "Plato as a Mystic," *Christianity as Mystical Fact and the Mysteries of Antiquity*, 2nd ed. (London: Rudolf Steiner Press, 1972), pp. 47–62.

all writing would be futile. It must be a feeling, a sentiment, an experience, which is not gained by momentary communication, but by making oneself with it, in heart and soul. The reference is to the inner education which Plato was able to give to his chosen pupils. For them, fire flashed forth from his words; for others, only thoughts.

The manner of our approach to Plato's *Dialogues* is not a matter of indifference. They will mean more or less to us, according to our spiritual condition. Much more passed from Plato to his disciples than the literal meaning of his words. In the place where he taught, his listeners lived in the atmosphere of the Mysteries. His words awoke overtones which vibrated in tune with them, but these overtones needed the atmosphere of the Mysteries, or they died away without having been heard.

In the center of the world of the Platonic Dialogues stands the personality of Socrates. We need not here touch upon the historical aspect of his personality. We are concerned with the character of Socrates as it appears in Plato. Socrates is a person consecrated by his having died for the truth. He died as only an initiate can die, as one to whom death is merely a moment of life like other moments. He approaches death as he would any other event in existence. His attitude towards it was such that even in his friends the feelings usual on such an occasion were not aroused. Phaedo, in the *Dialogue on the Immortality of the Soul*,* says: "Truly I found myself in a strange state of mind. I felt no compassion for him, as is usual at the death of a dear friend. So happy did the man appear to me in his demeanor and speech, so steadfast and noble was his end, that I was confident that he was not going to the underworld without a divine mission, and that even there it would be well with him, if it ever is with anyone. No tender-hearted emotion overcame me, as might have been expected at such a mournful event, nor on the other hand was I in a cheerful mood, as is usual during philosophical pursuits, although our conversation was of this nature; but I found myself in a wondrous state of mind, an unwonted blending of joy and grief, when reflecting that this man was about to die." The dying Socrates

---

Phaedo.—ED.

instructs his disciples about immortality. His personality, having learnt by experience the worthlessness of life, furnishes a kind of proof quite different from logic and arguments founded on reason. It seems as if it were not a man speaking, for this man was passing away, but the voice of eternal truth itself, which had taken up its abode in a perishable personality. Where the temporal dissolves into nothing, there seems to be a breath of the air in which the eternal can resound.

We hear from Socrates no logical proofs of immortality. The whole discourse is designed to lead his friends to where they may behold the eternal. Then they will need no proofs. Would one have to prove that a rose is red to someone who has a rose before him? Why should one need to prove that the spirit is eternal to someone whose eyes we have opened to behold the spirit? Socrates points to experiences, inner events, and first of all to the experience of wisdom itself.

What is denied by someone who aspires after wisdom? He wishes to free himself from all that the senses offer him in everyday perception. He seeks for the spirit in the sense-world. Is not this a fact which may be compared with dying? "For," according to Socrates, "those who occupy themselves with philosophy in the right way are really striving after nothing else than to die and be dead, without this being noticed by others. If this is true, it would be strange if, after having aimed at this all through life, when death itself comes they should be indignant at something for which they have so long striven and exerted themselves." To corroborate this, Socrates asks one of his friends: "Does it seem to you fitting for a philosopher to take trouble about so-called pleasures of the senses, such as eating and drinking? Or about sexual pleasures? And do you think that such a man pays much heed to other bodily needs, or to fine clothes, shoes and other adornments? Do you think he values or despises them any more than his bare needs require? Does it not seem to you that it should be such a man's whole preoccupation not to turn his thoughts to the body, but as much as possible away from it and towards the soul? Therefore the first mark of the philosopher is that he, more than all other men, frees his soul from association with the body."

Socrates is then entitled to say that aspiration after wisdom has this much in common with dying: it turns man away from the physical. But whither does he turn? Towards the spiritual. But can he desire the same from the spirit as from the senses? On this, Socrates says: "But how is it with rational knowledge itself? Is the body a hindrance or not, if we take it as a companion in our search for knowledge? I mean, do sight and hearing bring us truth? Or are the poets wrong in always telling us that we never see or hear anything accurately. . . . When does the soul catch sight of truth? For when it tries to examine something with the help of the body, the body evidently deceives it."

Everything we perceive through our bodily senses comes and goes. And this coming into being and passing away is the cause of our being deceived. But if we look with rational insight more deeply into things, the eternal element in them is revealed to us. Thus the senses do not offer us the eternal in its true form. The moment we trust them implicitly, they deceive us. They cease to deceive us if we confront them with our thoughtful insight and submit what they tell us to its examination.

But how could our thoughtful insight sit in judgment on the reports of the senses unless there were something living within it which transcends sense-perception? Therefore the truth or falsity in things is decided by something within us which opposes the physical body and so is not subject to its laws. Above all, this something cannot be subject to the laws of growth and decay, for it bears truth within itself. Now truth cannot have a yesterday and a today; it cannot be one thing one day and another the next, as happens with objects of sense. Therefore truth must be something eternal. And when the philosopher turns away from the perishable things of sense and towards truth, he is turning towards an eternal element that lives within him. If we immerse ourselves wholly in spirit, we shall live wholly in truth. The things of sense around us are no longer present merely in their physical form. "And he accomplishes this most perfectly," says Socrates, "who approaches everything as much as possible with the spirit only, without either looking around when he is thinking, or letting any other sense interrupt his reflecting; but, making use of pure thought only, he strives to grasp everything as it is in itself, separating it as much as possible from eyes and ears, in short from the whole body, which only disturbs the soul and does not allow it to attain truth and insight when associated with the soul. . . . Now is not death the release and separation of the soul from the body? And it is only true philosophers who are always striving to release the soul as far as they can. This, therefore, is the philosopher's vocation, to deliver and separate the soul from the body. . . . Hence it would be foolish if a man, who all his life has taken measures to be as near death as possible, should rebel against it when it comes. . . . In fact the real seekers after wisdom aspire to die, and of all men they are those who least fear death."

Moreover, Socrates bases all higher morality on liberation from the body. A man who follows only the demands of his body is not moral. Who is valiant? asks Socrates. He is valiant who does not obey his body but the demands of his spirit when these demands imperil the body. And who is self-controlled? Is it not he who "does not let himself be carried away by desires, but maintains an indifferent and seemly demeanor towards them? Therefore is not self-control most typical of those who set least value on the body and live in the love of wisdom?" And so it is, in the opinion of Socrates, with all the virtues.

Socrates goes on to characterize rational insight. How do we come to know something? Undoubtedly, by forming judgments. I form a judgment about some object; for instance, I say to myself that the thing in front of me is a tree. How do I arrive at saying that? I can do it only if I already know what a tree is. I must recall my image of a tree. A tree is a material thing. If I remember a tree, I am therefore remembering a material thing. I say of something that it is a tree if it resembles other things I have previously observed and know to be trees. Memory is the key to this knowledge. It enables me to compare all sorts of material things with one another. But this does not exhaust my knowledge. If I see two similar things, I form a judgment and say they are alike. Now, in reality two things are never exactly alike. I can find a likeness only in certain respects. The idea of a perfect similarity therefore arises within me although it has no counterpart in the external world. And this idea helps me to form a judgment, just as memory helps me towards judgment and knowledge. Just as one tree reminds me of others, so am I reminded of the idea of

similarity by looking at two things in relation to each other. Within me, therefore, thoughts and memories arise which are not due
to physical reality.

All kinds of knowledge not borrowed from sense-reality are
grounded on such thoughts. The whole of mathematics consists of
them. It would be a bad geometrician who could bring into mathematical relations only what he can see with his eyes and touch
with his hands. Thus we have thoughts which do not orignate in
perishable nature, but arise out of the spirit. And it is these that
bear in them the mark of eternal truth. The findings of mathematics will be eternally true, even if the whole cosmic system were to
collapse tomorrow and an entirely new one were to arise. In another cosmic system conditions might prevail to which our
present mathematical truths would not be applicable, but they
would still be true in themselves.

It is when the soul is alone with itself that it can bring forth
these eternal truths. It is then related to the true and eternal, and
not to the ephemeral and apparent. Hence Socrates says: "When
the soul, returning into itself, reflects, it goes straight to what is
pure and everlasting and immortal and like unto itself; and being
related to this, cleaves to it when the soul is alone, and is not
hindered. And then the soul rests from its mistakes, and is in
communion with that which is like unto itself. And this state of
soul is called wisdom. . . . Look now whether it does not follow,
from all that has been said, that the soul is most like the divine,
immortal, reasonable, unique, indissoluble, unchanging; while
the body is most like the human and mortal, the unreasonable,
multiform, dissoluble and everchanging. . . . If, therefore, this is
so, the soul goes to what is like itself, to the immaterial, to the
divine, immortal, reasonable. There it attains to bliss, freed from
error and ignorance, from fear and undisciplined love and all
other human evils. There it lives, as the initiates say, through all
aftertime truly with God."

It is not within the scope of this book to indicate all the paths
along which Socrates leads his friend to the eternal. These paths
all breathe the same spirit. They all tend to show that man finds
one thing when he goes the way of transitory sense-perception,
and another when his spirit is alone with itself. It is to this origi-

nal nature of spirit that Socrates points his hearers. If they find it, they see with their own spiritual eyes that it is eternal. The dying Socrates does not prove the immortality of the soul; he simply lays bare the nature of the soul. And then it comes to light that growth and decay, birth and death, have nothing to do with the soul. The essence of the soul lies in the true, and this can neither come into being nor perish. The soul has no more to do with becoming than the straight has with the crooked. But death belongs to the process of becoming. Therefore the soul has nothing to do with death. Must we not say of what is immortal that it admits of mortality as little as the straight admits the crooked? Must we not say, Socrates continues, that "if the immortal is imperishable, it is impossible for the soul to come to an end when death arrives? For from what has been already shown, it does not admit of death, nor can it die any more than three can be an even number."

Let us trace the whole development of this dialogue, in which Socrates brings his hearers to behold the eternal in human personality. The hearers accept his thoughts, and they look into themselves to see if they can find in their inner experiences something which assents to his ideas. They make the objections which strike them. What has happened to the hearers when the dialogue is finished? They have found something within them which they did not possess before. They have not merely accepted an abstract truth; they have gone through a development. Something has come to life in them which was not living in them before. Is not this to be compared with an initiation? And does not this throw a light on why Plato set forth his philosophy in the form of conversation? These dialogues are meant to be nothing else than a literary form of the events which took place in the sanctuaries of the Mysteries. We are convinced of this from what Plato himself says in many passages. As a teacher of philosophy, he wished to be what the initiator into the Mysteries was, as far as this was possible in a philosophical style of communication. How clear it is that Plato feels himself to be in harmony with the Mysteries! He thinks he is on the right path only when it is taking him where the mystic should be led. He expresses this in the *Timaeus:* "All those who are of right mind invoke the gods for their small or great enterprises; but we who are concerned with teachings about the universe—how far it is created or uncreated—have the special duty, if we have not quite lost our way, to call upon and implore the gods and goddesses that we may teach everything first in conformity with their spirit, and next in harmony with ourselves." And Plato promises those who follow this path that the Godhead, as savior, will ensure that their inquiry, so prone to error and ranging so far from the beaten track, will lead them finally to an illuminating teaching.

It is especially the *Timaeus* that reveals to us how the Platonic cosmogony is connected with the Mysteries. At the very beginning of this dialogue an "intiation" is referred to. Solon is "initiated" by an Egyptian priest into the formation of worlds, and the way in which eternal truths are symbolically expressed in traditional myths. "There have already been many and various destructions of part of the human race," says the Egyptian priest to Solon, "and there will be more in the future; the most extensive by fire and water and lesser ones through countless other causes. It is related also in your country that Phaeton, the son of Helios, once mounted his father's chariot, and as he did not know how to drive it, everything on the earth was burnt up, and he himself slain by lightning. This sounds like a fable, but the truth in it concerns changes in the movements of the celestial bodies revolving round the earth and of the destruction of everything on the earth by fierce fire. This annihilation happens periodically, after the lapse of certain long periods of time." This passage gives a clear indication of the attitude of the initiate towards folk-myths. He recognizes the truths hidden in their images.

The drama of the creation of the world is brought before us in the *Timaeus*. Whoever wishes to follow the traces which lead back to this creation will come to the point of divining the primordial force from which all things have sprung. "Now to find the Creator and Father of the universe is difficult indeed, and then, having found Him, to speak about Him so that all may understand is impossible." The mystic knew what this "impossible" means. It signifies the drama of Divinity. God is not present for him in the materially comprehensible world. There He is present only as nature, where He is spell-bound. Only one who awakens the divine within himself is able to approach Him. Thus He cannot at once be made comprehensible to everyone. But even to one who approaches Him, He does not Himself appear. The *Timaeus* says this also. The Father made the universe out of the body and soul of the world. He mixed together, in harmony and perfect proportions, the elements which came into being when, pouring Himself out, He gave up His separate existence. Thereby the body of the world came into being, and stretched upon it, in the form of a cross, is the soul of the world. It is the divine element in the world. It met with the death on the cross so that the world might come into existence. Plato can therefore call nature the tomb of the divine; a grave, however, in which there lies nothing dead, but rather the eternal, to which death only gives the opportunity of bringing to expression the omnipotence of life. And man sees nature in the right light when he approaches it in order to release the crucified soul of the world. It must rise again from its death, from its spell. Where can it come to life again? Only in the soul of the initiated man. Then wisdom finds its right relation to the cosmos. The resurrection, the liberation, of God—that is what the attainment of true knowledge means.

In the *Timaeus* the development of the world is traced from the imperfect to the perfect. An ascending process is represented imaginatively. Beings develop. God reveals Himself in their development. The process of evolution is the resurrection of God from the tomb. Within evolution, man appears. Plato shows that with man something special comes in. True, the whole world is divine, and man is not more divine than other beings. But in other beings God is present in a hidden way; in man, God is manifest. At the end of the *Timaeus* we read: "And now we might say that our discourse concerning the universe has reached its end, for after the world has been provided with mortal and immortal living beings and thereby fulfilled, it becomes itself a visible being embracing everything visible, and an image of the Creator. This one and only begotten world has become the God perceptible to the senses, and the greatest and best world, the fairest and most perfect there could be." But this one and only begotten world would not be perfect if the image of its Creator were not to be found among the images it contains. This image can be engendered in the human soul. Not the Father Himself, but God's offspring, the Son, living in the soul and like unto the Father—he it is who can be born of man.

Philo, of whom it was said that he was Plato reborn, characterized as the "Son of God" the wisdom born of man, which lives in the soul and has as content the reason present in the world. This cosmic reason, or Logos, appears as the book in which "everything enduring in the world is recorded and engraved." It also appears as the Son of God: "following in the paths of the Father, he creates forms, while contemplating their archetypes." Philo, the Platonist, addresses this Logos as though he were speaking of the Christ: "As God is the first and only king of the universe, the way to Him is rightly called the 'royal road.' Consider this road as philosophy . . . the road taken by the ancient company of ascetics, who turned away from the entangling fascination of pleasure and devoted themselves to a noble and earnest cultivation of the beautiful. The Law names this royal road, which we call true philosophy, the Word and Spirit of God."

It is like an initiation for Philo when he enters upon this path, in order to meet the Logos who, for him, is the Son of God. "I do not shrink from relating what has happened to me innumerable times. Often when I wished to put my philosophical thoughts in writing in my accustomed way, and saw quite clearly what was to be set down, I found my mind barren and rigid, so that I was obliged to give up without having accomplished anything, and seemed to be beset with idle fancies. At the same time I marveled at the power of the reality of thought, with which it rests to open and close the womb of the human soul. At other times, however, I would begin empty and arrive, without any trouble, at fullness. Thoughts came flying like snowflakes or grains of corn invisibly from above, and it was as though divine power took hold of me and inspired me, so that I did not know where I was, who was with me, who I was, or what I was saying or writing; for then a flow of ideas was given me, a delightful clearness, keen insight, and lucid mastery of material, as if the inner eye were now able to see everything with the greatest clarity."

This is a description of a path to knowledge so expressed that we see how anyone taking it is conscious of flowing in one current with the divine when the Logos becomes alive within him. This is again put clearly in the words: "When the spirit, moved by love, takes its flight into the most holy, soaring joyfully on divine wings, it forgets everything else and itself. It holds to and is filled only with the Power of which it is the follower and servant, and to this it offers the incense of the most sacred and chaste virtue."

For Philo there are only two ways. Either man follows the world of sense, open to observation and intellect, in which case he limits himself to his personality and withdraws from the cosmos; or he becomes conscious of the universal cosmic force, and experiences the eternal within his personality. "He who wishes to escape from God falls into his own hands. For there are two things to be considered, the universal Spirit, which is God, and one's own spirit. The latter flees to and takes refuge in the universal Spirit, for one who goes out beyond his own spirit says to himself that it is nothing and relates everything to God; but one who turns away from God discards Him as First Cause, and makes himself the cause of everything that happens.

The Platonic view of the universe sets out to be a form of knowledge which by its very nature is also religion. It brings knowledge into relation with the highest to which man can attain through his feelings. Plato allows knowledge to hold good only when it completely satisfies human feelings. It is then not a knowledge merely of images; it is the very substance of life. It is a higher man within man, that man of which the personality is only an image. Within man is born a being who surpasses him, a primordial, archetypal man; and this is another secret of the Mysteries brought to expression in the Platonic philosophy. Hippolytus, one of the early Fathers, alludes to it: "This is the great secret of the Samothracians (the guardians of a certain Mystery cult); an ineffable secret which only the initiates know. They speak in detail of Adam as the primordial, archetypal man."

Plato's dialogue on love, the *Symposium*, also represents an initiation. Here love appears as the herald of wisdom. If wisdom, the eternal word, the Logos, is the Son of the eternal creator of the cosmos, love is related to the Logos as a mother. Before even a spark of the light of wisdom can flash up in the human soul, an obscure impulse, a longing for the divine, must be present. Man must be drawn unconsciously towards the experience which, when it is raised into his consciousness, will constitute his supreme happiness. What Heraclitus calls the "daimon" in man is connected with the idea of love. In the *Symposium*, people of the most various ranks and with the most diverse views of life speak about love—the ordinary man, the politician, the learned man, the satiric poet Aristophanes and the tragic poet Agathon. Each has his own view of love, in keeping with their different experiences of life. How they express themselves shows the stage at which their "daimon" stands. By love one being is drawn to another. The manifold diversity of the things into which divine unity has been poured aspires towards unity and harmony through love. Hence love has something divine in it, and so each individual can understand it only as far as he participates in the divine.

After these men at different stages of maturity have set forth their ideas about love, Socrates takes up the discussion. He considers love from the point of view of a man in search of knowledge. For him, love is not a divinity, but something which leads man to God. Eros, or love, is for him not divine. God is perfect, and therefore possesses the beautiful and good; but Eros is only the desire for the beautiful and good. Eros thus stands between man and God. He is a "daimon," a mediator between the earthly and the divine.

It is significant that Socrates does not claim to be giving his own thoughts when speaking of love. He says he is only relating what a woman once imparted to him as a revelation. It was through mantic art that he came to his conception of love. Diotima, the priestess, awakened in Socrates the daimonic force which was to lead him to the divine. She "initiated" him.

This passage in the *Symposium* is highly suggestive. Who is the "wise woman" who awakened the daimon in Socrates? She is more than a merely poetic mode of expression. For no wise woman on the physical plane could awaken the daimon in the soul, unless the daimonic force were latent in the soul itself. It is surely in Socrates' own soul that we must look for this "wise woman." But there must be a reason why that which brings the daimon to life within the soul should appear as a real external being. This force cannot work in the same way as the forces we can observe in the soul as belonging to and native to it. Clearly, it is the soul-force which precedes the coming of wisdom that Socrates represents as a "wise woman." It is the mother-principle which gives birth to the Son of God, Wisdom, the Logos. The unconscious soul-force which brings the divine into consciousness is here represented as a feminine element. The soul which as yet is without wisdom is the mother of that which leads to the divine. This brings us to an important conception in mysticism. The soul is recognized as the mother of the divine. Unconsciously it leads man to the divine, with the inevitability of a natural force.

This conception throws light on the view of Greek mythology taken in the Mysteries. The world of the gods is born in the soul. Man looks upon the images he himself creates as his gods. But he must force his way through to another conception. He must transmute into divine images the divine force which is active within him before the creation of those images. Behind the divine appears the mother of the divine, which is nothing else than the original force of the human soul. So man places goddesses side by side with the gods.

Let us look at the myth of Dionysus in this light. Dionysus is the son of Zeus and a mortal mother, Semele. Zeus wrests the still immature infant from its mother when she is slain by lightning, and shelters it in his own thigh until it is ready to be born. Hera, the mother of the gods, incites the Titans against Dionysus and they dismember the body. But Pallas Athene rescues his heart, which is still beating, and brings it to Zeus. Out of it he engenders his son for the second time.

In this myth we can accurately trace a process which is enacted in the depths of the human soul. Interpreting it in the manner of the Egyptian priest who instructed Solon about the nature of myths, we might say: It is related that Dionysus was the son of a god and of a mortal mother, that he was torn in pieces and afterwards born again. This sounds like a fable, but it contains the truth of the birth of the divine and its destiny in the human soul. The divine unites itself with the earthly, temporal human soul. As soon as the divine, Dionysiac element stirs within the soul, it feels a vehement desire for its own true spiritual form. Ordinary consciousness, which again appears in the form of a female goddess, Hera, becomes jealous at the birth of the divine out of the higher consciousness. It stirs up the lower nature of man (the Titans). The still immature divine child is torn in pieces. Thus the divine child is present in man as dismembered material science. But if there be enough of the higher wisdom (Zeus) in man to be active, it nurses and cherishes the immature child, which is then born again as a second son of God (Dionysus). Thus from knowledge, the fragmented divine force in man, is born undivided wisdom, the Logos, the son of god and of a mortal mother, who is the transitory human soul, which unconsciously aspires after the divine. As long as we see in all this merely a process in the soul and look upon it as a picture of this process, we are a long way from the spiritual reality which is enacted in it. In this spiritual reality the soul is not merely experiencing something in itself; it has been entirely released from itself and is taking part in a cosmic event, which in reality is not enacted within the soul, but outside it.

Platonic wisdom and Greek myths are closely linked together; so too are the myths and the wisdom of the Mysteries. The created gods were the object of popular religion; the history of their origin was the secret of the Mysteries. No wonder that it was held to be dangerous to "betray" the Mysteries, for thereby the origin of the gods of the people was "betrayed." And a right understanding of that origin is salutary; a misunderstanding of it is destructive.

Human Evolution and the Christ Principle*

We have seen that we come closer to the profound meaning of the Gospel of St. John when we seek to approach it from various sides, and yesterday we were able from a certain point of view to indicate one of the most significant mysteries of this Gospel. In order that we may gradually reach a complete understanding of the mystery presented yesterday, it will not be necessary to consider the advent of Christ-Jesus in our Post-Atlantean period. We have gathered together the most varied material in order that we might trace the evolution of the human being and within it the Christ Principle. Today we shall try to understand why, just at this point of time in our evolution, the Christ appeared as a human being walking upon the earth, and we shall in this way form a connection with what we have already heard in part in the last lectures. Now we shall have to consider especially the evolution of our humanity in the Post-Atlantean period.

We have repeatedly stated that at a time very far in the past our forefathers dwelt out there in the west in a region now occupied by the Atlantic Ocean. Our forebears dwelt upon old Atlantis. In the lecture of the day before yesterday we were able to call attention especially to the external bodily appearance of these our Atlantean forefathers. We have seen that the physical body, visible now to the external human sense organs, only slowly and gradually reached the present density of flesh which it now possesses. We said that not until the last part of the Atlantean period

---

* Editor's title. From Maud B. Monges, trans., "Human Evolution in its Relation to the Christ Principle," *The Gospel of St. John* (Hamburg Cycle, 1908), rev. ed. (New York: Anthroposophic Press, 1962), pp. 123–36.

did men bear some resemblance to their present form. Even toward the last third of the Atlantean period they were still essentially very different creatures from the men of today, although to the external senses they appeared much the same. We can best make clear what progress the human being has made, if we compare him in his present state with any of the existing higher animals. However highly developed the animal may be, it must now be clear for various reasons how the human being differs essentially from the animal. We find that upon the physical plane or in the physical world, every animal consists of physical body, ether or life body and astral body; that these three parts compose its animal being in the physical world.

You must not imagine that only what is *physical* exists in the physical world. It would be a great mistake if you were to seek all that is etheric or in fact all that is astral only in the supersensible world. It is true you can see only what is physical with the physical senses in the physical world, but that is not because only what is physical exists here. No, the ether and astral bodies of the animals are present in the physical world and the clairvoyantly endowed person can see them. It is only when he wishes to reach the real ego of the animal that he can no longer remain in the physical world; he must then mount into the astral regions. There the group-soul or group-ego of the animals is to be found and the difference between the human being and the animal consists in the ego of the former also being present here below in the physical world. This means that here in the physical world, the human creature consists of a physical, ether and astral body and an ego, although the three higher members, from the ether body upwards, are only perceptible to clairvoyant consciousness. This difference between the human being and the animal is expressed clairvoyantly in a certain way. Let us suppose that a person endowed with clairvoyance is observing a horse and a man. Extending beyond the horse's head, which is lengthened out to a muzzle, he finds an etheric appendage. This etheric head protrudes beyond the physical head of the horse and is magnificently organized; these two do not coincide in the horse. But he finds that in the human being of the present, the etheric head corresponds almost exactly in form and size to the physical. Clairvoyantly observed, the elephant makes an extremely grotesque appearance with its extraordinarily huge etheric head; it is, indeed, etherically a very grotesque animal. In the human beings of the present, the physical and etheric heads coincide and in form and size they are very nearly alike. This, however, has not always been the case. We find it so only in the last third of the Atlantean period. The ancient Atlanteans' etheric head protruded far beyond his physical head, then by degrees these two grew together and it was in the last third of the Atlantean period that the physical and the etheric heads exactly coincided. In the brain, near the eyes, there is a point which coincides with a very definite point in the etheric head. These points were apart in ancient times; the etheric point was outside of the brain. These two important points have drawn together and only when this occurred did the human being learn to say "I" to himself. Then appeared what we yesterday called the "Consciousness Soul." Through the coincidence of the etheric and physical heads, the appearance of the human head changed very greatly, for the head of the ancient Atlantean was still very different in appearance from the head of present human beings. If we wish to understand how the present evolution became possible, we must consider a little the physical conditions in ancient Atlantis.

If you had been able to walk through ancient Atlantis, out there in the west, you would not have been able to experience the conditions of rain, fog, air, and sunshine that we have now in our present earth. At that time mists pervaded especially the northern regions, west of Scandinavia. Those human beings who lived in ancient Atlantis, in the region where Ireland now stands and even further to the West, never saw rain and sunshine as separate phenomena as is now the case. They were always immersed in mist and only with the Atlantean Flood did the time come when the fog banks separated from the air and were precipitated into the ocean. You might have searched through the whole of Atlantis and you would not have found that spectacle which is now well known to you all as an extraordinary phenomenon of nature; it would have been impossible to discover a rainbow. That is only possible through a separation of rain and sunshine such as can now exist in the atmosphere. On Atlantis before the Flood, you would have found no rainbow. Only gradually, after the Flood, did this phenomenon appear, that is, it became a physical possibility. If after having received these communications of Spiritual Science, you recall that the memory of the Atlantean Flood is preserved in the various sagas and myths of the Deluge and that after the Deluge, Noah came forth and first saw the rainbow, then you will get some idea of how literally and profoundly true the religious documents are. It is a fact that human beings first saw a rainbow after the Atlantean Flood. These are the experiences which can be had by one who acquaints himself with occultism, and then bit by bit learns to understand how literally the religious documents must be taken. Of course one must first learn to understand the alphabet.

Towards the end of the Atlantean period, the external and internal human conditions proved to be most favorable in a certain region of the earth's surface which was in the vicinity of present Ireland. This region is now covered with water. At that time the conditions there were especially favorable and in this region the most highly gifted of the Atlantean races developed, a race that was especially endowed with the capacity to rise to an independent human self-consciousness. The leader of this people, which in Spiritual Science literature is usually designated the ancient Semites, was a great initiate who sought the most highly developed individuals of this people and migrated with them to the East through Europe as far as Asia into a region occupied now by the present Tibet. Thither migrated a relatively small but spiritually very highly developed fraction of the Atlantean peoples. Toward the end of the Atlantean period, it so happened that gradually the westerly portions of Atlantis disappeared and became covered by the sea. Europe in its present form gradually arose. In Asia, the great Siberian regions were still covered with extensive bodies of water, but, especially in the south of Asia, there were regions of land which had already appeared, differntly formed, however. Some of the less advanced of the great mass of people joined with this germinal group which migrated from west to east. Many went with them a long distance, others not so far. But the peopling of ancient Europe came about for the most part through the migrations of great hordes of people out of Atlantis who settled there. Other great groups of people who had been driven from other parts of Atlantis, even some from ancient Lemuria, had come into Asia at a still earlier period and now encountered each other during this migration. Thus peoples variously endowed and of very different spiritual capacities settled in Europe and Asia. The small number who were led by that great spiritual individuality, Manu, settled there in Asia in order to foster the greatest possible spirituality. From there streams of culture flowed out into the various regions of the earth and among the various peoples.

The first cultural stream flowed down into India and through the impulse given by the spiritual mission of that great individuality, Manu, there developed what we may call the ancient Indian civilization. We are not speaking now of that Indian culture of which we have only echoes in those wonderful books of the Vedas, nor are we speaking of what has been handed down to posterity as tradition. Previous to all that can be known of this external culture, there existed a much more glorious and more ancient culture, that of the ancient Holy Rishis, those great teachers who in the far distant past gave to mankind the first Post-Atlantean civilization. Let us transplant ourselves into the souls of the people of this first Post-Atlantean cultural stream. This was the first really religious human culture. Those Atlantean cultural periods which preceded this one were not religious cultural epochs in the true sense of the word. Religion is, in fact, a characteristic of the Post-Atlantean age. You will ask, why is this the case?

Let us see how Atlanteans lived. Since the etheric head was still outside of the physical head, the ancient hazy clairvoyance was not yet completely lost. Therefore, at night, when the Atlantean was outside of his physical body, he could look into the furthest reaches of the spiritual world. Although during the day— when he dipped down into his physical body—he saw physical things here in the physical world, at night he still saw, to a certain degree, the regions of the spiritual world. Transfer yourselves now for a moment into the middle or first third of the Atlantean period. What was the condition of the human being then? He awakened in the morning and his astral body was drawn into his physical and ether bodies. At that time the objects of the physical world were not yet so sharply and clearly contoured as they are now. When a city is enveloped in fog, and you observe the lanterns in the evening as though surrounded by an aura of color with undefined edges and streams of color, you have in this a picture of how things appeared at that time on Atlantis. The outlines were not clearly defined, but it was like seeing the lanterns in the mist. Hence, there was likewise no such sharp division between the clear day-consciousness and the unconsciousness of the night as appeared after the Atlantean period. During the night the astral body slipped out of the ether and physical bodies, but since the ether body still remained partly united with the astral body, there were always reflections of the spiritual world; the human being could always have a hazy clairvoyance, could live within the spiritual world and could behold about him spiritual beings and spiritual activities. The scholars who sit in their studies say that the common people have composed, for example, the Germanic myths and sagas out of their folk phantasy. Wotan and Thor and all the other gods were only personifications of nature forces. There are complete mythological theories which deal in this way with the folk creative phantasy. When one hears such a thing, it is easy to believe that such a learned individual is like the Homunculus in Goethe's *Faust*, born out of a retort, who had never seen a real human being. For anyone who has really observed the people, it is not possible to speak in this way of the creative folk imagination. The legends of the gods are nothing less than what remains of actual events which people of earlier ages really beheld clairvoyantly. This Wotan really existed. During the night human beings wandered about among the gods in the spiritual world and knew Wotan and Thor there as well as they knew people of flesh and blood like themselves here upon the earth. What primitive people of that age beheld, for a long time dimly and clairvoyantly, has now become the content of myth and sage, especially of those of the Germans.

People who at that time migrated from west to east into the regions later called Germany were those who had retained, more or less, some degree of clairvoyance and who were still able at a certain time to perceive in the spiritual world. And simultaneous-

ly with the migrations of that greatest of initiates and his followers
into Tibet, whence he sent forth the first cultural colony into
India, initiates who fostered the Spritual Life in the Mysteries
were left behind everywhere among the peole of Europe. Mysteries existed among these people, the Druid Mysteries, for example, but men no longer have any knowledge of them—for what is
recounted is merely fantastic rubbish. It is a significant fact that at
that time when the higher worlds were mentioned among the
Druids or among the peoples of the regions of western Russia and
Scandinavia where the Mysteries of the Trotts existed, there was
always a large number who knew of these spiritual worlds. When
they spoke of Wotan or of the incidents that occurred between
Baldur and Hodur, they were not talking of something wholly
unknown to them. There were many who had themselves experienced such incidents in special states of consciousness, and those
not having the experiences themselves heard it from their neigh-
bor in whom they had confidence. Wherever you might have
gone in Europe, you would still have found vivid memories of
what existed in Atlantis. What did exist there? Something one
might call a natural, living companionship with the beings of the
spiritual world, with what is today called Heaven. The human
being continually entered into the spiritual world and lived there.
In other words he needed no special religion to point out to him
the existence of a spirit-land.

What is the meaning of "religion"? It signifies *union,* union of
the physical world with the spiritual. At that time the human
being needed no special means of union with the spiritual world,
because for him it was a world of natural experience. Just as there
is no need now for anyone to impart to you a belief in the flowers
of the field or in the beasts of the forest, because you see them
with your own eyes, so similarly the Atlanteans "believed" in the
gods and spiritual beings, not through religion, but because they
experienced them. As human evolution progressed, mankind acquired a clear day-consciousness. It was in the Post-Atlantean age
that people acquired this clear *waking* consciousness and they
gained it by renouncing their ancient *clairvoyant* consciousness.
It will be theirs again in the future in addition to the present clear
day-consciousness. For our ancestors here in Europe, the sagas

and myths often aroused memory-pictures of the distant past. One might ask, what was the nature of these most developed human beings? Strange as it may sound, these highly developed individuals whom the leader guided eastward into Tibet were for the most part advanced, because they had lost their ancient, dreamlike consciousness.

What does it signify to progress from the fourth over into the fifth root-race? It means becoming day-conscious; it means losing the ancient clairvoyance. The great initiate and guide led away the members of his little group in order that they might not have to live among people who were still at the stage of the ancient Atlanteans. Among the first, only those could be guided into the higher worlds who had been trained artificially, who had gone artificially through an occult training. It may be asked, what did the people of the first Post-Atlantean epoch have left of that ancient relationship with the spiritual, divine world? Only the longing for the spirit world, the door to which had been closed. They felt that there had been a time—for they heard it in their sagas—when their forefathers had gazed into the spirit world, had lived there among spirits and gods and had discovered themselves in the midst of deep spiritual realities. "Oh, could we but experience this too!" they said and out of this longing the ancient Indian way of initiation was created. This method of initiation arose out of the longing for what was past and caused the pupil to lose, for a time, the clear day-consciousness which he had acquired in order that he might force himself back in consciousness to his former state. "Yoga" is the method of the ancient Indian initiation which, through its technique and exercises, restored what had been lost in a quite natural way.

Imagine, for example, an ancient Atlantean whose ether head protruded far beyond his physical head. When the astral body withdrew, a large part of the ether head was still united with it. Therefore what it experienced could be imprinted upon the ether body and thus he became conscious of his experiences. When, in the last part of the Atlantean period, the ether part of the head was drawn wholly into the physical head, the astral body left the ether body entirely each night. Thus in the ancient initiations, the teacher had to try to draw out the ether body of his pupil by artificial means; in other words, the pupil had to be brought into a sort of lethargic condition, into a kind of deathlike sleep which lasted about three and a half days. During this time the ether body protruded from the physical body and was loosened from it. What the astral body then experienced was impressed upon the ether body. Then when the ether body was redrawn into the physical body, the pupil knew what he had experienced in the spiritual world.

That was the ancient method of initiation, the Yoga initiation, by means of which the pupil was lifted out of the world wherein he found himself in order to be transported back again into the spiritual world. And the cultural mood which resulted from this kind of initiation found its echo in the later Indian culture. It was this mood that gave rise to the words: Truth, Reality, Being exist only in the spiritual world, in that world into which a person enters when he lifts himself out of the physical sense-world. Here he is in the midst of the physical world, surrounded by the mineral, plant and animal kingdoms. But what surrounds him is not reality, it is only an outer semblance; he lost the reality ages ago and now lives in a world of appearance, of illusion, of Maya.

The world of the physical, therefore, was the world of Maya for the ancient Indian civilization. We must comprehend this, not as a dull theory, but in accordance with the cultural mood itself—in accordance with the feelings of the people themselves of that time. When the ancient Indian wished to be especially holy, the world of illusion became worthless to him. This physical world became to him an illusion; the true world existed for him when he withdrew from the physical, when through Yoga he was permitted to live again in the world in which his forefathers still lived during the Atlantean period.

The significance of further evolution consists in the human being of this Post-Atlantean period becoming gradually accustomed to value the physical world which is allotted to him, according to its worth and meaning. The second epoch, the next step after the ancient Indian period, is also a prehistoric cultural epoch which is named after the people who later lived in the region of Persia; we designate it the primitive Persian civilization. However, we have not the later Persian civilization in mind, but a prehistoric culture.

The second period differs very essentially in its mood, in its feeling-content from the primeval Indian period. It became more and more difficult to loosen the ether body during initiation, but it was still possible and in a certain way it was always done even up to the time of Christ.Jesus. But there was one thing these men of the primitive Persian civilization had attained; they began to appreciate Maya or illusion as something of value. The ancient Indian was happy when he could flee from illusion. For the Persian, it became a sphere of activity. It is true, illusion still continued to appear to him as something hostile, something which must be overcome. Later this gave rise to the myth of the battle between *Ormuzd* and *Ahriman* in which the human being allied himself with the good gods against the power of the gods of evil existing in matter. Out of this, the mood of that age was created. The Persian was still not fond of this physical "reality" (Maya), but he no longer fled from it like the ancient Indian; he worked upon it and considered it a stage upon which he could be active, a place where there was something that must be overcome. In this second cultural stage, a step in the conquest of the physical world had been made.

Then came the third cultural stage. We are now approaching closer and closer to historical times. This cultural period is designated in Occult Science the Chaldaic-Babylonian-Assyrian-Egyptian civilization. All these civilizations were founded by colonies sent out under the guidance of great leaders. The first colony founded the civilization of the ancient Indians, the second founded what we have just described as the ancient Persian cultural center and a third cultural stream traveled still further to the West and laid their the foundation of the Babylonian-Chaldaic-Assyrian-Egyptian civilization. Thus an important step was taken in the conquest of the physical world. To the Persian it still seemed an intractable mass which he had to manipulate if he wished to work in it with those Beings whom he considered the good Spirits of the true Spiritual Reality. He had now become more familiar, more intimate with physical reality. Just consider the ancient Chaldean astronomy. It is one of the most extraordinary and tremendous creations of the human spirit of the Post-Atlantean age. There you see how the course of the stars was explored, how the laws of the heavens were examined. The ancient Indian would have looked out at this heaven and said: The course of the stars with its laws is not worth the trouble to investigate! To the people of the third cultural epoch it was even then very important to penetrate into these laws. To those belonging to the Egyptian civilization, it was of special importance to examine the earthly relationships and to develop the science of geometry. Maya or illusion was explored and physical science came into being. Men studied the thoughts of the gods and felt that they must make a connection between their own individual activity and what they found inscribed in matter as the script of the gods.

If you were to investigate spiritually the earlier conditions of Egyptian political life, you would gain a concept of a political organism very different from any that people of the present day can possibly imagine. The individualities who directed and guided those political states were wise men who knew the laws governing the course of the stars, of the movements of the cosmic bodies, and at the same time they knew that everything in the cosmos must mutually correspond. They had studied the course of the stars and knew that there must be a harmony between what was taking place in the heavens and what was happening upon the earth. According to the events in the heavens they decreed what, in the course of time, is to occur on earth. Even in the earliest part of the Roman period (the fourth cultural epoch) there still existed the consciousness that what transpires upon the earth must correspond to what is happening in the heavens. For long periods in the ancient Mysteries it was known at the beginning of a new epoch what events would transpire in the following period.

It was known through the Mystery-wisdom, for example, at the beginning of Roman history that a period would follow in which the most varied historical events would be enacted and that they would take place in the region of Alba Longa. For anyone who can read it, it is clear that a deeply symbolical expression is suggested here and that it was, so to say, priestly wisdom that laid out or planned the civilization of ancient Rome. "Alba Longa" was the long priestly garment. In these ancient regions the future historical events were in this way laid out—if we may be allowed to use a technical expression. They knew that seven epochs must follow one after another in succession. The future was divided according to the number seven and an outline of the future history was foretold. I could easily show you how prophetic historical plans were concealed in the story of the seven Kings of Rome which had already been inscribed in the *Sibylline Books* even as early as the beginning of the Roman epoch. In those days people knew that they had to live through what was written there and on important occasions they consulted the Holy Books. This then accounts for the holy and mysterious character of the *Sibylline Books*.

Thus humanity of the third cultural epoch worked Spirit into Matter, permeated the outer world with Spirit. There are countless historical evidences of this concealed in the development of the epochs of this third cultural stream—this Assyrian-Babylonian-Chaldean-Egyptian civilization. Our own age can be understood only when we know the important relationships which exist between that age and our own. I should like now to call attention to one of the relationships between these two epochs, in order that you may see how wonderfully things are connected for anyone who can penetrate more deeply into them and who knows that what is called egotism and utilitarianism has now reached its culmination. Never before was a cultural epoch as purely egotistic and unidealistic as our own and it will become even more so in the near future. For, at the present time, spirit has descended completely into a materialistic civilization. Tremendous spiritual forces have had to be employed by men in the great discoveries and inventions of the new age, that is, of the nineteenth century. Just think, for instance, how much spiritual force exists in the telephone, in the telegraph, in the railroads, etc.! How much spiritual force has been materialized, crystallized in the commercial relationships of the earth! How much spiritual energy it requires to cause a sum of money to be paid, let us say in Tokyo, by means of a piece of paper, a check written here in this place! Thus one may ask: Does the use of this spiritual force mean spiritual progress? Whoever faces the fact must acknowledge the following:

You build railroads indeed, but they carry, practically, only what you need for your stomachs; and when you yourself travel, you do so only because of something that has to do with your physical needs.

Does it make any difference from the standpoint of Spiritual Science whether we grind our own corn with a few stones or obtain it from a distance by means of the telegraph, ships, etc.? A tremendous spiritual force is employed, but it is used in an entirely personal sense. What then will be the meaning of what men thus negotiate? Apparently not Anthroposophy, in other words, not spiritual realities. When the telegraph and steamships are used, it is in the first place a question of how much cotton will be ordered to be sent from America to Europe, etc.; in other words it is a question of something that has to do with personal needs. Mankind has descended to the profoundest depths of personal necessity, of physical personality. But just such a egotistic, utilitarian principle had to come sometime, because through it, the ascening course of all human evolution will be facilitated. What has happened to cause the human being to attach so much importance to his own personality, thus causing him to feel himself so much a separate individual? And, moreover, what was it that prepared him for this strong feeling of self in his life between birth and death?

In the third period of civilization a most important preparation was made for this, in the desire to retain the form of the physical body beyond death in the "mummy," in the wish to prevent the dissipation of the form of the body by embalming it. Thus, this holding fast to the separate individuality became imprinted upon the soul in such a way that now it appears again in another incarnation as the feeling of personality. That this feeling of personality is so strong today is the result of the embalming of the body in the Egyptian period. So we see that in human evolution everything is correlated. The Egyptians mummified the bodies of the dead in order that people of the fifth epoch might have the greatest possible consciousness of their own personality. Certainly, profound mysteries exist within human evolution.

Thus you see how the human being has gradually descended deeper and deeper into Maya and has permeated matter with what he is able to achieve. In the fourth cultural period, the Greco-Latin age, he placed his inner being out in the external world. Thus you see in Greece how he objectified himself in matter and form. He concealed his own form in the figures of the Grecian gods. In Aeschylus there still resounds, in dramatic form, men's desire to convert their own individuality into artistic form. They step out upon the physical plane and create a copy of themselves. In the Roman period men created an image of themselves in the institutions of the State. It is a sign of the greatest dilettantism when one traces what is now called Jurisprudence back beyond the Roman period. What existed previously is, in concept, something quite different from *jus* or "justice," "right" (*Recht*), for the concept of the human being as an outer personality, the concept of human rights did not exist prior to that time. In ancient Greece there was the *polis,* the little municipal state, and men felt themselves as members of it. It is difficult for people to enter into the consciousness of the Greek epoch. In the Roman epoch, the path into the physical world had been trod so far that the individual human personality—as a Roman citizen—appears also as possessing rights. Everything progresses by stages and we shall trace in detail how the personality emerges by degrees and how at the same time the physical world is being conquered more and more with the progress of history, and how the human being is plunging deeper and deeper into matter.

Our own epoch is the first after the Greco-Latin; in other words, it is the fifth epoch of the Post-Atlantean age. There will follow after it a sixth and a seventh epoch. The fourth, the Greco-Latin, is the middle period, and during this *middle* period, *Christ-Jesus* came upon the earth. This event was prepared for within the third Post-Atlantean epoch, because everything in the world has to be prepared beforehand. The third epoch made ready for that greatest of all events which was to be enacted upon the earth during the fourth Post-Atlantean epoch at a time when men had progressed far enough in their feeling of personality to step outside themselves and create their gods in their own image. In the art of the Grecian period, men created a world of gods after their own image. They repeated this in the form of the State. An understanding of physical matter was reached even to the degree of the union of Maya (the world of illusion, matter) and Spirit. This is the moment when men also attained an understanding of personality. You will comprehend that this was also the time when they were able to understand God as a personal manifestation, the time when the spirit belonging to the earth also progressed to the point of becoming a personality. Thus we see how in the middle of the Post-Atlantean civilization God Himself appeared as a man, as a separate personality. When we see how in Greek art the human being fashioned an image of himself, we may say: What happened in the middle of the Post-Atlantean civilization appears to us as an image. When we pass from the Greek to the Roman period and observe the types of human beings of the great Roman Empire, does it not actually seem as though the Greek images of the gods had descended from their pedestals and were walking about in their togas? One can fairly see them!

Thus the human creature had progressed from the time he felt himself as a member of the Godhead to a feeling of himself as a personality. He could comprehend as a personality even the Godhead Itself which, embodied in the flesh, had descended and dwelt among men.

It has been our desire here to picture to our souls the reason for the appearance of Christ-Jesus just at this period of human evolution. How this mystery developed further, how in the earlier evolutionary periods it shone forth prophetically, and how it works prophetically into the distant future, we shall consider next time.

IV
ESOTERIC
CHRISTIANITY

Christ—Representative of Mankind. Sculpture by Rudolf Steiner.

Esoteric Christianity

INTRODUCTION

Esoteric Christianity and the Gospel of St. John

When one first looks into the life and teaching of Rudolf Steiner, it is perhaps unclear whether he is in fact a Christian, and
whether Spiritual Science and Anthroposophy follow from or are
compatible with Christianity. Steiner and his teaching would presumably have to be read in Christian terms if only because of his
experience, described in *An Autobiography*, of "standing in the
spiritual presence of the Mystery of Golgotha in a most profound
and solemn festival of knowledge" (p. 319). Further, he delivered
more than a dozen lecture cycles on the Gospels, and in response
to a plea for help, transmitted the ideas for a spiritual organization
and the words and actions for a ritual which are the root of The
Christian Community. On the other hand, Steiner's approach to
the various sciences, arts, and education are not explicitly Christian and apparently can be practiced with some measure of success by individuals with little or no Christian commitment. The
readings in this chapter will clarify the relationship between Rudolf Steiner's life and teaching on the one side and Christian practice and teaching on the other. The present introduction and the
following three lectures from Steiner's *The Gospel of St John* are
intended as a brief introduction to the esoteric stream of Christianity which is the aim as well as the source of Steiner's Spiritual
Science.

First, the troublesome term esoteric: although it is little known
to the vast majority of Christian believers, a tradition of esoteric
Christianity based on the writings and influence of John and Paul
has existed alongside institutional Christianity from the time of
Jesus to the present. When the Christian Church became the

established religion of Europe, esoteric Christian groups and their teachings were opposed by Rome. Throughout the Middle Ages esoteric communities were persecuted as heretical. During the last several centuries, esoteric Christianity, to the extent that it has survived at all, has existed in monastic orders (for example, as practiced by the Eastern Orthodox monks in the monastery on Mt. Athos), and in a very small number of esoteric Christian teachers such as Emanuel Swedenborg. Because he is thoroughly modern in his approach to knowledge in general, and in his approach to knowledge of Christian mysteries in particular, Steiner would seem to be one of the few sources of an esoteric Christian revelation which is generated by and intended for the present age.

The earlier chapters in this book prepare the reader for the fact that it is the esoteric, or secret, spiritual dimension of Christianity with which Steiner is primarily concerned. And anyone who has seriously studied the Christian scriptures will have noticed the many references to knowledge or teachings which are intended for some but not for all. The specific purpose of this chapter, however, is to show the intimate, and essential, relationship between the esoteric and exoteric levels of meaning. In the following lectures, Steiner contends that the Gospel of St. John, precisely because of its unrivaled spiritual profundity, is not likely to be understood by a modern reader without the aid of esoteric schooling such as is provided by Spiritual Science.

In the opening statement of the first lecture, Steiner explains the ideal positive relationship between the spiritual truths contained in the Gospel of St John and the knowledge of higher worlds made possible by Spiritual Science:

Our lectures upon the Gospel of St. John will have a double purpose. One will be the deepening of the concepts of Spiritual Science themselves and their expansion in many directions, and the other will be to make this great document itself comprehensible by means of the thoughts that will arise in our souls in consequence of these deepened and expanded concepts. (p. 15)

To the extent that a follower of Steiner were to succeed in the practice of Spiritual Science, he or she would come to know the truths of this Gospel in the same way, and perhaps approximately to the same depth, as Steiner himself did. When reading these lectures, it is worth remembering that they are not the results of scholarly research, but issued directly from Steiner's power of spiritual perception. As we read his account of the raising of Lazarus, and of the "Holy Spirit" overshadowing Virgin Sophia, we might also wish to picture Rudolf Steiner standing before fewer than a dozen members of the Theosophical Society as he articulates the living ideas contained in the Gospel of St. John which are inaccessible to all but those few Christians who can penetrate its mysteries. It is worth asking, why should such an important document be so difficult to understand? In that connection, Steiner asks:

Should the most profound mysteries of the world be expressed in trivial language? Is it not a strange point of view, a real insult to what is holy when one says, for example, that in order to understand a watch, one must penetrate deeply into the nature of the thing with the understanding, but for a comprehension of the divine in the world, the simple, plain, naive human intelligence should suffice? It is a very bad thing for present humanity that it has reached the point of saying, when reference is made to the profoundness of religious documents: Oh! Why all these complicated explanations? It should all be plain and simple. However, only those who have the good intention and good will to plunge down into the great cosmic facts can penetrate into the deep meaning of such words as those at the very beginning of the most profound of the Gospels, this Gospel of St. John, words that are in fact a paraphrase of Spiritual Science.

Let us now translate the introductory words of this Gospel:

In the beginning was the Word and the Word was with God and the Word was a God (or divine). This was in the beginning with God. Through the same all things were made and save through this Word, nothing was made. In It was Life, and Life became the Light of men. And the Light shone into the darkness. But the darkness comprehended it not.

How the darkness, little by little, comes to an understanding of the Light is recounted later on in the Gospel. (p. 42)

Showing the way by which the darkness comes to the understanding of the Light is the aim not only of the Gospel of St. John, but equally of the Spiritual Science of Rudolf Steiner, and for both spiritual teachings, the concept and experience of initiation are fundamental. In the lecture, "The Raising of Lazarus," Steiner explains that the profoundly mysterious account of the raising of Lazarus, which appears only in the Gospel of St. John, is in fact an esoteric account of Christian initiation.

Lazarus and Initiation

In "Christian Initiation," Steiner characterizes an initiate as one who is able to transcend the outer physical world and experience the spiritual worlds directly, as ordinary people experience the physical world through their senses. Second, the initiate is able to transcend the feelings and sensations which belong to the physical world but which have no place in the spiritual worlds. In sum, the initiate of all ages is characterized by direct knowledge of the spiritual world and absolute objectivity. Both of these characteristics are evident in the experience and teachings of the great yogis, exemplars of what Steiner refers to as the first of three main types of initiation. These characteristics are also evident in the Gospel of St. John, written by the one whom the Christ Himself initiated as the archetypal representative of the Christian esoteric tradition. Spiritual knowledge and objectivity are also characteristic of the spiritual experience and teachings of Rudolf Steiner, the foremost exponent-exemplar of the modern, Rosicrucian type of Christian initiation. To understand the combination of Christian and modern in Steiner's teaching concerning initiation, it is important to build on an understanding of Christian initiation as revealed by the Christ to the author of the Gospel of St. John.

In the lecture "The Raising of Lazarus" Steiner explains the meaning of the words "love" and "beloved" in this Gospel: These words are used for only two individuals, Lazarus and the Beloved Disciple who is the author of the Gospel of St. John. He also explains that the statement by Jesus, "this sickness is not unto death," refers to the three-and-a-half day deathlike sleep during which the initiate undergoes a radical spiritual transformation. Steiner emphasizes that the first ten chapters of the Gospel of St. John presents a kind of ordinary spiritual knowledge available to informed, or even inspired observers such as the writers of the three synoptic Gospels and other followers of Jesus. Beginning with chapter 11, however, the writer of the Fourth Gospel reveals a spiritual knowledge available only to one who has been initiated by a spiritual master such as the Christ. This is precisely the experience which John, then known as Lazarus, underwent when he was initiated (raised from "the dead"). We may refer to first ten chapters as Lazarus consciousness, and chapters 11 to 21 as "Beloved Disciple" or initiate consciousness.

In the same lecture, Steiner also describes John the Baptist as an initiate whose access to the spiritual world enabled him to recognize Jesus as the Christ. In the third of the following three lectures, Steiner explains that Mary Magdalene, one of the closest disciples of the Christ, "had received through the Event of Palestine the powerful force needed for spiritual perception." Mary Magdalene had received the clairvoyance which enabled her to see the resurrected Christ and to see the two spiritual forms (angels) that Steiner says are clairvoyantly visible on either side of a recently deceased individual.

These great spiritual figures at the beginning of the Christian tradition—John the Baptist, Lazarus-John, Mary Magdalene—represent, in the technical terms articulated in Steiner's *Theosophy* (chapter 2, above), the transforming power of the ego within the astral body. Beginning with Christian initiation, and continuing thereafter with increasing force and effect, the human ego has had the ability to influence the astral body during sleep when both the ego and the astral body are separated from the physical and etheric bodies. In time, the ego will be able to work its way down into the etheric and the physical bodies as well. This kind of multilayered transformation is, of course, one of the essential aims of Rudolf Steiner's Spiritual Science. As Steiner's spiritual teaching begins with an affirmation of the etheric or formative forces in the physical world, his work and mission culminate in the affirmation of the working in the etheric of the resurrected Christ. According to recent anthroposophical teaching, it is the resurrected Christ appearing in the etheric who can be perceived by increasing numbers of people within the realm of formative forces. Steiner argues that although science and traditional Christianity are inadequate interpretations of the physical and spiritual worlds, both have been necessary building blocks, representative of the powers and limitations of recent stages of the evolution of consciousness.

The Raising of Lazarus*

From the three foregoing lectures, it should have become some-what clear that in the Gospel of St. John the truths of Spiritual Science can be found again. However, it must be very clear that in order to discover these truths, it will be necessary to weigh every word thoroughly. In fact the important thing in a consideration of this religious document is that the true, exact meaning be perfectly understood, for as we shall see in particular instances everything in it has the deepest possible significance. Moreover, not only the wording of special passages is of importance, but something else must be considered, namely, the division, the composition, the structure of the document. As a matter of fact, people no longer have the right feeling for such things. Authors of the past—if I may so designate them— introduced into their works much more of an architectural structure, much more of an inner arrangement than is usually imagined. You need only to recall from among them a relatively modern poet, Dante, to find this confirmed. Here we see that the *Divine Comedy* is architecturally composed of parts based upon the number three. And it is not without meaning that each division of Dante's Comedia closes with the word "Stars." This I mention only to suggest how architecturally ancient writers constructed their works, and especially in the great religious documents we should never lose sight of this architectural form, because in certain cases the form signifies a very great deal. To be sure, we must first discover this meaning.

Here at the end of the 10th Chapter of this Gospel of St. John we should recall the following verse, which we should keep clear-ly in mind. In the 41st verse we read:

* From Maud B. Monges, trans., "The Raising of Lazarus," *The Gospel of St. John* (Hamburg Cycle, 1908), rev. ed. (New York: Anthroposophic Press, 1962), pp. 60–77.

And many came to him and said: John performed no miracles, but all that he said of this man is true.

This means that we find in this verse of the 10th chapter an indication that the testimony given of Christ Jesus by John is true. He expresses the truth of this testimony in very special language. Then we come to the end of the Gospel and there we find a corresponding verse. Here we read in the 24th verse of the 21st chapter:

This is the disciple which testifieth of these things, and wrote these things: and we know that his testimony is true!

Here at the end of the entire Gospel, we have a statement that the testimony of the one who reported these things is a true one. The coincidence that something very special is being said, here and there, by means of some particular word, is never without significance in ancient writings and just behind this coincidence is concealed something very important. We shall proceed with our considerations in the right manner if we direct our attention to the reason for this.

In the middle of the Gospel of St. John a fact is presented which, if not understood, would render this Gospel incomprehensible. Directly following the passage in which these words are introduced as confirmation of the truth of the testimony of John the Baptist stands the chapter concerning the raising of Lazarus. With this chapter the whole Gospel falls into two parts. At the end of the first part it is pointed out that the testimony of John the Baptist should be accepted for everything that is maintained and affirmed concerning Christ Jesus and at the very end of the Gospel it is pointed out that all that follows the chapter on the raising of Lazarus should be accepted on the testimony of the Disciple whom we have often heard designated as "the Disciple whom the Lord loved." What then is the real meaning of the "raising of Lazarus?"

Let me remind you that following the narration of the raising of Lazarus there stands an apparently enigmatical passage. Let us picture the whole situation: Christ Jesus performs what is usually called a miracle—in the Gospel itself it is called a "sign"— namely, the raising of Lazarus. And subsequently we find many passages which attest that "this man performs many signs," and all that follows indicates that the accusers did not wish to have intercourse with Him because of these signs. If you read these words, whatever their translation (this has already been referred to in my book *Christianity as Mystical Fact*), you would need to ask: What is really at the bottom of it all? The raising of some one provoked the enemies of Christ Jesus to rise up against Him. Why should just the raising of Lazarus so provoke these opponents? Why does the persecution of Christ Jesus begin just at this stage? One who knows how to read this Gospel will understand that a mystery lies hidden within this chapter. The mystery concealed therein is, in truth, concerned with the actual identity of the man who says all that we find written there. In order to understand this, we must turn our attention to what in the ancient Mysteries is called "initiation." How did these initiations in the ancient Mysteries take place?

A man who was initiated could himself have experiences and personal knowledge of the spiritual worlds and thus he could bear witness of them. Those who were found sufficiently developed for initiation were led into the Mysteries. Everywhere—in Greece, among the Chaldeans, among the Egyptians and the Indians— these Mysteries existed. There the neophytes were instructed for a long time in approximately the same things which we now learn in Spiritual Science. Then when they were sufficiently instructed, there followed that part of the training which opened up to them the way to a perception of the spiritual world. However, in ancient times this could only be brought about by putting the neophyte into a very extraordinary condition in respect of his four principles—his physical, ether and astral bodies, and his ego. The next thing that occurred to the neophyte was that he was put into a deathlike sleep by the initiator or hierophant who understood the matter and there he remained for three-and-a-half days. Why this occurred can be seen if we consider that in the present cycle of evolution, when the human being sleeps in the ordinary sense of the word, his physical and ether bodies lie in bed and his astral body and ego are withdrawn. In that condition he cannot observe any of the spiritual events taking place about him, because his astral body has not yet developed the spiritual sense organs for a

perception of the world in which he then finds himself. Only
when his astral body and ego have slipped back into his physical
and ether bodies, and he once more makes use of his eyes and
ears, does he again perceive the physical world, that is, he perceives a world about him. Through what he had learned, the neophyte was capable of developing spiritual organs of perception in
his astral body and when he was sufficiently evolved for the astral
body to have formed these organs, then all that the astral body
had received into itself had to be impressed upon the ether body
just as the design on a seal is impressed upon the sealing wax.
This is the important thing. All preparations for initiation depend-
ed upon the surrender of the man himself to the inner processes
which reorganized his astral body.

The human being at one time did not have eyes and ears in his
physical body as he has today, but undeveloped organs instead—
just as animals who have never been exposed to the light have no
eyes. The light forms the eye, sound fashions the ear. What the
neophyte practiced through meditation and concentration and
what he experienced inwardly through them acted like light
upon the eye and sound upon the ear. In this way the astral body
was transformed and organs of perception for seeing in the astral
or higher world were evolved. But these organs are not yet firmly
enough fixed in the ether body. They will become so when what
has been formed in the astral body will have been stamped upon
the ether body. However, as long as the ether body remains
bound to the physical, it is not possible for all that has been accomplished by means of spiritual exercises to be really impressed
upon it. Before this can happen, the ether body must be drawn
out of the physical. Therefore when the ether body was drawn out
of the physical body during the three-and-a-half days deathlike
sleep, all that had been prepared in the astral body was stamped
upon the ether body. The neophyte then experienced the spiritual world. Then when he was called back into the physical body
by the Priest-Initiator, he bore witness through his own experience of what takes place in the spiritual worlds. This procedure
has now become unnecessary through the appearance of Christ-
Jesus. This three-and-a-half day deathlike sleep can now be re-

placed by the force proceeding from the Christ. For we shall soon see that in the Gospel of St. John strong forces are present which render it possible for the present astral body, even though the ether body is still within the physical, to have the power to stamp upon the etheric what had previously been prepared within it. But for this to take place, Christ-Jesus must first be present. Up to this time without the above characterized procedure, humanity was not far enough advanced for the astral body to be able to imprint upon the ether body what had been prepared within it through meditation and concentration. This was a process which often took place within the Mysteries; a neophyte was brought into a deathlike sleep by the Priest-Initiator and was guided through the higher worlds. He was then again called back into his physical body by the Priest-Initiator and thus became a witness of the spiritual world through his own experience.

This took place always in the greatest secrecy and the outer world knew nothing of the occurrences within these ancient Mysteries. Through Christ-Jesus a new initiation had to arise to replace the old, an initiation produced by means of forces of which we have yet to speak. The old form of initiation must end, but a transition had to be made from the old to the new age and to make this transition, someone had once more to be initiated in the old way, but initiated into Christian Esotericism. This only Christ-Jesus Himself could perform and the neophyte was the one who is called Lazarus. "This sickness is not unto death," means here that it is the three-and-a-half day deathlike sleep. This is clearly indicated.

You will see that the presentation is of a very veiled character, but for one who is able to decipher a presentation of this kind it represents initiation. The individuality Lazarus had to be initiated in such a way that he could be a witness of the spiritual worlds. An expression is used, a very significant expression in the language of the Mysteries, "that the Lord loved Lazarus." What does "to love" mean in the language of the Mysteries? It expresses the relationship of the pupil to the teacher. "He whom the Lord loved" is the most intimate, the most deeply initiated pupil. The Lord Himself had initiated Lazarus and as an initiate Lazarus arose from the grave, which means from his place of initiation. This same expression "Whom the Lord loved" is always used later in connection with John, or perhaps we should say in connection with the writer of the Gospel of St. John, for the name "John" is not used. He is the "Beloved Disciple" to whom the Gospel refers. He is the risen Lazarus himself and the writer of the Gospel wished to say: "What I have to offer, I say by virtue of the initiation which has been conferred upon me by the Lord Himself." Therefore the writer of the Gospel distinguishes between what occurred *before* and what occurred *after* the raising of Lazarus. Before the raising, an initiate of the old order is quoted, one who has attained a knowledge of the Spirit, one whose testimony is repeatedly announced to be true. "However, what is to be said concerning the most profound of matters, concerning the Mystery of Golgotha, I myself say, I the Risen One; but only after I have been raised, can I speak concerning it!" And so we have in the first part of the Gospel, the testimony of the *old* John—in the second half, the testimony of the *new* John whom the Lord Himself had initiated, for this is the risen Lazarus. Only thus do we grasp the real meaning of this chapter. These words are written there because John wished to say: I call upon the testimony of my supersensible organs, my spiritual powers of perception. What I have related I have not seen in the ordinary physical world, but in the spiritual world in which I have dwelt by virtue of the initiation which the Lord has conferred upon me.

Thus we must attribute the characterization of Christ-Jesus, which we find in the first chapters of the Gospel of St. John as far as the end of the 10th Chapter, to the knowledge which might be possessed by any one who had not yet, in the deepest sense of the word, been initiated through Christ-Jesus Himself.

Now, you will say: "Yes, but we have already in these lectures listened to profound words about Christ-Jesus as the incarnated Logos, the Light of the World, etc." It is no longer surprising that these profound words concerning Christ-Jesus were spoken even in the very first chapters, for in the ancient Mysteries, Christ-Jesus, who was to appear in the world at a future time, in other words, the Christ, was not perhaps an unknown being. And all the Mysteries point to One who was to come. For this reason the ancient initiates were called "prophets" because they prophesied concerning something that was to take place. Thus the purpose of initiation was to let it be clearly understood that in the future of mankind the Christ would be revealed, and in what he had already learned at that time, the Baptist found the truth which made it possible to state that He, who had been spoken of in the Mysteries, stood before him in the person of Christ-Jesus.

How all this is connected and what the relationship was between the so-called Baptist and Christ-Jesus will become clearer to us if we answer two questions. One of these questions is the following: What was the position of the Baptist in his own age? The other leads back to the explanation of various passages at the beginning of the Gospel.

What was the position of the Baptist in his own age? What, in fact, was the Baptist? He was one of those who—like others in their initiation—had received indications of the coming Christ, but he was represented as the only one to whom the true mystery concerning Christ-Jesus had been revealed, namely, that He who had appeared was the Christ Himself. Those who were called Pharisees or were designated by other names saw in Christ-Jesus some one who in fact opposed their old principles of initiation, one who in their eyes did things to which they in their conservatism could not accede. Just because of their conservatism they said: We must adhere to the old principles of initiation. And this inconsistency of constantly speaking about the future Christ, yet never admitting that the moment had arrived when He was really present, was the reason for their conservatism. Therefore when Christ-Jesus initiated Lazarus, they looked upon it as a violation of the ancient Mystery-traditions. "This man performs many signs! We can have no intercourse with him!" According to their understanding, He had betrayed the Mysteries, had made public what should be confined within their secret depths. Now we can see how to them this was like a betrayal and seemed to be a valid reason for rising up against Him. From that time because of this, a change takes place; the persecution of Christ-Jesus begins.

How did the Baptist represent himself in the first chapters of this Gospel? In the first place, as one who was well acquainted with the Mystery-truths of the Christ Who was to come; as one who knew very well that the writer of the Gospel of St. John himself could repeat all that he, the Baptist, already knew, having become convinced of its truth through what we are now about to learn.

We have heard what the very first words of the Gospel mean. We shall now consider for a moment what is said there about the Baptist himself. Let us present it once more in the best possible translation. Thus far we have only read the very first words:

In the beginning was the Word, and the Word was with God and the Word was a God.

The same was in the beginning with God.

All things came into being through It and save through It was not anything made that was made.

In It was Life and Life was the Light of men.

And the Light shown into the darkness but the darkness comprehended it not.

There was a man; he was sent from God, bearing the name John.

The same came as a witness in order to bear witness of the Light that through him all might believe.

He was not the Light but was a witness of the Light.

For the true Light which lighteth every man should come into the world.

It was in the world and the world came into being through It, but the world knew It not.

It entered into individual men (that is, the ego-men); but individual men (the ego-men) received it not.

But they who received it could reveal themselves as Children of God.

They who trusted in His name were not born of the blood, nor of the will of the flesh, nor of the will of man—but of God.

And the Word was made flesh and dwelt among us and we have heard His teaching, the teaching of the once-born Son of the Father filled with Devotion and Truth.

John bore witness of Him and proclaimed clearly: He it was of whom I said: He will come after me, who was before me. For He is my forerunner.

For out of His fullness have we all received Grace upon Grace.

For the law was given through Moses, but Grace and Truth came through Jesus-Christ.

Hitherto hath no one beheld God with his eyes. The once-born Son, who was in the bosom of the Universal Father, has become the leader of this beholding. (1:1–18)

These are the words which give again approximately the meaning of those first verses of the Gospel of St. John. However, before we come to their interpretation, we must add something else. How did John describe himself? You will remember that people were sent to discover who John the Baptist was. Priests and Levites came to him to ask him who he was. Why he gave the foregoing answer, we have yet to discover. Just at present we shall only consider what he said.

He said, "I am the voice of one calling in solitude." These are the words which stand there. "I am the voice of one calling in solitude." "In solitude" stands there quite literally. In Greek, the word *eremet* signifies the "solitary one." You can then understand that it is more correct to say, "I am the voice of one calling in solitude," than "I am the voice of one preaching in the wilderness." We shall better understand all that is presented in the opening words of the Gospel, if we call to mind John's own characterization of himself. Why does he call himself "the voice of one calling in solitude?"

We have seen that in the course of human evolution, the true Earth-mission is the evolution of love, but that love is only conceivable when it is given as a voluntary offering by self-conscious human beings. We have also seen that the human being little by little gains control of his ego and that slowly and gradually this ego sinks into human nature. We know that the animal, as such, has no individual ego. If the individual lion were able to say "I" to itself, the individual animal would not be meant thereby, but the group-ego in the astral world. All lions would say "I" to this group-ego. Thus whole groups of animals of like form say "I" to the supersensibly perceptible group-ego in the astral world. The great advantage human beings have over the animals is that of possessing an individual ego. The latter, however, only evolved by degrees, for human beings also began with a group-ego, with an ego belonging to a whole group of individuals.

If you were to go back to ancient peoples, to ancient races, you would find that originally human beings were everywhere formed into little groups. With the Germanic peoples you would not need to go very far back. In the writing of Tacitus it is quite evident that the German thought more of his whole tribe than of himself as an individual. The individual felt himself more as a member of the *Cheruskian* or of the *Sigambrian* tribe than as a separate personality. Therefore he partook of the fate of the whole tribe and when an individual member or the entire tribe received an affront, it did not matter who was the avenger.

Then in the course of time it happened that individual personalities gave up their tribal membership, and this resulted at last in the breaking up of the tribes so that they no longer held together. Human beings also evolved out of this group-soul characteristic and little by little they developed to a point where they could experience the ego in their own individual personalities. We can only understand certain things, especially religious documents, when we understand this mystery of the group-souls, of the group-egos. For those peoples who had come already to a certain conception of the individual ego, there still always existed a greater ego that spread out not only over groups living contemporaneously in a certain place, but also far beyond these groups. Human memory at the present time is of such a character that the individual remembers only his own youth. But there was a time when a different kind of memory existed, a time when the human being not only remembered his own deeds but also those of his father and of his grandfather as though they were his own. Memory reached out beyond birth and death as far as the blood relationship could be traced. The memory of an ancestor whose blood, as it were, flowed down through generations was preserved for centuries in this same blood, and a descendant or offspring of a tribe said "I" to the deeds and the thoughts of his forebears as though to himself. He did not feel himself limited by birth and death, but he felt himself as a member of a succession of generations, the central point of which was the ancestor. For what held the ego together was the fact that the individual remembered the deeds of the fathers and of the grandfathers. In ancient times this had its outer expression in the giving of names. The son remembered not only his own deeds but also those of his father and of his grandfather. Memory extended far back through generations and all that the memory thus encompassed was called in ancient times, for example, Noah or Adam. The individual human beings were not meant by these names, but the egos which for centuries had preserved the memory. This mystery was also concealed behind the names of the Patriarchs. Why did the Patriarchs live so long? It would never have occurred to the people of ancient times to denominate an individual human being by a special name during his life between birth and death. Adam was looked upon as a common memory, because the limits of time and space in ancient days played no part in the giving of names.

By degrees the human individual ego slowly freed itself from the group-soul, from the group-ego. The human being came gradually to a consciousness of his own individual ego. Formerly he felt his ego in his tribal membership, in the group of human beings to whom he was related through the blood tie, either as to time or space; hence the expression, "I and Father Abraham are one," which means one ego. The individual felt himself safe within the whole, because a common blood ran through the veins of all of the members of his particular people. Evolution progressed and the time became ripe for individuals right within their race to feel their own separate egos. It was the mission of the Christ to give to human beings what they needed in order that they might feel themselves secure and firm within their separate individual egos. In this way we should also interpret those words which can be so easily misunderstood, namely, "He who does not deny wife and child, father and mother, brother and sister, cannot be my disciple!" We must not understand this in the trivial sense of instruction to run away from the family. But it means that every one should feel that he is an individual ego and that this individual ego is in direct union with the spiritual Father who pervades the world. Formerly a follower of the Old Testament said, "I and Father Abraham are one," because the Ego felt itself resting within the blood relationship. At that moment this feeling of oneness with the spiritual Father-Substance had to become independent; no longer should the blood relationship be a guarantee of membership in the whole, but the knowledge of the pure spiritual Father-Principle in whom all are one.

Thus we are told in the Gospel of St. John that the Christ is the great bestower of the Impulse which gives to men what is needed to make them feel themselves forever within their own separate, individual egos. This is the transition from the Old Testament to the New, for the old had always something of a group-soul character in which one ego felt itself associated with the others, but in reality never felt either itself or the other egos. Instead, it experienced the folk or tribal ego within which they all had a common shelter.

What must be the feeling of an ego that has become so matured that it no longer feels the connection with the other individual personalities of the group-soul? What must have been the feelings of the individualized ego in a period in which it could be said, "The time is now past when union with other persons, union with all egos belonging to a group-soul, can be felt as an actual life-reality; first, however, One must come who will give the spiritual Bread of Life to the soul from which the individual ego may receive nourishment"? This separate ego had to feel itself solitary, and the forerunner of the Christ was compelled to say: I am an ego that has broken away, that feels itself alone, and just because I have learned to feel solitary, I feel like a prophet to whom the ego gives real spiritual nourishment in solitude. Therefore the herald had to designate himself as one calling in solitude, which means the individual ego isolated from the group-soul calling for what can give it spiritual sustenance. "I am the voice of one calling in solitude." Thus we hear again the profound truth: Each human individual ego is one wholly dependent upon itself; I am the voice of the ego that is freed, seeking a foundation upon which it, as an independent ego, can rest. Now we understand the passage, "I am the voice of one calling in solitude."

In order that we may accurately understand the words of the Gospel, we shall need to familiarize ourselves a little with the way names and designations were then usually given. The giving of names at that time was not so abstract and devoid of meaning as it is at present, and if the exponents of biblical documents would only consider a little how much is expressed in this way, many trivial interpretations would never come to the light of day. I have already pointed out that when the Christ said, "I am the Light of the World," He really meant that He was the first to give expression to the "I AM" and was the Impulse for it. Therefore in the first chapters wherever "I AM" is to be found, it must be especially emphasized. All names and designations in ancient times in a certain sense are very real—yet at the same time they are used in a profoundly symbolical manner. This is often the source of tremendous errors made in two directions. From a superficial point of view, many say that according to such an interpretation a great deal is meant symbolically, but with such an explanation in which everything has only a symbolical meaning, they wish to have nothing to do, since historical, biblical events then disappear. On the other hand, those who understand nothing at all of the historical events may say: "This is only meant symbolically." Those, however, who say such things, understand nothing of the Gospel.

The historical reality is not denied because of a symbolic explanation, but it must be emphasized that the esoteric explanation includes both, the interpretation of the facts as historical and the symbolic meaning which we ascribe to them. Of course, if anyone sees only the prosaic external facts, namely, that a man was born somewhere, at some particular time, he will not understand that this man is something more than just a person with a particular name whose biography can be written. But whoever knows the spiritual relationship will learn to understand that besides being born in some particular place this living human being is also a symbol of his age and that what he signifies for the evolution of humanity is expressed in his name. It is something symbolic and historical at the same time, not simply the one or the other. This is the important thing in a true interpretation of the Gospel. Therefore in almost all of the events and allusions, we shall see that John—or the author of the Gospel bearing his name—really has a supersensible perception; he sees at one and the same time the outer events and the manifestation of deep spiritual truths. He has in mind the historical figure of the Baptist; he is considering the historical figure. But the true historical figure is for him at the same time a symbol for all men who were in ancient times called upon to receive the imprint of the Christ Impulse upon their egos, a symbol for those into whose individual egos the Light of the World might shine, although they had just started on the path. It was not, however, a symbol for those who in their darkness were not yet able to apprehend the Light of the World. What appeared as Life, Light, and Logos in Christ-Jesus has always shone in the world, but those who were first to become matured did not recognize it. The Light was always there, for had it not been there, the germ of the ego could not possibly have come into existence.

Only the physical, ether, and astral bodies of the present human being existed within the Moon Evolution; there was no ego in them. Only because the Light became transformed into that light which now shines down upon the earth did It have the power to enkindle the individual egos and to bring them gradually to maturity. "The Light shone in the darkness but the darkness could not yet comprehend it." It entered into the individual human being—right into the human ego—for an ego-humanity could not have come into existence at all, had not the Light been rayed into it by the Logos. However, ego-humanity as a whole did not receive It, but only certain individuals, the initiates. They raised their souls to the spiritual worlds and they always bore the name "Children of God," because they possessed knowledge of the Logos, of the Light, and of Life and could always bear witness of These. There were certain ones who already knew of the spiritual worlds through the ancient Mysteries. What was present there in these initiates? It was the eternal human living within them in full consciousness. In the mighty words, "I and the Father are one," they felt, in fact, I and the great Primal Cause are one! And the most profound thing of which they were conscious, their individual ego, they received not from father and mother but through their initiation into the spiritual world. Not from the blood nor from the flesh did they receive it, nor from the will of father or mother, but "from God," which means from the spiritual world.

Here we have an explanation of why it was that although the majority of mankind had already received the rudiments of an ego-being they could not as individuals receive the Light which had only descended, in fact, as far as the group-ego. Those, however, who received the Light—and they were few, indeed—could by means of it make themselves "Children of God." Those who put their trust in the Light were through initiation born of God.

This gives us a clear picture. But in order that all men might perceive the living God, with their earthly senses, He, the Christ, had to appear upon earth in a way that made it possible for Him to be seen with physical eyes; in other words, He had to take on a form of flesh, because only such a form can be seen with physical eyes. Prior to this, only the initiates could perceive Him through the Mysteries, but now He took on a physical form for the salvation of every soul. "The Word or the Logos became flesh." Thus the writer of the Gospel of St. John links the historical appearance of Christ-Jesus together with the whole of evolution. "We have heard His teaching—the teaching of the once-born Son of the Father!" What manner of teaching is this? How were other men born?

In the ancient times in which the Gospels were written, those who were born of the flesh were called "twice-born." They were called twice-born—let us say—because of the intermingling of the blood of father and mother. Those who were not born of flesh and did not come into existence through a human act or through the mingling of blood, were "born of God," that is to say, they were "once-born." Those who were previously called "Children of God" were always in a certain sense the "once-born" and the teaching about the Son of God is the teaching of the "once-born." The physical man is "twice-born," the spiritual man is "once-born." You must not understand it to mean born in to *(hineingeboren)*—no, "once-born" *(eingeboren)* is the antithesis of "twice-born" *(zweigeboren)*. These words point to the fact that besides the physical birth, the human being can experience also a spiritual birth, namely, union with the Spirit, a birth through which he is "once-born," a child or a son of the Godhead.

Such a teaching had first to be heard from Him who represented the Word-made-Flesh. Through Him this teaching became general—"this teaching of the once-born Son of the Father, filled with Devotion and Truth." Devotion is the better translation here, because we have to do not only with being born out of the Godhead, but also with continued union with It, with the removal of all illusions which only come from being "twice-born" and which surround men with sense-deceptions. On the contrary it is a teaching, the truth of which is substantiated by Christ-Jesus

Himself, living and dwelling among men as the incarnated Logos.

John the Baptist called himself—literally interpreted—the forerunner, the precursor, the one who goes before as herald of the ego. He designated himself as one who knew that this ego must become an independent entity in each individual soul, but he also had to bear witness of Him who was to come, in order that this be brought about. He said very clearly, "That which is to come is the 'I AM,' which is eternal, which can say of Itself, "Before Abraham was, was the I AM." John could say, "The I (the ego) which is spoken of here existed before me. Although I am Its forerunner, yet It is at the same time my Forerunner. I bear witness of what was previously present in every human being. After me will come One Who was before me."

At this point in the Gospel very significant words are spoken: "For of His Fullness have we all received grace upon grace." There are men who call themselves Christians, who pass over this word, "Fullness," thinking that nothing very special is meant by it. "Pleroma" in Greek means "Fullness." We find this word also in the Gospel of St. John: "For from the Pleroma have we all received grace upon grace." I have said that if we wish really to understand this Gospel, every word must be weighed in the balance. What is then, Pleroma, Fullness? He alone can understand it who knows that in the ancient Mysteries Pleroma or Fullness was referred to as something very definite. For at that time it was already being taught that when those spiritual beings manifested themselves who during the Moon period evolved to the stage of divinity, namely, the Elohim, one of them separated from the others. One remained behind upon the Moon, and thence *reflected* the power of Love until humanity was sufficiently matured to be able to receive the *direct* Light of the other six Elohim. Therefore they distinguished between Jahve, the individual God, the reflector, and the Fullness of the Godhead, "Pleroma," consisting of the other six Elohim. Since the full consciousness of the Sun Logos meant to them the Christ, they called Him the "Fullness of the Gods" when they wished to refer to Him. This profound truth was concealed in the words: "For out of the Pleroma, we have received grace upon grace."

Now let us continue by transplanting ourselves back into the age of the group-souls, when each individual felt his own ego as the group-ego. Let us now consider what kind of a social organization existed in the group. As far as they were visible human beings, they lived as individuals. They felt inwardly the group-ego, but outwardly they were individuals. Since they did not yet feel themselves as separate entities, they were also unable yet to experience inner love to its fullest extent. One person loved another because he was related to him through blood. The blood relationship was the basis of all love. First those related by blood loved each other and all love, as far as it was not sex-love, sprang from this blood relationship. Men must free themselves more and more from this group-soul love and proffer love as a free gift of the ego.

At the end of the earth evolution, a time will come for mankind when the ego, now become independent, will receive into its inner being, in full surrender, the impulse to do the right and good. Because the ego possesses this impulse, it will do the right and the good. When love becomes spiritualized to such a degree that no one will wish to follow any other impulse than this, then that will be fulfilled which Christ-Jesus wished to bring into the world. For one of the mysteries of Christianity is that it teaches the seeker to behold the Christ, to fill himself with the power of His image, to seek to become like Him, and to follow after Him. Then will his liberated ego need no other law; it will then, as a being free in its inner depths, do the good and the true. Thus Christ is the bringer of the impulse of freedom from the law, that good may be done, not because of the compulsion of any law, but as an indwelling Impulse of Love within the soul. This Impulse will still need the remainder of the Earth period for its full development. The beginning has been made through Christ-Jesus, and the Christ figure will always be the power which will educate humanity to it. As long as men were not yet ready to receive an independent ego, as long as they existed as members of a group, they had to be socially regulated by an outwardly revealed law. And even today men have not, in all things, risen above the group-egos.

In how many things in the present are men not individual human beings, but group-beings? They are already trying to become free, but it is still only an ideal. (At a certain stage of esoteric discipleship, they are called the homeless ones.) The man who voluntarily places himself within the cosmic activities is an individual; he is not ruled by law. In the Christ Principle lies the victory over law. "For the law was given by Moses, but Grace through Christ." According to the Christian acceptance of the word, the soul's capacity for doing right out of the inner self was called Grace. Grace and an inner recognition of truth came into being through the Christ. You see how profoundly this thought fits into the whole of human evolution.

In earlier ages, those who were initiated developed higher spiritual organs of perception; previously no one ever saw God with physical eyes. The once-born Son who rests in the bosom of the Father is the first who made it possible for us to behold a God in the way we see a human being upon earth with the physical earthly senses. Previously God had remained invisible. He revealed Himself in the supersensible world through dreams or in other ways in the places of Initiation. Now God has become an historical fact, a form in the flesh. We read this in the words: "Before this no one had beheld God. The once-born Son who dwelt in the bosom of the Universal Father became the guide to this perceiving." He brought mankind to the point where it could behold God with earthly senses.

Thus we can see how sharply and clearly the Gospel of St. John points to the historical event of Palestine and in what exemplary and concise words which must be accurately weighed in the balance if we wish to use them for an understanding of Esoteric Christianity.

Now we shall see in the following lectures how this theme is further developed and at the same time how it is shown that the Christ is not only the guide of those who are united with the group-soul, but how He enters into each individual human being and endows the individual ego itself with His Impulse. The blood-tie indeed remains, but the spiritual aspect of love is added to it, and to this love which passes over from one individual, independent ego to another. He gives His Impulse.

Day by day, one truth after another was revealed to the neophyte in the course of his initiation. A very important truth is always disclosed, for example, on the third day. Then it is that one learns fully to understand that there is a point in the evolution of the earth when physical love, bound up with the blood, becomes ever more spiritualized. This point of time is the event which demonstrated the transition from a love dependent upon the blood-tie to a spiritualized form of love. In significant words Christ-Jesus makes reference to this when He says: "A time will come which is my time, a time when the most important things will no longer be accomplished by men bound by the tie of blood, but by those who stand alone by themselves. This time however is yet to come."

The Christ Himself, who gave the first impulse, says on one important occasion that this ideal will sometime be fulfilled, but that His time is not yet come. He prophetically points to this when His mother stands there and asks Him to do something for mankind, hinting that she has the right to induce Him to an important deed for humanity. He then replies, "What we are able to do today is still connected with the blood bond, with the relationship between thee and me, for My time is not yet come." That such a time will come when each must stand alone is expresed in the narrative of the Marriage at Cana when the announcement: "They have no wine," was answered by Jesus with the words: "That is something that has still to do with *thee and me*, for My time is not yet come." Here we have the words, "between thee and me" and "My time is not yet come." What stands there in the text refers to this mystery. Like many others, this passage also is usually very roughly translated. It should not read: "Woman, what have I to do with thee? "but: "This has to do with me and thy blood relationship." The text is very fine and subtle, but comprehensible to those who have the will to understand it. But when, in our age, these religious documents are repeatedly interpreted by all kinds of people, one would like to ask, have those who call themselves Christians then no feeling for all this, that they make the Christ utter the words, incorrectly translated, "Woman, what have I to do with thee?"

In much that today calls itself Christianity which rests upon the teaching of the Gospel, we are inclined to ask, *Do they really possess the Gospel?* The important thing is that *they should first possess it.* And with such a profound document as the Gospel of St. John every word must be weighed in order that its proper value be recognized.

Christian Initiation*

If in this whole lecture course we are to concentrate our efforts on gaining a deeper understanding of the words "Father and Mother of Jesus," and consequently of the essence of Christianity in general according to the Gospel of St. John, we must first acquire the material for an understanding of the concept, Mother and Father, in its spiritual sense, as it is intended in this Gospel and at the same time in its actual meaning. For it is not a question of an allegorical or a symbolic explanation.

We must first understand what it means to unite oneself with the higher spiritual worlds, to prepare oneself to receive the higher worlds. We must at the same time consider the nature of initiation, especially in regard to the Gospel of St. John. Let us ask: What is an initiate?

In all ages of the Post-Atlantean human evolution, an initiate has been a person who could lift himself above the outer physical sense-world and have his own personal experiences in the spiritual worlds, a person who could experience the spiritual worlds just as the ordinary human being experiences the physical sense-world through the outer senses, eyes, ears, etc. Such an initiate becomes then a witness of those worlds and their truths. That is one aspect. But there is also something else very essential which every initiate acquires as a very special characteristic during his initiation, that is, he lifts himself above the feelings and sensations which are not only justified but also very necessary within the physical world, but which cannot, however, exist in the same way in the spiritual world.

Do not misunderstand what is said here and imagine that any-

---

* From Maud B. Monges, trans., "Christian Initiation," *The Gospel of St. John* (Hamburg Cycle, 1908), rev. ed. (New York: Anthroposophic Press, 1962), pp. 164–173.

one who is able, as an initiate, to experience the spiritual world as well as the physical world must give up all other human feelings and sensations which are of value here in the physical world and exchange them for those of the higher worlds. This is not so. He does not exchange one for the other, but he acquires one in addition to the other. If, on the one hand, he has to spiritualize his feelings, he must, on the other, strengthen much more those feelings which are of use for working in the physical world. In this way we must interpret those words used in connection with an initiate, namely, that he must, in a certain sense, become a homeless person. It is not meant that in any sense he must become estranged from his home and his family as long as he lives in the physical world, but these words have at least this much significance, that by acquiring the corresponding feelings in the spiritual world, the feelings for the physical world will experience a finer, more beautiful development.

What does it mean to be homeless? It means that one without this designation cannot, in the true sense of the word, attain initiation. To be a homeless man, means that he must develop no special sympathies in the spiritual world similar to those he possesses here in the physical world for special regions or relationships. The individual human being in the physical world belongs to some particular folk or to some particular family, to this or that community of the state. That is all quite proper. He does not need to lose this; he needs it here. If, however, he wished to employ these feelings in the spiritual world, he would bring a very bad dowry to that world. There, it is not a question of developing sympathy for anything, but of allowing everything to work upon him objectively, according to its inherent worth. It could also be said, were this generally understood, that an initiate must be, in the fullest sense of the word, an objective human being.

It is just through its evolution upon the earth that humanity has emerged out of a former homeless state connected with the ancient dreamy, clairvoyant consciousness. We have seen how mankind has descended out of the spiritual spheres into the physical world. In the primal spiritual spheres, patriotism and such things did not exist. When humanity descended from the spiritual spheres, one part peopled the earth in one region and another part in another region, and thus the individual groups of human beings of different regions became stereotype copies of those regions. Do not imagine that the negro became black solely from inner reasons; he became black also through adapting himself to the region of the earth in which he lived. And so it was also with the white people. Just as the great differences of colour and race came into existence because human beings have acquired something through their connection with their environment, so is it also true in respect of the smaller differences in folk individuality. But this has again to do with the specialization of love upon the earth. Because men became dissimilar, love was at first established in small communities.

Only gradually will humanity be able to evolve out of the small communities into a large community of love which will develop concretely through the very implating of the Spirit-Self. The initiate had to anticipate whither human evolution is tending in order to overcome and bridge over all barriers and bring about great peace, great harmony and brotherhood. In his homelessness, he must always, at the very beginning, receive the same rudiments of great brotherly love. This was symbolically expressed in ancient times in the descriptions of the wanderings experienced by the initiate, such as those, for example, of Pythagoras. Why was this described? In order that the initiate might become objective toward every thing in the feelings he had developed within the heart of the community. It is the task of Christianity to bring to the whole of humanity the Impulse of this Brotherhood which the initiate always possessed as an *individual* impulse.

Let us hold clearly in mind that most profound idea of Christianity, that the Christ is the Spirit of the earth and that the earth is His body or vesture. And let us take it literally, for we have said that we must weigh in the balance each separate word of such a document as the Gospel of St. John. What do we learn with respect to the "vesture of the earth" when we make a survey of evolution? We learn, first of all, the fact that the vesture of the earth—that is, the solid parts of it—was divided. One person took possession of this part, another of that part. This part belonged to one person, that part to another. Possession, i.e., the extension of the personality through the acquisition of property, is in a certain sense that into which the garment worn by the Christ, the Spirit of the earth, has, in the course of time, been divided. One thing alone could not be divided, but belonged to all; this was the airy envelope surrounding the earth. And from this airy covering, the breath of life was breathed into the human being, as we are shown in the myths of Paradise. Here we have the first rudiments of the ego in the physical body. The air cannot be divided. Let us try to find out whether the one who described Christianity most profoundly in the Gospel of St. John has anywhere indicated this: And they parted His garments; but His coat they did not divide.

Here you have the words which give you an explanation of how the earth as a whole, together with its airy envelope, is the body or garment, and the coat of the Christ. The garments of the Christ were divided into continents and regions; but not the coat. The air has not been divided; it remains a common possession of all. It is the external, material symbol for the love which is hovering about the earthly globe, which will later be realized.

And in many other connections, Christianity must bring mankind to an acceptance of some of the ancient principles of initiation. If we wish to understand this, we must now characterize initiation. It will suffice, if we consider especially the three main types of initiation; the ancient Yoga, the really specific Christian initiation, and that initiation which is entirely appropriate for men of the present day, the Christian-Rosicrucian initiation. We intend now to describe what course initiation, in general, takes in all three of these forms; what it is and what it represents.

How does a human being become capable of perception in spiritual worlds? First, let me ask, how have you become capable of observing in the physical world? The physical body has sense-organs that make this possible. If you trace human evolution very far back, you will find that in primeval times, the human creature did not yet possess eyes for seeing and ears for hearing in the physical world, but that, as Goethe says, all organs were still undifferentiated. As proof of this, just recall how certain lower animals today still have these undifferentiated organs. Certain lower animals have points through which they can distinguish only light and darkness, and out of these undifferentiated organs, eyes and ears have been moulded and formed. They have been worked into the plastic substance of the physical body. Because your eye has been moulded, there exists for you a world of color, and because your ear has been sculptured, a world of tone is audible to you. No one has the right to say that a world does not really exist; he may only say, "I do not perceive it." For to see the world in the true sense of the word, means that I have the organs with which to perceive it. One may say: "I know only this or that world," but one may not say: "I do not admit of the existence of a world that someone else perceives." A person who speaks in this manner demands that others too should perceive only just what he himself perceives, but nothing else; he claims authoritatively that only what he perceives is true.

When at present someone appears and says: "That is all Anthroposophical imagining, what Anthroposophists declare exists, does not exist," he only proves that he and those like him do not perceive these worlds. We take the positive standpoint. Whoever grants only the existence of what he himself perceives, demands not only that we acknowledge what he knows, but he wishes to make an authoritative decision about something of which he knows nothing. There is no greater intolerance than that shown by official science toward Spiritual Science, and it will become even worse than it has ever been before! It appears in the most varied forms. People are not all conscious of saying something which they should not allow themselves to say. In many gatherings of very good Christians, one can hear it said: "Anthroposophists talk of some kind of an esoteric Christian teaching, but Christianity needs no esoteric teaching; for only that can be true which a simple, unpretentious mind can perceive and understand," which means, of course, only what the speaker can perceive and understand. He therefore requires that no one should perceive and understand anything different from what he himself perceives and understands. The infallibility of the Pope is quite properly not acknowledged in such Christian assemblies, but the infallibility of the individual is claimed today in the widest circles even by the Christians. Anthroposophy is attacked as a result of this papal standpoint in consequence of which each individual sets himself up as a kind of little pope.

If we consider that the physical sense-world exists for us because the individual organs have been carved into the physical body, it will no longer seem extraordinary when it is said that perception in a higher world rests upon the fact that higher organs have been formed in the higher members of the human organism, in the ether and astral bodies. The physical body is, in this way, already provided with its sense organs, but the ether and astral bodies are not yet so provided; these have still to be carved into them. When this has been done, there exists what is called perception in the higher worlds.

We shall now speak of the way in which these organs are built into the ether and astral bodies. We have said that in anyone who aspires to initiation and has attained it, higher organs have been developed. How is this accomplished? It is a matter of understanding the human astral body in the state in which it exists in its purity. During the day this astral body is immersed in the physical body. There the forces of the physical body act upon it; it is not then free. It carries out the demands of the physical body; hence it is impossible to begin the development of these higher organs during the day. It can be begun when the astral body is out of the physical body, in sleep; only then can the astral body be molded. The human astral body can only have its higher sense organs developed when they are carved into it during sleep, while outside the physical body. But we cannot manipulate a sleeping human being; that would not be possible for the modern man, if he wishes to perceive what is happening to him in sleep. If you have him in an unconscious condition, then he cannot observe this. Here there seems to be a contradiction, for the astral body is not conscious of its connection with the physical body during sleep. But *indirectly* it is possible that during the day the physical body is acted upon and the impressions which it then receives remain within the astral body when this is withdrawn at night.

Just as the impressions which the astral body receives from the surrounding physical world have been impressed upon it, so in like manner we must do something quite specific with the physical body, in order that this something be imprinted upon the astral body and then be formed in it in the proper manner. This happens when the human being ceases to live in his customary way during the day, allowing random impressions to enter his consciousness, and takes his inner life in hand by means of a methodical schooling in the manner described. This is called Meditation, Concentration, or Contemplation. These are exercises which are as strictly prescribed in the schools for the purpose, as microscopy is prescribed in the laboratories. If a person carries out these exercises, they act so intensely upon him that the astral body is plastically reshaped when it withdraws during sleep. Just as this sponge adapts itself to the form of my hand as long as I hold it there, but forms itself again according to the forces inherent in it as soon as I release it, so in like manner is it with the astral body; when in sleep it withdraws from the corporality, it follows the astral forces invested in it. Thus it is during the day that we must undertake those spiritual activities by means of which the astral body, during the night, is plastically formed so that organs of higher perception are developed in it.

Meditation can be regulated in a threefold manner. 1. There can be more consideration given to the thought-matter, to the so-called elements of Wisdom, the pure element of thought. This is the Yoga training which deals especially with the element of thought, Contemplation. 2. One can work more upon the feeling through its special cultivation. This is the specifically Christian course. 3. Again one can work through a combination of feeling and will. This is the Christian-Rosicrucian method. To consider the Yoga practice would carry us too far, and it would also have no relationship to the Gospel of St. John. We shall consider the specifically Christian initiation and explain its basis. You must think of this form of initiation as one which a person belonging to the present social order could hardly undergo. It demands a temporary isolation. The Rosicrucian method, however, is the method by which we can work ourselves into the higher worlds without interfering with our duties. What, however, is applicable in principle, we can also fully explain by means of Christian initiation.

This method of initiation has to do exclusively with the feelings, and I shall now have to enumerate seven experiences of the feeling-life; seven stages of feeling, through the experiencing of which the astral body is actually so affected that it develops its

organs during the night. Let us describe how the Christian neophyte must live in order that he may pass through these stages.
The first stage is called "Washing the Feet." Here the teacher
says to the pupil: "Observe the plants. They have their roots in
the ground; the mineral earth is a lower being than the plant. If
the plant were able to contemplate its own nature, it would have
to say to the earth: it is true I am a higher being, but if thou wert
not there, I could not exist; for from thee, O earth, I draw most of
my sustenance. If the plant were able to translate this into feeling, it would then bow itself down to the stone and say: I bow
myself before thee, O stone, thou humbler being, for I am in-
debted to thee for my very existence! Then if we ascend to the
animal, it would have to behave in a similar manner toward the
plant and say: Indeed it is true, I am higher than the plant, but to
the lower kingdoms I owe my existence! If in this manner we
mount higher and reach the human being, then each individual
who stands somewhat higher in the social scale must incline himself to the lower and say: To those on the lower social level I owe
my existence! This continues on up to Christ-Jesus. The Twelve
who are about Him are at a level lower than Christ-Jesus; but as
the plant develops out of the stone, so does the Christ grow out of
the Twelve. He bows down to the Twelve and says: I owe you My
existence."

When the teacher had explained this to the pupil, he then said
to him: "For weeks must thou surrender thyself to this cosmic
feeling of how the superior should incline to the inferior and
when thou hast thoroughly developed this feeling within thee,
then wilt thou experience an inner and an outer symptom!" These
are not the essential things, they only indicate that the pupil has
practiced sufficiently. When the physical body was sufficiently
influenced by the soul, this was indicated to him by an external
symptom in which he feels as though water were lapping over his
feet. That is a very real feeling! And he has another very real
feeling in which the "Washing of the Feet" appears to him as in a
mighty vision in the astral, the inclining of the Higher Self to the
lower. Thus the occult student experiences in the astral world
what is found depicted in the Gospel of St. John as an historical
fact.

At the second stage, the pupil is told: "Thou must develop within thyself yet another feeling. Thou must picture how it would be were all the suffering and sorrow possible in the world to come upon thee; thou must feel how it would be wert thou exposed to the piling up of all possible hindrances, and thou must enter into the feeling that thou must stand erect even though all the adversity of the world were to bear down upon thee!" Then when the pupil has practiced this exercise for a sufficient length of time, there are again two symptoms; in the first he has the feeling of being beaten from all sides, and in the second he has an astral vision of the "Scourging." I am relating what hundreds of people have experienced whereby they have acquired the ability to mount into the higher worlds.

In the third exercise, the pupil had to imagine that the holiest thing that he possesses, which he defends with his whole ego-being, is subjected to jeers and gibes. He must say to himself: "Come what may, I must hold myself erect and defend what is holy to me." When he had accustomed himself to this, he felt something like pricking upon his head, and he experienced the "Crown of Thorns" as an astral vision. Again it must be said that the important thing is not the symptoms; they appear as a result of the exercises. Care was also taken that there was no question of suggestion and autosuggestion.

In the fourth exercise, the pupil's body must become as foreign to his feelings as any external object—a stick of wood for example —and he must not say "I" to his body. This experience must become so much a part of his feelings that he says: "I carry my body about with me as I do my coat." He connects his ego no longer with his body. Then something occurs which is called the Stigmata. What in many cases might be a condition of sickness is in this case a result of Meditation, because all sickness must be eliminated. On the feet and hands and on the right side of the breast appear the so-called Stigmata; and as an inner symptom, he beholds the "Crucifixion" in an astral vision.

The fifth, sixth and seventh grades of feeling, we can only briefly describe. The fifth grade consists of what is called "The Mystical Death." Through feelings which the pupil is permitted to experience at this stage, he feels as though, in an instant, a black curtain were drawn before the whole physical, visible world and as though everything had disappeared. This moment is important because of something else that must be experienced, if one wishes to push on into Christian initiation, in the true sense of the word. The pupil then feels that he can plunge into the primal causes of evil, pain, affliction, and sorrow. And he can suffer all the evil that exists in the depths of the human soul, when he descends into Hell. That is the "Descent into Hell." When this has been experienced, it is as though the black curtain had been rent asunder and he looks into the spiritual world.

The sixth step is what is called the "Interment and Resurrection." This is the stage at which the pupil feels himself one with the entire earthbody. He feels as though he were laid within and belonged to the whole earth planet. His life has been extended into a planetary existence.

The seventh experience cannot be described in words; only one could describe it who is able to think without the physical brain instrument—and for that there is no language, because our language has only designations for the physical plane. Therefore, only a reference can be made to this stage. It surpasses anything that the human being can possibly conceive. This is called the "Ascension" or the complete absorption into the spiritual world.

This completes the gamut of feelings into which the pupil, during waking day-consciousness, must place himself with complete inner equanimity. When the pupil has surrendered himself to these experiences, they act so strongly upon the astral body that, in the night, inner sense organs are developed, are plastically formed. These seven steps of feeling are not practiced in the Rosicrucian initiation, but the result is the same as that of which we have just spoken.

Thus you see that the important thing in initiation is to influence the astral body in such a way by the indirect means of the day-experiences, that it may, when it is wholly free during the night, take on a new plastic form. When the human being in this manner, as an astral being, has given himself a plastic form, the astral body has become actually a new member of the human organism. He is then wholly permeated by Manas or Spirit-Self.

When the astral body is thus divided, that part which has in this way been plastically formed is brought over into the ether body. And just as you press the seal upon the sealing wax, and the name on the seal appears not only on the seal, but on the wax as well, so too must the astral body dip down into the ether body and impress upon it whatever it may now possess. The inner process, the working over of the astral body, is the same in all methods of initiation. Only in the method of transmission into the ether body do the individual methods differ. We shall speak tomorrow of these differences and show how the three methods of initiation, which have proved to be the most profound evolutionary impulses in the course of the Post-Atlantean age, differ from each other and what significance initiation, in general, has for human evolution. Then these parts of the Gospel of St. John upon which we have not yet been able to touch will also become clear.

Virgin Sophia and the Holy Spirit*

Yesterday we reached the point of discussing the change which takes place in the human astral body through meditation, concentration, and other practices which are given in the various methods of initiation. We have seen that the astral body is thereby affected in such a way that it develops within itself the organs which it needs for perceiving in the higher worlds and we have said that up to this point, the principle of initiation is everywhere really the same—although the forms of its practices conform wholly to the respective cultural epochs. The principal difference appears with the occurrence of the next thing which must follow. In order that the pupil may be able actually to perceive in the higher worlds, it is necessary that the organs which have been formed out of the astral part, impress or stamp themselves upon the ether body, be impressed into the etheric element.

The *refashioning of the astral body indirectly through medita-tion and concentration,* is called by an ancient name "katharsis," or purification. Katharsis or purification has as its purpose the discarding from the astral body all that hinders it from becoming harmoniously and regularly organized, thus enabling it to acquire higher organs. It is endowed with the germ of these higher or-gans; it is only necessary to bring forth the forces which are present in it. We have said that the most varied methods can be employed for bringing about this katharsis. A person can go very

* From Maud B. Monges, trans.,"The Nature of the Virgin Sophia and of the Holy Spirit," *The Gospel of St. John* (Hamburg Cycle, 1908), rev. ed. (New York: Anthroposophic Press, 1962), pp. 174–192.

far in this matter of katharsis if, for example, he has gone through and inwardly experienced all that is in my book, *Philosophy of Freedom*, and feels that this book was for him a stimulation and that now he has reached the point where he can himself actually reproduce the thoughts just as they are there presented. If a person holds the same relationship to this book that a virtuoso, in playing a selection on the piano, holds to the composer of the piece, that is, he reproduces the whole thing within himself— naturally according to his ability to do so—then through the strictly built up sequence of thought of this book—for it is written in this manner—katharsis will be developed to a high degree. For the important point in such things as this book is that the thoughts are all placed in such a way that they become active. In many other books of the present, just by changing the system a little, what has been said earlier in the book can just as well be said later. In the *Philosophy of Freedom* this is not possible. Page 150 can as little be placed fifty pages earlier in the subject matter as the hind legs of a dog can be exchanged with the forelegs, for the book is a logically arranged organism and the working out of the thoughts in it has an effect similar to an inner schooling. Hence there are various methods of bringing about katharsis. If a person has not been successful in doing this after having gone through this book, he should not think that what has been said is untrue, but rather that he has not studied it properly or with sufficient energy or thoroughness.

Something else must now be considered, namely, that when this kastharsis has taken place, when the astral organs have been formed in the astral body, it must all be imprinted upon the ether body. In the pre-Christian initiation, it was done in the following manner. After the pupil had undergone the suitable preparatory training, which often lasted for years, he was told: The time has now come when the astral body has developed far enough to have astral organs for perception, now these can become aware of their counterpart in the ether body. Then the pupil was subjected to a procedure which today—at least for our cultural epoch—is not only unnecessary, but is not in all seriousness feasible. He was put into a lethargic condition for three-and-a-half days, and was treated during this time in such a way that not only the astral body left the physical and ether bodies—a thing that occurs every night in sleep—but to a certain degree the ether body also was lifted out; but care was taken that the physical body remained intact and that the pupil did not die in the meantime. The ether body was then liberated from the forces of the physical body which act upon it. It had become, as it were, elastic and plastic and when the sensory organs that had been formed in the astral body sank down into it, the ether body received an imprint from the whole astral body. When the pupil was brought again into a normal condition by the hierophant, when the astral body and ego were again united with the physical and ether bodies—a procedure which the hierophant well understood—then not only did he experience katharsis, but also what is called Illumination or Photismos. The pupil could then not only perceive in the world around him all those things that were physically perceptible, but he could employ the spiritual organs of perception, which means, he could see and perceive the spiritual. Initiation consisted essentially of these two processes, purification or purging, and illumination.

Then the course of human evolution entered upon a phase in which it gradually became impossible to draw the ether body out of the physical without a very great disturbance in all its functions, because the whole tendency of the Post-Atlantean evolution was to cause the ether body to be attached closer and closer to the physical body. It was consequently necessary to carry out other methods of initiation which proceed in such a manner that without the separating of the physical and ether bodies, the astral body, having become sufficiently developed through katharsis and able of itself to return again to the physical and etheric bodies, was able to imprint its organs on the body in spite of the hindrance of the physical body. What had to happen was that stronger forces had to become active in meditation and concentration in order that there might be the strong impulse in the astral body for overcoming the power of resistance of the physical body. In the first place there was the actual specifically Christian initiation in which it was necessary for the pupil to undergo the procedure which was described yesterday as the seven steps. When he had undergone these feelings and experiences, his astral body had been so intensely affected that it formed its organs of perception plastically—perhaps only after years, but still sooner or later—and then impressed them upon the ether body, thus making of the pupil one of the Illuminati. This kind of initiation which is specifically Christian could only be described fully if I were able to hold lectures about its particular aspects every day for about a fortnight instead of only for a few days. But that is not the important thing. Yesterday you were given certain details of the Christian initiation. We only wish to become acquainted with its principle.

By continually meditating upon passages of the Gospel of St. John, the Christian pupil is actually in a condition to reach initiation without the three-and-a-half day continued lethargic sleep. If each day he allows the first verses of the Gospel of St. John, from "In the beginning was the Word" to the passage "full of devotion and truth," to work upon him, they become an exceedingly significant meditation. They have this force within them, for this Gospel is not there simply to be read and understood in its entirety with the intellect, but it must be inwardly fully experienced and felt. It is a force which comes to the help of initiation and works for it. Then will the "Washing of the Feet," the "Scourging" and other inner processes be experienced as astral visions, wholly corresponding to the description in the Gospel itself, beginning with the 13th Chapter.

The Rosicrucian initiation, although resting upon a Christian foundation, works more with other symbolic ideas which produce katharsis, chiefly with imaginative pictures. That is another modification which had to be used, because mankind had progressed a step further in its evolution and the methods of initiation must conform to what has gradually evolved.

We must understand that when a person has attained this initiation, he is fundamentally quite different from the person he was before it. While formerly he was only associated with the things of the physical world, he now acquires the possibility likewise of association with the events and beings of the spiritual world. This presupposes that the human being acquires knowledge in a much more real sense than in that abstract, dry, prosaic sense in which we usually speak of knowledge. For a person who acquires spiritual knowledge finds the process to be something quite different. It is a complete realization of that beautiful expression, "Know thyself." But the most dangerous thing in the realm of knowledge is to grasp these words erroneously and today this occurs only too frequently. Many people construe these words to mean that they should no longer look about the physical world, but should gaze into their own inner being and seek there for everything spiritual. This is a very mistaken understanding of the saying, for that is not at all what it means.

We must clearly understand that true higher knowledge is also an evolution from one standpoint, which the human being has attained, to another which he had reached previously. If a person practices self-knowledge only by brooding upon himself, he sees only what he already possesses. He thereby acquires nothing new, but only knowledge of his own lower self in the present meaning of the word. This inner nature is only one part that is necessary for knowledge. The other part that is necessary must be added. Without the two parts, there is no real knowledge. By means of his inner nature, he can develop organs through which he can gain knowledge. But just as the eye, as an external sense organ, would not perceive the sun by gazing into itself, but only by looking outward at the sun, so must the inner perceptive organs gaze outwardly, in other words, gaze into an *external spiritual* in order actually to perceive. The concept "Knowledge" had a much deeper, a more real meaning in those ages when spiritual things were better understood than at present. Read in the Bible the words, "Abraham knew his wife!" or this or that Patriarch "knew his wife." One does not need to seek very far in order to understand that by this expression fructification is meant. When one considers the words, "Know thyself," in the Greek, they do not mean that you stare into your own inner being, but that you fructify yourself with what streams into you from the spiritual world. "Know thyself" means: Fructify thyself with the content of the spiritual world!

Two things are needed for this, namely, that the human being prepare himself through katharsis and illumination, and then that he open his inner being freely to the spiritual world. In this connection we may liken his inner nature to the female aspect, the

outer spiritual to the male. The inner being must be made susceptible of receiving the higher self. When this has happened,
then the higher human self streams into him from the spiritual
world. One may ask: Where is this higher human self? Is it within
the personal man? No, it is not there. On Saturn, Sun, and Moon,
the higher self was diffused over the entire cosmos. At that time
the Cosmic Ego was spread out over all human kind, but now
men have to permit it to work upon them. They must permit this
Ego to work upon their previously prepared inner natures. This
means that the human inner nature, in other words, the astral
body, has to be cleansed, purified and ennobled, and subjected to
katharsis, then a person may expect that the external spirit will
stream into him for his illumination. That will occur when the
human being has been so well prepared that he has subjected his
astral body to katharsis, thereby developing his inner organs of
peception. The astral body, in any case, has progressed so far that
now when it dips down into the ether and physical bodies, illumination or phocismos results. What actually occurs is that the astral
body imprints its organs upon the ether body, making it possible
both for the human being to perceive a spiritual world about him
and for his inner being, the astral body, to receive what the ether
body is able to offer it, what the ether body draws out of the
entire cosmos, out of the Cosmic Ego.

This cleansed, purified astral body, which bears within it at the
moment of illumination none of the impure impressions of the
physical world, but only the organs of perception of the spiritual
world, is called in esoteric Christianity the "pure, chaste, wise
Virgin Sophia." By means of all that he receives during katharsis,
the pupil cleanses and purifies his astral body so that it is transformed into the Virgin Sophia. And when the Virgin Sophia encounters the Cosmic Ego, the Universal Ego which causes illumination, the pupil is surrounded by light, spiritual light. This
second power that approaches the Virgin Sophia is called in esoteric Christianity—is also so called today—the "Holy Spirit."
Therefore according to esoteric Christianity, it is correct to say
that through his processes of initiation the Christian esotericist
attains the purification and cleansing of his astral body; he makes
his astral body into the Virgin Sophia and is illuminated from

above—if you wish, you may call it overshadowed—by the "Holy Spirit," by the Cosmic, Universal Ego. And a person thus illumined, who, in other words, according to esoteric Christianity has received the "Holy Spirit" into himself, speaks forthwith in a different manner. How does he speak? When he speaks about Saturn, Sun, and Moon, about the different members of the human being, about the processes of cosmic evolution, he is not expressing his own opinion. *His* views do not at all come into consideration. When such a person speaks about Saturn, it is Saturn itself that is speaking through him. When he speaks about the Sun, the Spiritual Being of the Sun speaks through him. He is the instrument. His personal ego has been eclipsed, which means that at such moments it has become impersonal and it is the Cosmic Universal Ego that is using his ego as its instrument through which to speak. Therefore, in true esoteric teaching which proceeds from esoteric Christianity, one should not speak of views or opinions, for in the highest sense of the word this is incorrect; there are no such things.

According to esoteric Christianity, whoever speaks with the right attitude of mind toward the world will say to himself, for instance: If I tell people that there were horses outside, the important thing is not that one of them pleases me less than the other and that I think one is a worthless horse. The important point is that I describe the horses to the others and give the facts. In like manner, what has been observed in the spiritual worlds must be described irrespective of all personal opinions. In every spiritual-scientific system of teaching, only the series of facts must be related and this must have nothing to do with the opinions of the one who relates them.

Thus we have acquired two concepts in their spiritual significance. We have learned to know the nature of the Virgin Sophia, which is the purified astral body, and the nature of the "Holy Spirit," the Cosmic Universal Ego, which is received by the Virgin Sophia and which can then speak out of this purified astral body. There is something else to be attained, a still higher stage, that is the ability to help someone else, the ability to give him the impulse to accomplish both of these. Men of our evolutionary epoch can receive the Virgin Sophia (the purified astral body) and the Holy Spirit (illumination) in the manner described, but only Christ Jesus could give to the earth what was necessary to accomplish this. He has implanted in the spiritual part of the earth those forces which make it possible for that to happen which has been described in the Christian initiation. You may ask how did this come about?

Two things are necessary to understanding this phenomenon. First we must make ourselves acquainted with something purely historial, that is, with the manner of giving names which was quite different in the age in which the Gospels were written from the way in which it is done at present.

Those who interpret the Gospel at present do not at all understand the principle of giving names at the time the Gospels were written and therefore they do not speak as they should. It is, in fact, exceedingly difficult to describe the principle of giving names at that time. We can, however, make it comprehensible even though we only indicate it in rough outlines. Let us suppose, in the case of someone whom we meet, that instead of holding to the name which does not at all fit him, and which has been given to him in the abstract way customary today, we were to harken to and notice his most distinguishing characteristics, were to notice the most prominent attribute of his character and were in a position to discern clairvoyantly the deeper foundations of his being, and then were to give him his name in accordance with those most important qualities which we believe should be attributed to him. Were we to follow such a method of giving names, we should be doing something at a lower elementary stage, similar to what was done at that time by those who gave names in the manner of the writer of the Gospel of St. John. In order to make very clear his manner of giving names, let us consider the following:

The author of the St. John's Gospel regarded the physical, historic Mother of Jesus in her most prominent characteristics and asked himself, Where shall I find a name for her which will express most perfectly her real being? Then, because she had, by means of her earliest incarnations, reached those spiritual heights upon which she stood; and because she appeared in her external personality to be a counterpart, a revelation of what was called in esoteric Christianity, the Virgin Sophia, he called the Mother of Jesus the "Virgin Sophia," and this is what she was always called in the esoteric places where esoteric Christianity was taught. Esoterically he leaves her entirely unnamed in contradistinction to those others who have chosen for her the secular name, Mary. He could not take the secular name for he had to express in the name the profound, world historic evolution. He does this by indicating that she cannot be called Mary, and what is more, he places by her side her sister Mary, wife of Cleophas and calls her simply the "Mother of Jesus." He shows thereby that he does not wish to mention her name, that it cannot be publicly revealed. In esoteric circles, she is always called the "Virgin Sophia." It was she who represented the "Virgin Sophia" as an external historical personality.

If we now wish to penetrate further into the nature of Christianity and its founder, we must take under consideration yet another mystery. We should understand clearly how to make a distinction between the personality who, in Esoteric Christianity, was called "Jesus of Nazareth" and Him who was called "Christ Jesus," the Christ dwelling within Jesus of Nazareth.

Now what does this mean? It means that in the historical personality of Jesus of Nazareth, we have to do with a highly developed human being who had passed through many incarnations and after a cycle of high development was again reincarnated; a person who, because of this, was attracted to a mother so pure that the writer of the Gospel could call her the "Virgin Sophia." Thus we are dealing with a highly developed human being, Jesus of Nazareth, who had progressed far in his evolution in his previous incarnations and in this incarnation had entered upon a highly spiritual stage. The other evangelists were not illuminated to such a high degree as the writer of this Gospel. It was more the actual sense-world that was revealed to them, a world in which they saw their Master and Messiah moving about as Jesus of Nazareth. The mysterious spiritual relationships, at least those of the heights into which the writer of the Gospel of St. John could peer, were concealed from them. For this reason they laid special emphasis upon the fact that in Jesus of Nazareth lived the Father, who had always existed in Judaism and was transmitted down through the generations as the God of the Jews. And they expressed this when they said: "If we trace back ther ancestry of Jesus of Nazareth through generation after generation, we are able to prove that the same blood flows in Him that has flowed down through these generations."

The evangelists give the genealogical tables and precisely show at what different stages of evolution they stand. For Matthew, the important thing is to show that in Jesus of Nazareth we have a person in whom Father Abraham is living. The blood of Father Abraham has flowed down through the generations as far as Jesus. He thus traces the genealogical tables back to Abraham. He has a more materialistic point of view than Luke. The important thing for Luke was not only to show that the God who lived in Abraham was present in Jesus, but that the ancestry, the line of descent, can be traced back still further, even to Adam. Adam was a son of the very Godhead, which means that he belonged to the time when humanity had just made the transition from a spiritual to a physical state. Both Matthew and Luke wished to show that this early Jesus of Nazareth has His being only in what can be traced back to the divine Father-power. This was not a matter of importance for the writer of the Gospel of St. John who could gaze into the spiritual world. The important thing for him was not the words, "I and Father Abraham are one," but that at every moment of time, there exists in the human being an Eternal which was present in him before Father Abraham. This he wished to show. In the beginning was the Word which is called the "I AM." Before all external things and beings, He was. He was in the beginning. For those who wished rather to describe Jesus of Nazareth and were only able to describe him, it was a question of showing how from the beginning the blood flowed down through the generations. It was important to them to show that the same blood flowing down through the generations flowed also in Joseph, the father of Jesus.

If we could speak quite esoterically it would naturally be necessary to speak of the idea of the so-called "virgin birth," but this can be discussed only in the most intimate circles. It belongs to the deepest mysteries that exist and the misunderstanding connected with this idea arises because people do not know what is meant by the "virgin birth." They think that it means there was no fatherhood. But it is not that; a much more profound, a more mysterious something lies at the back of it which is quite compatible with what the other disciples wish to show, that is, that Joseph is the father of Jesus. If they were to deny this, then all the trouble they take to show this to be a fact would be meaningless. They wish to show that the ancient God exists in Jesus of Nazareth. Luke especially wished to make this very clear, therefore he traces the whole ancestry back to Adam and then to God. How could he have come to this conclusion, if he really wished only to say: I am showing you that this genealogical tree exists, but Joseph, as a matter of fact, had nothing to do with it. It would be very strange if people were to take the trouble to represent Joseph as a very important personality and then were to shove him aside out of the whole affair.

In the event of Palestine, we have not only to do with this highly developed personality, Jesus of Nazareth, who had passed through many incarnations, and had developed himself so highly that he needed such an extraordinary mother as the Virgin Sophia, but we have also to do with a second mystery. When Jesus of Nazareth was thirty years of age, he had advanced to such a stage through what he had experienced in his present incarnation that he could perform an action which it is possible for one to perform in exceptional cases. We know that the human being consists of physical, ether and astral bodies, and an ego. This fourfold human being is the human being as he lives here among us. If a person stands at a certain high stage of evolution, it is possible for him at a particular moment to draw out his ego from the three bodies and abandon them, leaving them intact and entirely uninjured. This ego then goes into the spiritual worlds and the three bodies remain behind. We meet this process at times in cosmic evolution. At some especially exalted, enraptured moment, the ego of a person departs and enters into the spirit world —under certain conditions this can be extended over a long period—and because the three bodies are so highly developed by the ego that lived in them, they are fit instruments for a still higher being who now takes possession of them. In the thirtieth year of Jesus of Nazareth, that Being whom we have called the

Christ took possession of his physical, ether and astral bodies. This Christ-Being could not incarnate in an ordinary child's body, but only in one which had first been prepared by a highly developed ego, for this Christ-Being had never before been incarnated in a physical body. Therefore from the thirtieth year on, we are dealing with the Christ in Jesus of Nazareth.

What in reality took place? The fact is that the corporality of Jesus of Nazareth which he had left behind was so mature, so perfect, that the Sun Logos, the Being of the six Elohim, which we have described as the spiritual Being of the Sun, was able to penetrate into it. It could incarnate for three years in this corporality, could become flesh. The Sun Logos Who can shine into human beings through illumination, the Sun Logos Himself, the Holy Spirit, entered. The Universal Ego, the Cosmic Ego, entered and from then on during three years, the Sun Logos spoke through the body of Jesus. The Christ speaks through the body of Jesus during these three years. This event is indicated in the Gospel of St. John and also in the other Gospels as the descent of the dove, of the Holy Spirit, upon Jesus of Nazareth. In esoteric Christianity it is said that at that moment the ego of Jesus of Nazareth left his body, and that from then on the Christ is in him, speaking through him in order to teach and work. This is the first event, according to the Gospel of St. John. We now have the Christ within the astral, ether and physical bodies of Jesus of Nazareth. There He worked as has been described until the Mystery of Golgotha occurred. What occurred on Golgotha? Let us consider that important moment when the blood flowed from the wounds of the Crucified Savior. In order that you may understand me better, I shall compare what occurred with something else.

Let us suppose we have here a vessel filled with water. In the water, salt is dissolved and the water becomes quite transparent. Because we have warmed the water, we have made a salt solution. Now let us cool the water. The salt precipitates and we see how the salt condenses below and forms a deposit at the bottom of the vessel. That is the process for one who sees only with physical eyes. But for a person who can see with spiritual eyes, something else is happening. While the salt is condensing below, the spirit of the salt streams up through the water, filling it. The salt can only become condensed when the spirit of the salt has departed from it and become diffused into the water. Those who understand these things know that wherever condensation takes place, a spiritualization also always occurs. What thus condenses below has its counterpart above in the spiritual, just as in the case of the salt, when it condenses and is precipitated below, its spirit streams upward and disseminates. Therefore, it was not only a physical process that took place when the blood flowed from the wounds of the Savior, but it was actually accompanied by a spiritual process; that is, the Holy Spirit which was received at the Baptism united Itself with the earth; that the Christ Himself flowed into the very being of the earth. From now on, the earth was changed, and this is the reason for saying to you, in earlier lectures, that if a person had viewed the earth from a distant star, he would have observed that its whole appearance was altered with the Mystery of Golgotha. The Sun Logos became a part of the earth, formed an alliance with it and became the Spirit of the Earth. This He achieved by entering into the body of Jesus of Nazareth in this thirtieth year, and by remaining active there for three years, after which He continued to remain on the earth.

Now, the important thing is that this Event must produce an effect upon the true Christian; that it must give something by which he may gradually develop the beginnings of a purified astral body in the Christian sense. There had to be something there for the Christian whereby he could make his astral body gradually more and more like a Virgin Sophia, and through it, receive into himself the Holy Spirit which was able to spread out over the entire earth, but which could not be received by anyone whose astral body did not resemble the Virgin Sophia. There had to be something which possesses the power to transform the human astral body into a Virgin Sophia. What is this power? It consists in the fact of Christ Jesus entrusting to the Disciple whom He loved —in other words to the writer of the Gospel of St. John—the mission of describing truly and faithfully through his own illumination the events of Palestine in order that men might be affected by them. If men permit what is written in the Gospel of St. John to work sufficiently upon them, their astral body is in the process of becoming a Virgin Sophia and it will become receptive to the

Holy Spirit. Gradually, through the strength of the impulse which emanates from this Gospel, it will become susceptible of feeling the true spirit and later of perceiving it. This mission, this charge, was given to the writer of the Gospel by Jesus Christ. You need but read the Gospel. The Mother of Jesus—the Virgin Sophia in the esoteric meaning of Christianity—stands at the foot of the Cross, and from the Cross the Christ says to the Disciple whom He loved: "Henceforth, this is thy Mother" and from this hour the Disciple took her unto himself. This means: "That force which was in My astral body and made it capable of becoming bearer of the Holy Spirit, I now give over to thee; thou shalt write down what this astral body has been able to acquire through its development." "And the Disciple took her unto himself"; that means he wrote the Gospel of St. John. And this Gospel of St. John is the Gospel in which the writer has concealed powers which develop the Virgin Sophia.

At the Cross, the mission was entrusted to him of receiving that force as his mother and of being the true, genuine interpeter of the Messiah. This really means that if you live wholly in accordance with the Gospel of St. John and understand it spiritually, it has the force to lead you to Christian katharsis. It has the power to give you the Virgin Sophia. Then will the Holy Spirit, united with the earth, grant you illumination or phocismos according to the Christian meaning. And what the most intimate disciples experienced there in Palestine was so powerful that from that time on they possessed at least the capacity of perceiving in the spiritual world. The most intimate disciples had received this capacity into themselves. Perceiving in the spirit, in the Christian sense, means that the person transforms his astral body to such a degree through the power of the Event of Palestine that what he sees need not be before him externally and physically sensible. He possesses something by means of which he can perceive in the spirit. There were such intimate pupils.

The woman who anointed the feet of Christ Jesus in Bethany had received through the Event of Palestine the powerful force needed for spiritual perception, and she is, for example, one of those who first understood that what had lived in Jesus was present after His death, that is, had been resurrected. She possessed this faculty. It may be asked: Whence came this possibility? It came through the development of her inner sense organs. Are we told this in the Gospel? We are indeed; we are told that Mary Magdalene was led to the grave, that the body had disappeared and that she saw there two spiritual forms. These two spiritual forms are always to be seen when a corpse is present for a certain time after death. On the one side is to be seen the astral body, and on the other, what gradually separates from it as ether body, then passing over into the cosmic ether. Wholly apart from the physical body, there are two spiritual forms present which belong to the spiritual world.

Then the disciples went away again into their own home. But Mary stood without at the sepulchre weeping; and as she wept she stooped down and looked into the sepulchre, and seeth two angels in white sitting.

She beheld this because she had become clairvoyant through the force and power of the Event of Palestine. And she beheld something more: she beheld the Risen Christ. Was it necessary for her to be clairvoyant to be able to behold the Christ? If you have seen a person in physical form a few days ago, do you not think you would recognize him again if he should appear before you?

And when she had thus said, she turned herself back and saw Jesus standing and knew not that it was Jesus.

Jesus saith unto her, Woman why weepest thou? Whom seekest thou? She, supposing it to be the gardener . . .

And in order that it might be told to us as exactly as possible, it was not only said once, but again at the next appearance of the Risen Christ, when Jesus appeared at the sea of Gennesareth.

But when the morning was now come, Jesus stood on the shore: but the disciples knew not that it was Jesus.

The esoteric pupils find Him there. Those who had received the full force of the Event of Palestine could grasp the situation and see that it was the Risen Jesus who could be perceived spiritually.

Although the disciples and Mary Magdalene saw Him, yet there were some among them who were less able to develop clairvoyant power. One of these was Thomas. It is said that he was not present the first time the disciples saw the Lord, and he declared he would have to lay his hands in His wounds, he would have to touch physically the body of the Risen Christ. You ask: What happened? The effort was then made to assist him to develop spiritual perception. And how was this done? Let us take the words of the Gospel itself:

And after a week His disciples were again within, and Thomas with them: then came Jesus the doors being shut, and stood in their midst, and said, Peace be unto you.

Then saith He to Thomas, reach hither thy fingers and behold My hands, and reach hither thy hand and thrust it into My side: and be not faithless, but believing. And thou shalt behold something if thou dost not rely upon the outer appearance, but art impregnated with inner power.

This inner power which should proceed from the Event of Palestine is called "Faith." It is no ordinary force, but an inner clairvoyant power. Permeate thyself with inner power, then thou needest no longer hold as real that only which thou seest externally; for blessed are they who are able to know what they do not see outwardly!

Thus we see that we have to do with the full reality and truth of the Resurrection and that only those are fully able to understand it who have first developed the inner power to perceive in the spirit world. This will make comprehensible to you the last chapter of the Gospel of St. John in which again and again it is pointed out that the closest followers of Christ Jesus have reached the stage of the Virgin Sophia because the Event of Golgotha had been consummated in their presence. But when they had to stand firm for the first time, had actually to behold a spiritual event, they were still blinded and had first to find their way. They did not know that He was the same One Who had earlier been among them. Here is something which we must grasp with the most subtle concepts; for the grossly materialistic person would say: "Then the Resurrection is undermined!" The miracle of the Resurrection is to be taken quite literally, for He said: "Lo, I remain with you always, even unto the end of the age, unto the end of the cosmic age."

He is there and will come again, although not in a form of flesh, but in a form in which those who have been sufficiently developed through the power of the Gospel of St. John, can actually perceive Him and possessing the power to perceive Him, they will no longer be unbelieving. The mission of the Spiritual Science Movement is to prepare those who have the will to allow themselves to be prepared for the return of the Christ upon earth. This is the cosmo-historical significance of Spiritual Science, to prepare mankind and to keep its eyes open for the time when the Christ will appear again actively among men in the sixth cultural epoch, in order that that may be accomplished for a great part of humanity which was indicated to us in the Marriage of Cana.

Therefore, the world concept obtained from Spiritual Science appears like an execution of the testament of Christianity. In order to be lead to real Christianity, the men of the future will have to receive that spiritual teaching which Spiritual Science is able to give. Many people may still say today: Spiritual Science is something that really contradicts true Christianity. But those are the little popes who form opinions about things of which they know nothing and who make into a dogma: What I do not know does not exist.

This intolerance will become greater and greater in the future and Christianity will experience the greatest danger just from those people who, at present, believe they can be called good Christians. The Christianity of Spiritual Science will experience serious attacks from the Christians in name, for all concepts must change if a true spiritual understanding of Christianity is to come about. Above all, the soul must become more and more conversant with and understanding of the legacy of the writer of the Gospel of St. John, the great school of the Virgin Sophia, the St. John's Gospel itself. Only Spiritual Science can lead us deeper into this Gospel.

In these lectures, only examples could be given showing how Spiritual Science can introduce us into the Gospel of St. John, for it is impossible to explain the whole of it. We read in the Gospel itself:

And there are also many other thing which Jesus did; and I suppose that were they all written down one after the other, the world could not contain all the books that would have to be written.

Just as the Gospel itself cannot go into all the details of the Event of Palestine, so too is it impossible for even the longest course of lectures to present the full spiritual content of the Gospel. Therefore we must be satisfied with those indications which could be given at this time; we must content ourselves with the thought that through just such indications in the course of human evolution, the true testament of Christianity becomes executed. Let us allow all this to have such an effect upon us that we may possess the power to hold fast to the foundation which we recognize in the Gospel of St. John, when others come to us and say: You are giving us too complicated concepts, too many concepts which we must first make our own in order to comprehend this Gospel. The Gospel is for the simple and naive, and one dare not approach them with many concepts and thoughts. Many say this today. They perhaps refer to another saying: "Blessed are the poor in spirit, for theirs is the kingdom of heaven." One can merely quote such a saying as long as one does not understand it, for it really says: "Blessed are the beggars in spirit, for they shall reach the kingdom of heaven within themselves." This means that those who are like beggars of the spirit, who desire to receive more and more of the spirit, will find in themselves the kingdom of heaven!

At the present time the idea is all too prevalent that everything religious is identical with all that is primitive and simple. People say: We acknowledge that science possesses many and complicated ideas, but we do not grant the same to faith and religion. Faith and religion—so say many "Christians"—must be simple and naive! They demand this. And many rely upon a conception which is little quoted perhaps, but which in the present is haunting the minds of men and which Voltaire, one of the great teachers of materialism, has expressed in the words: "Whoever wishes to be a prophet must find believers, for what he asserts must be believed, and only what is simple, what is always repeated in its simplicity, that alone finds believers."

This is often so with the prophets, both true and false. They take the trouble to say something and to repeat it again and again and the people learn to believe it because it is constantly repeated. The representative of Spiritual Science desires to be no such prophet. He does not wish to be a prophet at all. And although it may often be said: "Yes, you not only repeat, but you are always elucidating things from other sides, you are always discussing them in other ways." When they speak thus to him, he is guilty of no fault. A prophet wishes that people believe in him. Spiritual Science has no desire to lead to *belief*, but to *knowledge*. Therefore let us take Voltaire's utterance in another way. He says: "The *simple* is *believed* and is the concern of the prophet." Spiritual Science says: the *manifold* is *known*. Let us try to understand more and more that Spiritual Science is something that is manifold—not a creed, but a path to knowledge, and consequently it bears within it the manifold. Therefore let us not shrink from collecting a great deal in order that we may understand one of the most important Christian documents, the Gospel of St. John.

We have attempted to assemble the most varied material which places us in the position of being able to understand more and more the profound truths of this Gospel; able to understand how the physical mother of Jesus was an external manifestation, an external image of the Virgin Sophia; to understand what spiritual importance the Virgin Sophia had for the pupil of the Mysteries, whom the Christ loved; again to understand how, for the other Evangelists—who view the bodily descent of Jesus as important—the physical father plays his significant part when it was a question of the external imprint of the God-idea in the blood; and further, to understand what significance the Holy Spirit had for John, the Holy Spirit through which the Christ was begotten in the body of Jesus and dwelt therein during the three years and which is symbolized for us in the descent of the Dove at the Baptism by John.

If we understand that we must call the father of Christ Jesus the Holy Spirit who begot the Christ in the bodies of Jesus, then if we are able to comprehend a thing from all sides, we shall find it easy to understand that those disciples who were less highly initiated could not give us so profound a picture of the Events of

Palestine as the Disciple whom the Lord loved. And if people, at present, speak of the Synoptics—which are the only authoritative Gospels for them—this only shows that they do not have the will to rise to an understanding of the true form of the Gospel of St. John. For everybody resembles the God he understands. If we try to make into a feeling, into an experience, what we can learn from Spiritual Science about the Gospel of St. John, we shall then find that this Gospel is not a text-book, *but a force which can be active within our souls*.

If these short lectures have aroused in you the feeling that this Gospel contains not only what we have been discussing here, but that indirectly, through the medium of words, it contains the force which can develop the soul itself further, then what was really intended in these lectures has been rightly understood. Because in them, not only was something intended for the understanding, for the intellectual capacity of understanding, but that which takes its roundabout path through this intellectual capacity of understanding should condense into feelings and inner experiences, and these feelings and experiences should be a result of the facts that have been presented here. If, in a certain sense, this has been rightly understood, we shall also comprehend what is meant when it is said that the Movement for Spiritual Science has the mission of raising Christianity into Wisdom, of rightly understanding Christianity, indirectly through spiritual wisdom. We shall understand that Christianity is only in the beginning of its activity, and its true mission will be fulfilled when it is understood in its true spiritual form. The more these lectures are understood in this way, the more have they been comprehended in the sense in which they were intended.

V
SOCIETY AND
EDUCATION

The Goetheanum, designed by Rudolf Steiner in 1923 as the center for the Anthroposophical Society. Photo by Hans Gross, Basel, Switzerland.

Society and Education

INTRODUCTION

The Spiritual Basis of Society and Education

According to Rudolf Steiner, society, or the social order, consists of three separate but mutually dependent spheres: economic, political or rights, and the cultural-spiritual. This third sphere includes religion, science, arts, and education. The essential characteristic of the cultural-spiritual realm, and therefore of education, is human freedom. Within the cultural-spiritual sphere, education requires, and in turn enhances, the individual's freedom within the economic and political spheres. In Steiner's view, all three spheres of society benefit from education but only the cultural-spiritual sphere should exercise influence over education and then only in a way compatible with a true understanding of human development. Although Steiner argues that the needs of society will be ideally met by a system of education such as Waldorf, the basis and aim of his pedagogy is the child. All of Steiner's suggestions for curriculum and pedagogy issue from his understanding of child development. If his suggestions seem unusual, and perhaps controversial, the difference of opinion will rightly revolve around conflicting interpretations of the inner life of the child. Similarly, objections to Steiner's social theories will ultimately focus on his contention that the ideal social order is, or ought to be, determined by the spiritual needs of each individual. With respect to both education and society, Steiner's suggestions are concrete, detailed, and consistently based on his reading of spiritual developments.

Two examples, one concerning child development and one concerning the mission of the child in the adult world, may prove instructive. One of the best known, and least understood, features of Waldorf education is its reluctance to teach reading to children until they are seven years old, or more accurately until their teeth begin to change. Obviously, this is a topic which lends itself to ridicule: critics and skeptics have no doubt noted that children do not read with their teeth. What now appears to be dogma was presented by Steiner as a supersensible observation of what is happening in the inner life, and reflected in the physical life of the child. The change of teeth is not significant in itself, but it signals the important change taking place in the child at this time. The inner significance of the change of teeth, which is an important topic in the three chapters from *The Roots of Education* reprinted below, is well summarized at the beginning of the fourth lecture in the same book:

We have been speaking of how reading and writing can be taught in accordance with the needs of the soul and spirit of the child. Now if you can come to an inner understanding of the relationship of soul and spirit to the physical body at the change of teeth, then you will not only see the truth of what has been said, but you will be able to work it out in practical details.

Up to the change of teeth the child lives entirely in his senses. He gives himself up to his environment and is thus by nature religious. But at the change of teeth the senses, which permeate the whole being of the little child, now come to the surface; they separate off from the rest of the organism and go on their separate ways, as it were. This means that the soul and spirit are freed from the physical body and the child can develop its own inner nature. The soul and spirit become independent, but you must remember that the soul and spirit are not really intellectual until puberty, for the intellect does not take its natural place in the child's development until then. Before that time the child has no power to meet an appeal to the intellect. His powers of comprehension and whole activity of soul between the change of teeth and puberty have a pictorial quality. It is a kind of aesthetic comprehension which we may characterize in the following way: Up to the change of teeth the child wants to imitate what is happening around him, what is being done in front of him. He exerts his activities in such a way, both in general and in individual instances, that he enters into an inward and loving relationship with all that is around him. This alters at the change of teeth, for then the child no longer goes by what he sees, but by what is being revealed in the teacher's feelings and mood of soul. (pp. 66–67)

Steiner's discussion of the significance of the change of teeth at age seven is but one of many examples of his attempt to explain an inner spiritual development by reference to physical change. Puberty, of course, is another important example concerning which Steiner lectured at length. Steiner also offered many important observations concerning the transformation which takes place between age twenty and twenty-one—specifically, the birth of the "I," or spirit, in the individual, and the consequent ability to chart one's free spiritual life. Steiner discussed from a spiritual perspective all of the stages of transition beginning with birth and proceeding every seven years through the change of teeth at age seven, puberty at age fourteen, descent of spirit at age twenty-one, and through each seven-year phase until death. All of these phases, and the appropriate educational processes which ought to accompany them, take place in a social context which Steiner also reads from the vantage point of spiritual perception.

We turn now to the second example of Steiner's inner view, this one concerned with the social significance of the special message brought to humanity through the spiritual instrumentality of the child. In the first lecture in *The Inner Aspect of the Social Question*, the volume from which the second lecture is reprinted below, Steiner explains the inner meaning of the deep and rewarding relationship between adults and the child. We are all familiar with the special relationship that can develop between the child and an older adult. We are as capable of observing this special relationship as we are of observing the change of teeth in a seven-year-old. The outer meaning in both cases is clear, and for most observers entirely satisfying. For those who wish an inner, spiritual meaning, Steiner offers an account of the adult-child relationship which is based on his reading of spiritual destiny in the same way that his understanding of the change of teeth is based on his understanding of the spiritual progression of the individual. Briefly, Steiner indicates that as a kind of substitute for the old clairvoyance, entirely lost to our contemporary state of consciousness, the child brings to humanity, specifically to the individuals who enter into a loving relationship with a child, some indication of the spiritual sense which humanity needs and which it can observe in or through the child. He writes:

A great deal that was formerly revealed through atavistic clairvoyance now remains hidden from a person who pays attention only to himself, who seeks for knowledge only within himself. It remains hidden from the cradle to the grave. This is also a consequence of the state of consciousness belonging to our age. We can strive for clear insight, yet much remains hidden—and precisely in the realm where we need to see clearly. This is a special characteristic of our time: we enter the world as children bearing some quality which is important for the world, for the social life of humanity, for the understanding of history. But we cannot reach a knowledge of this, not in childhood, or in maturity, or in old age, if we remain shut up in ourselves. Knowledge of it, however, can be reached in a different way. We can reach it if we look at the child with finely-tuned perception, and realize that in the child is revealed something which the child does not and cannot ever know, but which *can* be understood by the soul of another person who in old age gazes on the child. It is something revealed *through* the child—not to the child himself and not to the man or woman who the child becomes but to the *other* person who from a later age looks with real love on his youngest contemporaries.

I draw special attention to this, my dear friends, so that from this characteristic of our age you may see how a *social* impulse, in the broadest sense, weaves and surges through our time. Is there not something profoundly social in this necessity: the necessity which ordains that life becomes fruitful only when age seeks its highest goal through fellowship with youth—the fellowship not merely of this or that man with another, but of the old with the very young? (pp. 21–22).

This is the second example, among many possible examples, of Steiner's reading an inner or spiritual meaning in externally observable phenomena. As in all of Steiner's thought and work, his indications for spiritual truth in the two areas of society and education are intended as disclosures which await verification by future observers. Steiner in effect says: let future spiritual scientists observe the validity of my spiritual perception, and let the scientist limited to empirical observation note the extent to which observable phenomena not only correspond to, but are illumined by, the insights of Spiritual Science. This approach will become more obvious both in the following selections and in the discussions of Steiner's theories of society and education found in the Guide to Further Reading ("Social Sciences" and "Education").

Applications in Society and Education

In his Foreword to Rudolf Steiner's *The Boundaries of Natural Science*, Nobel Laureate Saul Bellow states that we cannot begin to think of social renewal until we begin to attain knowledge of the spiritual and raise to consciousness what we would otherwise do unconsciously. Bellow agrees with Steiner and Owen Barfield in viewing the modern West as a world of outsides without insides. Bellow recommends Steiner as an initiate whose experience and teaching will help the West to move beyond the boundaries of materially bound scientific thinking to the imaginative and free experience of psychic and spiritual forces. He warns that failure to develop a closer, truer relation to the external world and to the interior self will leave a civilization characterized by quantities without qualities, of souls devoid of mobility and of communities which are more dead than alive.

Throughout his writings on society and education, as well as in his lectures of 1920 recently published as *The Boundaries of Natural Science*, Steiner seeks to solve the double problem of society and education by recommending imagination, inspiration, and intuition. As explained in Steiner's basic works, imagination is cultivated by the etheric body, inspiration by the astral body, and intuition by the Ego or "I." In its attempt to enable the student to learn in a way appropriate to his or her development, Waldorf education treats these three progressively advanced modes of knowledge as the distinctive goals of the second, third, and fourth seven-year stages of development. The curriculum and pedagogy of the second stage, ages seven to fourteen, emphasizes imagination. The teacher's task in working with students of this age-range is to transform, with the aid of pictures, stories, and imaginative experience, the intellectual content of the elementary school curriculum. For children of these ages, science and history, as well as music and art, ought to be activities rich in personal and imaginative experience. This approach, under the direction of a teacher who advances through each grade with his or her class, the feeling for knowledge is rooted in exact imagination which will prepare each student in later years for the scientific study of the facts and laws of life.

With the development of the astral body during puberty, the student is capable of inspired knowledge—scientific and artistic knowledge rooted in direct experience of laws and relationships underlying phenomena (the same phenomena experienced in the earlier grades through stories). Again, the arts and sciences, literature and history, are treated as complementary ways of enabling the student to develop an imaginative and inspired knowledge of the world, and of his or her own rapidly changing personal history. When, approximately at age twenty-one, the "I" incarnates in the person, one gains the capacity and responsibility for self-education. However imperfectly, the young adult enters in a new way on the double task of harmonizing the self and developing a creative relationship to the external world. This life task, which Steiner refers to as intuition, is at once the aim of Waldorf education and the restoration of a holistic, integral thinking so needed in the contemporary world. In this respect, the details of Waldorf pedagogy issue from, serve, and impact on the larger question of social values. A few examples will be useful.

If, as Steiner and others agree, personal and social life in the modern West are disabled by several dualisms, including thinking/feeling, inner/outer, physical/spiritual, scientific/artistic, then the teaching of physics through acoustics, and acoustics through the experience of qualitatively different sounds, might have a significance that transcends a Waldorf high school classroom. In the classroom of an intuitive and well-trained Waldorf teacher, students can experience the interplay of the threefold social order through a disciplined exercise with primary colors. In earlier grades, these students learn to take responsibility for the artistic as well as organizational and conceptual quality of their work by generating their own textbooks. Instead of monotonous workbooks, the children listen to stories, read and perform them, and write their own stories accompanied by drawings and watercolor paintings. As they learn rhythm and pattern by knitting, and sound qualities by playing recorders that they craft in shop, they combine botany and art by rendering leaves, plants, and other living forms in artistic creations. In later classes, they will study projective as well Euclidean geometry, and express the complex visual relationships through equally complex and artful drawings. These and countless other examples help to show the myriad ways in which the scientific, social, and artistic aspects of experience and knowledge are given their distinctive and interdependent functions.

For many adults stifled by conventional educational methods, it may prove difficult to develop a capacity for intuition, or even imagination. More shocking, however, are the lost and failed opportunities for growth in a preschool child whose imagination, whose attention to sight and sound, whose ability to focus and take responsibility for learning, are already limited by television, mechanical toys, and the standard retinue of automatic, unengaging substitutes for the world of play and imagination.

These examples of Waldorf curriculum and pedagogy are important not in themselves, but as a way of pointing back to a spiritual base and ahead to practical applications. Steiner regarded Waldorf education as an example of the kind of educational advance that is possible when teacher and educational philosophy are rooted in a spiritual awareness of the child and the learning process. He did not intend the Waldorf School movement to spread worldwide, or to become an enormous system, but rather he wanted his countless pedagogical and curriculum indications to serve as a model for future experiments in educational processes based on the true development of the child. Whether or not Steiner would have been pleased or impressed by the fact that fifty thousand students are now educated in five hundred Waldorf schools, and that new schools are being founded at an astonishing rate, he would surely have insisted that the real test of Waldorf education lies in the degree to which its students learn to replace the dead thinking of modern Western scientism and commercialism by a thinking that is alive, whole, imaginative, and socially sensitive. Like Spiritual Science, of which it is a practical application, Waldorf education should be judged by the quality of its influence on individuals and on society.

Interestingly, a high percentage of the parents of Waldorf School students know as little about Steiner or his philosophy, spiritual or educational, as do their grade-school children. In Waldorf schools, students neither read Steiner's writings nor learn of his ideas—except, ordinarily, that he developed the discipline of movement called eurythmy, which is taught in all Waldorf schools. The following selections from Steiner's *The Roots of Education* provide an introductory account for parents and others interested in Waldorf education. However, without the spiritual base, a commitment to imagination (scientific as well as artistic) and a concern for the inner development of each child, Waldorf education will seem another method, another technique, another one-sided experiment—precisely the fate that Rudolf Steiner and the vast majority of Waldorf School teachers have sought to avoid.

The Inner Aspect of the Social Question*

A week ago I was saying that we here, as anthroposophists, are able to grasp in a much deeper sense all that is necessary for reaching a judgment on the burning questions of the present day. We can do much more in this way than is possible in wider circles. In a sense we can look on ourselves as a kind of leaven—if I may use the biblical word—so that everyone in his own situation may try to contribute something, out of a strong warmth of impulse, towards the needs of the time.

If we recall what has been said as the keynote of the public lectures, we shall appreciate that the immediate essential is to strive towards a certain differentiation—a certain "membering"— of the social organism. I say always "strive towards"—there is no question of wanting to effect a revolutionary change overnight. We must strive towards a differentiation of a great deal which under modern influences has become centralized. What we must work for—instead of the so-called unitary State—is that a certain realm of society, embracing all that has to do with *spiritual life*, should unfold freely and independently alongside the other realms. This realm will include the upbringing of children, education, art, literature, and also (as I have remarked already and shall mention in the public lecture tomorrow) everything concerned with the administration of civil and criminal law.

As a second "limb" of the social organism we should recognize, but in a restricted sense, that which has been known as the "State." It is precisely on the shoulders of this "State" that men

---

* From Charles Davy, trans., *The Inner Aspect of the Social Question* (London: Rudolf Steiner Press, 1974), pp. 23–47.

nowadays want to pile as much as possible—State schools, State childcare, and so on. That has been the great tendency of the last four hundred years. And today, under the influence of social ideas and socialistic thinking, people want to weld economic life into a single whole with political life. These two realms must be separated once more. The *political* State must stand on its own independent ground, as the second sphere of society; and the same relative independence must distinguish the realm of domestic economy, where commodities circulate—that is, economic life.

Now, my dear friends, we will look at this question from a point of view not easily reached by anyone outside our movement. And we will carry the matter to a certain culmination, so that out of this culmination a deeper understanding of the human situation today may spring forth.

Let us look first at what is called, in an earthly sense, spiritual life. Spiritual life in this earthly sense embraces everything which in one way or another lifts us out of our solitary egoism and draws us into community with other human beings. Let us take, as the most important manifestation of earthly spiritual life for most people still, that aspect of it which should bring us into relation with superearthly spirtitual life—I mean the practice of religion, as this takes its course in the various congregations.

In the human soul are needs which cause people to seek each other out; people are united by experiencing similar needs. The upbringing of a child means that one soul is caring for another. Anyone who reads a book is drawn out of the egoistic circle of his individual life, for it is not he alone who absorbs the author's thoughts; even when he is only halfway through a book he is already sharing these thoughts with a great company of other readers. And so, through this kinship of soul-experience, a certain human community is formed. This is an important characteristic of spiritual life: it has its springs in freedom, in the individual initiative of the single human being, and yet it draws men together, and forms communities out of what they have in common.

Here, for anyone who seeks deeper understanding, is a fact to be kept in mind—a fact which brings every kind of human fellowship into relation with the central event of earth-evolution—the Mystery of Golgotha. For since the Mystery of Golgotha everything concerned with human fellowship belongs in a sense to the Christ Impulse. That is the essential thing—the Christ Impulse belongs not to single men but to the fellowship of men. In truth, according to the mind of Christ Himself, it is a great mistake to suppose that the solitary individual can establish a direct relation with Christ. The essential thing is that Christ lived and died, and rose from the dead, for humanity as a whole. Since the Mystery of Golgotha, therefore, the Christ Event is immediately relevant (we shall return to this point) wherever human fellowship unfolds. And accordingly, for anyone who really understands the world, the earthly spiritual life which springs from the most individual source, from personal circumstances and gifts, leads to the Christ Event.

Let us now first consider this earthly spiritual life—religion, education, art and so forth—on its own account. We gain through it a certain connection with other human beings. Here we must distinguish between the connections we form through our individual destiny and karma, and those which in this narrow sense are not dependent on our karma. Some of the connections we establish in the course of life are the direct outcome of relationships formed in earlier lives; some will bear karmic fruit in future lives. Human beings form connections with one another in manifold ways. The connections formed directly through our karma must be distinguished from the wider connections that arise when we meet people through joining a society, or a religious body or a fellowship of belief, and also from those that come through reading the same book or through common enjoyment of a work of art, and so on. The people we encounter in these ways on earth are not always related to us karmically from an earlier life. Certainly, there are communities which point to a common destiny in earlier lives; but with the wider groupings of which I have just spoken it is generally not so. This brings us to a further point.

Towards the end of our time in the supersensible world, between death and a new birth, when we reach the period just before our next incarnation, we enter into relations—as far as we are ripe for them—with Angels, Archangels and Archai, and with the higher Hierarchies as well. But also we come near to other human souls, due to be incarnated later than ourselves—souls which have to wait longer, one may say, for their incarnations. During this period we have a whole range of supersensible experiences to go through, according to our individual stage of development, before we are plunged again into earthly life. And the forces we thus receive place us on earth in the situation which will enable us to find our way into those experiences of earthly spiritual life of which I have just spoken.

The essential point to grasp is that our spiritual life on earth— all that we experience through religion, or through upbringing and education, through artistic impressions and so on—is not determined solely by earthly circumstances. Our earthly spiritual life takes its character from the experiences we have had in supersensible realms before birth. Just as an image in a mirror indicates what is being reflected, so does earthly spiritual life point to what the human being has experienced before entering his physical body.

Nothing on earth stands towards the supersensible world in so intimate, real and living a relationship as this earthly spiritual life—which indeed shows aberrations, many aberrations . . . but these very aberrations have a relation full of meaning to all that we experience—certainly, in a quite different way—in the supersensible. This connection with pre-earthly life places spiritual life on earth in a quite special situation. Nothing else in earthly life is so closely bound up with our life before birth!

This is a fact to which the spiritual investigator is bound to draw particular attention. He distinguishes spiritual life from man's other earthly activities, because supersensible observation shows him that spiritual life on earth has its roots and impulse in the life before birth. So for the spiritual investigator this earthly spiritual life marks itself off from other human experiences.

It is different with what can be called, in a strict sense, political life, the life of civic rights, which brings administrative order into human affairs. You see, however hard one may try to discover, with the most exact methods of spiritual science, the deeper connections of political life . . . one can find no relation between this political life and the supersensible. Political life is entirely of the earth! We must clearly understand what this signifies.

For example, what shall we take as a preeminently earthly type of legal relationship? The relation to property, to ownership. If I own a plot of land, then it is solely by political means that I am given an exclusive right and tenure of the land. It is this which enables me to exclude all others from using the land, building on it, etc. So it is with everything that has to do with public law. The sum total of public law, together with the means taken to protect a society from external interference—all that makes up political life in the strict sense.

This is the genuine earth-life—the life connected solely with impulses which take their course between birth and death. However much the State may imagine itself to be God-given . . . the truth to which all religious creeds, in their deeper meaning, bear witness is as follows. The first truth was conveyed by Christ Jesus when in the old phraseology he said: "Render unto Caesar the things that are Caesar's, and to God the things that are God's." Faced with the pretensions of the Roman Empire, He wished above all to separate everything to do with political life from all that bears the imprint of the supersensible. But when the purely earthly State seeks to make itself the bearer of a superearthly impulse—when, for example, the State seeks to assume responsibility for religious life, or for education (this last responsibility, unfortunately, is taken for granted in our day)—then we have the situation characterized by the deeper teachings of religion, when they said: Wherever an attempt is made to mix the spiritual-supersensible with the earthly-political, there rules the usurping Prince of this world.

What is the meaning of the "usurping Prince of this world?" You know, perhaps, my dear friends, that people have thought a great deal about this, without getting anywhere. Only through spiritual science can one reach the meaning. The usurping Prince of this world rules whenever an authority which should be concerned only with the ordering of earthly affairs arrogates to itself the spiritual—and seeks also, as we shall see later, to assimilate economic life. The rightful Prince of this world is he for whom the political realm includes only those things which belong wholly to the life between birth and death.

So we have come to an understanding of the second "limb" of the social organism, in the sense of spiritual science. It is the realm orientated towards those impulses which run their course between birth and death.

Now we come to the third, the economic realm. Just think, my dear friends, how economic life draws us into a particular relation with the world. You will readily understand what this relation is if you compel yourselves to imagine that it were possible for us to be entirely absorbed in economic life. If that could happen, what should we be like? We should be thinking animals, nothing else. We are not thinking animals for the reason that besides economic life we have a life of rights—a political life—and a knowledge of the spirit, an earthly spiritual life. Through economic life we are thus plunged, more or less, into the midst of human relationships. And because of this, interests are kindled. Precisely in this field of human relations we are able to develop interests which in the true sense of the word are fraternal. In no other realm than that of economic life are fraternal relationships so easily and obviously developed among human beings.

In the spiritual life . . . what is the ruling impulse in earthly spiritual life? Fundamentally, it is personal interest—an interest arising out of the soul-nature, certainly, but none the less egoistic. Of religion, people demand that it shall make them holy. Of education, that it shall develop their talents. Of any kind of artistic representation, that it shall bring pleasure into their lives, and perhaps also stimulate their inner energies. As a general rule, it is egoism, whether of a grosser or more refined sort, which leads a person—quite understandably—to seek in spiritual life whatever satisfies *himself*.

In the political life of rights, on the other hand, we have to do with something which makes us all equal before the law. We are concerned with the relation of man to man. We have to ask what our rights should be. No question of rights exists among animals. In this respect, also, we are raised above the animals, even in our earthly affairs. But if we are connected with a religious community, or with a group of teachers, then—just as much as in civic relationships—we come up against personal claims, personal wishes. In the economic sphere, it is through the overcoming of self that something valuable, not derived from personal desires, comes to expression—brotherhood, responsibility for others, a way of living so that the other man gains experience through us.

In the spiritual life we receive according to our desires. In the sphere of rights we make a claim to something we need in order to make sure of a satisfactory human life as an equal among equals. And in the economic sphere is born that which unites men in terms of feeling: that is, brotherhood. The more this brotherhood is cultivated, the more fruitful economic life becomes. And the impulse towards brotherhood arises when we establish a certain connection between our property and another's, between our need and another's, between something we have and something another has, and so on.

This fraternity, this brotherly relation between men which must radiate through economic life if health is to prevail there, may be thought of as a kind of emanation rising from the economic sphere—and in such a way that if we absorb it into ourselves we are able to take it with us through the gate of death and carry it into the supersensible life after death.

On earth, economic life looks like the lowest of the three social spheres, yet precisely from this sphere arises an impulse which works on into superearthly realms after death. That is how the third member of the social organism presents itself in the light of Spiritual Science. Its character is such that in a certain sense it drives us into regions below the human level; yet in fact this is a blessing, since from the fraternity of economic life we carry through the gate of death something which remains with us when we enter the supersensible world. Just as earthly spiritual life points backward, like a mirrored image, to supersensible spiritual life before birth, so does economic life, with all that arises from its influence on men—social interests, feeling for human fellowship, brotherhood—so does economic life point forward to supersensible life after death.

Thus we have distinguished the three social spheres, in the light of spiritual science: spiritual life, pointing back to supersensible life before birth; political life, bound up with the impulses which take their course between birth and death; and economic life pointing forward to the experiences we shall encounter when we have passed through the gate of death.

Now, just as it is true that the being of man belongs not only to earthly but to superearthly realms—that he bears in himself the fruits of his prenatal life in the supersensible, and develops in himself the seeds (if I may use this image) of the experiences that will be his in the life after death—just as it is true that in this connection human life is threefold, unfolding on earth between these two reflections of the superearthly, so in truth must the social organism be itself "three-membered" if it is to serve as foundation for human soul-life as a whole.

For those, accordingly, who through Spiritual Science understand man's place in the cosmos, there are much deeper reasons for recognizing that the social organism must have a threefold structure, and that if everything is centralized, if everything is piled on to a chaotically jumbled social life, then man is bound to degenerate . . . as indeed in modern life he has, in some respects, which has led on to the frightful catastrophe of the last four years.*

You see: to grasp human life in such a way as to realize that every human fellowship is inwardly related to the whole of humanity and to the wider world—this is what ought more and more to come home to men from the deepening of spiritual-scientific knowledge. This is also the true Christ-Knowledge for our time and the immediate future. That is what we shall learn if we are willing, today, to listen to the Christ. He Himself said—I have often quoted it: "I am with you always, even unto the end of the world." This means: Christ did not speak only during His time on earth; His utterance continues, and we must continue to listen for it. We should not wish merely to read the Gospels (though certainly they ought to be read over and over again); we should listen to the living revelation that springs from His continued presence among us. In this epoch He declares to us: "Make new your ways of thinking" (as His forerunner, John the Baptist said: "Change your thinking"), so that they may reveal to you man's threefold nature which demands also that your social environment on earth shall have a threefold membering."

You see, it is absolutely true to say: The Christ died and rose again for the whole of mankind; the Mystery of Golgotha is an

---

* World War I. —ED.

event which concerns the whole of humanity. At the present time it is particularly necessary to be aware of that—at this time when nation has risen against nation in savage struggle, and when even now, after events have led on to a crisis, we find no thoughtfulness, no consciousness of the community of mankind, but on manifold sides a delirium of victory! Make no mistake: all that we have lived through in the last four years, all that we are experiencing now and have still to experience—to anyone who looks below the surface all this shows that mankind has reached a kind of crisis with regard to knowledge of the Christ. And the reason for this is that the true spirit of fellowship, the true relationship between men, has been lost. And it is very necessary that men should ask themselves: How can we find our way again to the Christ-Impulse?

A simple fact will show that the way is not always found. Before the Christ-Impulse entered into earth-evolution through the Mystery of Golgotha, the people from whom Christ Jesus was born looked on themselves as the chosen people, and they believed that happiness would come to the world only if all other peoples were to die away, and their own stock to spread over the entire face of the earth. In a certain sense that was a well-founded belief, for Jehovah, the God of this people, had chosen it as *his* people, and Jehovah was regarded as the one and only God. In the time before the Mystery of Golgotha this was a justified perception for the old Hebrew people, since out of this old Hebrew people Christ Jesus was to emerge. But with the enactment of the Mystery of Golgotha this way of thinking should have come to an end. After that, it was out of date: in place of the recognition of Jehovah should have come the recognition of Christ—the recognition which compels one to speak always of *humanity,* just as, for those who looked up to Jehovah, one people only was in question. Not to have understood that is the tragic fate of the Jewish people. Today, however, we are coming up against all sorts of reversions. What is it but a reversion when every nation—though it may suppose itself to be doing something quite different and may use other names—wants to worship a sort of Jehovah, a special national goal of its own!

Certainly, the old religious formulae are no longer used, but the outcome of present-day mentality is that every nation wants to set up its own national god and so confine itself within a strictly national existence. And the inevitable result is that nation rages against nation! We are experiencing a reversion to the old Jehovah-religion—with the difference that the Jehovah-religion is breaking up into a multitude of Jehovah-religions. Today we are really confronted with an atavistic reversion to the Old Testament. Humanity is bent on dividing itself up into separate sections all over the earth—quite contrary to the spirit of Christ Jesus, who lived and stood for the whole of humanity. Humanity is trying to organize itself under the sign of national deities, Jehovah fashion. Before the Mystery of Golgotha that was quite proper; now it is a reversion. This must be clearly understood: the way of nationalism is a reversion to the Old Testament.

This reversion is preparing heavy ordeals for mankind, and against it only one remedy will suffice: to draw near once more to the Christ by the path of the spirit.

Those concerned with Spiritual Science are therefore bound essentially to ask the question: How, out of the depths of our own hearts and souls, under the conditions of the present time, shall we find Christ Jesus?

This is a very serious question (I have often spoken of it before from other points of view in this group), as you can see from the fact that many official exponents of Christianity have lost the Christ! There are plenty of well-known parsons, pastors, etc., who talk about the Christ. The burden of their discourse is that men can reach the Christ through a certain deepening of the inner life, a certain inner experience. But if one comes close to what these people mean by the Christ, one finds that no distinction is made between this Christ and God in general—the Father-God, in the sense of the Gospels.

You will agree that Harnack, for example, is a celebrated theologian. He is emulated by many here in Switzerland. Harnack has published a small book, *The Nature of Christianity;* in it he speaks a great deal about the Christ. But what he says concerning Christ . . . why should it apply to Christ? It could apply just as well to the Jehovah-God. For this reason the whole book, *The Nature of Christianity,* is inwardly untruthful. It would become truthful only if it were hebraicized—if it were so translated that wherever the word "Christ" stands, "Jehovah" were written instead.

This is a truth of which people today have scarcely any inkling. From countless pulpits all over the world Christ is spoken of, and people believe simply because they hear the word 'Christ,' that the preacher is really speaking about the Christ. They never come to the point of thinking: "Strike out the word 'Christ' from what the pastor says and substitute 'Jehovah'—that and nothing less will make it right!" You see, a definite untruth lies at the root of the deepest ailments of our time.

Do not think that in saying this I want to accuse or criticize any individual. That is not so. My wish is simply to bring out the facts. For those persons who often fall into the deepest inner untruth—one could even say, into an inner lie—have thoroughly good intentions, in their own way. It is hard today for humanity to reach the truth, since what I have called an inner untruth has an exceptionally strong backing of tradition. And this inner untruth, which has come to prevail in immeasurably wide circles, gives rise to another, so that in the most diverse realms of life the question is asked: Is anything still true? Where is any genuine truth left?

For this reason, those who are striving along the path of Spiritual Science are specially moved to ask earnestly: How shall I find the true way to the Christ—to that unique Divine Being Who may rightly be called the Christ?

Indeed, if here on earth our soul-life follows customary lines of development from birth to death, then we have no inducement to come to the Christ. We may be as spiritual as we like: we have no inducement to come to the Christ!

If, without doing a certain thing—which I will indicate in a moment—we simply pass on from birth to death, as most people do today, we remain far from the Christ. How, then, do we come to the Christ?

The impulse to take the way to the Christ—even though it be ofttimes an impulse rising from the subconscious or from an obscure realm of feeling—must come from ourselves. Any person who is normally healthy can come to the God whom we have identified with the Jehovah-principle. Not to find the Jehovah-God is nothing else than a sort of illness in mankind. To deny God, to be an athiest, means that you are in some way ill. Anyone who has developed normally and healthily cannot be a denier of God, for it is merely laughable to believe that the healthy human organism can have other than a divine origin. The *Ex Deo Nascimur* is something which declares itself to a healthily developed man in the course of human life. For if he does not recognize—*I am born out of the Divine*—then he must have some defect, which expresses itself in the fact that he becomes an athiest. But to come to that generalized conception of the Divine, which out of inner falsehood is called Christ by modern pastors—that is not to come to the Christ.

We come to the Christ only—and here I am speaking with special reference to the immediate present—if we go beyond customary conditions of health, given by nature. For we know that the Mystery of Golgotha was enacted on earth because mankind would not have been able to maintain a worthy human status without the Mystery of Golgotha—that is, without finding its way to the Christ-Impulse. And so we must not merely discover our human nature between birth and death: we must rediscover it, if we are to be Christians in the true sense, able to draw near to the Christ. And this rediscovery of our human nature must take place in the following way. We must strive for the inner honesty—we must nerve ourselves to the inner honesty—to say: "Since the Mystery of Golgotha we have not been born free from prejudice with regard to our world of thought—we are all born with certain prejudices." If we regard the human being as perfect, after the manner of Rousseau or in any other way, we can by no means find the Christ. This is possible only if we know that the human being living since the Mystery of Golgotha has a certain defect, for which he must compensate through his own activity during his life here on earth. I am born a prejudiced person, and freedom from prejudice in my thinking is something I have to achieve during life.

And how can I achieve it? The one and only way is this: instead of taking an interest merely in my own way of thinking, and in what *I* consider right, I must develop a selfless interest in every opinion I encounter, however strong I may hold it to be mistaken. The more a man prides himself on his own dogmatic opinions and is interested only in them, the further he removes himself, at this moment of world-evolution, from the Christ. The more he develops a social interest in the opinions of other men, even though he considers them erroneous—the more light he receives into his own thinking from the opinions of others—the more he does to fulfill in his inmost soul a saying of Christ, which today must be interpreted in the sense of the new Christ-language.

Christ said: "Inasmuch as ye have done it unto one of the least of these my brethren, ye have done it unto me." The Christ never ceases to reveal Himself anew to men—even unto the end of earthly time. And thus He speaks today to those willing to listen: "In whatever the least of your brethren thinks, you must recognize that I am thinking in him; and that I enter into your feeling, whenever you bring another's thought into relation with your own, and whenever you feel a fraternal interest for what is passing in another's soul. Whatever opinion, whatever outlook on life, you discover in the least of your brethren, therein you are seeking Myself."

So does the Christ speak to our life of thought—the Christ Who desires to reveal Himself in a new way—the time for it is drawing near—to the men of the twentieth century. Not in such a way that people should speak in Harnack's style of the God who may equally well be the Jehovah-God, and is in fact nothing else, but so that it may be known: Christ is the God for all men. We shall not find Him if we remain egotistically bound up with our own thoughts, but only if we relate our own thoughts to those of other men, if we expand our interest to embrace, with inner tolerance, everything human, and say to ourselves: "Through the fact of my birth I am a prejudiced person; only through being reborn into an all-embracing feeling of fellowship for the thoughts of all men shall I find in myself the impulse which is, in truth, the Christ-Impulse. If I do not look on myself alone as the source of everything I think, but recognize myself, right down into the depths of my soul, as a member of the human community"—then, my dear friends, one way to the Christ lies open. This is the way which must today be characterized as the *way to the Christ through thinking.* Earnest self-training so that we gain a true perception for estimating the thoughts of others, and for correcting bias in ourselves—this we must take as one of life's serious tasks. For unless this task finds place among men, they will lose the way to the Christ. This today is the way through thinking.

The other way is through the *will.* Here, too, people are much addicted to a false way, which leads not to the Christ but away from Him. And in this other realm we must find again the way to the Christ. Youth still keeps some idealism, but for the most part humanity today is dry and matter-of-fact. And men are proud of what is often called practical technique, though the expression is used in a narrow sense. Humanity today has no use for ideals which are drawn from the fountain of the spirit. Youth still has these ideals. Never was the life of older people so sharply severed from the life of the young as it is today. Lack of understanding among human beings is indeed the great mark of our time.

Yesterday I spoke of the deep gulf which exists between the proletariat and the middle class. Age and youth, too—how little they understand each other today! This is something we ought to take most seriously into account. We may try to reach an understanding with youth on the ground of its idealism. Yes, that is all very well, but today efforts are made to drive the idealism out of young people. The aim is to do this by depriving youth of the imaginative education which is given by fairytales and legends, by all that leads away from dry, external perceptions. All the same— it will not be too easy to drive all the youthful, natural, primitive idealism out of young people! But what is this youthful idealism? It is a beautiful thing, a great thing—but it ought not to be all-sufficient for human beings, for this youthful idealism is in fact bound up with the *Ex Deo Nascimur,* with that aspect of the Divine which is identical with the Jahve aspect. And that is just what must not remain sufficient, now that the Mystery of Golgotha has been enacted on earth. Something further is required— idealism must spring from inner development, from *self-education.* Besides the innate idealism of youth, we must see to it that in human society something else is achieved—precisely an *achieved idealism:* not merely the idealism that springs from the instincts and enthusiasm of youth, but one that is nurtured, gained by one's own initiative, and will not fade away with the passing of youth. This is something which opens the way to the Christ, because—once more—it is something acquired during the life between birth and death.

Feel the great difference between instinctive idealism and achieved idealism! Feel the great difference between youthful enthusiasm and the enthusiasm which springs from taking hold of the life of the spirit and can be ever and again kindled anew, because we have made it part of our soul, independently of the course of our bodily existence—then you will grasp this second idealism, which is not merely the idealism implanted in us by nature. This is the way to the Christ through *willing*, as distinct from the way through thinking.

Do not ask today for abstract ways to the Christ; ask for these concrete ways. Seek to understand the way through thinking, which consists in becoming inwardly tolerant towards the opinions of mankind at large, and developing social interest for the thoughts of other men. Seek also for the way through willing— there you will find nothing abstract, but an inescapable need to cultivate idealism in yourselves. And if you cultivate this idealism, or if you introduce it into the education of young people— which is particularly necessary—then you will have something which inspires men not to do only what the outer world impels them to do. For from this idealism arises the resolve to do *more* than the sense-world suggests—to act out of the spirit. When our actions spring from this achieved idealism we are acting in accordance with the intentions of the Christ, Who did not descend from worlds above the earth in order to achieve merely earthly ends, but came down to the earth from higher realms in order to fulfill a superearthly purpose. We shall grow towards Him only if we cultivate idealism in ourselves, so that Christ, Who represents the superearthly within the realm of earth, can work through us. Only in achieved idealism can there be realized the intention of the Pauline saying about Christ: "Not I, but Christ in me."

Anyone who refuses to develop this second idealism through a rebirth of his moral nature can say only: "Not I, but Jehovah in me." But whoever cultivates this second idealism, which must essentially be cultivated, he can say: "Not I, but Christ in me."

These are the two ways through which we can find the Christ. If we pursue them, we shall no longer speak in such a way that our speech is an inward lie. Then we shall speak of Christ as the Divine Power active in our rebirth—while Jehovah is the Divine Power active in our birth.

People today must learn to appreciate this distinction, for it is this which leads also to genuine social feeling, a genuine interest in our fellowmen. Whoever develops an achieved idealism in himself, he will have love for humankind. You may preach as much as you like from pulpits, telling men they ought to love one another: it is like preaching to a stove. The most excellent exhortations will not persuade the stove to heat the room. It will heat the room all right if you stoke it with coal—there is no need to preach to it that its ovenly duty is to heat the room. In just the same way you can keep on preaching to men—love, love, love . . . that is mere sermonizing, mere words. Strive rather that men should experience a rebirth of idealism, that besides instinctive idealism they should achieve in their souls an idealism which persists throughout life, then . . . then you will kindle a warmth of soul in the love of man for man. For as much as you nurture an idealism in yourselves, by so much will you be led in your soul life away out of egoism towards a concern for other men.

And if you follow this twofold way, the way through thinking and the way through willing, which I have shown you with regard to the renewal of Christianity, there is one thing you will certainly experience and discover. Out of a thinking which is inwardly tolerant and interested in the thoughts of others, and out of a willing reborn through the achievement of idealism, something unfolds. And this can be described only as a heightened feeling of responsibility for every action one performs.

Anyone with an inclination to examine the unfolding of his soul will feel in himself, if he follows the two ways—it is a feeling different from anything encountered in the course of an ordinary life which does not follow the two ways—this heightened and refined sense of responsibility towards everything one thinks and does. This heightened feeling of responsibility will impel one to say: Can I justify this that I am doing or thinking, not merely with reference to the immediate circumstances of my life and environment, but in the light of my responsibility towards the supersensible spiritual world? Can I justify it in the light of my knowledge that everything I do here on earth will be inscribed in an akashic record of everlasting significance, wherein its influence will work on and on? Oh, it comes powerfully home to one, this supersensible responsibility towards all things! It strikes one like a solemn warning, when one seeks the twofold way to Christ—as though a Being stood behind one, looking over one's shoulder and saying repeatedly: "Thou are not responsible only to the world around thee but also to the Divine-Spiritual, for all thy thoughts and all thy actions."

But this Being who looks over our shoulder, who heightens and refines our sense of responsibility and sets us on a new path—he is the one who first directs us truly to the Christ, Who went through the Mystery of Golgotha. It is of this Christ-Way, how it may be found and how it reveals itself through the Being I have just described, that I wanted to speak to you today. For this Christ-Way is most intimately connected with the deepest social impulses and tasks of our time.

The Roots of Education*

Lecture 1

After having so often spoken to you, here in Bern, about Anthroposophy in general, it is a special pleasure to be able to speak to you now, out of the spirit of Anthroposophy, on the subject of education—that sphere of life which must above all things lie close to the heart of man. For it is essential that we should develop an art of eduction which will lead us out of the social chaos into which we have fallen during the last few years and decades. And the only way out of this social chaos is to bring spirituality into the souls of men through education, so that out of the spirit itself men may find the way to progress and the further evolution of civilization.

We know in our hearts that this is true, for the world is created in spirit and comes forth out of spirit, and so also human creation can only be fruitful if it springs forth from the fountain head of spirit itself. But to achieve such fruitful creation out of spirit, man must be educated and taught in the spirit also. And as I believe that Anthroposophy has indeed much to say about the nature of education and teaching, it affords me great satisfaction to be able to give these lectures here.

Now there are numbers of people all over the world who feel that in education and teaching a new impetus of some kind is needed. True, in the course of the Nineteenth Century, which was full of progressive ideas, a great deal was done in the cause of education, but the tendency of recent civilization is such that man is seldom brought into touch with man himself. For many centuries we must record the most wonderful progress in the domain of

* From Helen Fox, trans., *The Roots of Education* (London: Rudolf Steiner Press, 1968), pp. 13–65. Some stylistic revisions by editor.

natural science and all the technical knowledge which has grown out of it. We have also seen how a kind of world conception has gradually been crystallized out of this scientific progress in civilization. We have seen how in the whole structure of the world man is thought of exclusively in terms of what the senses can teach us about the phenomena of nature, and what the intellect, which is connected with the brain, is able to state about the world of the senses. But all the knowledge that has been acquired in recent times about the world of nature does not really lead us to man himself. This fact is not clearly recognized today, for although great numbers of people feel that it is true they are not prepared to admit it.

And this impossibility of approaching man himself must especially be felt when we try to understand the growing human being —the child. We feel that a barrier is set up between the teacher and the child. Anthroposophy on the basis of a true and comprehensive knowledge of man would give ear to this appeal which comes to us from all sides, give ear to it, not by setting up theories about education and teaching but by showing men and women how to enter as teachers into the practical life of the school. Anthroposophical education is in reality school life in practice, and our lectures must include practical details of how to deal with this or that in teaching. But something else must come first, for if we were to begin by speaking of practical details in this way, then the spirit out of which all this is born would not be able to reveal itself. Therefore you must kindly allow me to speak today about this spirit of anthroposophical education as a kind of introduction. We shall speak of it out of a comprehensive knowledge of man, a truly penetrating knowledge of man, the active force of Anthroposophy in education.

A penetrating knowledge of man! What does this mean to us? If we have a growing human being before us, a child, it is not enough, as I have said, to have certain rules of how he should be taught and educated, and then just conform to the rules as one does in a technical science. This will never lead to good teaching. We must bring an inner fire, an inner enthusiasm, to our work; we must have impulses which are not intellectually transmitted from teacher to child according to certain rules, but which pass over from teacher to child in an intimate way. The whole of our being must work in us as educators, not only the thinking man; the man of feeling and the man of will must also play their part.

The mode of thought and world conception of natural science has taken possession of man in recent times more than he thinks. Even those who have not had a specially scientific training exercise their thinking, feeling, and willing in a scientific way. This is impossible for a teacher, for the scientific mode of thought only gives one an understanding of one member of the whole human being, namely, the physical body and body of the senses. But this is only one member of the whole human being. It is Antroposophy which shows us that if we have a true knowledge of man, we see that the human being possesses three clearly distinguished members: the physical body, the soul, and the spirit. We can only see the whole man if we have the wisdom and knowledge to recognize the soul in its true nature as clearly as we recognize the physical body; and, further, if we are able to recognize the spirit in man as an independent being. But the connections between body, soul and spirit in the child are different from those of the grown man. And it is just this loosening of the connection with the physical body that allows us to observe the soul and spirit of the child as the greatest wonder of knowledge and practical life to be found in human existence.

Let us look for a moment at the tiny child, and see how he is born into the world. Here we see a truly magical process at work. We see how spirit, welling forth out of the innermost being of the little child, flows into his undefined features, his chaotic movements, into all his actions that seem as yet so disjointed and disconnected. Order and form enter into his glance, into the movements of his face and the other members of the human body, his features gain more and more in expression. Increasingly in the eye and other features the spirit manifests itself, working from within towards the surface, and the soul which permeates the whole bodily nature is revealed. We must take a serious and unprejudiced view of these things and we can see how they come about by observing the growing child and thereby gazing reverently into the wonders and the riddles of cosmic and human existence. If we watch the child's development in this way we shall see that his life is divided into clearly differentiated epochs, and the only reason why these epochs are not usually so distinguished is that this depends on a deep and intimate knowledge, and men of today with their cruder scientific ideas are not going to give themselves the trouble of acquiring an intimate knowledge of this kind.

The first significant change in the life of a child occurs round about the seventh year when his second teeth appear. The outward physical process of the coming of the second teeth is in itself of great interest: first we have the milk teeth, then the others force their way through and the first ones are pushed out. A superficial view of this process will not get further than the actual changing of the teeth. But if we look into it more deeply with the means which will be described in this course of lectures, then we shall discover that this transformation can be observed in the whole body of the child, though in a more delicate manner than in the change of teeth itself. The changing of the teeth is the most physical and fundamental expression of a fine process which actually takes place in the whole body. For what is it that really happens? You can all see how the human organism develops; you cut your nails, you cut your hair, you find that your skin peels off. All this shows that the physical substance is cast off on the surface, and is being pushed out from within. This pushing from within, which we observe in the changing of the teeth, is present in the whole human body. A more exact knowledge will show us that in point of fact the child has gradually driven forth the body which he received by inheritance—he has cast it out. Just as the first teeth are driven forth, so the whole first body is driven forth.

At the time of the change of teeth the child stands before us with a body which, in contrast to the body he was born with, is entirely newly formed. The body of his birth has been cast forth like the first teeth, and a new body is formed. What is this more intimate process which has taken place? The child received his first body by inheritance. It is, so to speak, the product of the working together of father and mother, and is formed out of the physical conditions of the earth. But what is it, this physical body? It is the model that the earth gives to man for his true development as a human being. For the soul and spiritual part of man descends from a world of soul and spirit in which it lived before the events of conception and birth. Before we became earthly man in a physical body, we were all beings of soul and spirit in a soul and spirit world. And that which our parents give us in inherited physical substance unites itself in the embryonic life with what descends as pure spirit and soul from a higher world. The spirit and soul lay hold of the physical body that has its origin in the stream of inheritance. This physical body becomes its model, and on this model an entirely new human organism is formed, and the inherited organism is thereby driven out. So that when we consider the child between birth and the change of teeth we must say: the physical body owes its existence to physical inheritance alone, but there are then two forces which combine together to work upon this physical body: the first is the force of what the human being himself brings with him on to the earth, and the second is what he assimilates from the matter and substance of the earth itself. With the change of teeth man has fashioned a second body on the model of the inherited body, and this second body is the product of the soul and spiritual being of man.

Those who come to such conclusions as I have spoken of out of a more intimate observation of man will of course be aware of the objections which can be raised against them. These objections are obvious. One is bound to hear it said: Can you not see that a likeness to the parents often appears after the change of teeth, and that therefore man is still subject to the laws of inheritance even after the change of teeth has taken place? Many such objections could be raised. But now consider the following: We have a model that comes from the stream of inheritance. On this model the spirit and soul work out the second man. But just as when something is being built up on a model, so it must be clear that the spirit and soul of man make use of the presence of the model to build up the second human organism in likeness to it. Nevertheless, if you are able to perceive and recognize what really happens you will make the following discovery. There are certain children who show in their ninth, tenth, or eleventh year how their second organism, which has already come into being, is almost exactly similar to the first inherited organism. With other children, one sees how dissimilar this second organism is to the first, how something quite different from the first inheritance is working itself out from the center of their being. Every variation between these two extremes can appear in human life. For when the spiritual soul part of man is working out the second organism it strives, above all, to obey the being which it brings with it when it descends from the world of spirit and soul. A conflict arises between that which has to work out the second organism and that which the first organism received by inheritance. And according to whether the human being has been stronger or weaker in his spiritual and soul existence (in the following lectures we shall see why this is so) he can either give his second organism an individual form, strongly impregnated with soul forces, or, if he descends with weaker forces from the spiritual world he will keep as near as possible to the model.

But just consider what it is we have to deal with if we are to educate the child in the first epoch of life from birth to the change of teeth. With what reverence we are inspired when we see how the divine spiritual powers work down out of supersensible worlds! We see them at work from day to day, from week to week, from month to month and year to year in the first epochs of the life of the child, and we see how their work carries them right on to the formation of a second individual body. In education we take part in this work of the spirit and soul, we continue for man's physical existence what the divine spiritual forces have begun. We take part in a divine labor. Such things should not be comprehended with the intellect alone, but with the whole person. Then indeed, brought face to face, as we are, with the creative powers of the world, we can come to a feeling of the magnitude of the task of education, especially in the early years. But I should like to point out to you that the way in which the spirit and soul enter upon the work of creating a second human organism shows us how in the child the formation of the body, the working of the soul and the creation of the spirit are a unity.

All that comes to pass in the forming of the new organism and the casting forth of the old is in the child a unity of spirit, soul and body. For this reason the child reveals himself quite differently from the adult. This can be clearly observed in single instances. When we as adults have something sweet to eat, it is the tongue and palate that perceive the sweetness, and the perception of sweetness then ceases. As adults we no longer follow its further course with our taste. With the child this is different. In the child the taste permeates the whole organism; he does not taste with tongue and palate alone, he tastes with his whole organism; he draws the sweetness through his whole organism. The child is indeed completely an organ of sense. Of what does the essence of a sense organ consist? Let us take the human eye. Impressions of color are made on the eye. In considering the act of sight in the human being, anyone who regards will and perception as one in the human eye does not get beyond the surface, the periphery of the human being.

In the first years of life, from birth to the change of teeth, this activity permeates the whole organism, albeit in a delicate manner. The whole organism of the child looks upon itself as a comprehensive sense organ. That is why all impressions which work on the child from his environment affect him quite differently from the adult. What is going on in the environment and can be seen with the eye is the expression of the soul element in man, of human morality. Subconsciously, or even unconsciously, the child has a delicate and intimate capacity for perceiving what is being expressed in every movement and every action of those around him. If a choleric person gives rein to his fury in the presence of a child and lets the child see what he is doing in the unconscious way I have spoken of, then believe me, we are quite mistaken if we think that the child only sees the outward movements. The child has a clear impression of what lies within these moral actions, even if it is an unconscious impression. The sense impressions of the eye are also unconscious. All ‛impressions which are not of the senses, but which are expressions of the moral and soul life, stream into the child just as colors stream into his eye, because the organism of the child is a sense organ.

But this organism is of such a delicate structure, that every impression permeates the whole of it. The first impression that the child receives from any moral manifestation is an impression of the soul. But in the child the soul always works down into the bodily nature. Whether it be terrors that a child experiences in his environment, or whether it be joy and delight—all this passes over, not crudely but in a fine and delicate manner, into the processes of growth, circulation, and digestion. A child who lives in constant terror of what may come to him as expressions of fury and anger from a choleric person, experiences something in his soul which immediately penetrates the breathing, the circulation of the blood and even the digestive activities. This is of great significance: in the age of childhood it is impossible to speak of bodily education alone, because soul education is also an education of the body, and the whole of the soul element is metamorphosed into the body—it becomes body. And we shall only realize the significance of this when, out of a real knowledge of man, we do not merely look at the child and imprint certain educational maxims upon him, but when we consider the whole earthly life of man. This is not so easy as merely to observe the child as he is. In doing the latter we record what his memory is like, his power of thought, the sense impressions of the eye, the ear, and so on. These records are made for the moment or, at the most, over a short space of time. But this has in no way helped us to a true knowledge of man himself. For just as with the plant, in the seed which becomes root there already lies something which after a long time will appear as blossom and fruit, so in the child up to the change of teeth, when his bodily nature is susceptible to influences of the soul, there lies the germ of happiness and unhappiness, health and sickness, for his whole earthly life right up to the time of his death. And what we as teachers and educators allow to flow into the child in the first epoch of his life, which works down into the blood, the breathing and digestion, is like a germ which may perhaps only come to fruition in the form of health or sickness in the man of forty or fifty years. This is indeed true, that the way in which the educator behaves to the little child predisposes his inward tendencies to happiness or unhappiness, sickness or health.

This is especially noticeable if out of the facts of life we make a detailed observation of these effects of the teacher on the child. These facts can be observed just as well as the facts of botany or physics in the laboratories, only we seldom find this being done. Let us take single instances. Let us for instance consider what the teacher is like in his relationship to the child in school. Take the temperament of the teacher. We know that according to his temperament the teacher can be a man of energy but also of quick temper and anger—a choleric; or he can be one who withdraws inwardly into himself, gazes into his own nature, feels things in an inward manner, and shuns the world—a melancholic; or again he can be someone who is very quick to receive outward impressions, and flies from one impression to the next—a sanguine; or he is one who lets everything slide, is indifferent to it all, who is not affected by outward impressions but lets them pass by unnoticed—a phlegmatic.

Let us suppose, for the moment, that the Teachers' Training College had not concerned itself with modifying such temperaments and thereby giving the teachers their right place in the school life, but that these temperaments were allowed full and complete expression, without rein or curb. Take the choleric temperament: let us imagine that in the age before the change of teeth a child is exposed to a choleric temperament. If a teacher or educator lets himself go with a temperament of this kind, it will have a permanent effect on the soul of the child, leaving its mark on his circulation and all that constitutes his inner rhythmic life. These effects do not at first penetrate very deeply, they are really only there in germ, but this germ grows and grows, as all germs do. It can sometimes happen that in the fortieth or fiftieth year of life circulatory disorders of the rhythmic system can appear as direct effects of the unbridled choleric temperament of the teacher. For indeed we do not only educate the child for the age of childhood, we educate him for his whole earthly existence, and even, as we shall see later, for the time beyond. Or let us suppose that the melancholic gives rein to his temperament; not having found the impulse to harmonize it during his training and bring it into his work with the children in the right form, he gives himself up to his own melancholy in his intercourse with the children. But by living, feeling and thinking this kind of melancholy within him, he is continually withholding from the child just what ought to be flowing out from teacher to child, namely, warmth. This warmth which is so often lacking in education, works, first of all as warmth of soul, but then passes into the body and chiefly into the digestive system, and quickens the germ of certain tendencies which appear in later life in all kinds of disorders, and diseases of the blood.

Or take the phlegmatic, who is indifferent to what he does with the child. A very peculiar relationship arises between them. It is not exactly of the nature of coldness, but an exceedingly watery element exists in the realm of soul between the child and a teacher of this kind. There is not a strong enough basis for a right kind of interplay of soul between teacher and child. The child is not sufficiently aroused to inward activity. If you observe a person who had to develop under the influence of phlegma, of a phlegmatic temperament, and follow the course of his life right on into his later years, you will often notice how a tendency to brain weakness, a bloodless condition of the brain, or a dulling of the brain activity occurs in later life. And now let us see how a sanguine person who gives rein to his sanguinity affects the child. He gives himself up to every impression, but the impressions pass quickly by. True, he also lives within himself in a special way, but he takes his own nature right out into the things around him. The child cannot keep up with him, he hastens from one impression to the next, and thereby fails to stimulate the child in the right way, for in order to arouse sufficient inward activity in the child the teacher must hold him lovingly to one impression for a certain length of time. If we observe a child who grows up under the influence of uncontrolled sanguinity we shall see that in later life he will lack a certain vital force. He will have too little strength and content in his life.

So that if we have the power to see it (and education depends on the capacity for fine perception), we can recognize different types of men in their fortieth or fiftieth year of life and we can say: this man has been influenced by the temperament of his teacher, melancholic, phlegmatic, choleric, or sanguine.

I am mentioning this in the introduction to my lectures, not in order to give instructions as to how these things should be worked out in the training of teachers, but because I want to show you how what we do with the child in his soul life does not remain in the soul but passes over completely into his bodily nature. To educate the child in his soul life means to educate him for his whole earthly life in his bodily nature too. Anthroposophy is often criticized for wanting to speak of spirit in addition to the soul. Many people today are very critical and antagonistic if they even hear spirit spoken of, and Anthroposophy is easily taken to be just another of these fantastic ideas. In Anthroposophy the reality of the sense world is supposed to be reduced to a kind of misty abstraction, and people who speak rationally of spiritual things do not need to concern themselves with this kind of abstraction. The truth is that what Anthroposophy strives for in educational practice is to apply the right principles for bodily education, because we know that it is just in the first epoch of life that the whole bodily nature of the child is influenced by the impulses of soul. Let anyone but seek consciously to discover how all bodily activity rests fundamentally on a basis of soul and spirit, and then he can be a materialist if he will, and in the development of the child from birth to the change of teeth he can work on the material nature alone, for in the very way matter works in the child he is a unity of soul and spirit. No one can understand matter in the child unless he attaches these values to soul and spirit. But soul and spirit are indeed revealed in what appears outwardly as matter.

To be educators we must have a sense of responsibility. This sense of responsibility is very strongly aroused by such considerations as I have put before you, and must lay hold of your hearts. For if you take up educational work knowing that what affects the young child will continue through the whole of life as happiness or unhappiness, sickness or health, then at first this knowledge may seem a burden on your souls, but it will also spur you on to develop forces and capacities and above all an attitude of mind as a teacher strong enough to sow "seeds of the soul" in the young child which will only blossom later in life, perhaps even in old age. This is the knowledge of man which Anthroposophy sets forth as the basis of the art of education. It is not only the knowledge of what we find in man in one special epoch of his life, for instance, in childhood, but it springs from the contemplation of the whole earthly life of man. For what indeed is man in his life on earth? When we view him as he stands before us at any given moment, we say that he is an organism, because every single detail in him is in harmony with the formation of the whole. If a man can gain an insight into the inner connections of size or form in the single members of the human organism, how they fit in with each other, are harmonized one with the other and form a unity but at the same time a multiplicity within this unity—if a man can gain an insight of this kind, then let him look, for instance, at the little finger. Now even though he is only looking at the little finger he will have some idea of the shape of the lobe of the ear as well: for the form of the lobe of the ear will have a certain connection with the form of the little finger, and so on.

The smallest and the largest members of the human organism take their shape from the whole, but are also related in form to every other member, so that we cannot understand, let us say, an organ in the head of man unless we see it in connection and harmony with an organ in the leg or the foot. This is the case with the space organism, the organism that is spread out in space. But besides the space organism man has also a time organism. We have seen that within the space organism the lobe of the ear, for instance, takes it shape from the whole body and also from the form of, let us say, the little finger, or the knee. But the time organism must come into consideration also. A man's configuration of soul in his fiftieth year, his physical health or sickness, cheerfulness or depression, clarity or dullness of mind—all this is most intimately bound up with what he bore within him in the tenth, seventh or fourth year of his life. Just as the members of the space organism bear a certain relationship to each other, so also do the members of the time organism which are separated from each other in time. From a certain point of view we can assert that when we are five years old that which we bear within us is already in harmony with what we shall be when we are forty. (Of course the trivial objection that we might die young does not hold good, as in this case other considerations enter in). Besides being an organism of space, man is also an organism of time. And if you should ever find a finger lying about somewhere, this severed finger could still be a finger only if it had been just cut off; it would very soon be a finger no longer. A limb separated from the organism for long shrivels up, and ceases to be a human limb. A finger separated from the human organism is not a finger at all. It could never live apart from the body, it becomes nothing; it cannot exist on its own, it is not a reality. It can only be a reality when it is united with the whole physical body between birth and death.

These considerations will make it clear to us that in all our teaching we must take this time-organism into account. Imagine what would happen to the space-organism if it were influenced in the same way as a man often influences his organism of time. Let us suppose that we put into a man's stomach some substance that destroys his head, but that we only examined the stomach. We did not look to see what happened to this substance when it was dispersed in the organism and came at last to the head. To understand the human organism you must be able to examine the process that the substance undergoes in the human stomach and see what significance it has for the head. In passing from the stomach to the head the substance must continually be altered and changed, it must be mobile. In the time organism we are continually committing sins against the child. We teach him to have clear, sharply defined ideas; we are not satisfied if his ideas are elastic and not so sharply defined. Our aim is to teach the child something in such a way that he can keep it in his mind and retell it to us in the same form. We are often particularly gratified if we can teach a child something that he can reproduce in the same form several years later. But this is just as though we were to have a pair of shoes made for a child of three and expect him to wear them when he is ten.

In reality our task is to give the child living, flexible ideas which can grow in his soul as the outward physical limbs grow in his body. It is much less trouble to give the child definitions of this and that to memorize and keep in mind, but this is like expecting the shoes of a child of three to fit a child of ten. We must ourselves partake in the inward activities of the child's soul, and we must count it a joy to give him something that is inwardly flexible and elastic. Just as he grows with his physical limbs so he can grow up with these ideas, feelings, and impulses, and in a short time he himself can make something else out of what we have given him. For this we need to have an inward joy in growth and change. We have no use for pedantry or sharply defined ideas about life. All we have use for is active, life-forming forces, the forces of growth and increase. And a teacher who has a feeling for this growing, creative life has already found a relationship to the child, because he has life within him, and this life can then pass over to the child who demands it of him. This is what we need above all. Much that is dead in our pedagogy and educational systems must be transformed into life. We need a knowledge of man therefore which does not only say: man is like this or like that; man is this, that and the other. We need a knowledge of man which works on the whole human being, as physical nourishment works on the blood. The blood circulates in man. We need a kind of human knowledge which gives us blood in our souls too, which not only makes us sensible, clever, and intelligent, but which can also make us enthusiastic and inwardly mobile, which can enkindle love in us—for an art of education which springs forth from a true knowledge of man must be borne by love.

Such are the introductory remarks I wanted to make about the fundamental ideas which an art of education must receive at the hands of Anthroposophy. In the further lectures we shall see how in the details of school practice the spirit of anthroposophical education can be realized.

Lecture 2

You will have seen that education must be based on a more intimate knowledge of man than can be found in natural science. For natural science, the basis of all present-day knowledge, cannot lead us to a real knowledge of man himself. The world is permeated by spirit, and true knowledge of the world must be spiritual knowledge. Anthroposophy can give us this spiritual knowledge of the world, and with it a spiritual knowledge of man, which alone can lead us to a true art of education. But do not imagine—this is a mistake which can easily arise—that we have any intention of founding "anthroposophical" schools in the sense that Anthroposophy as such, as a world conception, should be taught in them in the place of other world conceptions of today, whether these be inspired more by intellect or by feeling. It is important to realize that this is in no way our intention. The kind of education we are speaking about here only wishes to concern itself with questions of method and teaching practice. Men and women who go deeply into Anthroposophy are rightly of the opinion that through the knowledge of man that it can give they can come to really practical rules for the treatment of children, and therefore it may also be assumed that in Anthroposophy the ways of teaching, the methods, and the whole treatment of our educational work may receive what they need.

Now in the Waldorf School at Stuttgart we have for many years been able to pursue an art of education based on Anthroposophy, and we have always made it clear to the outside world that Anthroposophy as such was never taught in the school. The Roman Catholic children have their religious instruction from a priest, the Protestant children from a Protestant pastor. It is only for those children whose parents specially wish it that we ourselves provide religion lessons in which a freer religious instruction is given on an anthroposophical basis. Our own anthroposophical conception of the world as such has really no place in the actual school work.

Moreover, I should like to point out to you that the real aim and object of our anthroposophical education is not to found as many anthroposophical schools as possible. It is of course necessary that there should be certain model schools where the methods are carried out in detail. It is a crying need of our days that there should be such schools. But our education concerns itself with the methods of teaching, and is essentially a new way and art of education, so every teacher can bring it into his work, in whatever kind of school he happens to be. There can be no question whatever of creating revolutions in existing institutions. Our task is rather to give indications of a way of teaching arising out of our anthroposophical knowledge of man.

Now, as you know, we need to acquire a more intimate observation of man than is customary at the present day. In certain spheres of life a very exact kind of observation is certainly taught, especially that which brings things nearer to the human eye. You find it for instance in the observation of the stars through the telescope, in surveying, and in many other spheres of knowledge, and it arises out of a feeling for exact observation in a mathematical sense. But the kind of intimate observation that reveals fine and delicate changes in man's soul or his bodily structure, does not evolve out of the scientific ideas of the last three or four centuries, nor is it to be found in the civilized life of today. That is why such important changes as those which happen at the changing of the teeth, at puberty, and again after the twentieth year, are simply not observed at all. These changes are spoken of, it is true, but only as they affect the more superficial dependence of the soul on this physical body. People have but little to say about the difference in the whole physical organization of a child before the changing of the teeth as against the period between the change of teeth and puberty. This requires a much more delicate method of observation. Now Anthroposophy takes its start by looking upon the world as an expression of spiritual forces (a fact which is seldom acknowledged today), and exercises are given for the soul-life by which a man may be trained to acquire an insight into the spiritual world itself. There are some who by reason of their destiny are not yet able to reach this point of seeing the spiritual facts for themselves, but the power of Anthroposophy is such that if they will only make a beginning with these exercises, this in itself will help them to acquire a much more delicate and intimate observation of man. For you must remember that all spiritual research depends upon the fact that in our soul and spirit, in that part of us which, as we have seen, descends, from a pre-earthly existence to unite itself with the inherited physical body, in this higher, supersensible part of us we have supersensible eyes and ears, organs of the soul like the eyes and ears of our physical body, so that we can come to certain perceptions independently of the body.

Every night in sleep man is unconsciously in a similar condition to that which is necessary for spiritual investigation. On falling asleep the soul and spirit of man leave the physical body and reenter it on awakening. In his waking life man uses his eyes and ears, and sets his limbs in motion, and the power to do these things proceeds from the spiritual and soul part of his being. A true knowledge of nature (which has not yet been acquired) would also affirm that in waking life physical actions are directed by soul and spirit, and that sleep is but an interruption of this activity. Here again, this is too fine a difference to be perceived by the methods of modern scientific thinking—that way of thinking on which the education of today is based, even for the earliest years of childhood. In sleep man is wholly given up to those activities of his organization to which plant and mineral are also subject. In Anthroposophy and Spiritual Science, however, we must be exact and accurate, and it would certainly not be true to say that man is a plant in his sleeping life. In a human being the mineral and plant substances have been raised to the stage of animal and man. Man's organization is not that of a plant, for a plant has no muscles and nerves, and man of course has both muscles and nerves, even in sleep. But the significant thing is this: the vegetable activity of the plant has nothing to do with nerves and muscles. In man this activity is united with muscles and nerves, and thereby transcends the physical; thus even the sleep activity of man is not merely a vegetable activity. (In a certain sense this applies to the animal, but this cannot be dealt with here.)

Although the same impulses are there in the plant as in the sleeping human being, yet something different from the plant life happens in the sleeping man. In his waking life man is permeated by soul and spirit. This soul and spirit has a certain similarity to the cosmos, the whole universe, but we must remember that it is *only* a similarity, and a careful observation of plant growth will show us the following: in spring, when the snow has melted, we see the plants springing forth from the earth and unfolding their being. Up to now the plant growth has been controlled by the sun forces within the earth, the stored up sunshine of the previous year. In spring the plants are, as it were, released by these earthly sun-forces and, as they shoot up out of the earth, they are received by the outward sunlight and guided through the summer time until the seeds are ripe. Then the plant growth is once more given over to the earth. Throughout the summer the forces of the sun gradually descend into the earth to be treasured up there, and the earth is always permeated by these accumulated sun forces. We have only to remember that the sun forces millions of years ago shone upon the plants, which then became coal in the earth, so that the sunlight is in reality now being burnt in our stoves. In the same way, though for a much shorter time, the sun-forces are preserved in the earth from one summer to the next. All through the winter the plants absorb the sun-forces which they find in the earth. In summer the sun pours its rays upon them straight out of the cosmos. So there is really a rhythm in the life of the plants: earthly sun-forces, cosmic sun-forces, earthly sun-forces, cosmic sun-forces, and so on. The plant life swings from one to the other like the pendulum of a clock.

Now let us turn to the human being. When he falls asleep he leaves behind in his body what is of a mineral and plant nature, although, as we have seen, the plant nature of man, in contrast to the plant itself, is organized in such a way that spirit and soul can dwell within it. What is thus left behind in sleep is wholly given over to its own plantlike activity. It begins to blossom and sprout, and when we fall asleep it is actually true that it is springtime within us. When we awaken, the plant-forces are driven back, and it is autumn within us. With the arising of soul and spririt on awakening, autumn enters into us. From the point of view of external analogies it is often said that waking is like spring and sleeping like autumn. But this is not so. True spiritual insight into human nature will show us that in the first moments of sleep spring-life sprouts and blossoms in us, and when we awaken autumn sinks into us like the setting sun. In waking life, when we are making use of all the faculties of the soul, then it is winter within us. Here again we have a rhythm, as in plant-life. In the growth of the plants we distinguish between earth activity and sun activity. In man there is fundamentally the same activity, in imitation of the plant; falling asleep—summer activity, awakening —winter activity, and so round again to summer activity, winter activity, only it takes place in the course of twenty-four hours. Man has condensed the rhythm of a year into the course of a day and a night. One rhythm is similar to the other but it is not identical. This is because the life of the soul and spirit in man is not of the same duration as the life of the spirit in the world of nature. For a year is but a day in the life of those spirits who pervade the cosmos and permeate the whole course of the year, as the soul and spirit of man directs the course of his day.

I must warn you that what I am now going to say may seem quite fantastic to you, but I put it forward as a hypothesis to show you more clearly what I mean. Let us suppose that a man falls

asleep, and has within him what I have described as the summer
activity. Let us suppose that he goes on and on sleeping and does
not awaken. What happens then? The plant element within him
—the element that is not of soul and spirit—would eventually
pass over into the rhythm of the plant realm. It would pass from
the rhythm of the day into the rhythm of the year. Such a rhythm
does not of course exist in the human being, so that if the physical
body were to go on sleeping in the way I have described, man
would no longer be able to keep it together, and death would
ensue. The spirit would be subject to other laws of nature if there
were only a plant activity within it. In this case the man's body
would fall away from soul and spirit, and in passing over to the
rhythm of the year he would become a plant. We can conceive of
physical death, the destruction of his organism, as follows: man is
born out of the cosmos into a physical body and thereby passes
over from the greater rhythm into the smaller. If he is left to
himself and cannot arouse the soul and spirit within him, as he is
not directly able to find his place in the cosmic rhythm, he will
fall prey to the forces of destruction.

We shall see that if we can develop a more delicate faculty of
observation, we can really gain an insight into the true essence of
human existence. That is why I said that those who have entered
on the path of spiritual knowledge, though they may not yet have
attained spiritual vision for themselves, will yet feel within themselves the stirrings of forces which lead to spiritual insight, and
these selfsame forces are the messengers and mediators of all the
spirits which work in the cosmos. For in the cosmos is spirit, and
there we find the beings who guide the life cycle of the year. This
is a new world to us but when we observe a human being we can
see how soul and spirit are present in all human life, and here we
are on familiar ground. For this reason, it is always easier to exercise a fine faculty of perception with regard to the soul and spiritual qualities of man than to perceive the workings of the spirit in
the world itself. When we think in ordinary life, this thinking,
this forming of mental images, perpetually escapes us. When we
knock against something, or feel an object with our fingers—a
piece of silk or velvet, for instance—then we perceive at once that
we have come up against the object in question and can feel its

shape by touching its surface. We know then that as human beings we have made a contact with our environment. But when we think, we do not appear to touch the objects around us in this way. When we have thought about something and made it our own we can say that we have "apprehended" or "grasped" it *(begreifen)*. What is this apprehending? If the outside objects are foreign to us, as is mostly the case with our thinking, then we do not say we have grasped them. If for instance the chalk is lying there and I am standing here and move my hand as one does when speaking, then we do not say, "I have grasped the chalk." But if we really take hold of the chalk with our hand, then we can say we have grasped it.

The men of former times knew better what thinking really was, and out of this knowledge words and expressions flowed into the languages which expressed the real thing far better than our modern abstractionists are aware of. If we have had a mental picture of something, we say we have grasped it. This means we have come into touch with the object, we have seized upon it *("erfasst,"* another word for "grasp"). Today man no longer knows that he can come into intimate contact with the objects of his environment even in the expressions he uses for his mental life. We have for example a word in the language of today which conceals its own meaning in a quite hypocritical fashion. We say *"Begriff"* (concept—from *"begreifen"* to grasp, see above). I have a *"Begriff."* The word *"greifen"* (to seize) is contained within it! I have something that I have grasped, seized upon. We have only got the word left now, the life has gone out of what the word indicates.* Such things, taken from everyday life, can show us the aim and purpose of the exercises you will find described as anthroposophical methods of research in my books, *Knowledge of the Higher Worlds*, or in the later half of *Occult Science*, or in other works. Take the exercises in mental imagery. Certain thoughts are held in the mind, so that the concentration on these thoughts may strengthen the life of the soul. These exercises are founded neither on superstition nor on mere fantasy, but on clear thinking and deliberation as exact as that used in mathematics,

---

* Compare our English word concept, from Latin *concipio*, to lay hold of completely. —TRANS.

and they lead man to develop his capacity of thought in a much more lively and active way than is found in the abstract-minded people of today. If these people work with their arms and legs all day, then they feel a necessity to sleep off their fatigue, for they know that when they move their arms and legs, their own real being has been active. What they do not know is that when they think, their own being is just as active. They cannot see that when they think, their own being streams out actively, and seizes hold of the objects of their thinking. This is because they do not perceive the lowest supersensible member of the human being, the etheric body, that lives within the physical body, just as the physical body lives within the outside world.

The etheric body can actually be perceived at the moment when, by carrying out the exercises I have referred to, man develops the eye of the soul and the ear of the spirit. He can then see how thinking, which is principally an activity of the etheric body, is really a spiritual grasping, a spiritual handling *(begreifen, befühlen")* of the objects around us. When we have condensed and concentrated our thoughts by means of the exercises mentioned above, we come to experience the spiritual in such a way that we no longer have the abstract feeling so prevalent today that objects are far away from us. Rather, we have a true feeling about them which arises out of our practiced, concentrated thinking. Then thinking too will bring fatigue, and particularly after using our powers of thought we shall want to sleep. It is not the actual materialistic ideas which are the worst product of this age of materialism in which we live. The educator must consider another aspect of it. He may be comparatively indifferent to the degree of fatigue which results from the activities of, let us say, a Monist. Such things can be put right when men have become a little more sensible. But the very worst thing for the educator is to see how a child can go through his school life and receive no other nourishment for his soul and spirit than that which bears the stamp of natural science, that is, of material things. This does not apply only to actual science lessons in the schools; *all* education today, even in the lowest classes, is based on a scientific way of thinking. It is absorbed by the child, grows up within him and works into his whole physical organizaition in such a way that in later years it appears as a condition of insomnia.

What is the cause of this sleeplessness in our materialistic age? The cause is that when we only think materialistically, this activity of thought, this "grasping" or "handling" in our environment through thought, does not allow the corresponding organs of the etheric body to become tired. In this case it is only the physical body which tires; the physical body can fall asleep, but the etheric begins to fidget and be restless, and cannot sleep. It draws the soul and spirit back into it, and this condition must gradually develop into an epidemic of insomnia. This is already taking place today. Only by considering such facts as these can we understand the significance of the materialistic age.

It is bad enough that men think materialistic theoretical thoughts, but this is not so serious. It is worse still that in their moral and economic actions they experience the consequences of materialism. But the worst thing of all is that through materialism they ruin the whole of their childhood and thereby come to the point where they can no longer take in any moral or spiritual impulses at all. These things must be known by all who recognize the necessity of transforming our teaching and education. For such transitions as we have spoken of, such as those which take place at the change of teeth and at puberty, can be understood only by an intimate observation of the human being. We have to see how man is inwardly active, so that the feelings man has about his physical body also apply to the etheric, and he must know that when he thinks about any particular object he is really carrying out in the etheric what is otherwise carried out in the physical body of man. If I want to know what an object is like I feel it, I make a contact with it, and thereby I gain a knowledge of its surface. If I think about it afterwards, I do the same thing with my etheric body. I "feel" (*"befühlen"*) in an etheric, supersensible way the object which I want to "grasp," of which I want to make a concept. The etheric body is as active as the physical, and it is only out of this knowledge and consciousness of the activity of the etheric body that a right knowledge of man and his development can proceed.

If we can make our thinking active in this way, and then with this inwardly active thinking watch a very young child, we shall see how every action that is performed in his environment, every look which is the expression of some moral impulse (for in the moral quality of the look lies that which passes over to the child as an imponderable force)—how every such action and look streams right into the child and continues to work on in the breathing and the circulaton of the blood. The clearest and most concrete statement that we can come to with regard to the child is as follows: The child is an imitative being through and through. The way a child breathes or digests in the more delicate and intimate processes of breathing or digesting is a reflection of how the people around him are behaving. The child is completely given up to his environment. In adult life the only parallel to this devotion is in religion, expressed in the soul and spirit of man. In the religious life we are spiritually given up to our environment. The religious life unfolds rightly if with our own spirit we pass out of ourselves and give ourselves up to a spiritual world order. We should flow out into a divine and world order. The religious life of an adult depends on the emancipation of his soul and spirit from the physical body. His own soul and spirit are given up to the divine spirit of the world. The child gives up his whole being to his environment. In the adult the activities of breathing, digestion, and circulation are within himself, cut off from the outside world. In the child all these activities are given up to his environment and are therefore by nature religious. This is the essential feature of the life of the child between birth and the change of teeth: his whole being is permeated with a kind of "natural-religious" element, and even the physical body is in religious mood.

But the child is not only surrounded by good forces, such as can inspire religious devotion in later life. There are bad spiritual forces also, proceeding from human beings around him and from other spiritual powers in the world, so that this natural-religious element in the physical body of the child can also be exposed to evil in his environment. He can come up against evil forces, and when I say that even the physical body of a little child is of a religious nature, that does not mean that children cannot be little demons! Many children are little demons, because they have given themselves up to evil spiritual forces around them. It is our task to overcome and drive out these forces, by applying the right methods for this age. As long as the child is an imitative religious being, admonitions are of no avail. Words can only be listened to when the soul is to some extent emancipated, and can direct its attention to itself. Words of reproof cannot help us with a little child. What does help us is what we ourselves do in the presence of the child, for when the child sees this it flows right into him and becomes sense-perception. But our actions must contain a moral quality. When a color blind person looks at a colored surface he sees only grey, and in the same way a grownup person looks at a man's actions, his look, gestures, or the movement of his limbs. He observes the speed or manner of his movements, but all this is only physical. He no longer sees the moral qualities of a man's actions. But the child sees these, even if only unconsciously, and we must see to it that in the presence of the child we not only do no actions which he should not imitate, but that we think no thoughts which should not have entry into the child's soul. This education through thinking is the most important part of a child's first seven years of life, and we must not allow ourselves to think any impure, ugly, or angry thoughts when we are with little children. You may say: But I can think what I like, this alters nothing in my outward behaviour; the child cannot see it or be influenced by it. In this connection it is interesting to consider those very peculiar and rather stupid shows which were given at one time with so-called thinking horses—horses which could count, and other animals performing intelligence tricks. These things were interesting, but not in the way that most people thought.

I have not seen the Elberfeld horses (I only want to speak out of my own observation), but I did see the horse which belongs to Herr von Osten, and I could observe how it gave answers to its master. Its master gave it sums to do, not very complicated, it is true, but difficult enough for a horse. It had to add and subtract and gave the correct answers by stamping with its feet. Now you can either look at this from the point of view of a scientific man of today as, for instance, the professor who wrote a lengthy book about the horse, or else you can look at it from an anthroposoph-

ical standpoint. Now the professor began by repudiating all lay
opinions on the matter. (Please do not think that I want to speak
against natural science in any way, for indeed I know its value.)
Then at the end he says that the horse was able to perceive very
delicate movements that the man made, the slight twitching of an
eyelid, the most delicate vibrations of certain muscles, and the
like. And from this he gradually learnt what answers corresponded to certain vibrations, and could give the requisite number of
stamps with his feet. This is a very clever and intelligent hypothesis. Then he comes to the inevitable question of whether these
things have actually been observed. He puts this question himself, for indeed people are learning to be most conscientious in
their research. But he answers it by saying that the human senses
are not organized to perceive such fine delicate movements and
vibrations, but the horse can see them. In point of fact all he
proves by this is that a horse can see more in a man than a professor can. But for me there was something else which was important: the horse could only give the correct answers when Herr
von Osten stood beside him and talked to him. And all the time
he talked he kept taking lumps of sugar and putting them in the
horse's mouth. The horse was permeated by a taste of sweetness
all the time. This is the important thing, that the horse felt himself "inwardized" by the sweetness. In this condition even a horse
can experience things that it could not otherwise have done. Actually I should like to put it like this: In the "horse of sweetness"
which, as etheric horse, had permeated the physical horse, Herr
von Osten himself was constantly living. His thoughts lived and
were diffused there, just as they were in his own body. The
thoughts lived on in the horse. It was not because a horse has a
finer perception than a professor but because he is not yet so
highly organized and is therefore susceptible to influences from
outside while his physical body is continually absorbing the
sweetness.

There are indeed such influences which pass from man to man,
aroused by things which are almost if not wholly imperceptible to
men today. These things occur in the intercourse between men
and animals, and they occur also in man to an enhanced degree
when the soul and spirit are not yet free of the body, namely, in
early childhood. The little child can really perceive the morality

which underlies every look and gesture of the people around him, though this may be no longer possible for those who are older. It is therefore of the utmost importance that we should never allow ourselves to think ugly thoughts in the presence of the child, for not only will this live on in his soul, but will work right down into his physical body.

True, the addresses delivered by doctors and others from the standpoint of modern science can be of great interest to us. But the time will come when there will be something quite new in this domain. Let me give you a concrete example to show you what I mean. There will come a time when a man may write a thesis for his doctor's degree, in which he shows that a disease occurring, let us say, in the forty-eighth year of life, can be traced back to certain evil thoughts in the environment of the child in his fourth or fifth year. This way of thought can bring us to a real understanding of man, and to the capacity for seeing the life of a human being as a whole.

Thus we have gradually to learn that it is not so much a question of inventing, out of our abstract thoughts, all kinds of things for little children to do, such as stick-laying and the like. The child does not do things like this out of himself. His own powers of soul must be aroused, and then he will imitate what the adults are doing. A little girl plays with her doll because she sees her mother nursing the baby. What is to be seen in adults is present in the child as the tendency to imitation. This tendency must be taken into account in the education of children up to the seventh year. But we must remember that what we are educating is subject to change in the organism of the child. In the child everything is carried out in a more living and animated way than with the adult, because the child is still a unity in body, soul, and spirit. In the adult the body has been freed from the soul and spirit, and the soul and spirit from the body. Body, soul, and spirit stand side by side as single entities; in the child they are firmly united. This unity even penetrates into the thinking. You can see this quite clearly from the following example. A little child is often given what is regarded as a beautiful doll, a painted creature with glass eyes, made to look just like a human being. These little horrors are made to open and shut their eyes and do all kinds of other things, and then they are given to children as "beautiful dolls." Even from an artistic point of view they are hideous, but I will not enlarge upon that now. But just consider what really happens to a child when I give him a doll of this kind, a doll that can open its eyes and what not. At first he will love it because it is a novelty, but that does not last. Compare this with what happens to a child if I just take a piece of rag and make a doll out of that. Tie it together for a head, make two dots for eyes, and perhaps a big nose, and there you have it. Give this to the child and then, in his imagination, in the soul and spirit, which are so closely bound up with the body, he can fill out all the rest for himself. Then every time he plays with his doll he awakens inwardly and remains inwardly active and alive. If you make these experiments you will see what a difference there is in giving a child playthings that leave as much as possible to his own power of imagination, or in giving him finished toys which leave nothing over for his own inner activity. Handwork for little children should only give indications, leaving much for the child's own imagination to carry out. To work in set forms which can perfectly well remain as they are, awakens no inward activity in the child, because his imagination cannot get beyond what lies open to his senses.

This throws light on what kind of teachers and educators we ought to be if we really want to approach the child in the right way. We need an art of teaching which is based on a knowledge of man—a knowledge of the child. Such an art of education can arise when we find a doctor's thesis dealing with a case of diabetes at the age of forty which he traces back to the harmful effects of a wrong kind of play in the third or fourth year. For then people will see what it means when we say that man consists of body, soul, and spirit, and that in the child the body, soul, and spirit are still a unity. Later the spirit and soul become freed from the body, and a trinity is formed. In the grown man body, soul, and spirit are, as it were, pushed asunder, and only the body preserves what was absorbed into the man in his early development as the germ of his later life. Now the strange thing is this: in the soul the consequences sink down into the unconscious and we then experience them physically in the body when we are seven or eight times as old. If you educate a child of three or four years old in such a way that you give him what will influence his soul life, then the effect of this will appear in his eighth year. People are still careful to avoid doing anything with a child of four or five which may affect his soul life in an unhealthy way in his eighth or ninth year. The effect on the physical body takes much longer to manifest itself because it has to free itself from the soul and spirit. An influence on the soul life at four or five may come to fruition in the physical body when the man is seven or eight times as old, let us say in the thirty-fifth year. Thus a man may have an illness in the late thirties or early forties which is caused by bad influences in his play which affected his soul life as a child of three or four. If you wish to understand the whole human being you must also realise that the freeing of the body from soul and spirit in the grown man, as against the unity of body, soul, and spirit in the child, is not an abstract theory, but a matter of concrete knowledge, for it protracts the time when various influences take effect in a man's life. The time that the body takes to work anything out becomes longer and longer compared with the time taken by the soul. The physical body remains behind, and harmful influences are manifested much later in the body than in the soul. So one can often see that if one transgresses against a little child in his very early years, then many wrong things will show themselves in his soul life when he is a teenager. But this can be made good. It is not so difficult to find means of helping even apparently ungovernable children in their teens. They may even become quite good and respectable citizens later on. That is not so serious. But the body develops more and more slowly as life goes on and the end will be long after all the soul difficulties of early youth have been overcome. Physical effects will gradually emerge, and in later life a man will have to contend with gout and other illnesses.

A concrete knowledge of man is of the utmost importance in human life. With its power of seeing right into man himself, a concrete knowledge of man is the only possible basis for a true art of education—an art of education whereby men may find their place in life, and subject to the laws of their own destiny develop all their powers to the full. Education should never work against a person's destiny, but should achieve the full development of his own predispositions. The education of a man today so often lags

behind the talents and tendencies which his destiny has implanted in him. We must keep pace with these powers to such an
extent that the human being in our care can win his way to all that
his destiny will allow—to the fullest clarity of thought, the most
loving deepening of his feeling, and the greatest possible energy
and ability of will.

This can only be done by an art of education and teaching
which is based on a real knowledge of man. We will speak more
of this in the next lectures.

Lecture 3

In the preceding lectures I have repeatedly shown you how
important it is for a teacher to consider the drastic changes that
take place in the life of a child at, for instance, the change of
teeth, or at puberty. Observation of these changes is not fully
developed at the present day, because one is only accustomed to
notice the more obvious external expressions of man's nature according to so-called natural laws, while what concerns the teacher
springs in reality from the innermost center of the child's being.
What the teacher can do for the child works right into this inner
nature. Thus we must pay special attention to the fact that at this
significant changing of the teeth, for instance, the soul itself undergoes a transformation. Let us examine just one aspect of this
soul life—the memory, the capacity for remembering. The memory of a child before and after the change of teeth is quite a different thing. The transitions and developments in a child's life take
place of course only slowly and gradually, and therefore a fixed
time such as the changing of the teeth can only be approximate.
But this point of time stands in the middle of the child's development, and we must consider very intensively what takes place
then. If we observe a very young child, we shall find that in effect
his capacity to remember has the quality of a habit in the soul.
When, during the first period of life up to the change of teeth, a
child remembers something, this remembering is a kind of habit
or skillfulness. So we may say that when as a child I acquire a
certain accomplishment—let us say, writing—this arises very
largely out of a certain suppleness of my physical constitution—a
suppleness which I have gradually acquired. If you watch a little

child grasping something you will find that in this the concept of habit can be grasped. The child gradually finds out how to move his limbs this way or that way, and this becomes habit and skill. Out of the child's imitative actions the soul develops skillfulness, which permeates his finer and more delicate organism. A child imitates something one day. The next day, and the day following, he does it again, and the action is not only performed outwardly but right into the innermost parts of his physical body. This is the basis of memory in the early years. After the change of teeth the memory is quite different, for then, as I have said, the spirit and soul are freed from the body, and a picture content can arise of what has been experienced in the soul, a formation of images which are not of a bodily nature. And every time we meet the same thing or same process, whether through an outward or an inward cause, then the same picture is called to mind. The little child does not yet make these inward pictures. No image emerges for him when he remembers something. With the older child a thought or an idea which he has experienced rises up again for him as a remembered thought, a thought "made inward."* A child under seven lives in his habits which are not inwardly pictured in this way. This fact is significant for the whole life of man.

If you observe man's development with the means of inner vision of which I have already spoken—with the eyes and ears of the soul—then you will see that man does not consist only of a physical body which you can see with your eyes and touch with your hands, but that he also has supersensible members of his being. I have already drawn your attention to the first so-called "supersensible man," living within the physical body, namely, the etheric man. There is also a third member of man's nature. One need not be put off by names—it is, after all, always necessary to have a certain terminology—and we call this third member the astral body, which develops the capacity of feeling. The plant has an etheric body; the animal has an astral body in common with man, and has feeling and sensation. Man, standing alone, as the crown of earthly creation, has within him a fourth member—the

---

* The German word for remember, *"erinnern,"* means literally to "make inward."

ego. These four members are entirely different from each other, but because they play into one another, the ordinary observer does not usually distinguish them. The ordinary observation never goes so far as to recognize the revelation of human nature in the etheric body, the astral body, or the ego. But it is not really possible to teach and educate without a knowledge of these things. One hesitates to make such a statement, for it would be regarded as fantastic and absurd in the widest circles of society today. But it is the truth, and an unprejudiced knowledge of man can raise no objection to it.

Now the way in which the nature of man works through the etheric and astral bodies and the ego is something peculiar to itself and is of significance for the educator. As you know, we are accustomed to find out about the physical body by making observations on the body, either living or dead, and by using our intellect which is connected with the brain, to elucidate what we have thus perceived with our senses. But with this kind of observation we shall never come to know the higher members of man's nature. They are inaccessible to methods of observation based on mere sense perception and the activity of the intellect. If you think only in terms of natural laws you will, for instance, never understand the etheric body. For this reason new methods should be introduced into the training colleges and universities. The observation of the senses and the work of the intellect connected with the brain can only enable man to observe the physical body. Quite a different university training is needed to enable him to perceive, for example, how the etheric body manifests itself in man. This is really a necessity, not only for teachers of all subjects, but also particularly for doctors. The first thing would be to learn to model, as a sculptor models, from within outwards, according to the unfolding of man's own nature, so that one could really come to the point of creating forms out of their own inner laws. The form of a muscle or of a bone can never be comprehended by the methods of present-day anatomy and physiology. Only a true sense of form can reveal to you what the forms of the human body really are. Now if we say such things we shall immediately be considered half-crazy. But Copernicus was con-

sidered half-mad in his day, and even as late as 1828 there were
some leaders of the Church who considered the Copernican theories madness and forbade the faithful to believe in them!

Now the physical body is heavy. It has weight and is subject to
the laws of gravity. The etheric is not subject to gravity. On the
contrary, it is always trying to get away—it always has the tendency to disperse and be scattered into the far spaces of the cosmos. And this is what actually happens immediately after death.
The first experience after death is that the etheric body is dispersed. The dead physical body follows the laws of earth when it
is lowered into the grave, or if it is cremated it burns according to
physical laws just like any other physical body. This is not the
case with the etheric body, which strives away from the earth just
as much as the physical body strives towards the earth. But the
etheric body does not necessarily extend equally in all directions,
nor does it strive away from the earth in a uniform manner. Here
we come to what may seem to you very peculiar, but it can truly
be perceived by the kind of observation of which I have spoken.

If you look up into the heavens you will see that the stars are
collected together into definite groups and that these groups are
all different from each other. It is these groups of stars which
attract the etheric body of man; they draw it out into the far
spaces. Let us imagine that a man is here in the center (see dia-
gram).

Now different groups of stars are drawing out his etheric body in varying degrees. There is a much stronger attraction from one group of stars than from another, so that the etheric body is not drawn out equally on all sides, but in varying degrees in the different directions of space. The result is that the etheric body does not have a spherical form, but through this dispersion of the etheric certain definite forms can arise in man through the cosmic forces working down from the stars. These forms remain in us as long as we live on earth and bear an etheric body within us. If we take for example the upper part of the thigh we shall see that what forms both the muscle and the bone comes from the stars. We have to discover how these different forms can arise from all directions of cosmic space. We must try to model these varying forms out of clay, and then we shall find that in one particular form the cosmic forces work to produce length; in another the form is rounded off sooner. Examples of the latter are the round bones, of the former the tubular bones.

We must be sculptors and as such we must develop a feeling for the world, the kind of feeling that was present in the humanity of olden times as a sort of instinctive consciousness. It was clearly expressed in the orientalism of prehistoric times, thousands of years before our era, but we still find it in Greek culture. Just think how the materialistic artists of today are often baffled by the forms of the Greek sculptors. They are baffled because they think that the Greeks worked from models, which they examined from all sides. But the Greeks still had a feeling that man is born out of the cosmos, and that the cosmos itself forms the human being. When the Greeks created their Venus de Milo (which is the despair of modern sculptors), then they took what streamed out of the cosmos, and although this could only reveal itself imperfectly in any earthly work, they strove to express it in the human form they were creating as far as they were able to do so. The point is that if you really set out to mould the form of a man according to nature, you cannot possibly do it by slavishly following a model, which is the method of the studios of today.

You must be able to turn to the great cosmic sculptor who forms man out of the "feeling for space" which man himself can also acquire. This then is the first thing you have to develop.

People imagine that they can gauge the form of a man by drawing a line through him like this, another through his outstretched arms and another so. But in doing this they are slaves to the three dimensions of space, and this is pure abstraction. If you draw a line through a man in the right way you will see that it is subject to many different forces of attraction, this way or that, in all directions of space. This "space" of geometry—about which Kant produced such unhappy definitions and spun out such abstract theories—is in reality an organism, putting forth varied forces in all directions. Man is apt to develop only his grosser physical senses, and he does not come to the point of unfolding within himself this fine delicate feeling for space which can be experienced in all directions. If he can only let this feeling for space hold sway, then the true image of man will arise. Out of an active inward feeling you will see how man arises in a modeled form. A feeling for the handling of soft plastic substance in this way will give you the right conditions for an understanding of the etheric body, just as the activity of man's intelligence, which is bound up with the brain, gives him the right conditions for an understanding of the physical body.

We have first to create a new method of acquiring knowledge, namely, a kind of plastic perception, together with an inward plastic activity. Unless we have this our knowledge stops short at the physical body, for we can only get to know the etheric body through pictures, and not through ideas. For truly, we can only understand these etheric images if we are able to refashion them ourselves in some way, in imitation of the cosmic fashioning.

Now we pass on to the next highest member of man. What is the thinking on this topic today? On the one hand we have the exponents of natural science who have become the authority for human knowledge in contemporary life. On the other hand we find anthroposophists isolated and misrepresented because they speak of the existence of etheric and astral bodies and describe them, and people try to understand the descriptions with the same methods of thought which they apply to an understanding of the physical body. This cannot be done. True, the astral body expresses itself in the physical body, and this physical expression of it can be comprehended according to the laws of natural science. But the astral body itself in its true inner being and function cannot be grasped by these laws. It can only be comprehended by an understanding of music, not only an outward but an inner understanding such as could be found in the East, and in a modified form was still present in Greek culture. In modern times it has disappeared altogether. Just as the etheric body works out of cosmic sculpture, so the astral body works out of cosmic music, cosmic melodies. The only thing that is earthly about the astral body is the time, the musical measure. Rhythm and melody come direct from the cosmos, and the astral body consists of rhythm and melody.* It is of no use to approach the astral body with what we know of the laws of natural science. We must approach it with what we have acquired for ourselves as an inner understanding of music. Then you will find, for example, that when the interval of a third is played it can be felt and experienced in the inner nature of man. So you can have a major and minor third, and considerable variations in the feeling life of man can be aroused by this division of the scale. This is still something inward in man. When we come to the fifth, we experience this on the surface, on the boundary of ourselves, as though with the fifth we were only just inside ourselves. The sixth and seventh we feel to be pursuing their way outside us. With the fifth we pass out of ourselves, and as we enter into the sixth and the seventh we experience them as something external, whereas the third is completely inward. This is the work of the astral body which is a musician in every human being, and imitates the music of the cosmos. And all this is again active in man and finds expression in the human form. If we can really come near to such a thought in striving to comprehend the world, it can be a stupendous experience for us.

You see, we are speaking now of something which we can study quite objectively—something which flows out of the astral body into the human form, arising in this case not out of cosmic sculpture, but out of the fact that the impulse of music streams into man from his astral body. Here again, we must take our start from an understanding of music, just as a plastic understanding was necessary for studying the activities of the etheric body. If you

---

* Cf. John Dryden: *A Song for St. Cecilia's Day.* —Trans.

take that part of man which goes from the shoulderblades to the arms, that is the work of what lives in man as the tonic, the keynote. In the upper arm we find the interval of the second (you can see all this in Eurythmy), and in the lower arm the third (major and minor as we have it in music). When you come to the third you find two bones in the lower arm, and so on right down into the fingers. This may sound like mere words and phrases, but by means of a real observation of man founded on Spiritual Science one can see these things just as exactly as a mathematician sees his mathematical problems. You cannot arrive at this through an inferior kind of music. You must investigate it with exactitude. If students of medicine and education are really to comprehend these things, their college training should be based on an inner understanding of music. Such an understanding, permeated by clear conscious thinking, can lead one back to the musical understanding of Oriental times, even before Greek culture began. Oriental architecture can be comprehended only if we understand how religious perception, as it were, flashed into the form. As music lends expression only in experiences of time, so architecture in experiences of space. The astral and etheric bodies of man must be grasped in the same contrasting way. You can never explain the life of feeling and passion by natural laws and so-called psychological methods. You can understand it only if you consider man himself in terms of music.

There will come a time when a diseased condition of the soul life will not be described as it is today by the psychologists, but it will be spoken of in musical terms, as one would speak, for instance, of a piano that was out of tune. Please do not imagine that Anthroposophy is not aware of what the difficulties will be of putting forth such a view at the present day. I can very well understand that there may be many people who will consider what I have set forth as purely fantastic if not half-crazy. But a so-called "reasonable" way of thinking can unfortunately never portray man as he really is. We have to develop a new and wider reasonableness in these things. In this connection it is extraordinary how people look at Anthroposophy today. They cannot imagine that there could be anything which their powers of comprehension cannot presently reach but could reach eventually.

Not long ago I read a very interesting book by Maeterlinck translated into German. In it there was a chapter about me, and it ended up in an extraordinary and also very amusing way. He says: "If you read Steiner's books you will find that the early chapters are logically correct, intelligently thought out, and presented in a perfectly scientific form. But if you read on further you will get the impression that the author has gone mad." Now Maeterlinck has a perfect right to his opinions. Why should he not have the impression that the writer was a clever man when he wrote the first part of the book, but went mad when he wrote the later part? But, now just consider what the situation really is. Maeterlinck believes that in the first chapters of these books the author was clever, but in the last chapters he had gone mad. So we get the following extraordinary fact. This man writes several books, one after the other. This means that in the first few chapters he seems to be quite clever, in the later chapters he seems mad, then clever again, then mad, and so on. You see how ridiculous it is when one has such an untrue picture. When writers, deservedly famous, write in such a way, people do not notice what nonsense it is. It just shows how hard it is even for such an enlightened personality as Maeterlinck to reach reality. On the firm basis of Anthroposophy we have to speak of a reality which today is considered unreal.

Now we come to the ego. As the astral body in music, so the true nature of the ego-organization can be studied in language. It may be assumed that everyone, even the doctors and teachers, accept the form of language of today as a finished product. If this is their standpoint they can never understand the inner configuration of language. This can only be understood if you regard language not as the product of our modern mechanism but as that in which the *genius* of language works in a living and spiritual way. You can do this if you set yourself to understand the way in which a word is formed. In words there lies untold wisdom, far beyond the grasp of man. All men's characteristics are expressed in the way in which they form their words, and the special peculiarities of any nation can be recognized in their language. Take for instance the German word *"Kopf"* (head). This is originally connected with the rounded form of the head which you also find in the word *"Kohl"* (cabbage), and in the expression *"Kohlkopf"* (head of cabbage). Thus the word arises out of a feeling for the form of the head. Here you see the ego has quite a different conception of the head from what we find, for instance, in *"testa,"* the word for head in the Romance languages, which comes from "testifying," "bearing witness." So that in this case the feeling out of which the word is formed comes from quite a different source. If you understand language in this inward way, then you will see how the ego-organisation works. There are some districts where lightning is not called *"Blitz"* but *"Himmlitzer."* This is because the people there do not think of the single flashes of lightning so much as the snakelike form. People who say *"Blitz"* picture the single flash and people who say *"Himmlitzer"* picture the zig-zag form. This then is how man really lives in language as far as his ego is concerned, although in the civilization of today he has lost connection with his language, which has consequently become something abstract. I do not mean to say that if you have this understanding of language you will already have attained inward clairvoyant consciousness, whereby you will be able to behold beings similar to the ego. But you will be on the way to such a perception if you accompany your speaking with inner understanding.

Thus our education in medical schools and teachers' training colleges should be fostered in the direction I have indicated so that the students' training may arouse in them an inner feeling for space, an inner relationship to music and an inner understanding of language. Now you will say: The lecture halls are already so empty, and in the end the teachers' training colleges will be just as empty if you put in all the things you have spoken of. What will all this lead to? And the medical course is always being made longer and longer. If you go on with your present methods a man will not be qualified till he is sixty. This does not arise out of the inner conditions themselves, but because these inner conditions are not fulfilled. If you fail to pass over from abstract conceptions to a conceiving of things plastically and musically and to an understanding of the cosmic word, that is, if you stop at abstract ideas, then your horizon will be endless. You will go on and on and never come to a boundary, to a point whence you can survey the whole. The understanding which will arise from an inward comprehension of modeling and music will make men inwardly more rational, and then, believe me, their training will in fact be accelerated rather than delayed. And so such an inner course of development will be the right method of training for educationists, and not only for the teachers but for those who have so much to contribute to educational work—the doctors.

From what was said in the introductory lectures about the connection between the methods of education and the physical health of the children it will be clear to you that true education cannot possibly be developed without having regard to medicine. The teacher should be able to judge the different conditions of health or disease among his children. Otherwise there will arise what is already being felt, namely, the need for a doctor in the schools. This is strongly felt, and the doctor is brought in *from outside*, which is the worst possible method that could be adopted. How does such a doctor stand in relation to the children? He does not know them, nor does he know, for example, what mistakes the teacher has made with them, and so on. The only possibility is to cultivate an art of education which has so much therapy within it that the teacher will constantly be able to see whether his methods are having a good or bad influence on the health of the children. But no reform is effected by bringing a doctor into the school from outside, necessary though this may appear to be.* With the kind of training which is given to doctors at the present day, they do not know what to do when they are sent into the schools.

In aiming at an art of education we must provide a training which is based on a knowledge of man. One hesitates to say these things because they are so difficult to grasp. But it is an error to believe that the ideas which have arisen from natural science can give us an understanding of man, and to be sensible concerning this error is one of the vital conditions for the progress of the art of education. It is only when one looks at the child from this point of view that one can see, for example, what radical and far-reach-

---

* Dr. Steiner means a doctor from outside the school with no knowledge of its methods. A doctor working with his methods of therapy, who was also a teacher, played an important part in the first Waldorf School. —TRANS.

ing changes occur with the coming of the second teeth, when the memory becomes a pictorial memory and is no longer attached to the physical body but to the etheric body. For what is it that really brings forth the second teeth? It is the fact that up to this time the etheric is almost completely bound up with the physical body, and when the first teeth are driven forth something is separated from the physical body. If it were not so, we should get new teeth every seven years. (As people's teeth decay so rapidly nowadays this would seem to be quite a good thing, and dentists would have to look for another job!)

When the etheric body is separated off, then what formerly worked in the physical body now works in the realm of soul. If you have a perception for these things and can examine a child's mouth without his knowledge, you will see for yourself that it is so. It is always better that a child does not know that he is being observed. This is why experimental psychology so often fails, because the child knows what is being done. You examine the child's second teeth which have been formed by the etheric body into a modeled image of the memory, and the shape of the teeth created by the etheric will be an indication of how the memory of the child will develop. With the exception of slight alterations of position, here or there, you cannot materially change the second teeth once they are through, unless you can really go so far as, for example, the dentist professor Romer has done. On the lines of a new art of medicine based on anthroposophical principles he has written a book on dentistry, where he speaks of certain changes which can be effected even when the second teeth are all through.

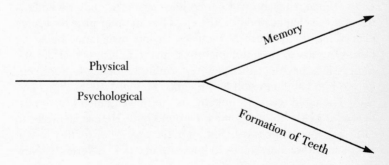

But this need not concern us further. When at the change of teeth the etheric body is loosened and stands alone, then the building up of the memory is separated off from the physical, and remains almost entirely in the element of soul, and this fact can really put the teachers on the right track. For before this change the soul and spirit formed a unity with the physical and etheric. After this the physical, which formerly worked together with the soul, is expressed in the form of the second teeth, and what collaborated with the physical in this process is separated off and is revealed as an increase in the power of forming ideas, and in the formation and reliability of the memory. If you have acquired this insight into human nature you will discover a great deal that will help you in your teaching. You must permeate yourselves with this spiritual knowledge of man in a living way, and then your observations of the child will inspire you with ideas and methods for your teaching, and this inner inspiration and enthusiasm will pass over into your practical work. The rules laid down in introductory books on education only produce an abstract activity of the soul, whereas what arises out of an anthroposophical knowledge penetrates into the teacher's will and into his work, and becomes the impulse for all that he does in the classroom.

A living knowledge of man brings life and order into the soul of the teacher, but if he studies only methods which arise out of natural science then he may get some clever ideas of what to do with the child but he will not be able to carry them out. The teacher's skill and practical handling of the child must arise out of the living spirit which is within him, and here purely scientific ideas can find no place. If the teacher can acquire a true knowledge of man, then he will notice how, when the etheric body is freed at the change of teeth, the child has an inner urge to receive everything in the form of pictures. In his own inner being he himself wants to become "picture." In the first epoch of life the impressions have not this picture-forming tendency but are converted into habit and skill in the child. Memory itself is habit and skill. The child wants to imitate, in the movements of his limbs, everything that he sees going on around him. He has no desire to form any inward pictures. But after the change of teeth you will notice how the child comes to know things quite differently. Now he wants to feel that pictures are arising in his soul, and therefore the teacher must bring everything into a pictorial element in his lessons. This creating of pictures is what the teacher has to understand above everything else.

But when we begin to look at the facts we are immediately confronted with certain contradictions. The child has to learn to read and write, and when he comes to school we take it for granted that he will learn to read first and then to write in connection with his reading. But let us consider the nature of the letters which we use when we take pen to paper and try to express in writing what is in our mind. What relationship have the printed letters of today to the original picture-language of olden times? How were we taught these things? We have to teach the children what a capital "A" and a small "a" are like, but whatever in the world have these letters to do with the sound "A" (as in "father")? There is no connection at all between the form of the letter A and the sound A. At the time when the art of writing arose, things were different. In certain parts of the world pictorial signs were used, and a kind of pictorial painting was employed. True, this became conventionalized later, but to begin with, these drawings were copies of the process and feeling of the sounds, so that what one had on the paper was to a certain extent a reproduction of what was living in the soul. But the modern characters are alien to the nature of the little child, and it is small wonder that when certain primitive peoples first saw printed letters they had a peculiar effect on them. When the civilized people of Europe came amongst the Red Indians of America and showed them how they expressed their thoughts on paper, the Red Indians were quite alarmed and thought it was the work of the devil. They were terrified of the little demons who were lurking behind the written letters. They immediately concluded that the Europeans dealt in black magic, for people have a habit of attributing to black magic whatever they cannot understand.

How should this topic be understood today? We know that when we utter the sound "Ah" we express wonder, admiration. Now it is quite a natural thing to try to reproduce this sound with your whole body and express it in this gesture of your arms. If you copy this gesture (stretching the arms obliquely above the head) then you get the capital A. In your teaching you can for instance begin with such a feeling of wonder, and proceed with the children to a kind of painting-drawing, and thus you can bring their inward and outward experiences into this painting-drawing and drawing-painting.

Now take another example. I tell the child to think of a fish, and I get him to paint it (awkward though this may be). He must do it in a special way, or just anyhow as he might like to, but with the head in front, like this, and the rest of the fish here. The child paints the fish, and thus, by a kind of painting-drawing, drawing-painting, he has produced a written character. You then tell him to pronounce the word "fish"—f-i-sh. Now take away the "i-sh," and from "fish" you have passed over to his first written letter, "f."

In this way the child will come to understand how pictorial writing arose, and how it developed into the writing of the present day. The forms were copied and the pictures were abandoned. This is how the drawing of the different sounds arose. You do not need to make a special study of how these things evolved. This is not absolutely necessary for a teacher, for he can develop them out of his own intuition and power of fancy.

Or take for instance the mouth. Let the child paint the upper lip and then pronounce the word "mouth." Leave out the "outh," and you get the "M."

In this way you can relate all the written characters to some reality, and the child will constantly be developing a living, inward activity. So you should teach the children writing first, and let the abstract letters of our present-day writing arise out of concrete reality. If a child learns to write in this way his whole being is engaged in the process. Whereas if you start with reading, then only the head organization takes part, in an abstract way. In writing the hand must participate also, and the whole human being is roused into activity. Thus if you begin with writing, a writing which is developed out of this shaping in pictures, drawing in forms, then in your teaching you will approach the whole being of the child. After this you can proceed to the teaching of reading, and what the child has developed out of his whole being, in this painting-drawing, can then be understood by the head. This method of teaching writing and reading will of course take longer, but it will have a far greater health-giving effect on the whole earthly life from birth to death.

These things can be done when the practical work of the school flows out of a real spiritual knowledge of man. Such a knowledge can, out of its own inner force, become the teaching method in our schools. It is this which lives in the desires of those who are earnestly seeking for a new art of education, but it can only be found in its true inner being if we are not afraid to seek after a full knowledge of the human being, body, soul, and spirit.

Guide to Further Reading

INTRODUCTION

Anyone coming to the teachings or writings of Rudolf Steiner for the first time cannot help but be bewildered, and perhaps incredulous, in the face of a bibliography of several hundred volumes. Without counting lectures in typescript or booklets and pamphlets, Steiner's publications in the authoritative Gesamtausgabe (Collected Works) edition in German number 354 volumes. Thus far approximately 200 volumes have been translated into English. Many are new editions rather than exact equivalents of the German editions. Approximately twenty volumes were written by Steiner as books; the remaining volumes consist of lecture cycles. It is important to recognize that most of the lecture courses have been published as they were delivered—without the benefit of Steiner's edit-

NOTE: Full bibliographic information current through 1983 on the volumes discussed below, as well as on other anthroposophical literature, can be found in the Bibliography.

ing. By contrast, Steiner wrote the following foundation works with great care and expected them to withstand careful scrutiny: *Philosophy of Freedom* (or *Philosophy of Spiritual Activity*), *Knowledge of the Higher Worlds and Its Attainment*, *Theosophy*, and *Occult Science*. These works, to which *Christianity as Mystical Fact* (also titled *Christianity and Occult Mysteries of Antiquity*) is sometimes added, serve as the carefully constructed base on which all of Steiner's lectures were built. In his *Autobiography*, Steiner offers the following explanation of the two forms of his published works:

The results of my anthroposophical work are, first, the books available to the general public; second, a great number of lecture-courses, originally regarded as private publications and sold only to members of the Theosophical (later Anthroposophical) Society. The courses consist of more or less accurate notes taken at my lectures which, for lack of time, I have not been able to correct. I would have preferred the spoken word to remain the spoken word, but the members wished to have the courses printed for private circulation. Thus they came into existence. Had I been able to correct them, the restriction "for members only," would have been unnecessary from the beginning. As it is, the restriction was dropped more than a year ago [Christmas Conference, 1923].

He continues:

In these private circles I could formulate what I had to say in a way I should have been obliged to modify had it been planned initially for the general public.

Thus the public and the private publications are in fact two quite different things, built upon different foundations. The public writings are the direct result of my inner struggles and labors, whereas the privately printed materials included the inner struggle and labor of the members. I listened to the inner needs of the members, and my living experience of this determined the form of the lectures. (*An Autobiography*, pp. 386–88)

The following annotated review of approximately 150 books by Steiner and fifty by other anthroposophic authors cannot claim to be comprehensive, but it does cover all of the basic works and many of the more revealing volumes of lectures. In the following pages, the basic books are not given attention proportionate to their importance because selections from these books are reprinted in this volume, and because their main ideas are discussed in the introductions to previous chapters. Since the primary purpose of the bibliography, and of this book, is to render Steiner more accessible and intelligible to students and the general reading public, the following pages contain many suggestions concerning the order in which to approach Steiner's vast and complex writings. While these suggestions may prove to be helpful in some cases, it is nevertheless true that many individuals have come to Steiner's writings through some unlikely routes, while others, armed with good intentions and good advice, sample and then move on. Reading (or not reading) in such materials is, above all, a personal choice.

1. LIFE AND WORK

By the usual standards of bibliographical guidance to Steiner's writings, the first work listed should probably be either *An Autobiography* or one of his basic works such as *Theosophy* or *Knowledge of the Higher Worlds*. Any one of these three works will well serve as an introduction to Steiner's teaching. Furthermore, no secondary source will be in the long run as rewarding as Steiner's own basic works, most of which deserve to be reread at regular intervals. Despite these reservations, however, readers new to Steiner's thinking may best be introduced to Steiner and Anthroposophy by the expert assistance provided in Stewart C. Easton's *Man and World in the Light of Anthroposophy*. This work effectively surveys all of the major areas of Steiner's thought: history of consciousness, human freedom, knowledge of higher worlds, karma and rebirth, esoteric Christianity, spirit and nature, art, social theory, education, biodynamic agriculture, medicine, nutrition, and the Anthroposophical Society. As *Man and World in the Light of Anthroposophy* is the best introduction in English to Anthroposophy in its basic teaching and varied applications, Stewart Easton's biography, *Rudolf Steiner: Herald of a New Epoch*, recreates, to the extent possible, the unique personal and spiritual drama of Rudolf Steiner's life. In contrast to Steiner's autobiography, which chronicles his life only until 1907, Easton's biography offers a detailed account of Steiner's entire life, culminating in a moving description of his last year, "The Annus Mirabilis of 1924." Easton's biography ably introduces and supplements Steiner's autobiographical account—written in his last year—of his childhood, education, intellectual development, spiritual experience, and the early years of his public mission.

Steiner's autobiography is available in two editions: *The Course of My Life* and *An Autobiography*. The more readable translation by Stebbing and the editorial notes by Paul M. Allen make the second far preferable to the earlier version. Regrettably, neither edition has an index. Valuable information is to be found in a minutely detailed out-of-print work by Guenther Wachsmuth, *The Life and Work of Rudolf Steiner: From the*

Turn of the Century to His Death. Friedrich W. Rittelmeyer's *Rudolf Steiner Enters My Life* describes Steiner's influence on a Protestant pastor who later founded The Christian Community with Steiner's help. Frans Carlgren's *Rudolf Steiner: 1861–1925* offers a summary sketch of Rudolf Steiner's life, writings, and practical activities, along with photographs. In *A Scientist of the Invisible: An Introduction to the Life and Work of Rudolf Steiner,* A. P. Shepherd, an Anglican clergyman, offers an informed and enthusiastic introduction to Steiner and Anthroposophy.

Since Easton's *Man and World* is more than 500 pages, some readers will prefer Francis Edmunds's *Anthroposophy—A Way of Life,* a clear introduction to Steiner's life, theory of human nature, historical vision, and interpretation of Christianity—all in readable prose and in less than 200 pages. George [Kaufman] Adams's *Fruits of Anthroposophy: An Introduction to the Work of Rudolf Steiner,* the first of many introductions, contains a sixty-page essay by George Adams, specialized essays by Carolyn Heydebrand, Eugen Kolisko, and Arild Rosenkrantz, as well as a bibliography and a survey of Anthroposophic activities up to 1922.

The following two works are collections of essays on the varied applications of Steiner's teaching, and will serve to complement the second half of Easton's *Man and World in the Light of Anthroposophy.* A. C. Harwood's *The Faithful Thinker: Centenary Essays on the Work and Thought of Rudolf Steiner, 1861–1925* contains essays by leading anthroposophists such as Owen Barfield, Alfred Heidenreich, A. C. Harwood, George Adams, Karl König, and Michael Wilson, and covers such topics as evolution, the Cosmic Christ, natural science and human freedom, color, architecture, the child with Down's Syndrome, farming, and the threefold commonwealth. A more recent volume, John Davy's *Work Arising: From the Life of Rudolf Steiner,* covers a similar range of topics: education, medicine, agriculture, arts, architecture, and industry—all theoretical and practical works based on the thought of Rudolf Steiner. As appropriate, there will be references in each section to individual chapters in Easton's *Man and World,* and to various articles in Harwood's *Faithful Thinker* and Davy's *Work Arising.*

2. EARLY WRITINGS

Goethe and Philosophy

Steiner wrote the material for his first book, *Goethe the Scientist,* from 1883, when he was twenty-two years old, until 1896. This work, which consists of essays on chapters of the Kuerschner edition of Goethe's natural science, is less systematic than *The Theory of Knowledge Based on Goethe's World-Conception* (1886). In 1897 Steiner published a second substantial work on Goethe's natural science and philosophy, *Goethe's Conception of the World*, a chapter of which is published in the present volume. Between his two major works on Goethe (1886 and 1897), Steiner published *Truth and Knowledge*, an enlarged version of his doctoral dissertation, his major work in philosophy, *The Philosophy of Freedom: The Basis for a Modern World Conception*. The philosophical attitude and some of the specific points in *The Philosophy of Freedom* are introduced in *Truth and Knowledge: Introduction to Philosophy of Freedom*, first published in 1892. In its first English translation, this work was entitled *Truth and Science* and published with *Philosophy of Freedom* in *The Philosophy of Spiritual Activity*. *Philosophy of Freedom* has often been published as *Philosophy of Spiritual Activity*. This was Steiner's recommendation for the English title which would at that time give the fullest meaning to his conception of freedom and which he hoped would most effectively impress on English-speaking people their need for a fuller realization of freedom. This work has two main sections: "Knowledge of Freedom," Steiner's epistemology based on Goethe and his own supersensible perception, and "The Reality of Freedom," Steiner's metaphysics and ethics of freedom. It is also a path of spiritual development capable of leading to supersensible perception solely through thinking. Steiner remarked that *Philosophy of Freedom* would outlast all of his other works. Although not all readers of Steiner are likely to be as engaged by *Philosophy of Freedom* as Steiner hoped, many others, both with and without philosophical training, may join those who regard it as the single most profound and personally influential book in their library.

Steiner's statements on the importance he attached to *Philosophy of Freedom* are collected in Otto Palmer's *Rudolf Steiner on His Book "The Philosophy of Freedom."* This volume would be helpful to anyone attempting to work through *The Philosophy of Freedom* on one's own, although it does assume a prior acquaintance with Anthroposophy. In addition to presenting Steiner's explanations concerning the origin, aim, and specific meaning of *The Philosophy of Freedom*, Palmer offers helpful explanations concerning both Steiner's comments and the use to which the book should be put. Palmer's book complements an earlier work with the same intent: Olin D. Wannamaker's *Rudolf Steiner's Philosophy of Spiritual Activity [Philosophy of Freedom]: Man's Freedom of Will—A Student's Introduction and Analysis*. This ninety-two-page booklet provides an outline and explanation for each chapter of *The Philos-*

ophy of Freedom. As helpful as Palmer, Wannamaker, and other second-ary sources may be, *Philosophy of Freedom* deserves and needs to be read on its own. The exercise of pondering this book is intended by Steiner as one of the surest methods for the development of a spiritually-based (inner, free) mode of thinking.

Carl Unger's *Principles of Spiritual Science* and Steiner's first course in the Goetheanum, *Boundaries of Natural Science,* with a lucid introduction by Nobel prize-winning author Saul Bellow, help to create a bridge from the earlier epistemological work to its later restatement and expansion as Anthroposophy.

Nietzsche

During this same period Steiner wrote a substantial study of Nietzsche, whom he visited and admired: *Friedrich Nietzsche: Battler Against His Time* (1895). At first glance, Steiner and Nietzsche might seem an odd combination, but it was the spiritual depth of Nietzsche that impressed Steiner, and on which Steiner's book focuses. Steiner refers to this book as "no more than a mere stammering," but one that is nevertheless inspired by his meeting with Nietzsche, a meeting which affords a revealing glimpse of Steiner's clairvoyance at work.

Ordinarily there would be little to be gained by a visit to Nietzsche during the last decade of his life when he was already insane and incapable of meaningful conversation. But Steiner's visit confirmed his belief that Nietzsche was to be revered more for his suffering than for his ideas. Steiner concludes his book with a memorial address, "The Personality of Friedrich Nietzsche," the last paragraph of which reads:

Nietzsche has produced no new ideas for a world conception. One will always recognize that his genius does not lie in the production of new ideas. But he suffered deeply because of the thought surrounding him. In compensation for this suffering he found the enraptured tones of his *Zarathustra*. He became the *poet* of the new world conception, the hymns in praise of the problems and results of the more recent natural science. All that the Nineteenth Century produced in ideas, would also have been produced without Nietzsche. In the eyes of the future he will not be considered an original philosopher, a founder of religions, or a prophet; for the future he will be a martyr of knowledge, who in poetry found words with which to express his suffering. (p. 212)

In subsequent writings, particularly in *Karmic Relationships* (Vol. 1, pp. 153–58) and in his *Autobiography*, Steiner recounts the clairvoyant vision of Nietzsche's soul tenuously related to his body. Steiner also saw with his "inner perception" the kind of soul history that he would later establish as one of the essential goals of Anthroposophy.

In inner perception I saw Nietzsche's soul as if hovering over his head, infinitely beautiful in its spirit-light, surrendered to the spiritual worlds it had longed for so much, but had been unable to find before illness had clouded his mind; the soul was still fettered to the body that had known it only when filled with yearning for the spirit. Nietzsche's soul was there still, but able to hold the body together only outside, the body in which it had met such strong resistance to the unfolding of its spiritual powers.

Previously I had *read* Nietzsche. Now I *saw* the actual bearer of ideas from the highest spirit-realms, ideas that even here shone in beauty despite having lost their original radiance on the way. A soul who had brought from former lives on earth golden riches of great spirituality but was unable to let it shine fully in the present life. I admired what Nietzsche had written; now I saw his radiant spirit behind what I so greatly admired.

Only in stammering words could I express what I thus beheld; this stammering became my book, *Friedrich Nietzsche: Battler Against His Time*. That the book is no more than a stammering conceals the nevertheless true fact that it was inspired by Nietzsche himself. (*An Autobiography*, p. 223)

Depending on the degree of our understanding and acceptance of Steiner's clairvoyance, the phrase "inspired by Nietzsche" can refer to a visit to a deranged, dying philosopher or to an inner vision of a soul-history suffering the torments of human blindness and cruelty.

Steiner slowly came to accept the fact that his clairvoyant reading of a thinker such as Nietzsche would not find favor with readers who reject the possibility of an interpretation based on spiritual experience. In the foreword to a work published in 1901, on mystics of the Renaissance, Steiner recounts some of the criticisms of his "world of ideas." While he dismisses these criticisms as unimportant in themselves, he nevertheless sees them as revealing "symptoms" of the serious resistance to a mode of thinking aiming at or based on higher knowledge. This work, variously titled *Eleven European Mystics, Mysticism at the Dawn of the Modern Age,* and *Mystics of the Renaissance and Their Relation to Modern Thought,* is Steiner's first work after his "experience of the mystery of Golgotha" which profoundly altered his spiritual and intellectual perspective. Writings after 1900—specifically works beginning with *Christianity as Mystical Fact* (1902)—all reflect Steiner's experience of the Christ event both in his own consciousness and in human history. In *Christianity as Mystical Fact,* which is also published as *Christianity and Occult Mysteries of Antiquity,* Steiner treats some of the themes which form the core of his spiritual teaching, including the centrality of the Christ event in the evolution of human consciousness, the preparatory function of ancient Egyptian, Greek, and Buddhist spiritual streams, and the esoteric dimension of early Christianity. This brief book is one of the most accessible and vivid of Steiner's works but it should not be taken as representative of his mature work on the history of consciousness or on Christology (for which see "The Evolution of Consciousness" and "Esoteric Christianity," below).

3. SPIRITUAL ANTHROPOLOGY

Basic Books

In 1904 Rudolf Steiner published two works which remain basic to his entire teaching. Although neither is explicitly concerned with the impact of the Christ event which he experienced in 1899, they do show the decisive effect of this spiritual experience and clearly mark the beginning of his esoteric-spiritual or anthroposophic teaching. *Knowledge of the Higher Worlds and Its Attainment,* which was published serially in *Lucifer-Gnosis* (1904),* may seem to some readers rather disorganized and occasionally obscure, but nevertheless it is one of the surest introductions to the method and effects of Steiner's spiritual discipline. A partial list of its contents accurately reflects its centrality to Steiner's entire teaching: method for attaining knowledge of the higher worlds, states of initiation, training, meeting the guardian of the threshold, death, and afterlife. *The Stages of Higher Knowledge* (previously *The Gates of Knowledge*) is a continuation of the series of articles that became *Knowledge of the Higher Worlds,* to which it forms a kind of sequel.

When anthroposophists are asked, as they invariably are, for the one book which most adequately represents the essential core of Steiner's teaching, most recommend *Theosophy: An Introduction to the Supersensible Knowledge of the World and the Destination of Man.* Accordingly, three of the four chapters of this basic work have been reprinted in this anthology.

Occult Science—An Outline is perhaps equally basic as a summary of anthroposophic teaching, but far more detailed and demanding of the reader. In addition to presenting Steiner's definitive articulation of his theory of human nature (in chapters 2 and 3), *Occult Science* contains his most systematic account of past, present, and future evolution, initiation, and other topics in spiritual science. As do *Knowledge of the Higher Worlds* and *Theosophy, Occult Science* will require repeated readings, ideally supplemented by works on more specific and applied topics, the

---

* Steiner also pulished *Cosmic Memory: Prehistory of Earth and Man* in *Luzifer-Gnosis,* a periodical which he edited at irregular intervals from 1903 to 1908.

most central of which are those dealing with karma and rebirth, initiation and spiritual discipline.

In *Theosophy of the Rosicrucian*, Steiner lectured on some of the same topics treated in *Theosophy* and *Occult Science*—specifically, theory of human nature, and initiation—in a briefer and less systematic fashion. As with most lecture series, this volume can be used effectively not as a substitute but as an introduction or supplement to such basic works as *Theosophy* and *Occult Science*. The lectures collected in *Reincarnation and Immortality* may be useful individually, but they are entirely unrelated (despite the title, reincarnation and immortality are barely discussed). Such disparate collections require the systematic framework provided by a more basic work, such as *At the Gates of Spiritual Science* or a secondary source such as Easton's *Man and World*.

Karma and Rebirth

Steiner wrote at great length on all aspects of the double topic of karma and rebirth. Perhaps the best place to start, after the second chapter of *Theosophy* (reprinted in this volume) is chapter four of Easton's *Man and World*. Most readers would do well to follow these readings with one or more of the following: *Reincarnation and Karma: Their Significance in Modern Culture*; Eugen Kolisko's *Reincarnation and other Essays*; Rudolf Frieling's *Christianity and Reincarnation*; and René Querido's, *Questions and Answers on Karma and Reincarnation*. *Manifestations of Karma* consists of eleven lectures on karma in individual life, including disease, accidents, freewill, and karma in relation to higher beings. Each of these volumes argues for the reality and spiritual significance of both karma and rebirth, with examples and explanations that avoid the simplistic mechanical view prevalent in writings on this topic. Each affords a glimpse of the inner workings of karma and rebirth available to a spiritual seer of Steiner's power.

Steiner's most complete and fascinating account of the passage of the discarnate human individuality through the planetary spheres after death is to be found in *Between Death and Rebirth* (Berlin, 1912–1913; not to be confused with *Life Between Death and Rebirth*, various cities, 1912–1913, discussed below). This cycle contains some of Rudolf Steiner's most advanced explanations concerning the relation between earth and other planets, and the complex influences on the individual during, after, and on the return to earthly life. Lecture 5, "Christian Rosenkreutz and Buddha" (22 December 1912), complements the lectures in *From Buddha to Christ* (1909–1912). Steiner explains that *Between Death and Rebirth* provides the cosmic dimension of afterlife, while his book *Theosophy* depicts the afterlife "more from within by means of pictures which relate more to inward soul conditions" (p. 118). *Between Death and Rebirth* is ideally complemented by The *Inner Nature of Man and Life between Death and a New Birth,* six lectures delivered in Vienna in 1914. Since this especially beautiful lecture cycle has long been out of print, it is worth listing the lecture titles: "The Four Spheres of Man's Life of Soul and Their Strengthening in Space," "Emergence from the Body in Time," "Phantoms and the Store of Memories," "Experiences in the Spiritual World after Death: The True Relationship to Christ," "The Life after Death until the Cosmic Midnight Hour," "The Awakening through the Holy Spirit." *Supersensible Man* (five lectures given at The Hague, 1923) supplements both of the above-mentioned cycles by depicting the individual soul in the afterlife as it appears to higher beings. In this respect, Stewart Easton suggests, *Supersensible Man* may be unique in all of Rudolf Steiner's writings.

In contrast to the three books recommended above, all of which are out of print, *Life Between Death and Rebirth,* the one book in print which superficially appears to cover some of the same topics, is marred by an almost verbatim repetition of lengthy sections of several lectures, with virtually the same content, given in different cities.

The most important of Steiner's writings on karma and rebirth is the remarkable eight-volume series, *Karmic Relationships: Esoteric Studies.* Stewart Easton describes these highly revealing and potentially misunderstood esoteric studies as "the very culmination and crown of Rudolf Steiner's life work," and explains why they should not be read selectively or out of sequence:

It is really essential for any student who wishes to study these lectures to begin with Volume 1 and work carefully through it. This volume gives a wealth of information about karma as a whole, whereas most of the later volumes deal with specific personalities, and Steiner on numerous occasions tells us that no generalizations can be made from the successive incarnations of the particular personalities he has chosen. If after thoughtful study of Volume 1, the student wishes to pursue his study further, he should read the entire series as a whole, the only exception to this being perhaps the second lecture of Volume 3 given on July 4, 1924, which contains a moving and beautiful discussion of the role of the various hierarchies in man's life between death and rebirth. (*Man and World,* p. 171)

Some of the ideas contained in the second lecture of Volume 3 are summarized in the introduction to chapter 2, "Spiritual Anthropology," above.

A careful reading of *Karmic Relationships,* and some of the more introductory works on karma and rebirth cited in this section, will eventually disclose the extent to which an understanding of both karma and rebirth require an understanding of spiritual discipline and intuition; they must also be understood in relation to cosmic and historical forces. There are at least three lecture series in which Steiner discusses karma and rebirth in relation to these larger themes. (For a bibliographical survey of Steiner's works on spiritual beings, cosmic forces, and patterns of historical evolution, see sections 4 and 5.) *The Karma of Vocation in Connection with the Life of Goethe* opens with an account, from a spiritual-scientific perspective, of how Goethe's relationship to the spiritual world enabled him to create *Faust*. Steiner explains how and why "Faust constantly grows beyond Goethe" (p. 39). The second half of this lecture series focuses on modern esoteric movements, particularly on the Theosophical Society, the need for a christianization and sacramentalization of labor and social life, and on the relation of human experience to spiritual forces and cosmic realities. There are also three earlier lecture series which cover some of the same topics—karma, spiritual beings, heavenly bodies, and initiation: *The Influence of Spiritual Beings upon Man* (unfortunately marred by a substandard translation) discusses from the perspective of spiritual science various facts and beings of the higher worlds and their connection with man, including the influence of planets and spiritual hierarchies on human experience; *Initiation, Eternity and the Passing Moment* contains seven lectures concerned primarily with initiate consciousness, and includes a discussion of the importance of a relation to the Christ as a preparation for the vision and recognition of the Christ Being in the higher worlds (p. 43); *The Being of Man and His Future Evolution* discusses the theme of karma and destiny as it concerns the human body, with particular emphasis on illness, sin, and the rhythms in the physical, etheric, and astral bodies.

Man: Hieroglyph of the Universe treats broadly the spiritual relationship between the human constitution and the earth, planets and fixed stars. *The Wisdom of the Soul, and of the Spirit; Anthroposophy, Psychosophy, Pneumatosophy* is difficult reading but it is highly suggestive.

Spiritual Development

Steiner delivered many lecture cycles on the method and effects of spiritual discipline, but perhaps none are quite so compelling as *The Effects of Spiritual Development*, which describes the influences of anthroposophical life on the whole organization of the human being:

The physical body, the etheric body, the astral body, and the true Self of man are transformed in a certain way when he really assimilates Anthroposophy. I propose to discuss in turn the modifications which the human sheaths undergo under the influence of esotericism or through the exoteric study of Anthroposophy when taken seriously. (p. 7)

Anyone who takes seriously the promised results of anthroposophic discipline will be interested in a judiciously edited collection of lectures by Steiner on the method for attaining supersensible knowledge, or knowledge of the higher worlds, *Esoteric Development* (1982). In his brief but helpful introduction, Alan Howard describes both the nature of the thinking process that Steiner teaches and the subtle self-transformation at which it aims. A portion of Howard's good advice is worth quoting at length:

The reader should also be aware of what will be happening to him if he decides to follow this path, and although Steiner makes this abundantly clear, it will not hurt to underline one thing. One is engaged in transforming the soul into an organ of perception, and one is doing this largely as the result of exercises based on thinking. We usually imagine perception and thinking to be two entirely different activities, but we cannot really keep them apart. One need only recall how, after a strenuous bout of thinking, when the concept for which we are searching at last appears, we invariably say, "Ah! Now I see!" to realize that perceiving (in this case, perceiving concepts) is closely interwoven with thinking. One does "see" the concept that has appeared in consciousness; and it is this seeing in thinking that the aspirant will be exercising in everything he does. "As color is to the eye," says Steiner in *Goethe the Scientist*, "and sound to the ear, so are concepts and ideas to thinking: it [thinking] is an organ of perception." (ix)

Additional works on the method and effects of Anthroposophy as a spiritual discipline include the following shorter paperbacks: *The Spiritual Guidance of Man, The Spiritual Foundation of Morality: Francis of Assisi and the Mission of Love, A Road to Self-Knowledge and the Threshold of the Spiritual World,* and two collections of significant but internally unrelated lectures, *Methods of Spiritual Research* and *Results of Spiritual Investigation*.

There are several lectures in which Steiner concretely explicates the differences between ancient Oriental practices for self-realization (e.g., yoga) and modern requirements: "The Change in the Path to Supersensible Knowledge" (published as a booklet), the first lecture in *The Tension between East and West,* and the first three lectures of *The Spiritual Ground of Education.*

Another instrument for the daily exercise of spiritual discipline is provided by Rudolf Steiner's *Calendar of the Soul,* consisting of a brief verse or *mantram* for each week of the year. In his preface to the second edition of the *Calendar,* reprinted below, Rudolf Steiner explains the purpose and use of these verses:

The year's round has a life of its own, a life the human soul can share. Let the soul be influenced by the life of the year as it changes week by week and it will rightly be able to find itself. It will feel how forces spring up that strengthen it inwardly. It will perceive that such forces yearn to be awakened in it that can lead to an understanding of the workings of the world as they unfold in the course of time. The soul will then come to realize which of those delicate but meaningful threads connect it with the world into which it has been born.

In this Calendar an appropriate mantram is given for each week, enabling the soul to experience what that week fulfills as its part of the life of the year. The mantrams are meant to express what resounds in the soul when it rightly unites itself with that life. They were designed with the thought in mind that, from a healthy feeling of unity with nature, a strong sense of one's being can arise, and also with the belief that, when the soul truly understands itself, it longs to experience the workings of the world through the means of such mantrams.

Several secondary works on spiritual anthropology—karma and rebirth, initiation, and spiritual discipline—all by accomplished followers of Rudolf Steiner, are especially recomended: Carl Unger, a close collaborator of Rudolf Steiner, has written *Steiner's Theosophy: Notes on the Book "Theosophy,"* a brief, helpful commentary on *Theosophy*. Karl König, founder of the Camphill Movement, is author of *The Human Soul* (also published as part of *Aspects of Curative Education*, an exceptionally clear spiritual physiology covering many of the topics treated in *Theosophy* and *Occult Science*); Guenther Wachsmuth, who was Rudolf Steiner's private secretary, first treasurer of the Anthroposophical Society, and author of *The Life and Work of Rudolf Steiner*, is also author of a detailed study of rebirth, *Reincarnation as a Phenomenon of Metamorphosis*; Paul Eugen Schiller's *Rudolf Steiner and Initiation: The Anthroposophical Path of Inner Schooling—A Survey* is one of the clearest introductory surveys of Steiner's spiritual discipline, including preparation (particularly the preparation of thinking, feeling, and willing), schooling (particularly meditation practice), initiation, and levels of knowledge (imagination, inspiration, and intuition); and Francis Edmunds, founder of Emerson College, a center of adult education in England based on Steiner's teachings and pedagogy, and author of *Rudolf Steiner Education*, has recently written *Anthroposophy—A Way of Life*, a wise and compelling introduction to Steiner's teachings and their practical applications. It is probably safe to say that this work by Edmunds is the best introduction to Steiner and Anthroposophy short of Easton's larger and more comprehensive introduction, *Man and World in the Light of Anthroposophy*.

It is not accidental that basic secondary works such as Easton's *Man and World* and Edmunds's *Anthroposophy* are cited here as well as in

the first and tenth sections. A survey of Steiner's spiritual anthropology—
including karma, rebirth, initiation, and spiritual discipline—cannot help
but overlap with an introduction to Steiner's life and work and his founding a movement and society for the sharing and application of his teaching.

4. THE SPIRITUAL COSMOS

Steiner's most systematic account of the evolution of the earth and of
human nature is to be found in the fourth chapter of *Occult Science,*
"Man and the Evolution of the World" (pp. 102–221). In 1904, at the
same time as he was writing *Theosophy* and *Knowledge of the Higher
Worlds,* Steiner also published in *Lucifer-Gnosis* a series of articles concerning the earliest stages of prehistory. In 1939 these articles were
translated as *Atlantis and Lemuria;* in 1959 they were published as *Cosmic Memory: Prehistory of Earth and Man.* Although many readers will
find this work unusual and difficult to assess, others will find it a vividly
written account of the early evolution of earth and humanity. Most of
Steiner's works on the topic of evolution (and on virtually all other topics)
consist in lecture series, few of which offer the systematic coherence of
written works such as *Occult Science* and *Cosmic Memory.*

The works listed in the remainder of this section, all of which consist of
lecture series, cover a wide range of topics, from the spiritual function of
planets and stars to the nature and significance of spiritual beings. It is
probably safe to conject that readers unfamiliar with Anthroposophy, or
the kind of subjects treated in spiritual and esoteric studies, will find the
material covered in these works the most startling of all Steiner's writings. In a culture which generally denies spiritual realities, writings concerning the spiritual influence of planets or significance of angels in human affairs will typically be regarded as speculative nonsense. That such
speculation should come from one so sane and productive of prized practical creations, however, may give some readers pause to consider the
possibility that the kind of link between the cosmos and human consciousness central to the ancient world may still have validity. Readers
not open to this possibility may want to omit this section and most of the
works listed in the next two sections, "Evolution of Consciousness" and
"Esoteric Christianity." If so, skip to sections on practical works—Social
Sciences (section 7), Education (section 8), Arts (section 9), and Natural
Sciences (section 10).

Planets

Perhaps the first work to be recommended after *Cosmic Memory* and *Occult Science* is *The Spiritual Hierarchies and Their Reflection in the Physical World: Zodiac, Planets, Cosmos*. In this series of ten lectures, Steiner discusses the realm of invisible beings above man which can be investigated by supersensible cognition. A supplement to this wide-ranging work might be a course of five lectures entitled *The Inner Realities of Evolution*. In this series Steiner discusses the evolutionary stages of the "embodiment of the earth" by heavenly bodies, understood from a spiritual point of view. This highly esoteric series of lectures concludes with an argument for the impact on the physical earth of the Mystery of Golgotha. *The Influence of Spiritual Beings Upon Man* discusses both the influence of heavenly bodies (Saturn, Sun, Moon) on earth and man, and the influence of elemental beings such as nymphs, undines, and gnomes. *Planetary Spheres, and Their Influence on Man's Life on Earth and in the Spiritual Worlds* includes six lectures delivered in London, 1922: "The Threefold Sun and the Risen Christ," "The Cosmic Origin of the Human Form," "Man's Life in Sleep and After Death," "Life in the Spiritual Spheres and the Return to Earth," "Luciferic and Ahrimanic Powers Wrestling for Man," and "Christ and the Metamorphosis of Karma."

The following seven volumes consist of cycles of lectures on such topics as stars and planets, the formation of the human body, and the relation between cosmic and human evolution. In this set of seven volumes, as in general, the later lecture series are the more advanced and revealing. *True and False Paths in Spiritual Investigation*, for example, a cycle of eleven lectures which Steiner delivered at Torquay, England, in August 1924, less than a year before he died, is a powerful series which presupposes familiarity with anthroposophical teachings concerning the spiritual world. The seven volumes, in order of delivery, are as follows: *Macrocosm and Microcosm* (1912), *The Spiritual Beings in the Heavenly Bodies and in the Kingdoms of Nature* (1912), *The World of the Senses and the World of the Spirit* (1912), *Man and the World of the Stars; The Spiritual Communion of Mankind* (1922), *Man as Symphony of the Creative Word* (1923), *Man's Being, His Destiny, and World Evolution* (1923), and the work noted above, *True and False Paths in Spiritual Investigation* (1924).

Spiritual Beings

In addition to stars, planets, the hierarchies, and elemental beings, Steiner's account of the spiritual cosmos includes elaborate descriptions of three spiritual beings intimately involved in the course of human history: Lucifer, Ahriman, and the Archangel Michael. With the possible exception of Steiner's account of the two Jesus children (section 6), writings on Lucifer and Ahriman are perhaps the most likely to be ridiculed, or at least avoided, by readers new to his teachings. Steiner most effectively presents the spiritual functions of Lucifer and Ahriman in his description of the temptation of Christ at the start of Christ's mission, in his Mystery dramas, and his sculpture, "Christ—'Representative of Man'."

As Steiner reads the Akashic Record, the Christ was tempted not by one being, but by two, Lucifer and Ahriman. He explains that Lucifer is another name for the Devil; Ahriman is another name for Satan. In the gospels and the Christian tradition generally these two beings are collapsed into one and their two names are used interchangeably. Steiner insists that evil is actually polar and that the function and powers of these two beings are quite different, both in the temptation scene (as in *The Fifth Gospel*, section 6) and in human evolution. In the temptation scene, and throughout the course of history, Lucifer plays on human pride and offers the delusion of divinity. Ahriman takes the opposite tack, tempting man to deny his link with divinity and to live entirely on the material plane (Ahriman tries to tempt the Christ to turn stone into bread and thereby to lower His power to the material plane). Although they are tempters, and their own aims must be regarded as essentially evil, the workings of Lucifer and Ahriman nevertheless serve the purposes of higher gods and in any case are necessary for human progress. In the books listed below, Steiner emphasizes the positive function as well as the dangers of Lucifer and Ahriman. In fact, the primary intent of these writings is to show the proper balance between these competing forces. The second picture which might help render Lucifer and Ahriman intelligible is Steiner's thirty-foot wood sculpture of the Christ as the "Representative of Man" balancing the competing influence of Lucifer and Ahriman (see p. 228).

Probably the best introduction to Steiner's conception of Lucifer and Ahriman is a booklet containing three lectures, *The Balance in the World and Man: Lucifer and Ahriman*. Also to be recommended are: *The Secrets of the Threshold*, a course of eight lectures delivered in 1913; a six-lecture cycle entitled *Three Streams in the Evolution of Mankind: The Connection of the Luciferic-Ahrimanic Impulses with the Christ-Jahve Impulse; The Deed of Christ and the Opposing Spiritual Powers: Lucifer, Ahriman, Mephistepheles, Asuras;* and *The Influences of Lucifer and Ahriman: Man's Responsibility for the Earth*. In all of these works Steiner emphasizes that although each individual, as well as the entire course of human history, are at least partly the result of Luciferic and Ahrimanic influences, it is the free choice of man which determines the exact nature and extent of such influences. Lucifer and Ahriman exert a negative and evil effect on humanity because man allows their influence to be misplaced and one-sided.

The third spiritual being important for an understanding of Steiner's teaching on man's place in the cosmos is the Archangel Michael, whose function is explained in, among other places, *The Mission of the Archangel Michael*, in Stewart C. Easton's *And Another Strong Angel: A Study of the Cosmic Mission of the Archangel Michael in Antiquity and Now According to the Teachings of Anthroposophy*, and most authoritatively, in *Anthroposophical Leading Thoughts*, Rudolf Steiner's letters to members in 1924, subtitled "The Michael Mystery." In the last of these three works, Rudolf Steiner describes the mission of Michael on behalf of humanity in relation to Ahriman, Lucifer, and the Christ: *"Michael-Christ* will stand in future as the guiding word at the entrance to the path upon which man may arrive at his world-goal, in a way that is cosmically right, between the Luciferic and Ahrimanic powers" (p. 90). The concept *Michael-Christ* is a way of expressing "the most perfect" accord between the Mystery of Golgotha and the Being and Mission of Michael (p. 93). In this same work, in a section entitled "First Study: At the Gates of the Spiritual Soul (Consciousness-Soul)—How Michael in the Spiritual World is Preparing for His Earth-Mission through the Conquest of Lucifer," Steiner offers the following summary of Michael's mission:

Michael is already at this time active for humanity from the spiritual world. He is preparing his later work from out of the supersensible. He is giving humanity impulses which preserve the former relation to the Divine-Spiritual world, without this preservation adopting a Luciferic character.

Then in the last third of the nineteenth century Michael himself presses forward into the physical earthly world with the activities which he has exercised in preparation from out of the supersensible, from the fifteenth to the nineteenth century.

Humanity had to undergo a period of spiritual evolution for the purpose of freeing itself from that relation to the spiritual world which threatened to become an impossible one. Then the evolution was guided, through the Michael Mission, into paths which brought the progress of Earth-humanity once more into a good and healthy relation to the spiritual world.

Thus Michael stands in his activity between the Luciferic *World-picture* and the Ahrimanic *World-intellect*. The World-picture becomes through him a *World-revelation* full of wisdom, which reveals the World-intellect as Divine *World-activity*. And in this World-activity lives the care of Christ for humanity—even in the World-activity which can thus reveal itself to the heart of man out of Michael's World-revelation. (pp. 110–11)

Seasons and Festivals

Given his deep affinity with the Mystery traditions, the esoteric Christian tradition, and the rhythms of the cosmos, Steiner could not help but be sensitive to the spiritual dimension of the seasons and calendar of spiritual events. This concern is evidenced by a major collection of this work on the subject, *The Festivals and Their Meaning*, which includes thirty lectures on the four principal spiritual seasons: Christmas, Easter, Ascension and Pentecost (or Whitsun), and Michaelmas (the festival celebrating the epoch of the Archangel Michael). These lectures provide a comprehensive explanation of the spiritual significance of the four festival seasons both in their origin and in contemporary experience. *The Four Seasons and the Archangels* is a lecture series given at Dornach in 1923 which treats "the experience of the course of the year in four cosmic imaginations": the Michael Imagination, the Christmas Imagination, the Easter Imagination, and the St. John Imagination.

5. EVOLUTION OF CONSCIOUSNESS

Steiner's historical writings and lectures are essentially exercises in imaginative thinking and enlivened perception on the model of the Goethean scientific-artistic world conception. Steiner reads history the way Goethe read the plant world: the phenomena are important but can be adequately understood only as symptoms of deeper processes. In this sense, all of Steiner's historical writings are an attempt to reveal the spiritual forces which fashion the particular and observable. The preceding section annotates those writings in which Steiner attempts to disclose changes wrought by planets, stars, spiritual hierarchies, and spirit beings; the next section, "Esoteric Christianity," lists works in which he interprets the history of the West in light of the ongoing struggle for and against freethinking made possible by the incarnation of the Christ. Consequently, it could be argued that by academic standards, Steiner does not write (external) history at all. Rather, he approaches the historical process with the same method and capability as he approaches all other pursuits—in order to penetrate to the level or source at which he believes the real, or the more effectual, action is taking place.

Perhaps the best brief introduction to Steiner's historical method and vision is the second chapter of Easton's *Man and World*. Easton, who is a former professor of history at The City College of New York and the author of two textbooks on modern Western history, is at his best form in this one-hundred-page chapter, "History and the Evolution of Human Consciousness." In addition to this chapter by Easton, a particularly convincing application of Steiner's historical-spiritual method is to be found in several works by Owen Barfield, whose writings are annotated at the conclusion of this section. As for general or introductory works, any of the following four books, three by Steiner and one by a distinguished anthroposophist, will serve as an example of Steiner's supersensible reading of the evolving modes of human awareness and thought.

Ancient World

First, *Egyptian Myths and Mysteries* offers some important insights on Isis and Osiris, but the value of this book for an understanding of the evolution of consciousness lies in its comparisons between ancient and modern cultural streams and corresponding qualities of the human body. The second work worthy of special mention is *Christianity as Mystical Fact* (or *Christianity and Occult Mysteries of Antiquity*), cited in section 1 and to be discussed again in section 7. This early but seminal book, from which three chapters have been reprinted in the present work, offers Steiner's distinctive interpretation of the Greek esoteric tradition from Homer to Plato, Egyptian and Buddhist traditions, and several revealing chapters on early Christianity. The entire book exemplifies Steiner's attempt to locate and explain the role of spiritual knowledge in the dynamics of cultural change.

The third book to be recommended is *Riddles of Philosophy*, an uneven but occasionally powerful history of Western philosophy which traces the varieties of thinking (rather than philosophical systems) characteristic of each epoch from the Presocratics to the early twentieth century. This book consists of two unequal parts. Part 1 was written in 1914 both as a historical outline of philosophic expression of the evolution of consciousness and as a way of providing a historical context for his earlier work, *World and Life Conceptions of the Nineteenth Century*, first published in 1901 and republished as Part 2 of *Riddles of Philosophy*. This unusual process of composition of *Riddles of Philosophy* explains why more than 300 of its 470 pages are devoted to nineteenth-century philosophers, mostly German, including, of course, Kant and Goethe as well as some philosophers entirely neglected by contemporary scholarship. Fewer than one-hundred pages are devoted to the twenty-five centuries from Thales to Kant. Anglo-American philosophy is barely mentioned. Therefore, as a history of philosophy, this work has serious limitations. But it is generally successful as an example of Steiner's esoteric capability addressed to the exoteric history of thought. A fourth work which typifies Steiner's esoteric historical method, and does so in a readable style, is Frederick Hiebel, *The Gospel of Hellas: The Mission of Ancient Greece and the Advent of Christ*. This fascinating work, unfortunately long out of print, offers a Steinerian interpretation of the mode of consciousness exhibited by Greek religion, arts, philosophy, the Hellenic character of both Paul's epistles (particularly his conception of conscience), and The Gospel of John.

The remainder of this section consists in a listing of approximately twenty works in which Steiner offers an interpretation of epochs or strands in the evolution of human consciousness. These volumes are arranged in the approximate chronological order of their subject matter, from ancient Egypt to the modern West. The last component in this section is a survey of writings by Owen Barfield on the evolution of consciousness.

Ancient Myths: Their Meaning and Connection with Evolution covers some of the same historical periods as *Egyptian Myths and Mysteries*. In addition to many individual lectures, Steiner also delivered a lecture series on Hebrew consciousness: *Genesis: Biblical Secrets of Creation—The Six Days' Work in the First Book of Moses*. For highly suggestive interpretations of the Hebrew scriptures based on Steiner, see Emil Bock's *Genesis: Creation and the Patriarchs* and Valentin Tomberg's *Anthroposophical Studies of the Old Testament*. Steiner's *Turning Points in Spiritual History* contains six lectures, one each on Zarathustra, Hermes, Buddha, Moses, Elijah, and Christ. His *Wonders of the World, Ordeals of the Soul, Revelations of the Spirit* discusses the significance of the gods, mythology, and mystery centers of the ancient world.

Mystery Knowledge and Mystery Centers briefly describes the evolution of the earth, plants, and animals, and the relation of each to humanity. Fascinating accounts follow on the ancient mysteries of Artemis at Ephesos, Hibernia, Eleusis, Samothrace, and the Rosicrucian Mystery of the Middle Ages. The ancient mysteries, from Zarathustrian and Hermetic to the Grail tradition of the Christian Middle Ages, are also described in *The Mysteries of the East and of Christianity* and *The East in the Light of the West*. All three of the previously mentioned works make excellent complements to *Christianity as Mystical Fact*. In *The Mission of the Individual Folk Souls in Relation to Teutonic Mythology*, Steiner describes the place of the folk spirits in relation to the distinctive character of a nation or people, in this case focusing on the development of the ancient Germanic peoples.

Buddha, Krishna, and Christ

Steiner delivered two lecture cycles and several individual lectures on early Indian spirituality, specifically on Buddha and the Bhagavadgita, each of which warrants special emphasis. The five lectures on Buddha and Christianity collected in *From Buddha to Christ* date from 1909-12, the years during which Steiner was also lecturing on the Christian scriptures. These five lectures trace some of the spiritual (and startling) links between the Buddha and the Christ, as well as between Buddha and St. Francis of Assisi and Christian Rosenkreutz (a spiritual personality important to Steiner's mission).

In *The Occult Significance of the Bhagavad Gita,* Steiner depicts Krishna as that being who has been working since the eighth century B.C. to make the human organism capable of entering the epoch of self-consciousness. Steiner also indicates that although Krishna was able to guide individuals (such as Arjuna of the Gita) to the self-consciousness of their divine natures, it remained for the Christ to lead the whole of humanity to this possibility by absorbing into his consciousness the limitation of self-salvation at the expense of the world (pp. 134-37). *The Bhagavad Gita and the Epistles of Paul* includes five lectures on the spiritual streams running through the Gita—Veda, Sankhya and Yoga—and their relationship of the Christian stream in the person and mission of the Apostle Paul. As a result of his own clairvoyant perception, Steiner describes the sublime mystery by which the Christ took Krishna as his own soul sheath, which sheath was perceived by Paul in his conversion experience on the road to Damascus. Thus, in experiencing the light enveloping the Christ, the spiritual message and power of the Gita streamed from the resurrected soul of the Christ into Paul and thereby into Christianity. Steiner concludes: "So much in the revelations of the Testaments, even if in scattered fragments, comes from the ancient teaching of Krishna" (p. 98). These are not the only books by Steiner depicting the intricate relationships among Krishna, Buddha, and Christian figures such as the Christ, John the Evangelist, Paul the Apostle and St. Francis. All of these figures, as well as Moses, Zarathustra, and others are woven throughout Steiner's many volumes of lectures on the gospels (section 6).

Some of these same topics are covered in two popularized accounts by Edouard Schuré: *The Great Initiates: A Study of the Secret History of Religions* and a less reliable—perhaps even unreliable—work, *From Sphinx to Christ: An Occult History.*

Christianity and the Modern World

If Steiner's writings on esoteric Christianity were not a separate section, this survey of his writings on successive epochs would turn at this point to writings concerning the impact on the evolution of human consciousness wrought by the Christ and the history of Christianity. An account of this transformation, as interpreted in Rudolf Steiner's lectures on the Gospels (section 6), would describe the mission of the Hebrew people as the agent of the law for which Christ would be the fulfillment in freedom. Such an account would also describe the way in which the Christ impulse toward thinking and freedom used the philosophic prowess and mystery traditions of the Greeks. Some of these themes are briefly discussed in the chapters from *Christianity as Mystical Fact* and *The Gospel of St. John* reprinted in this book, as well as in *Christ and the Spiritual World: The Search for the Holy Grail*.

Steiner's lecture cycle *Occult History: Historical Personalities and Events in the Light of Spiritual Science* offers revealing insights on ancient cultures and on both ancient and Christian thinkers from Homer to Nicolas of Cusa. Steiner offers a few works on the medieval and renaissance experiences, and several on modern European thought. One work which covers both periods, though only briefly, is *Riddles of Philosophy* (cited above). The cursory treatment of medieval thought in *Riddles of Philosophy* is compensated for in *The Redemption of Thinking: A Study in the Philosophy of Thomas Aquinas*. The title of this important series of three lectures is rather misleading in that only the second lecture is concerned with Aquinas; the first lecture concerns Neoplatonism and Augustine and the third traces Thomism from the time of Aquinas to the early twentieth century. A lengthy epilogue relating Steiner's spiritual science to Thomism is provided by M. R. Nicoll and A. P. Shepherd.

The Driving Force of Spiritual Powers in World History includes seven brief lectures which serve as a transition from Steiner's lectures on the Renaissance mystics (in *Eleven European Mystics/Mysticism at the Dawn of the Modern Age*, section 3) to the modern period. Far more substantial lectures on the same period, approximately from the fifteenth to the early twentieth century, are in the cycle entitled *From Symptom to Reality in Modern History*. This work is especially valuable for its discussions of the rise of modern science, Goethe, modern European Christianity, and Steiner's comments on his *Philosophy of Freedom*. In *The Occult Movement in the Nineteenth Century and Its Relation to Modern Culture*, Steiner discusses the materialist character of nineteenth-century thought in relation to the efforts by some of the prominent esoteric movements, particularly the Theosophical Society, to stem the advance of materialism.

The Tension between East and West discusses the sciences and social structures of Asia and Europe (and briefly, America). These lectures on the conflicting philosophies of Eastern in relation to Western Europe and America have gained rather than lost relevance during the sixty years since they were delivered. *The East in the Light of the West* traces the history of consciousness and esoteric teaching from the Oriental to the European and American cultures and emphasizes the nature and function of the Christ influence in this evolution.

There are two additional lecture series on history and the evolution of consciousness, both of which Steiner delivered during the last two years of his life. Clearly intended for an audience well-versed in Anthroposophy, they are: *World History in the Light of Anthroposophy* and *The Evolution of Consciousness as Revealed through Initiation-Consciousness* (originally, and more accurately, titled: *The Evolution of the World and Humanity*). The latter lecture cycle, delivered in 1923, at Penmaenmawr, Wales, consists of thirteen esoterically advanced lectures on the complex relationships between human and cosmic history.

Owen Barfield's Contribution

Both Steiner and the case for the evolution of consciousness have been blessed by the rare blend of scholarship, precise argumentation, and brilliant writing found in the works of Owen Barfield. In *Romanticism Comes of Age*, Barfeld explains the reasons why his writings owe "a paramount debt to Rudolf Steiner" (p. 7). He also chides the literary and philosophical community for their "unwonted irresponsibility" in dismissing the thought of Rudolf Steiner without investigation. He includes in this criticism his lifelong friend, C. S. Lewis (p. 17). (For a fascinating account of the disagreement between Barfield and Lewis on Steiner and Anthroposophy, see Lionel Adey's *C. S. Lewis's "Great War" with Owen Barfield*.) In addition to the implicit presence of Steiner's teachings in all of Barfield's works, some of his writings are explicitly concerned with Steiner: "The Time-Philosophy of Rudolf Steiner" and "Rudolf Steiner's Concept of Mind," both in *Romanticism Comes of Age*, and his "Introduction" to *The Case for Anthroposophy*. Barfield's most widely read work, *Saving the Appearances: A Study in Idolatry*, offers a carefully argued defense of a spiritually-based interpretation of the evolution of consciousness; it is also effective as a critique of the modern Western scientistic mind-set.

Important works by Barfield, written throughout the past fifty years

(1928–79), include the following: *Poetic Diction: A Study in Meaning*,
first published in 1928, is a highly praised study in the theory and experience of language, metaphor and meaning; first published in 1944,
Romanticism Comes of Age, since the expanded 1966 edition, has included two essays on Steiner, one each on Coleridge and Goethe, as well
as essays on thinking, imagination, and literature; *Worlds Apart: A Dialogue of the 1960s* (1963) consists of a lively intellectual exchange between the exponents of eight diverse points of view—a professor of historical theology and ethics, a young man employed at a rocket research
station, a professor of physics, a retired teacher, a research biologist, an
analytic philosopher, a psychiatrist, and a lawyer interested in philology
(Barfield himself): *Unancestral Voice* (1965), another work in dialogue
form, is a kind of sequel to *Worlds Apart*.

The Case for Anthroposophy (1970), consisting of selections from
Steiner's *Von Seelenrätseln* ("Riddles of the Soul"), includes eight brief
but demanding chapters on philosophical psychology and an equally substantial introduction by Barfield. In his informed and rigorously argued
defense of spiritual science, Barfield characteristically begins with the
"isolation of matter from mind as a philosophical principle." This isolation
is traceable to Descartes and the methodology of natural science which
has issued from Cartesian dualism and the disentanglement of matter
from nonmaterial factors realized during the scientific revolution. He also
argues, however, that the freedom of operation and ensuing success on
the side of scientific thinking has not been attained by thinkers such as
Rudolf Steiner, who have attempted to create a science which systematically excludes all physical qualities from thinking. Barfield's summary of
this development is worth quoting:

> It might have been expected, then, that by meticulously disentangling itself
> from all reference, explicit or implicit, to material factors, the immaterial, as a
> field of knowledge, would also gain inestimable advantages. That is what did not
> happen. But it will be well to state at once that it is nevertheless precisely this
> correlative epistemological principle that is the basis of Rudolf Steiner's An-
> throposophy. It belongs to the post-Aristotelian age for the same reason that natu-
> ral science does; but in the opposite way. Thus, the parallel terms, "spiritual
> science" and "occult science," which he also used, do not betoken a fond belief
> that the methodology of technological science can be applied to the immaterial.
> The methodology of technological science is rightly based on the exclusion of all
> occult qualities from its thinking. The methodology of spiritual science is based on
> an equally rigorous exclusion of all "physical qualities" from its thinking. That is
> one of the things I hope this book will help to make clear. (pp. 8–9)

What Coleridge Thought (1971) is a major original study of the philosophical thought of Samuel Taylor Coleridge, which in the process re-

veals Barfield's philosophical and literary roots and affinities. *The Rediscovery of Meaning, and Other Essays* (1977) presents nineteen of Barfield's essays exemplifying the full range of his scholarly work: meaning,
language, allegory, matter and spirit, and philosophical theology. Barfield's next book, *History, Guilt and Habit* (1979) may be described as a
three-part study of the past, present, and future, or more specifically: the
evolution of consciousness, the idolatrous one-sidedness of contemporary
thought and culture, and a recommendation for the future that we must
individually and collectively develop and practice the kind of imagination
which Barfield describes as "thinking with a bit of will in it" (pp. 80).
Anyone who works through several of these volumes will then want to
return to Barfield's challenging and most systematic work, *Saving the
Appearances: A Study in Idolatry*. Shirley Sugarman's *The Evolution of
Consciousness: Essays in Honor of Owen Barfield* includes a dozen articles on topics prominent in Barfield's thought, as well as an extended
interview with him (pp. 3–28) and a complete bibliography of his writings
until 1974.

6. ESOTERIC CHRISTIANITY

Steiner delivered more than a dozen volumes of lectures on the events
depicted in the Christian scriptures, all of which continue to be largely
ignored by scripture scholars. Since Christian exegetes ordinarily are
thought to be comfortable with talk about matters of spirit, it might be
assumed that Steiner's volumes of lectures on the Gospels would be studied, if only to be criticized and rejected. In fact, however, Steiner's interpretations of the personalities and events depicted in the Gospels are
largely neglected by Christian exegetes. This neglect may not be a function of content at all, but owing simply to the fact that these writings,
none of which have been published by mainline publishers, have not
come to the attention of the academic world. While some of the books
cited in this section require a background in Steiner's teaching and a
receptivity to esoteric and spiritual teaching, others can be read profita-
bly by both skeptics and orthodox believers.

Once again *Christianity as Mystical Fact* can be recommended as an
excellent introduction to esoteric Christianity. This work is valuable because it traces a spiritual line from pre-Christian (particularly Greek)
mysteries to the mystery content in early Christianity, notably as evidenced in the "raising," or initiation, of Lazarus (whom Steiner identifies

as John the Evangelist, the Beloved Disciple, so called after his initiation experience). An excellent complement to *Christianity as Mystical Fact* is the chapter on "Anthroposophy and Christianity" in Easton's *Man and World* (pp. 173–216). This chapter covers five topics: Jesus of Nazareth, the Christ Being, the Mystery of Golgotha and the powers of evil (particularly concerning the nature and function of Lucifer and Ahriman), Christianity and reincarnation, and the Etheric Christ and the Second Coming.

The second work to be recommended as an introduction to esoteric Christianity, one far more sophisticated and substantial than *Christianity as Mystical Fact,* is *The Gospel of St. John,* a series of nine lectures delivered to a handful of Theosophists in a living room in Hamburg, 18–31 May 1908. A list of chapter topics conveys the central importance of this work in Steiner's representation of the spiritual events described in the Gospels: The doctrine of the Logos, raising (initiation) of Lazarus, seven degrees of initiation, "I AM," the Mystery of Golgotha, human evolution and the Christ principle, as well as the three chapters reprinted in this volume.

Perhaps the second gospel lecture series to be recommended is *The Gospel of St. Luke.* This series is noted for its treatment of the influence of the Buddha on the principle of love as depicted in the Gospel of Luke, the mission of the Hebrews, and the contribution of Zarathustra. It also introduces one of Steiner's most radical and controversial theses, the two Jesus-Children. This teaching, which Steiner develops in several lecture series, is too subject to misunderstanding to be summarized here; it is most clearly developed in *The Spiritual Guidance of Man and Mankind* and *From Jesus to Christ,* lecture 8. *The Gospel of St. Matthew* focuses on the physical and etheric sheaths of the Christ: "Through St. Matthew's Gospel we learn to know how the forces of the Cosmos worked through the human body borne by Christ and what He accomplished through His descent into the nature of man" (p. 16; cf. p. 204). *The Gospel of St. Mark* emphasizes the relationship between the new impulse of the gospels and the impulses of the ancient world, Asian and Western, signified by such personalities as Krishna and Moses; it also depicts the relationship between the Christ and His twelve disciples.

In addition to these lecture series on each of the four Gospels, Steiner delivered a second series on the Gospels of St. Matthew and St. Mark and several cycles on the Gospel of St. John. *The Gospel of St. John and Its Relation to the Other Gospels* treats, among other topics, the meaning of the baptism of Jesus by John the Baptist, the meaning of the Mysteries, prophecies, and miracles in the Gospels, particularly in the Gospel of

St. John. *Background to the Gospel of St. Mark* focuses on the continuity between the ancient Mystery teachings and the Gospel of St. Mark. *Deeper Secrets of Human History in the Light of the Gospel of St. Matthew* similarly traces some of the more important esoteric streams preparatory to the Christ event. Finally, this survey of Steiner's lecture series on the New Testament would be incomplete without reference to *The Apocalypse of St. John: Lectures on the Book of Revelation*, which discusses at length the symbolism of the seven seals, pre-Christian and Christian initiation, and the evolution of consciousness as revealed in the Apocalypse.

Building Stones for an Understanding of the Mystery of Golgotha places the Mystery of Golgotha in the center of myriad relationships, both persons and events, including the Mithras Mysteries, John the Baptist, Caligula and Nero, Julian the Apostate, Augustine, Manichaeism, Swedenborg, Kant, and Goethe. Perhaps because it is less detailed, with fewer examples, analogies, and tangents, *The Christ Impulse and the Development of Ego Consciousness* can be highly recommended as an introduction to Steiner's understanding of the significance of the Christ event in human history. In these seven lectures he relates the Christ impulse to such diverse topics as the pre-Christian (particularly Buddhist) conception of the ego, the law of karma, the significance of the Christ in the evolution of humanity, and the birth and development of conscience.

Esoteric Christology

There remain two significant series of lectures which are full of startling disclosures and at the same time typical of Steiner's Spiritual Science: *From Jesus to Christ* discusses the several modes of gaining knowledge of the Christ corresponding to several epochs of human consciousness, three pre-Christian streams (Buddhist, Hebrew, and Greek), the significance of the Resurrection and of Paul, and finally, as noted above, a summary account of the Jesus-child described in Matthew and the Jesus-child described in Luke. In addition to offering another description of the two-Jesus-children thesis, *The Fifth Gospel* is Steiner's most advanced account of the spiritual events surrounding the life of the Christ that are either veiled or omitted in the four Gospels. This lecture series teems with disclosures available to Steiner from the Akashic Record. While this is one of Steiner's most beautiful books, one capable of generating awe and reverence, it is likely to elicit disbelief or a response appropriate to fiction. Consequently, it is important not to read *The Fifth Gospel* until one has first come to terms with one of the more basic gospel lecture series such as the *Gospel of St. John* or *Gospel of St. Luke*.

One brief lecture series, a collection of lectures, and three pamphlets are each valuable additions to this collection of materials on the event which Rudolf Steiner refers to as the Mystery of Golgotha: *Christ and the Human Soul, The Reappearance of Christ in The Etheric, The Pre-Earthy Deeds of Christ, The Deed of Christ and the Opposing Spiritual Powers,* and *Christ in the Twentieth Century*.

Two works on the esoteric meaning of Christianity by disciples of Steiner are especially recommended: written by the widely published Dutch psychiatrist F. W. Zeylmans van Emmichoven, *The Reality in Which We Live* offers clear summaries of pre-Christian esoteric streams, the life, ministry, and resurrection of Jesus Christ, esoteric streams in Christianity, the significance of Goethe, as well as meanings and functions of the Christ in science, religion, art, and society; and Frederick Hiebel, author of *The Gospel of Hellas* (section 5) is also the author of *The Epistles of Paul and Rudolf Steiner's Philosophy of Freedom*.

The Christian Community

In 1921 Steiner received a request from German and Swiss pastors and theology students who were asking for help in their effort to bridge the widening gulf between modern science and the world of spirit. Such a bridge was felt necessary to renew Christian life and liturgy. In response to this need Steiner, acting as a private person rather than as the initiator of the Anthroposophical Society, heard and saw, and then disclosed, a liturgy called "The Act of Consecration of Man." With this profoundly Christian ritual, which is not unlike the Roman Catholic Mass but more obviously reflective of the modern stream of Johannine Christianity, Steiner also helped inaugurate and fashion an institutional and ecclesiastical structure called The Christian Community. This "Movement for Religious Renewal," as it is also called, consists of local congregations spread throughout the world whose community life is centered around the traditional seven sacraments in a renewed form. Although Steiner's spiritual insights formed the basis for a new understanding of Christian scripture and tradition found in The Christian Community, his emphasis was nevertheless on religion rather than on theology. The foundation is esoteric, as is true for all vital religious movements, but the practice is exoteric.

Some of the best writings on the Christian scriptures and in the esoteric Christian tradition influenced by Rudolf Steiner are by members of The Christian Community. This small Christian church or community has attracted and produced an impressive line of scholarly priests, including Emil Bock, Friedrich Rittelmeyer, Alfred Heidenrich, and Rudolf Frieling. The two clearest accounts of The Christian Community are a book and an article: Alfred Heidenrich's *Growing Point: The Story of the Foundation of the Movement for Religious Renewal—The Christian Community* and Oliver Mathews' "Religious Renewal—The Work of the Christian Community," in Davy's *Work Arising.* The following three works by Emil Bock are among the most spiritually advanced and intellectually penetrating interpretations of the scriptures: *Genesis: Creation and the Patriarchs, The Three Years: The Life of Christ between Baptism and Ascension,* and *The Apocalypse of St. John.* In writing *The Three Years,* Bock had the advantage of his own erudition and thorough grounding in Steiner's lectures on the gospels. *The Three Years* discusses some of the more essential and mysterious events depicted in the Gospels, including Jesus' healings and resurrection.

Another scholarly priest of The Christian Community, Alfred Heidenrich, is the author of *The Unknown in the Gospels* and *Healings in the Gospels.* Other works by members of The Christian Community, recommended for beginning as well as advanced students of Spiritual Science and esoteric Christianity, include two works by Rudolf Frieling, *Christianity and Reincarnation* and *Christianity and Islam;* three works by Frederick Rittelmeyer, *Rudolf Steiner Enters My Life, Reincarnation in the Light of Thought, Religion and Ethics, Meditation: Letters on the Guidance of the Inner Life According to the Gospel of St. John;* and Adam Bittleston's *Our Spiritual Companions: From Angels and Archangels to Cherubim and Seraphim.*

The Goethean approach to science in the service of Christianity is most clearly exemplified in the three booklets by Friedrich Benesch: *Ascension, Easter,* and *Whitsun: Community in the Age of Individualism.*

7. SOCIAL SCIENCES

Individual Freedom and Social Responsibility

By the time Rudolf Steiner undertook to provide a comprehensive analysis of the social and political ills of our time—a task thrust upon him by the suffering and chaos generated by the First World War—he had spent more than a decade applying his anthroposophical knowledge of man and the universe to a wide range of practical problems. Rudolf

Steiner's emphasis on individual freedom (e.g., in his *Philosophy of Freedom*) is to be expected in the arts and other value areas, but no area of human experience would seem to be less promising for his spiritual teachings than politics and economics. It is theoretically and practically significant that Steiner is equally insistent on individual freedom in the social as in the spiritual order.

In addition to drawing on his theory of human nature, Steiner's social philosophy also presupposes his reading of human history, particularly the evolution of free individuality during the Christian and modern Western epochs. In the *Mission of the Archangel Michael,* for example, Steiner argues for the distinctive combination of freedom and social solidarity which is possible for the first time in the present century, or more precisely since 1879, the year Steiner gives for the beginning of the Michaelic Age. Steiner views this age as a time of extraordinary challenge and opportunity. On the side of challenge, the present age has generated new problems and requires new solutions:

Externally, mankind today approaches serious battles. In regard to these serious battles which are only at their beginning—I have often mentioned it here—and which will lead the old impulses of *Earth* evolution *ad absurdum*, there are no political, economic or spiritual remedies to be taken from the pharmacy of past historical evolution. For from these past times come the elements of fermentation which, first, have brought Europe to the brink of the abyss, which will array Asia and America against each other, and which are preparing a battle over the whole earth. (p. 53)

On the side of opportunity, Steiner maintains that the Michaelic Age makes possible the realization of free social relationships. Such a realization, if wide-spread, should be seen as a viable solution to human chaos, violence, and loss of meaning. To follow the Michaelic path, which means living at the forefront of ideal contemporary consciousness, requires that each person respond to all other persons in terms of their concrete existence and their supersensible reality. More succinctly, it requires that social relations be firmly rooted in the spiritual.

In secular terms, Michaelic thinking may be understood as the ideal of a universal human community. According to Steiner's interpretation of the Michaelic Age, both individuality and social solidarity must be understood and practiced from a universal perspective. We are reminded of the slogan first coined by René Dubos: "Think globally, act locally." The obvious obstacle to Steiner's attempt to combine free individuality and universal fraternity is the nineteenth-century passion for nationalism in economics and politics. In rejecting the nationalistic outlook and its constant companion, patriotism, Steiner criticizes in a more general way the concept of "a people" in the Hebraic sense, and folk culture in the European sense. He offers concrete exercises for overcoming our tendency to view the world narrowly from the vantage point of our own people. He articulated this ideal in numerous lectures on social philosophy delivered after the First World War. The following lengthy passage, from "Specters of the Old Testament in the Nationalism of the Present," in *The Challenge of the Times*, delivered on 7 December 1918, well summarizes Steiner's social teaching:

The cultivation of the social life, which in earlier times had its source only in the bonds of blood, does not depend so much upon any sort of socialistic programs, but upon man's becoming a spiritual-social being. But he will become such a being by awakening within himself, in the manner I have described, the deeper forces which can bring to birth within him the capacity for conceiving pictorially the other human being. Otherwise we shall always remain antisocial beings, capable of approaching other persons only according to our sympathies and antipathies, incapable of approaching them according to the picture which may stream forth out of each person if we only develop the picture-forming forces in our intercourse with other human beings. Precisely in the social life of humanity must the principle come into existence: "Thou shalt make for thyself an image of thy fellow man." But then, when we form a picture of our fellow man, we enrich our own soul-life; then do we bestow a treasure upon our own inner soul-life with each human acquaintanceship. Then we do not any longer so live that A lives there, B there, C there, but A, B, and C live in D; A, B, and D live in C; C, D, and E live in A; etc. We gain the capacity to have other human beings live in us.

But this must be acquired: this is something not born within us. And, if we should continue simply to cultivate those characteristics which are born in us, we should continue within the limits of a mere blood culture, not the culture to which could be ascribed in the true sense of the word human brotherhood. For only when we carry the other human being within ourselves can we really speak of human brotherhood, which has appeared thus far only in an abstract word. When we form a picture of the other person, which is implanted as a treasure in our soul, then we carry within the realm of our soul-life something from him just as in the case of a bodily brother we carry around something through the common blood. This elective affinity as the basis of the social life must take the place in this concrete way of the mere blood affinity. This is something which really must evolve. It must depend upon the human will to determine how brotherhood shall be awakened among men.

Human beings have hitherto been separated. They ought to become socialized in brotherhood. In order that the manifoldness shall not be lost, that which is the innermost element in man, the thought, must be able to take form individually in every single person. With Jahve the whole folk stood in a relationship. With Christ each individual person must stand in relationship. But the fact that brotherhood will thus awaken requires that there shall be a compensation in an entirely different field—that is, through freedom of thought. (pp. 176–78)

As is obvious in the above passage, Steiner is not recommending a traditional concept of human brotherhood. As Stewart Easton points out, many people in our age, particularly young people, have a kind of intuitive feeling for this ideal community of free individuls but look for its models in the past. One such formulation of this ideal rooted in the past is the motto of the French Revolution, "Liberty, Equality, and Fraternity," which, according to Easton, is now capable of realization:

Its true meaning was revealed by Rudolf Steiner when he explained that each of the three ideals is the aim of one of the three domains in the Social Order: Liberty in the cultural spiritual life, that is, freedom of thought; equality in the life of rights, in which every man has the same rights as every other; and fraternity in the economic life, in which human, economic, and material needs are satisfied through a free exchange of goods throughout the world, unimpeded by national boundaries or other hindrances. . . . According to Steiner, nations should not as such disappear in the future, but their role becomes much more limited; if it is so limited, it cannot give birth to or foster the growth of nationalism. The Michaelic, Christian, principle of universalism, the overcoming of the bonds of the blood, is *required*, according to Steiner, in our age and in the future. The means by which we move toward it is above all through the recognition of the three domains of the Social Order. *(Man and World,* pp. 330–31)

The Threefold Social Order

Steiner's basic statement on the social nature of human life is contained in a book which he wrote in 1919, variously titled in English: *The Threefold Commonwealth* (1923), *The Threefold Social Order* (1966), and *Towards Social Renewal: Basic Issues of the Social Question* (1977). In this brief, carefully constructed work, Steiner argues that social life, in conformity with human nature, should ideally consist of three separate but related realms: economic, political or rights, and spiritual-cultural. According to this scheme, every member of society belongs to all three realms, but the realms themselves ought not exercise influence beyond their proper sphere. Steiner admits that in relation to modern Western institutions, particularly institutions prevalent throughout the twentieth century, some may view his proposal as altogether utopian. He also contends, however, that in the present age humanity is frustrated because the threefold social order which it unconsciously seeks has not yet come into being. Steiner's triune or threefold social order is analogous to the tripartite system of government prescribed by the United States Constitution: each of the three branches are necessary and equal, and no one branch should exercise control over either of the other two. Indeed, Steiner contends that the ills and injustices of modern Western social life are largely attributable to the imbalance between these realms. He is particularly critical of the economic and political realms' control of education, which belongs exclusively to the spiritual-cultural domain. All three of these realms, as well as their proper contributions and limitations, are described in Steiner's *Towards Social Renewal*.

In addition to the important chapter on the economic sphere in *Towards Social Renewal* (chapter 3: "Capitalism and Social Ideas," pp. 83–126), Steiner explained his conception of the economic sphere in a cycle of fourteen lectures, delivered in 1922, *World Economy: The Formation of a Science of World Economics*. In the face of an understandable tendency to regard as utopian all pleas for reform in the economic sphere, Steiner argues that his proposal is neither utopian nor ungrounded in the realities of human nature and social life. Indeed, Steiner argues that there is need for competition, but insists that it belongs in the cultural rather than the economic sphere. In the economic realm, the relationship between producers, distributors, and consumers should be one of fraternity and intelligent cooperation. Obviously, the economic realm cannot be reformed independently of the other two realms of human life—the political and cultural-spiritual—but all three need to be reformed, and the economic sphere is a useful place to discern the imbalances which have proved so disastrous in contemporary social life. The three parts of the social order require independence, balance, and reciprocity.

From the concrete facts of economic life, such as production and circulation, capital and labor, and the individual human actions which generate these relationships, Steiner offers the following example and summary of the entire threefold social order:

The moment intelligence is to enter the economic life, we must allow to flow into the economic domain that which prevails in the free life of the Spirit. The three members of the social organism must stand in the right relation to one another, so that they may work on one another in the right way.

This way the real meaning of *The Threefold Commonwealth*—not the splitting of the three members into parts, since this splitting apart is always present. The point is rather to find how the three members can be brought together, so that they may really work in the social organism with inherent intelligence, just as the nerves-and-senses system, the heart-and-lungs system, and the metabolic system, for example, work together in the natural organism of man. (*World Economy*, pp. 133–34)

If it is to function properly and make a harmonious contribution to the integral working of the entire threefold social order, the economic sphere will need to be governed by a practical science which is responsive to the integral working of the entire threefold social order, the economic sphere will need to be governed by a practical science which is responsive to the partial but inevitable transition from national economies to world economies. Steiner's lectures on world economy are based on detailed analyses of production and distribution, but offer solutions to economic disharmonies by casting these processes in the light of a worldwide system of economic associations. As a local economic relationship must ultimately be conceived and reformed in light of a national network, so must each national economy increasingly recognize its essential interdependence within the world economic order. Such an expansion of the economic order on a global scale, however, should not lead to an expansion of the economic order into the realm of the political or cultural. With Marx and other dominant social economists, Steiner laments the conception of human labor as if it were a commodity. But as Stewart Easton points out, Steiner's solution to this problem is quite different from most social and economic thinkers in that he separates production and remuneration into separate social spheres:

> The first problem is how to produce economic goods as efficiently as possible with a minimum of wastefulness; the second is how to remunerate the workers. The first is an economic problem, the second is a question of human rights, and therefore does not belong to the economic domain at all, but rather to the "jural" or "rights-body." (*Man and World*, 339–40)

The exact lines of relationship and limitations between the economic and political spheres ought not be decided in the abstract. In making these distinctions, Steiner repeatedly turns to specific cases such as whether a tailor should purchase his clothing ready-made or make his own, and the value of peas for a farmer and consumers. If we are conscious of Steiner's work as a spiritual scientist, particularly the epistemology of picture-thinking articulated in *Philosophy of Freedom*, we can appreciate his insistence that economic life requires that each transaction be conceived and executed as an economic picture which is at once detailed and comprehensive. Steiner recommends the following approach to economic life:

> Even in economic science we must work towards such pictures, pictures taken from what is immediate perception. This means, in other words, that to act rightly in the economic sense, we must make up our minds to enter into the events of production, trade and consumption, with a picture-thinking. We must be ready to enter into the real process; then we shall get approximate conceptions—only approximate ones, it is true—but conceptions which will be of real use to us when we wish to take an actual part in the economic life. Above all, such conceptions will be of use to us when what we do not know by our own sensibility (supposing we ourselves have not arrived through sensibility at the corresponding pictures) is

supplemented or corrected by others who are associated with us. There is no other possibility. Economic judgments cannot be built on theory; they must be built on living association, where the sensitive judgments of people are real and effective; for it will then be possible to determine out of the association—out of the immediate experiences of those concerned—what the value of any given thing can be. (*World Economy*, p. 131)

According to Steiner, a picture or an economic association is right to the extent that it is in proper balance in itself as well as in harmony with the global network of economic associations. Such harmony in the economic sphere contributes to, and in turn is dependent upon, harmony in the political sphere.

The most distinctive feature of Steiner's theory of the political sphere —and historically the most novel—is its impartiality. As Easton observes: "Obviously, if the State provides education for its citizens, or if it owns or manages industry, it cannot be impartial in relation to either education or industry" (*Man and World*, p. 351). In the rights sphere, as in the economics sphere, Steiner insists that problems be solved concretely, and by imaginative thinking, rather than by abstract principles.

Of the three social spheres, Steiner lectured frequently concerning the cultural-spiritual sphere, and focused on the economic sphere both in the three lecture cycles on the threefold social order and in *World Economy*. He did not, however, write at length on the rights sphere. His primary point with respect to the rights sphere is to limit its task to the administration of police and armed forces, maintaining order in the state, and arbitration (*Man and World*, p. 341). Within this general framework, Steiner examines specific rights such as those affecting ownership, particularly land ownership, which in fact Steiner places not in the sphere of rights but in the economic sphere. As the economic sphere needs to be enlarged, without a loss of attention to detail, to a worldwide context, so does the sphere of rights need to be conceived globally or universally. In the same way that it is an enemy of sound economic thinking, partiality is also disastrous in the sphere of rights.

As the sphere of rights contributes impartiality and objectivity to the threefold social order, the spiritual-cultural domain contributes the creativity and freethinking of each individual human being. Consequently, for education to make its necessary and free contributions to the social order, the political sphere must allow schools, teachers, and the learning process to proceed unimpeded by political self-interest. In Steiner's view, all of the creative arts and intellectual activities of teachers, scientists, and other contributors to the intellectual and cultural life of humanity properly belong to the cultural-spiritual sphere and, as such, must be free from the self-interested domination of either economic or political influence.

In a sense, all of Steiner's writings and lectures on Waldorf education presuppose the kind of freedom—and the Waldorf Schools throughout the world intend such freedom—as is prescribed in his threefold social teaching. It is now possible to survey Steiner's writings on the three spheres of the social order—the economic, political, and cultural-spiritual.

Writings and Lectures

Steiner first announced his "fundamental social law" in *Anthroposophy and the Social Question,* three essays published in 1906–08:

In a community of human beings working together, the well-being of the community will be the greater, the less the individual claims for himself the proceeds of the work he has himself done; i.e., the more of these proceeds he gives over to his fellow workers, and the more his own requirements are satisfied, not out of his own work done, but out of work done by the others. (p. 24)

Steiner's basic text, as noted above, is *Toward Social Renewal*. This slim volume establishes the conception of the three social spheres, as well as the relationships between them. *Toward Social Renewal* is nicely complemented by *Threefolding: A Social Alternative,* a booklet consisting of two lectures delivered at Oxford in 1922: "Social Impulses of the Present Day" and "Man Within the Social Question: Individuality and Community." In *The Inner Aspect of the Social Question,* containing three lectures delivered to members of the Anthroposophical Society in Zurich in 1919, Steiner articulates the esoteric basis and significance of the social teaching which he developed exoterically in works such as *Towards Social Renewal*. The second of these three lectures is reprinted in the present volume. In *The Social Future,* Steiner offers six lectures on various aspects of social life from the perspective of the threefold social order. *The Threefold Order of the Body Social* is an extensive out-of-print collection of addresses and articles, mostly from 1920, on various practical and theoretical aspects of Steiner's threefold social conceptions.

In the economic sphere, in addition to Steiner's basic work, *World Economy,* it is important to note the work of two social economists influencned by Steiner: Dr. Bernard C. J. Lievegood, founder of the Netherland Pedagogical Institute in 1954, and Folkert Wilken, author of two important studies on work and capital. Stewart Easton offers the following brief description of the Netherland Pedagogical Institute (NPI):

This Institute, staffed entirely by experienced anthroposophists who have familiarized themselves with many aspects of Steiner's teachings, and not only those on the social order, has been self-supporting for many years, acting as consultant in many realms of social life. It has in particular done notable work on what may be called the "humanizing" of the economic organizations that have asked it for help. The staff tries to perceive the underlying realities of each particular industry, and give advice accordingly. As a result, the solutions offered, always tentative and organic, are invariably found *to conform to* the threefold membering of the social organism as described by Steiner, rather than being, as it were, *tailored to fit* the concepts. A great deal of experience in many fields has been amassed by the consultants, and the movement has now spread into several other countries, though the form it takes differs in each. Everywhere that it has spread, however, it is always the meetings of small groups for discussion and criticism, especially self-criticism, that proves to be the real heart of the work. (*Man and World,* p. 371)

Christopher Schaefer's "Helping Social Growth—The Work of the N.P.I.," in Davy's *Work Arising* (pp. 170–96), clearly explains the development and work of NPI as well as its relationship to Steiner's social teachings. Martin Large's *Social Ecology: Exploring Post-Industrial Society* provides a more complete description of the NPI approach to problem solving, along with a comprehensive analysis of individual development. Anyone seriously interested in social economics or management will want to study the following two works by Folkert Wilken: *The Liberation of Work: The Elimination of Strikes and Strife in Industry Through Associative Organization of Enterprise* and *The Liberation of Capital,* an informed, vigorous defense of Steiner's contention that access to capital is a right rooted in the proper structure of the social order. Two other original British studies on social questions based on Steiner's pioneering thought are Charles Davy's *Towards a Third Culture* and Christopher Budd's *Prelude in Economics*.

8. EDUCATION: THE WALDORF SCHOOL MOVEMENT

Between his first lecture series on education in 1909 and his last in 1924, Steiner delivered to educators and parents numerous lectures on the theory and practice of education. The 1909 lecture-essays, *The Education of the Child in the Light of Anthroposophy,* constitute perhaps Steiner's most basic statement, but since it is only forty-eight pages, it needs to be supplemented by later, more detailed works. One such later and slightly lengthier series, consisting of five lectures delivered in 1924, is *The Roots of Education*. The second and third lectures in this series were chosen for the present volume because of their emphasis on the place of the artistic in Waldorf education. Both *The Education of the Child* and *The Roots of Education* issue from Steiner's spiritual experience of the development of the child. When read together, they effectively frame his proposal for an educational perspective capable of addressing the child's individual development—physical, vital, intellectual, and spiritual. A third series of comparable importance, similar to *The Roots of Education*, is *The Essentials of Education*.

Education of the Child

Perhaps the most original and significant component in Steiner's educational philosophy is its conception of child development in seven-year stages. In addition to discussions of these stages in the works cited above and in virtually all of the secondary sources (particularly the two books by Harwood, cited below), the first two stages are especially well described in *The Kingdom of Childhood*. These seven lectures, followed by questions and answers, were Steiner's last lectures on education. Given the sudden upsurge of interest in Waldorf education and the founding in the United States between 1980 and 1983 of more than twenty Waldorf Schools, both recognized and unofficial, Steiner's last words on education, delivered to a group of teachers who had resolved to found a Waldorf School in England (and did in fact open Michael Hall, Sussex, in 1925), would seem to warrant repetition here:

Very much depends on how your first project is launched: from it the world must notice that the matter is neither something which is steeped in abstract, dilettante plans of school reform nor anything amateur, but something which arises out of a conception of the real being of man, and which is now to be brought to bear on the art of education. *(The Kingdom of Childhood,* p. 159)

As *The Kingdom of Childhood* is recommended for education during the first two stages of life, *Waldorf Education for Adolescence: Supplementary Course—The Upper School* is especially recommended for the spiritual understanding of adolescence and corresponding pedagogical and curricular considerations for this period of dramatic development.

A second important contribution of Steiner's educational teaching is his theory of temperaments, clearly explained in a booklet, *The Four Temperaments*. Steiner refers to a temperament as "the characteristic coloring of the human being":

We speak chiefly of four types, as you know: the *sanguine*, the *choleric*, the *phlegmatic*, and the *melancholic* temperament. Even though this classification is not entirely correct in so far as we apply it to individuals—in individuals the temperaments are mixed in the most diverse way, so we can only say one temperament predominates in certain traits—still we shall in general classify people in four groups according to their temperaments. (p. 12)

Practical pedagogical suggestions concerning temperaments form a prominent part of *Discussions with Teachers,* a series of fifteen revealing discussions with the teachers of the Waldorf School in Stuttgart. This volume concludes with a presentation of four principles which Steiner recommends as ideals for the Waldorf teacher: Initiative in matters large and small, interest in the entire world and humanity, unwillingness to compromise in mind and heart with what is untrue, and refusal to grow stale or sour. (p. 165)

Pedagogy

Steiner also delivered several lecture series for audiences, frequently teachers, familiar with his basic teachings on education. Of these, perhaps the most useful are: *The Renewal of Education through the Science of the Spirit* and *A Modern Art of Education,* previously published as *Education and the Modern Spiritual Life. The Renewal of Education* includes lectures on the theory of human nature which forms the base of Steiner's educational philosophy as well as lectures on curriculum—specifically on eurythmy, arts, language, and natural sciences. *A Modern Art of Education* includes lectures on the history of education, reading, sciences, and education toward inner freedom. With these two volumes as background, a lecture series consisting primarily of practical pedagogical suggestions may be recommended: *Practical Advice to Teachers,* consisting of fourteen lectures which Steiner delivered at the founding of the Stuttgart Waldorf School in 1919. These lectures offer specific directions concerning artistic activity, reading and writing, rhythms of the body and of the day, languages, geography, the development of moral principles, and the place of external regulations. *The Study of Man: General Education Course* is perhaps Steiner's most advanced lecture series on the spiritual character of his educational philosophy and psychology, and consequently requires a thorough familiarity with both Anthroposophy and his teaching on child development and education. A similar recommendation and caution is necessary for a second lecture series, *Balance in Teaching,* which Steiner delivered a year later to the same faculty at Stuttgart.

Steiner repeatedly emphasized that the Waldorf School Movement had a social and historical as well as an educational function—or, in terms truer to Steiner's intent, that true education is necessarily a social responsibility with social implications. He similarly emphasized that the ills of education were a by-product of social ills, and that an educational method based on a true understanding of human nature can effectively counter such ills. Steiner delivered several cycles of lectures on the social aspect of education, including: *Education as a Social Problem,* a series of six lectures delivered to members of the Anthroposophical Society at Dornach, *Human Values in Education,* and *A Social Basis for Primary and Secondary Education.*

Writings by Waldorf Teachers

There are numerous, highly readable accounts of Waldorf education as well as studies of teaching specific school subjects by Steiner's followers. Most of them are the fruit of decades of experience in Waldorf education. Henry Barnes, for many years the faculty chairman of the Rudolf Steiner School in New York City, and former chairman of the General Council of the Anthroposophical Society of America, offers a clear outline in "An Introduction to Waldorf Education," *Teachers College Record* (Spring 1980), 81:322–36. This excellent, brief summation of the history of the Waldorf School Movement and the philosophy and methods that under- lie it is the lead article in a special symposium sponsored by Teachers College, Columbia University, and published with two other important articles: Alan Howard, "Education and Our *Human* Future" (pp. 337–44) and John Davy, "The Social Meaning of Education" (pp. 345–59). Since many local and college libraries subscribe to *Teachers College Record* (and any library can secure a copy through interlibrary loan), this special symposium is perhaps the most readily available of all the writings on Waldorf education.

Stewart Easton's *Man and World* includes two chapters on education: "The New Art of Education—The Waldorf School Movement" (pp. 382– 411) and "Anthroposophy and Curative Education" (pp. 412–35). John Davy's lengthy, crisply informative article, "The Movement That Every- one Tries to Forget," *The (London) Times,* Educational Supplement, 23 March 1973, has been reprinted and is available from the Anthroposoph- ical Library (section 11).

Mary Caroline (M. C.) Richards's *Toward Wholeness: Rudolf Steiner Education in America* is also a readily accessible and very substantial introduction. M. C. Richards, the well-known author of *Centering—In Pottery, Poetry and the Person,* has been associated with Waldorf schools and anthroposophical educational endeavors for more than twenty years. Her *Toward Wholeness* includes an introduction to Rudolf Steiner, the history of Waldorf education in America, the artistic character of Waldorf pedagogy, Camphill (villages and schools for individuals in need of special mental and emotional care), three chapters on Waldorf education in the context of contemporary America, and appendices listing Waldorf schools, institutes, and adult education centers. Because it issues from a well-informed understanding of American culture and education, and because it effectively expresses the author's personal experience and enthusiasm, *Toward Wholeness* makes an especially convincing case for Waldorf education.

While the following five single-author volumes lack the concern for Waldorf education in the American context, they are nevertheless valuable as general introductory accounts of Steiner's theories of human nature, child development, learning, imagination, curriculum, and school structure: *Rudolf Steiner Education: The Waldorf Schools* is a summary of all of these topics by Francis Edmunds, whose work on behalf of Waldorf education in England includes: class teacher at Michael Hall, Chairman of The Rudolf Steiner Educational Foundation, and founder of Emerson College in 1962. A. C. Harwood, another English Waldorf teacher of impressive range and depth, is the author of two excellent studies: *The Recovery of Man in Childhood—A Study in the Educational Work of Rudolf Steiner*, a lengthy, substantial work, and, *The Way of a Child: An Introduction to the Work of Rudolf Steiner for Children*. Majorie Spock's *Teaching as a Lively Art*, offers the best account of Waldorf education by year: it provides a full chapter discussion of each year from six to thirteen, followed by chapters on the temperaments, the teacher, and the teacher-child relationship. René Querido, director of Rudolf Steiner College in Sacramento, Calif., is the author of *Creativity in Education: The Waldorf Approach*, which consists of five lectures on the distinctive qualities and on several specific subjects of Waldorf education.

Among multi-authored volumes, the following two works are quite different despite nearly identical titles: Paul M. Allen's *Education as an Art* includes two fine lectures by Steiner and brief, unrelated essays by three exponents of Waldorf education. Ekkehard Piening's and Nick Lyons's *Educating as an Art: Essays on the Rudolf Steiner Method—Waldorf Education* is an informative survey by more than twenty American Waldorf school teachers on teaching arts, reading, history, science, mathematics, and a variety of other subjects. This well-illustrated and enthusiastic volume is perhaps the most inviting introduction to the theory and reality of a Waldorf School. Finally, Frans Carlgren's *Education towards Freedom*, a large-format volume with extensive color reproductions of student work and a nearly comprehensive survey of elements and subjects from all grade levels, provides an appealingly concrete introduction to "education as an art."

9. ARTS

Theoretically, this section should begin with works on the spiritual roots and meaning of artistic activity, but in actual practice it more frequently happens that an individual will first experience one of Steiner's writings or artistic contributions and only subsequently (and perhaps gradually and reluctantly) approach his writings on the spiritual and esoteric basis of these contributions. Specifically, this section concerning Steiner's writings on, and contributions to, the arts uses the same approach as the order of chapter selections: It follows Steiner in beginning with Goethe. This is a legitimate approach to Steiner and his works in general, and particulary useful in approaching his work in the arts. After a brief account of Steiner's approach to the arts and the way in which he built on Goethe in his own contributions to architecture, sculpture, and color theory, this chapter will proceed to a discussion of painting, eurythmy, speech, drama, poetry, and works which treat the spiritual-esoteric basis of the arts.

There are two brief general introductions to Steiner's approach to the experience, method, and purpose of the arts: Stewart Easton's chapter, "Anthroposophy and Its Relation to the Arts," in *Man and World* (pp. 217–62) and Arne Klingborg's "The Arts in Life," in Davy's *Work Arising*. (pp. 40–60)

Steiner's serious involvement with art and aesthetics dates to 1888, when at age twenty-seven he lectured on Goethe's aesthetics before the Goethe Society of Vienna. This twenty-five page lecture, published under the title, *Goethe as the Founder of a New Science of Aesthetics*, is unfortunately long out-of-print. The extent to which Steiner's aesthetics issued from Goethe's is evident in this lecture and in several subsequent full-length studies, including *Goethe's Conception of the World*, particularly the sections on "Goethe and Schiller" and "The Phenomena of the World of Color" and *Goethe's Standard of the Soul as Illustrated in "Faust" and in the Fairy Story of "The Green Snake and the Beautiful Lily."*

For a deeper understanding of the significance of Goethe for Steiner's aesthetics, it is best to look past his writings on Goethe to the implementation of Goethean principles in Steiner's artistic works, most especially

in the Goetheanum, the impressive, distinctive building which he designed in two versions (1913 and 1923). Of the many expressions of Steiner's artistic work—drama, speech formation, eurythmy (movement to
speech and music), painting, sculpture, and architecture—the architectural impulse, particularly as manifested in the Goetheanum, the physical center of the Anthroposophical Society since 1913, is perhaps the
most impressive and revealing of his genius. One of the most useful brief
introductions to Steiner's architectural theories and influences is Rex
Raab's "Architecture—Buildings for Life," in Davy's *Work Arising*. (pp.
61–75)

Of the several books on the Goetheanum, two are especially well written and handsomely illustrated: *The Goetheanum: Rudolf Steiner's Architectural Impulse*, by Hagen Biesantz *et al.*, and *Eloquent Concrete* by
Ake Fant, Rex Raab, and Arne Klingborg. *The Goetheanum* is particularly useful for placing Steiner's architectural work, and the Goetheanum
specifically, in the context of early twentieth-century architecture. It includes a detailed discussion of the first and second Goetheanum (the first
Goetheanum was burned to the ground on New Year's Eve, 1922), as
well as photographs of the many buildings, primarily in Europe, designed on Steiner's architectural principles. Two chapters in this work,
both by Hagen Biesantz, are especially noteworthy: "Rudolf Steiner's
Architectural Impulse in Modern Architectural History" traces a strand
of the history of European architecture from Goethe, through Steiner, to
mid-century architects such as Bruno Taut, Walter Gropius, Frank Lloyd
Wright, and Le Corbusier, all arguably influenced to some degree by
Steiner's architectural principles; "Rudolf Steiner's Aesthetics" explains
Steiner's "aesthetic fragments" in relation to Goethe, imagination and
spiritual knowledge, the spiritual origin of art, and the psychology of art.

In addition to its importance for architecture, the Goetheanum is also
a living repository of Steiner's original sculptures. These sculptures are
handsomely presented in *Rudolf Steiner's Sculpture in Dornach* by Åke
Fant, Arne Klingborg, and A. John Wilkes. The major subject in this large,
handsome volume is Steiner's thirty-foot high wooden sculpture entitled
"Christ—'Representative of Man' " (see photograph, p. 228).

Steiner's major work on color theory, *Colour*, includes: "The Nature of
Colour," "Colour in Light and Darkness," "Dimension, Number
Weight," and "The Creative World of Colour." Two students of Steiner's
color theory, both artists, have written effectively on the application of
the theory of color developed by Goethe and further developed by Steiner: Maria Schindler's *Goethe's Theory of Colour* includes forty-two color
illustrations, and consequently is quite expensive; as a study of the appli-

cation of the Goethean-Steiner color theory, however, it is extremely useful. *The Individuality of Colour: Contributions to a Methodical Schooling in the Experience of Colour* by Elizabeth Koch and Gerard Wagner is both a comprehensive introduction to anthroposophical color theory and a graded path at painting exercises based on Steiner's training sketches for painters. A similar mixture of theory and praxis informs Hilde Boos-Hamburger's *The Creative Power of Colour*. *Beppe Assenza* includes many illustrations of Boos-Hamburger's paintings together with extensive text by Herbert Witzenmann on an anthroposophical aesthetics as well as on Assenza's applications of the Goethe-Steiner color principles. Collot D'herbois' *Colour, Part One: A Textbook for the Painting Group 'Magenta'* and *Colour, Part Two* represent a dynamic approach to color and watercolor "veil painting" increasingly influential among anthroposophical painters. British painter Gladys Mayer has written three booklets on color: *Colour and the Human Soul, Colour and Healing*, and *The Mystery Wisdom of Colour*. There are also two fine essays on color in Harwood's *The Faithful Thinker:* Michael Wilson's "Colour, Science and Thinking" (pp. 141–52) and Alec and Gladys Morison's "The Activity of Colour in the Art of Painting" (pp. 153–62).

Since eurythmy is a novel art form involving movement and sound, it cannot be adequately described by the printed word. Waldorf schools and other anthroposophical institutions generally offer courses and performances in eurythmy. Short of seeing a performance, some glimmer of this subtle, spiritually based form of movement to music and poetry may be gained from a booklet which includes Rudolf Steiner's sketches for eurythmy figures: *Eurythmy and the Impulse of Dance* by Marjorie Raffe, Cecil Harwood, and Marguerite Lundgren. The last two paragraphs of this booklet briefly describe the purpose of this art form introduced to the world by Rudolf Steiner in 1912:

The task, and the effectiveness, of Eurythmy in the spheres of education and healing spring from the fact that it is an art drawing its inspiration and its force from a modern knowledge of the spiritual world. Consciously or unconsciously all true art has done this. But in its origins the arts were religious and their impulse and direction sprang from the great Mystery Centers where a conscious relation with the Spiritual world and its divine powers was cultivated. In the process of becoming a free individual, man necessarily lost this connection with the Divine— he had to escape from the pressure of the divine presence in order to become free. Now his urgent need is to recover in freedom, and in full clarity of consciousness, the heritage he had necessarily to abandon. Materialism will only be overcome by a knowledge of the spiritual world as wide, as detailed, and as effective as our present knowledge of the material world.

The art of Eurythmy is one of the channels through which the spirit is again revealing itself to human consciousness. It is a path through which man may again find a way to that self-knowledge which is also a knowledge of the universe. (p. 27)

Steiner's own *Eurythmy as Visible Music* or *Eurythmy as Visible Song* include lectures on the experience of major and minor, the gestures of music, chords and the harmonic element in melody, choral eurythmy, and other topics.

In addition to his major work on speech eurythmy, *Eurythmy as Visible Speech,* Steiner also wrote extensively on speech formation and dramatic speech, particularly with respect to the performance of the four mystery dramas which he wrote, one per year, from 1910 through 1913. These full-length dramas are collected in *Four Mystery Dramas: The Portal of Initiation, The Soul's Probation, The Guardian of the Threshold and The Soul's Awakening.* The first mystery drama is also separately published: *The Portal of Initiation: A Rosicrucian Mystery.* Steiner delivered three lecture cycles, more specifically, on speech, including speech formation, dramatic recitation, and poetry. The most important is *Speech and Drama.* This work contains a helpful foreword by Marie Steiner and Rudolf Steiner and nineteen lectures which Steiner gave to the Section for the Arts of Speech and Music, School of Spiritual Science, at the Goetheanum in September, 1924. These lectures were among the last which Steiner delivered before illness and death. In this lecture series Steiner discusses such topics as the forming of speech, speech as gesture, style in speech and drama, the arts of producing and acting, the esoteric aspect of the actor's vocation, the stage, and the word. *Poetry and the Art of Speech* is a collection of technical lectures primarily concerned with a new approach to the art of recitation, particularly of poetry, pioneered by Rudolf Steiner and Marie Steiner. *Creative Speech: The Nature of Speech Formation,* a collection of "aphoristic records of courses on the cultivation of speech as an art," is far more technical and less well organized than *Poetry and the Art of Speech.*

The best book influenced by Rudolf Steiner concerning poetry is Owen Barfield's *Poetic Diction: A Study in Meaning.* Readers interested in an aid to writing poetry by poets who write from the perspective and presumed benefit of Anthroposophy will find useful suggestions in the following three works: Johanna Knottenbelt's *The Art of Poetry in the Light of Anthroposophy,* D. E. Faulkner Jones's *The English Spirit* and Daisy Alden's *The Art and Craft of Poetry.* In addition to her work on Waldorf education (*Toward Wholeness,* section 7), Mary Caroline (M. C.) Richards is the author of two splendid books on the arts, both deeply influenced by the teachings of Rudolf Steiner: *Centering—In Pottery, Poetry, and the Person* and *The Crossing Point: Selected Talks and Writings*.

These brief bibliographical introductions to the kind of artistic work which Rudolf Steiner produced and influenced, serve well as a background to his writings on the spiritual basis and function of the arts. It is perhaps not necessary to believe that the arts are the creation of the spiritual world in order to appreciate the artistic results of Steiner's spiritual work, but if one is interested in writings which argue for the spiritual realities underlying his artistic works, *The Arts and Their Mission* and *Art in the Light of Mystery Wisdom* are especially recommended. *The Arts and Their Mission* contains some of Steiner's most penetrating comments on a variety of art forms, including architecture, painting, music, drama, and eurythmy. The entire book is full of insights, explanations and hints concerning the spiritual mission of these arts and the artistic sphere in general. Virginia Moore's excellent introduction concludes with a passage worth quoting in full:

> Reaffirming with the ancient Mysteries the inseparability of the good (morality), the true (science) and the beautiful (art)—three spheres connected not by likeness but analogy—Dr. Steiner stresses the aridity of matter-bound thinking and its enmity to art; and in the process makes points which, owing to absence of the pontifical manner, may deceive by their simplicity, may seem at first flush of limited scope when, actually, their implication for culture and the well-being of mankind reach out and out; for example (choosing at random), his statement that true architecture offers man the lines along which, when projected into the cosmos, the soul in life or death can expand; that true sculpture builds on the life-giving formative forces lying behind physical structure; that true painting relies on not spatial but color-perspective, color being an entire world in itself; that modern music, seeking depth in the single tone rather than in harmony or melody, begins, just begins, to find its way back to the spirit from which it descended; that poetry depends upon the relation between breath and pulse, nerve system and blood system; that eurythmy, as "expressive gesture," is linked with the invisible gesture-system which is language; and that imagination is the child's power of growth transformed for loftier purposes. . . .
>
> Such insights can, by quickening creativity, multiply works "determined outwardly to use and inwardly to delight." And perhaps such insights have a special significance for America. Elsewhere Dr. Steiner has observed that, to achieve balance, Russia needs philosophy, America art. (ix–x)

The second important work concerning Steiner's spiritual approach to the arts is *Art in the Light of Mystery Wisdom*. This work contains seven lectures: "The Connection between the Artistic and the Knowledge Gained through Spiritual Science"; "Processes of Initiation as the First

Stage in a Momentous Transformation of Human Life"; "The Supersensible Origin of the Artistic"; "Truth, Beauty, and Goodness"; two lectures, or one lecture in two parts, entitled 'Tone Experience in Humanity: A Basis for the Cultivation of Musical Pedagogy"; and "The World of the Hierarchies and the World of Tone."

10. NATURAL SCIENCES

Natural Forms and Etheric Forces

This section lists works in projective geometry, evolution, theory of matter, human physiology, illness and health, nutrition, agriculture, and biodynamic gardening. Of the thirty works cited, five are by Steiner and the remainder are by natural scientists and physicians working within the theoretical framework generated by Steiner's spiritual science.

Projective geometry offers one of the clearest applications of the scientific method advanced by Goethe and Steiner. Perhaps the most accomplished examples of this mathematical art form (or mathematical art of forms) are Olive Whicher's *Projective Geometry: Creative Polarities in Space and Time* and George Adams's and Olive Whicher's *The Plant between Sun and Earth and the Science of Physical and Ethereal Spaces*. By text and illustrations these works show the creative interplay of the artistic and the scientific approaches to an understanding of natural forms. A more basic work applying projective geometry to physics is George Adams's *Physical and Ethereal Spaces*. As is indicated by its subtitle—"Research Concerning the Outer World of Living Forms and the Inner World of Geometrical Imagination"—the following work is an excellent complement to the work of George Adams and Olive Whicher: Lawrence Edwards' *The Field of Form*.

An equally delightful fusion of the scientific and artistic is evident throughout Theodor Schwenk's *Sensitive Chaos: The Creation of Flowing Forms in Water and Air*. Schwenk notes that "this book is based on scientific observations of water and air but above all on the Spiritual Science of Rudolf Steiner. In his life's work he has shown how scientific thinking, if carried through logically, can lead to the reality of life and its spiritual origins" (p. 11). Another work similarly influenced by Steiner is Walter Cloos's *The Living Earth: The Organic Origin of Rocks and Minerals*, whose introduction is worth quoting:

In this book we have attempted to look at scientific facts concerning the world of rocks in the light which Rudolf Steiner has shed on all spheres of human life and endeavor in his Anthroposophy or Spiritual Science. Seen from this point of view the Earth is a living organism whose life is interwoven spiritually with the life of the heavenly bodies in the solar system and the whole realm of the stars. What has developed gradually within this life as the kingdoms of nature—mineral, plant, and animal—are all stages left behind by the being which is the culminating goal of all Earth existence—MAN. (p. 11)

Two of the most scholarly and forceful books in science influenced by Rudolf Steiner are Guenther Wachsmuth's *The Etheric Formative Forces in Cosmos, Earth and Man: A Path of Investigation into the World of the Living* and Ernst Lehrs's *Man or Matter: Introduction to a Spiritual Understanding of Nature on the Basis of Goethe's Method of Training Observation and Thought.* Some years after completing a doctorate in mathematics and physics, including a thesis on high-frequency electric currents, Lehrs was attracted to a scientific conference organized by the Anthroposophical Society in Stuttgart. While in attendance he heard Rudolf Steiner's lecture series on "Mathematics, Scientific Experiment and Observation, and Epistemological Results from the Standpoint of Anthroposophy." In *Man or Matter,* Lehrs describes the consequences of that experience for his understanding of Goethe and the scientific method:

In the course of a comprehensive historical survey the lecturer characterized, in a way I found utterly convincing, the present mathematical interpretation of nature as a transitional stage of human consciousness—a kind of knowing which is on the way from a past premathematical to a future postmathematical form of cognition. The importance of mathematics, whether as a discipline of the human spirit or as an instrument of natural science, was not for a moment undervalued. On the contrary, what Rudolf Steiner said about projective (synthetic) geometry, for instance, its future possibilities and its role as a means of understanding higher processes of nature than had hitherto been accessible to science, clearly explained the positive feelings I myself had experienced—without knowing why—when I had studied the subject.

Through his lectures and his part in the discussions—they were held daily by the various speakers and ranged over almost every field of modern knowledge—I gradually realized that Rudolf Steiner was in possession of unique powers. Not only did he show himself fully at home in all these fields, he was able to connect them with each other, and with the nature and being of man, in such a way that an apparent chaos of unrelated details was wrought into a higher synthesis. Moreover, it became clear to me that one who could speak as he did about the stages of human consciousness past, present, and future, must have full access to all of them at will, and be able to make each of them an object of exact observation. I saw a thinker who was himself sufficient proof that man can find within the resources of his own spirit the vantage-ground for the deed which I had dimly surmised, and by which alone true civilization could be saved. Through all these things I knew that I had found the teacher I had been seeking.

Thus I was fully confirmed in my hopes of the conference; but I was also often astonished at what I heard. Not least among my surprises was Rudolf Steiner's presentation of Goethe as the herald of the new form of scientific knowledge which he himself was expounding. I was here introduced to a side of Goethe which was as completely unknown to me as to so many others among my contemporaries, who had not yet come into touch with Rudolf Steiner's teachings. For me, as for them, Goethe had always been the great thinker revealing his thoughts through poetry. Indeed, only shortly before my meeting with Rudolf Steiner, it was in his poetry that Goethe had become newly alive to me as a helper in my search for a fuller human experience of nature and my fellow-men. But despite all my Goethe studies I had been quite unaware that more than a century earlier he had achieved something in the field of science, organic and inorganic alike, which could help modern man towards the new kind of knowledge so badly needed today. This was inevitable for me, since I shared the modern conviction that art and science were fields of activity essentially strange to one another. And so it was again left to Rudolf Steiner to open the way for me and others to Goethe as botanist, physicist, and the like. (pp. 28–29)

Four major works on the biological sciences may also be cited as indications of how Anthroposophy does not apply to living organisms the scientific principles appropriate to the nonliving mineral world, but rather apprehends the living biological world with a similarly living thinking: Gerbert Grohmann's *The Plant*, Wolfgang Schad's *Man and Mammals: Toward a Biology of Form,* and two books by Hermann Poppelbaum, *Man and Animal: Their Essential Difference* and *A New Zoology*.

Guenther Wachsmuth, cited above for his *Life and Works of Rudolf Steiner* ("Life and Work"), is also the author of a three-volume study, the first two of which—*Earth and Man* and *The Evolution of the Earth*—have not been translated into English. The third volume, *The Evolution of Mankind,* is primarily concerned with prehistory and ancient history, and secondarily with medieval and modern history, thereby reversing the usual emphasis:

This means that we must go back to the remotest times. In so doing, the study of random discoveries of ruins, documents, artifacts, and bones must more and more be replaced by spiritual-scientific research which can recognize and describe the single steps of evolution from its grasp of higher impulses, laws, and processes. The basis for this is found in the work of Rudolf Steiner, without which this book could not have been written.

The span of time handled here is much larger than anything familiar to modern history. To divide it into manageable fragments, we have adopted the phases of the Platonic world-year. We hope to show that these phases represent steps in the unfolding of man that coincide with cosmic rhythms and periodicities. This would harmonize with our thesis that man's development is organically related to that of the earth. (p. 7)

Rudolf Steiner himself gave three specifically scientific courses, complete with experimental demonstrations, the first two of which have been published in English: *Light Course: First Scientific Lecture Course* and *Warmth Course*.

Medicine

Rudolf Steiner delivered several lecture series on physiology, health, illness, and medicine. *An Occult Physiology* consists of eight systematic lectures on the inner, or esoteric, physiology of the human being, including lectures on the human being's micro-inner cosmic system, the blood as the instrument of the human ego, conscious life, and the human form. The next two lecture series were given at the request of physicians: *Spiritual Science and Medicine* is probably Steiner's most detailed and informative lecture course on physiology and medicine. The twenty lectures in this volume cover at least eight to ten topics, each containing an explanation or recommendation based on Steiner's clairvoyant understanding of the human body. *Anthroposophical Approach to Medicine* consists of four lectures which range over topics similar to those covered in *Spiritual Science and Medicine*. In the first lecture Steiner explains that his spiritual-scientific view, in contrast to the spiritual teachings of the past, presupposes and has arisen in relation to the achievements of modern Western science:

But it must be emphasized that the conceptions put forward by me are founded on a basis quite different from that of the various mystical, theosophical, and so-called gnostic ideas which have arisen traditionally in the course of human history. In order to make myself clear, I need mention only the main points of difference between the conceptions which will be put forward here and those of earlier times. Those earlier conceptions arose in human thought at a time when there was no science in our sense; mine have been delivered in an age when science has not only come into being but has reached a certain—albeit provisional—perfection. This must always be remembered if we would understand the meaning and significance of our studies, for it applies to all that may be said and discovered by Anthroposophy in regard to the different domains of human knowledge and capacity. (p. 8)

I am not out to attack scientific research or scientific medicine in any sense. My aim is to show that in this scientific medicine there is a mine of opportunity for a much wider knowledge than can be attained by modern methods, and above all by the current outlook on the world. We have no wish to scoff at the scientific mode of observation but on the contrary to give it a true foundation. When it is founded upon the spirit, then, and only then, does it assume its full significance. (p. 26)

Health and Illness: Nine Lectures to the Workmen at the Goetheanum includes lectures on the ear, nose, glands, various illnesses and the spiritual-scientific foundations of physiology. In 1924, with Ita Wegman, his personal physician and close collabarator, Steiner wrote *Fundamentals of Therapy: An Extension of the Art of Healing through Spiritual Knowledge*. In her preface of 1925, Ita Wegman wrote:

It had always been Rudolf Steiner's endeavor—and in this I could meet him with fullest sympathy of understanding—to renew the life of the ancient mysteries and cause it to flow once more into the sphere of medicine. From time immemorial, the mysteries were most intimately suited with the art of healing, and the attainment of spiritual knowledge was brought into connection with healing the sick. We had no thought, after the style of quacks and dilettanti, of underrating the scientific medicine of our time. We recognize it fully. Our aim was to supplement the science already in existence by the illumination that can flow from a true knowledge of the Spirit, towards a living grasp of the processes of illness and of healing. Needless to say, our purpose was to bring into life, not the instinctive habit of soul which still existed in the Mysteries of ancient time, but a method of research corresponding to the fully evolved consciousness of modern man, which can be lifted into spiritual regions. (ix)

Another of Steiner's contributions to humanity lies in his teachings concerning children in need of special care. Readers with the least interest in the mentally or emotionally disabled owe it to themselves to read some of the following sources for this important work: "Anthroposophy and Curative Education," in Easton's *Man and World;* two articles in *The Faithful Thinker* by Karl Konig, M.D., "The Mystery of the Mongol Child" (pp. 179–91), and "The Challenge of the Handicapped Child" (pp. 205–13); and Thomas J. Weihs's "The Handicapped Child—Curative Education," in Davy's *Work Arising* (pp. 93–116), as well as Weihs's book-length introduction, *Children in Need of Special Care*. With the help of any one of these introductory writings, the reader will be able to take better advantage of Rudolf Steiner's lecture course, *Curative Education: Twelve Lectures for Doctors and Curative Teachers*.

Steiner's lectures to medical doctors were not without effect. In 1981 more than five hundred physicians attended a conference on Spiritual Science and medicine sponsored by the Medical Section of the Anthroposophical Society at Dornach. There are now more than two thousand physicians, mostly in Germany and Holland (there are only twenty in the United States), whose medical practice follows the indications left by Rudolf Steiner. There are several hospitals in Switzerland and in Germany which are guided entirely by anthroposophical methods. The following eight works, all by anthroposophists who are physicians in Germany, represent the major works in English, but are only a fraction of the published research in Germany, Switzerland, and Holland.

Friedrich Husemann, M.D., former Director of the Clinic at Wiesneck Buchenbach near Freiburg, is the author of two important volumes: *Goethe and the Art of Healing: A Commentary on the Crisis in Medicine* and *The Image of Man as the Basis of the Art of Healing*. Dr. Husemann also wrote, with Otto Wolff, M.D., and others, *The Anthroposophical Approach to Medicine: An Outline of a Spiritual Scientifically Oriented Medicine*. Otto Wolff, M.D., is also the author of a succinctly written introductory booklet, *Anthroposophically Oriented Medicine and Its Remedies*. For the reader new to Anthroposophy or new to the study of medicine and health, this booklet by Wolff is perhaps the single work most to be recommended; it is informed, clear, inexpensive, and readily available. The other volume with these positive characteristics (except that it is 200 pages in contrast to Wolff's fifty pages and proportionately more expensive) is Victor Bott's *Anthroposophical Medicine: An Extension of the Art of Healing*.

In 1973 Karl E. Schaefer, M.D., organized three conferences sponsored by the Rockefeller Foundation under the general heading, "Man-Centered Physiology and Medicine," resulting in three volumes under the title, *A New Image of Man in Medicine*. Many of the ideas expressed in these volumes are either directly influenced by or sympathetic to the Spiritual Science of Rudolf Steiner. Each volume is worthy of separate mention: Volume 1, *Toward a Man-Centered Medical Science*, edited by Karl E. Schaefer, M.D., Herbert Hensel, M.D., and Ronald Brady, Ph.D., includes a foreword by René Dubos and articles by Joseph Weizenbaum, Owen Barfield, Ronald Brady, and many medical scientists. Volume 2, *Basis of an Individual Physiology*, edited by Karl Ernst Schaefer, M.D., Gunther Hildebrandt, M.D., and Norman Macbeth, LL.D., is considerably more specialized than the first volume in that it focuses on specific medical and anatomical concerns such as functional, rhythmical, and respiratory systems. Vol. 3, *Individuation Process and Biographical Aspects of Disease*, edited by Karl Ernst Schaefer, M.D., Uwe Stave, M.D., and Wolfgang Blankerburg, M.D., focuses on childhood and adolescence, stages of human life, and the relation between biography and disease.

On a more popular level, there are two recently published paperbacks by medical doctors writing within the framework of the anthroposophical conception of the human body, birth, and child development: W. zur Linden's *A Child Is Born: Pregnancy, Birth, Early Childhood*, and Walter Bühler's *Living with Your Body*. In *Fulfillment of Old Age*, Norbert Glas, a physician who directed a nursing home in England for many years, offers a host of helpful insights on the process of aging as conceived within the life cycle described in writings by Rudolf Steiner. Dr. Glas is also the author of *Conception, Birth and Early Childhood*.

Nutrition and Biodynamic Farming and Gardening

The basic text for the theoretical and practical foundation of the biodynamic approach to agriculture and gardening is a course of eight lectures, entitled *Agriculture,* which Rudolf Steiner delivered in June, 1924. In his preface, Ehrenfried Pfeiffer, M.D., describes the practical, step-by-step method by which Steiner developed the biodynamic method. This book of eight lectures, along with four discussions between Dr. Steiner and the attending farmers and scientists, is full of practical, concrete solutions which cumulatively reveal an entirely new basis for agriculture and gardening. As Pfeiffer explains:

> In the Agriculture Course, which was attended by some sixty persons, Rudolf Steiner set forth the basic new way of thinking about the relationship of earth and soil to the formative forces of the etheric, astral, and ego activity of nature. He pointed out particularly how the health of soil, plants, and animals depends upon bringing nature into connection again with the cosmic creative, shaping forces. The practical method he gave for treating soil, manure, and compost, and especially for making the biodynamic compost preparations, was intended above all to serve the purpose of reanimating the natural forces which in nature and in modern agriculture were on the wane. "This must be achieved in actual practice," Rudolf Steiner told me. He showed how much it meant to him to have the School of Spiritual Science going hand in hand with the real-life practicality when he spoke on another occasion of wanting to have teachers at the School alternate a few years of teaching (three years was the period mentioned) with a subsequent period of three years spent in work outside, so that by this alternation they would never get out of touch with the conditions and challenges of real life. (pp. 8–9)

As a spiritually based agricultural method is essential for proper nutrition, so does nutrition exercise an essential influence on the human will forces necessary for the practice of spiritual discipline. Dr. Pfeiffer relates a conversation in which he asked Rudolf Steiner why the will forces necessary for carrying out spiritual activity seem to be so weak even in Steiner's disciples who seemed most eager to follow his directives. Pfeiffer recounts Steiner's response as follows:

> This is a problem of nutrition. Nutrition as it is today does not supply the strength necessary for manifesting the spirit in physical life. A bridge can no longer be built from thinking to will and action. Food plants no longer contain the forces people need for this. (p. 7)

Rudolf Steiner also left indications for a science of nutrition. Gerhard Schmidt, M.D., who is a physician in Dornach and has been a member of the faculty of the Rudolf Steiner (Summer) Institute since 1975, is the author of *The Dynamics of Nutrition: The Impulse of Rudolf Steiner's Spiritual Science for a New Nutritional Hygiene*. Schmidt's introduction is worth quoting for the light it sheds on the conception of nutrition influenced by Rudolf Steiner's Spiritual Science.

In the present volume it has been our task to examine the fundamental and general aspects of nutrition. Therefore we begin with the questions about the meaning and reality of nutrition, a sketch of the physiology of nutrition including the problems of rhythm and fragrance as well as the fundamental aspects of taking foods from the mineral, plant, and animal realms. Furthermore, we concern ourselves with the relationship of nutrition to human soul and spiritual life, with rational understanding of the evaluation of uncooked and cooked foods, and with the differentiation of foodstuffs into remedies, dietary foods, and delicacies. Finally, a contribution to the social significance of nutrition and its developmental history suggests possibilities for a contemporary nutritional hygiene.

The problem of nutrition is today without a doubt exceedingly important. Through the stimulation of Spiritual Science it has become ever more revelant. Rudolf Steiner himself said that it is "just the everyday things that are most difficult to be included into the spiritual life—because eating and drinking are included only when we are able to follow why, in order to fulfill man's role in the world, we have to ingest physical substances in a rhythmical manner and what relationship these physical substances have to the spiritual life."

Therewith we have broached the theme which will lead us into the consideration of the first chapter. For the unprejudiced reader of this book it will probably become clear, only after reading it, that a healthy further development of humanity in our time demands that a new light of consciousness illumine our conception of nutrition.

Finally, a few words about the title of our book, *The Dynamics of Nutrition*. Rudolf Steiner has often indicated that the substances we take up with our nourishment serve much more to stimulate and unfold activities in the organism than to serve as material deposits. "The primary concern is not with an arrangement of quantities of substances in metabolism, but rather, whether with foodstuffs we take up in us in a proper manner the vitality of forces." This expresses what the content of the teaching of a dynamics nutrition should be. . . .

In this sense we deal here with a dynamic nutrition as a foundation for a new science of the interaction of nourishment with man. In its basic principles, as well as in many details, this has been developed by Rudolf Steiner. What remains, however, is to make the existing building blocks visible, and to put them together, to allow the impressive edifice to appear with increasing clarity. (pp. 2–3)

There are at least five books which introduce a farmer, gardener, or curious nonexpert to the theory and practice of biodynamic agriculture and gardening: for agriculture, the most thorough, up-to-date introduction is probably Herbert A. Koepf's *Bio-Dynamic Agriculture—An Introduction*. For the application of biodynamic methods to the home garden, the following three books are practical, entirely readable introductions: Alice Heckel's *The Pfeiffer Garden Book: Bio-Dynamics in the Home Garden;* Ehrenfried Pfeiffer's and Erika Riese's *Grow a Garden and Be Self-Sufficient;* and John and Helen Philbrick's *Gardening for Health and Nutrition: The Organic Method*. Finally, anyone seriously interested in the understanding of agriculture and gardening in light of cosmic rhythms and influences will welcome the assistance handsomely provided by *The Kimberton Hills Agricultural Calendar for Farmers and Gardeners: A Beginner's Aid for Understanding the Influence of Cosmic Rhythms in Work on the Land* (issued annually by the Camphill Village at Kimberton Hills, Penn.).

11. THE ANTHROPOSOPHICAL SOCIETY

A clear understanding of the communal or societal structures of Rudolf Steiner's legacy requires the definition of three terms: Anthroposophical Movement, Anthroposophical Society, and The School of Spiritual Science. The Anthroposophical Movement refers to the loosely organized configuration of all the ideas, movements, and individuals in varying degrees of agreement and engagement with the Spiritual Science of Rudolf Steiner. Individuals who read this book with sympathy, and thereafter carry in their heart or mind (however unconsciously) Rudolf Steiner's vision and spiritual teachings, may to this extent be a part of the Anthroposophic Movement. As a movement, Anthroposophy was not founded at any given moment and has no specific limits as to scope, membership, or regulating principles—excepting the teachings and mission of Rudolf Steiner.

The Anthroposophical Society, by contrast, is a definite group of individuals who have consciously united themselves to study the teachings and advance the impulse of Rudolf Steiner. When he founded the earlier Anthroposophical Society in 1913, Rudolf Steiner in effect separated the Anthroposophical Movement from the Theosophical Society in which he had been working since 1900. The new Society, maintained as a visible spiritual society by which his teachings might be shared and implemented, proved predictably to be an imperfect instrument for its lofty spiritual task. It has been suggested that the imperfections and controversies which characterized the Anthroposophical Society from its inception led, karmically, to the burning of the first Goetheanum on New Year's Eve, 1922.

On Christmas, 1923, Steiner fused into one the seemingly separate tasks of rebuilding the Goetheanum and reconstituting the Anthroposophical Society. The result, which can be described here in only superficial terms, was the founding of the General Anthroposophical Society as a spiritual body both public and esoteric, of which the Goetheanum is both a physical and spiritual representation. Whereas the foundation stone of the first Goetheanum was a physical stone (albeit highly symbolic), the Foundation Stone of the Second Goetheanum, which is also the Foundation Stone of the General Anthroposophical Society, is a spiritual "stone" laid in the hearts of those who identify themselves with the Spiritual Science of Rudolf Steiner. Steward Easton discusses the founding and evolution of the Anthroposophical Society in both *Man and World* (chapter 14; section 1) and *Rudolf Steiner* (chapters 8 and 12; section 1).

The third step or level of spiritual commitment is the School of Spiritual Science, which Rudolf Steiner began to form during the early months of 1924. The School, often but erroneously referred to as the First Class, is to consist of those members of the General Anthroposophical Society who accept the responsibility of representing Anthroposophy, the Spiritual Science of Rudolf Steiner, in and to the world. A member of the School of Spiritual Science attempts to deepen spiritual-scientific knowledge and to attain personal experience in its field by special instruction and lessons. This includes attempts to meet other persons in terms of their individual struggle for spiritual life. Each member also seeks to participate in spiritual research, among the first steps of which is to penetrate by creative imagination as much of reality as possible, both in its supersensible and sensible aspects.

From its inception, the spiritual research of the School of Spiritual Science has been conducted according to the personnel available for leading and staffing the various sections. In recent years, subject areas have included general Anthroposophy, medicine, the arts of speech and music, plastic arts, belles lettres, mathematics and astronomy, natural science, pedagogy, spiritual striving of youth, social sciences, nutrition, and agriculture. Rudolf Steiner intended that the spiritual work of the School of Spiritual Science would be the spiritual root of the Society, as the Society is the spiritual core responsible for the Anthroposophic Movement.

With this brief, and necessarily inadequate, introduction to the Anthroposophical Movement, Anthroposophical Society, and School of Spiritual Science, it is now possible to turn to some of Rudolf Steiner's writings on these spiritual groups. The following works, whether lectures or books, were intended primarily for members of the Anthroposophical Society. They are listed here because the general reader might wish to know something of the communication which Steiner gave to those who attempt to practice his teachings both individually and in community. Works intended for members of the School of Spiritual Science are not listed.

Because they were written (or delivered as lectures) to anthroposophists, the basic documents for the spiritual life of the Anthroposophical Society are not entirely intelligible, and not particularly useful, to newcomers. The first such work is *Anthroposophical Leading Thoughts: Anthroposophy as a Path of Knowledge—The Michael Mystery*. The first two paragraphs constitute the most definitive statement, in Rudolf Steiner's own words, concerning the meaning of Anthroposophy:

1. Anthroposophy is a path of Knowledge, to guide the Spiritual in the human being to the Spiritual in the universe. *It arises in man as a need of the heart, of the life of feeling;* and it can be justified only inasmuch as it can satisfy this inner need. He alone can ackowledge Anthroposophy, who finds in it what he himself in his own inner life feels impelled to seek. Hence only they can be *anthroposophists who feel certain questions on the nature of man and the universe as an elemental need of life,* just as one feels hunger and thirst.

2. *Anthroposophy communicates knowledge that is gained in a spiritual way.* Yet it only does so because everyday life, and the science founded on sense-perception and intellectual activity, lead to a barrier along life's way—a limit where the life of the soul in man would die if it could go no farther. Everyday life and science do not lead to this limit in such a way as to compel man to stop short at it. For at the very frontier where the knowledge derived from sense-perception ceases, there is opened through the human soul itself the further outlook into the spiritual world. (p. 13)

Complementing this volume are two slim volumes of brief articles concerning the character, aims, and problems of the Society: *The Life, Nature, and Cultivation of Anthroposophy* and *The Constitution of the School of Spiritual Science*. There are also two volumes concerning the founding of the General Anthroposophical Society on 25 December 1923: F. W. Zeylmans van Emmichoven's *The Foundation Stone: Laying of the Foundation Stone of the Anthroposophical Society,* and Arvia Ege, *The Christmas Foundation Meeting, 1923.*

Finally, ten lectures delivered from January to March 1923, after the burning of the first Goetheanum and prior to the founding of the General Anthroposophical Society, are collected in *Awakening to Community,* an eloquent plea for the creation of anthroposophical communities. One passage in *Awakening to Community* is especially germane for an understanding of what Rudolf Steiner intends—and the weakness he intends to overcome—by the creation of a genuine community based on anthroposophic discipline:

When a number of people meet in an ordinary state of consciousness and fail to lift themselves and their full life of feeling to the supersensible level, when they meet to listen in a merely ordinary state of mind to what the spiritual world is saying, there is a great—an immeasurably great—chance of their coming to blows, because all such people become egotists as a natural consequence.

There is, to be sure, a powerful remedy for this, but it is available only if the human soul develops it. I am referring to tolerance of a truly heartfelt kind. But we have to educate ourselves to it. In a state of everyday consciousness a little tolerance suffices most people's needs, and social circumstances put many a situation right again. But where the ordinary, everyday state of mind prevails, it often happens that people talking together are not even concerned to hear what the other is saying. We all know this from our own personal experience. It has become a habit nowadays to give only scant attention to somebody else's words. When a person is partway through a sentence, someone else starts talking, because he is not the least interested in what is being said. He is interested only in his own opinion. One may be able, after a fashion, to get by with this in the physical world, but it simply cannot be done in the spiritual realm. There, the soul must be imbued with the most perfect tolerance; one must educate oneself to listen with the most positive inner calm even to things one cannot in the least agree with, listen not in a spirit of supercilious endurance, but with the most positive inner tolerance as one would to well-founded utterances on the other person's part. In the higher worlds there is little sense in making objections to anything.

A person with experience in that realm knows that the most opposite views about the same fact can be expressed there by, let us say, oneself and someone else. When he has made himself capable of listening to the other's opposite view with exactly the same tolerance he feels toward his own—and please notice this—then and then only does he have the social attitude required for experiencing what was formerly merely theoretical knowledge of the higher worlds.

This moral basis is vital to a right relationship to the higher realms. The strife that I have described as so characteristic of the societies we are discussing has its root in the fact that when people hear sensational things, such as that man has an etheric and astral body and an ego as well as a physical body, and so on, they listen for sensation's sake but do not undertake to transform their souls as these must be transformed if they are to experience spiritual reality differently than they would a chair or a table in the physical world, and one experiences even these objects differently in the physical world than one does in dreams. When people apply their ordinary soul habits to what they think they are understanding of teachings about the higher worlds, then this inevitably develops strife and egotism. (pp. 110–11)

Just a few months after delivering the lecture series entitled *Awakening to Community,* quoted above, Rudolf Steiner delivered a cycle of eight lectures entitled *The Anthroposophic Movement: Its History and Life-Conditions in Relation to the Anthroposophical Society—An Occasion for Self-Recollection.* This revealing series of lectures recounts Steiner's spiritual work in three phases: in the first phase, which lasted approximately until 1908 or 1909, and includes the years during which he wrote his basic work, he laid the foundations for a modern science of spirit. During the second phase, until 1913, he gave numerous lecture cycles aimed at the renewal of the Christian esoteric tradition; in the third phase, beginning in 1913, he directed, but did not actually join, the first Anthroposophical Society. Since these lectures were delivered in June, 1923, this historical survey does not include what might be called a fourth phase, the founding of the General Anthroposophical Society at the Christmas meeting of 1923.

The founding of the General Anthroposophical Society is described in some of the works cited above, particularly in Easton's *Man and World,* and the two volumes entitled *The Foundation Stone.* Along with *Anthroposophical Leading Thoughts,* perhaps the most complete description of Anthroposophy as a discipline and a spiritual society, is to be found in *Anthroposophy—An Introduction,* edited by Owen Barfield. This work, despite its subtitle, is an highly advanced account of the spiritual potentiality of Anthroposophy in contemporary experience. This cycle of nine lectures, delivered at the Goetheanum, January–February 1924, includes Rudolf Steiner's most carefully rendered thoughts on meditation, spiritual knowledge, initiation, and the ideal of a selfhood conscious of eternity. Since this lecture cycle is as demanding as it is important, it should not be read without the kind of preparation provided by works such as Easton's *Man and World,* Edmunds' *Anthroposophy,* Schiller's *Rudolf Steiner and Initiation,* and one or more of Steiner's foundation books.

12. ANTHROPOSOPHICAL ACTIVITIES

General Anthroposophical Society

Since it was given its final form by Rudolf Steiner during the Christmas Conference of 1923, the world center of the Anthroposophical Society has been in the Goetheanum, the building which Rudolf Steiner designed, at the foothills of the Jura Mountains in Dornach near Basel, Switzerland. The Goetheanum is the physical center of the Anthroposophical Society by virtue of housing the Executive Committee (the German term *Vorstand* is used even in English-speaking countries), leaders of the sections of the School for Spiritual Science, and a stage and auditorium which Rudolf Steiner designed for the presentation of his four Mystery Dramas and eurythmy. It is also the center for the worldwide network of communications between anthroposophists working in collaboration all over the world, and the repository for records. More significantly, as briefly explained in the previous section, the Goetheanum is also the spiritual center of the spiritual task which Rudolf Steiner sought to realize in the present age.

A demographic density map of anthroposophists, anthroposophical centers and activities would show an overwhelming concentration in Germany, Switzerland, and Holland, with a secondary concentration in Great Britain, France, and Italy, and a very low presence of anthroposophists and anthroposophical activities in the United States and Canada. It is revealing, for example, that there are more anthroposophists in the city of Stuttgart than in the entire United States. In Germany, the Waldorf schools constitute the second largest, and apparently most respected, system of private education. Another exmple of the acceptance of anthroposophic teaching in Germany is the recently established, fully accredited University at Witten/Herdecke, a complete university program including studies leading to the degrees of Ph.D., LL.D., and M.D. The Medical School of the university at Witten-Herdecke, which opened in April of 1983, will provide medical training along the lines indicated by the spiritual-medical teachings of Rudolf Steiner.

Similarly, there are many highly visible and respected anthroposophic institutions throughout Great Britain, the most prominent of which are Rudolf Steiner House, 35 Park Row, London, and Emerson College, Forest Row, Sussex. Rudolf Steiner House offers courses, lectures, eurythmy classes and performances, a library, and a bookstore. For the present, Rudolf Steiner Press is situated at 38 Museum Street, which also houses a large Anthroposophic bookstore. Emerson College offers a one-year foundation course in anthroposophical studies and three specialized courses of study: a school of education devoted essentially to Waldorf education; a school of biodynamic agriculture and earth sciences; and facilities for training in arts and crafts.

There are also active centers in Canada, particularly:

The Anthroposophical Society in Canada, Hill House, 81 Lawton Boulevard, Toronto, Ontario, M4V-126; and The Anthroposophical Society, Montreal Branch, 5291 Queen Mary Road, Montreal, P.Q., H3W 143.

Anthroposophical Society in America

Of the approximately two thousand members of the Anthroposophical Society in America, perhaps half live in or have access to anthroposophical communities or branches. Since the basic units, and the basic activity, of anthroposophical work are study groups which should consist of at least seven people, individual members who do not have access to a group of anthroposophists work at a disadvantge. Whereas some members must study entirely on their own, others have the benefit of a weekly or biweekly study group, and many others have access to a variety of activities available in major cities. From east to west, the major anthroposophical centers in the U.S. are as follows: Wilton, N.H.; Boston, Mass.; Harlemville, Great Barrington, and Copake, on the New York-Massachusetts border; Spring Valley, N.Y.; New York City; Princeton, N.J.; Kimberton Hills, Penn.; Washington, D.C.; Chicago, Ill.: Ann Arbor and Southfield (Detroit), Mich.; Milwaukee, Wisc.; Houston and Austin, Tex.; Denver and Woodland Park, Colo.; Los Angeles, San Francisco, and Sacramento, Calif. Addresses and additional information concerning these centers are available from the national headquarters of the Society, in Harlemville, New York, one hundred miles north of New York City: The Anthroposophical Society in America, RD 2, Box 215, Ghent, N.Y. 12075.

Education

There are three teacher-training institutes, each offering a one-year general foundation course in Anthroposophy, followed by a year of specific training courses in Waldorf pedagogy: Rudolf Steiner College: A Center for Anthroposophical Endeavors, 9200 Fair Oaks Blvd., Fair Oaks, Calif. 95628; Waldorf Institute of Mercy College of Detroit, 23399 Evergreen Road, Southfield, Mich. 48075; and Waldorf Institute of Southern California, 17100 Superior St., Northridge, Calif. 91324.

The Foundation Year (also called Orientation Year) is offered at Fair Oaks, Southfield, and Toronto. There are now more than sixty Waldorf schools in the United States, with new schools being established each year. There are twelve full schools, kindergarten to twelfth grade: Detroit Waldorf School, Detroit, Mich.; Green Meadow Waldorf School, Spring Valley, N.Y.; Hawthorne Valley School, Harlemville, N.Y.; Highland Hall School, Northridge, Calif.; High Mowing School, and Pine Hill High Mowing Waldorf School, Wilton, N.H.; Kimberton Farms School,

Kimberton, Penn.; Mohalapua Waldorf School, Honolulu, Hawaii; Rudolf Steiner School, New York, N.Y.; Sacramento Waldorf School, Fair Oaks, Calif.; Toronto Waldorf School, Thorn Hill, Ont., Canada; Vancouver Waldorf School, B.C., Canada; Waldorf School, Garden City, N.Y. A complete list of Waldorf schools and other schools sponsored by the Association of Waldorf Schools in North America is reprinted in M. C. Richards's *Toward Wholeness*, in Frances Edmunds' *Rudolf Steiner Education,* and is available from the Anthroposophical Society office in Harlemville (Ghent).

The Rudolf Steiner Institute, which meets for three weeks during each summer, offers college-level courses by professors well-versed in anthroposophical teaching. After meeting for five summers in Natick, Mass., the Institute moved to Wilson College, Chambersburg, Penn. in 1982. Information concerning the Institute program is available from: Registrar, Rudolf Steiner Institute, RD 2, Box 199, Phoenixville, Penn. 19460.

Specialized Groups and Activities

The School of Eurythmy at the Threefold Center for Adult Education, Spring Valley, N.Y., which is accredited by the Section for the Arts of Music and Speech of the School of Spiritual Science at the Goetheanum, Dornach, offers a four-year training course leading to a diploma in eurythmy. Yearlong programs in the visual arts are offered at the Rudolf Steiner College, Fair Oaks, Calif.; Waldorf Institute of Mercy College, Southfield (Detroit), Mich.: Donald Hall Painting School, Harlemville, N.Y.

There are Camphill villages (communities for people in need of special care), in Copake, N.Y. and at Beaver Run and Kimberton Hills, Penn. Physicians who are members of the Anthroposophical Society have formed a working group called The Fellowship of Physicians, 219 Hungry Hollow Road, Spring Valley, N.Y. The anthroposophic community of Spring Valley is also the center for several related activities and groups: The Fellowship Community (241 Hungry Hollow Road) cares for older individuals. Anthroposophical Therapy and Hygiene Association is concerned with the multiple-disciplinary approach of anthroposophy to the problems of hygiene and therapeutics (same address). Weleda, Inc. prepares remedies used by physicians in the practice of anthroposophically extended medicine (841 South Main Street).

There are three major biodynamic farming associations: Wyoming, R.I., Headquarters, Bio-Dynamic Farming and Gardening Association, Granada Hills, Calif.; Pfeiffer Foundation, Spring Valley, N.Y.

The Christian Community

Christian Communities, generally consisting of at least a priest, a congregation, and a chapel, can be found in the following locations: New York City; Copake, N.Y.; Devon, Penn.; Brookline, Mass.; Chicago; Denver; Los Angeles; San Francisco; Sacramento; Toronto; and Vancouver.

Libraries and Bookstores

The Rudolf Steiner Lending Library of the Anthroposophical Society in America is located at Harlemville. This library houses all of Rudolf Steiner's published works, both in German and English, as well as hundreds, if not thousands, of unpublished lectures in German and English. The library also contains a virtually complete collection of works influenced by Rudolf Steiner as well as a large and rapidly expanding collection of works in the following areas: medicine and nutrition, arts, Goethe, the esoteric tradition (including gnostic, medical, and alchemical writings), celtic (including Arthurian and grail legends), mysticism (including Jewish, Christian, and Islamic), folklore and fairy tales, and comparative theologies and religions. The library has developed lists of library holdings under these and other subject categories. Most of the books in the library can be borrowed by mail for a modest membership fee.

There are also books on anthroposophical subjects in the libraries of the larger anthroposophical centers, including: Berkeley, Los Angeles, and Fair Oaks, Calif.; Chicago; Toronto; Ann Arbor; Gainesville, Fla.; Honolulu; Newton Centre, Marlborough, and Belmont, Mass.; Spring Valley and New York, N.Y. Rudolf Steiner Library for the Blind (111 Gibbs St., Newton Centre, Mass. 02159; (617) 969–0388) distributes writings by Rudolf Steiner on tapes and in braille.

The main anthroposophical bookstore is connected with the Anthroposophic Press, 258 Hungry Hollow Road, Spring Valley, N.Y. 10977. There are also anthroposophical bookshops in New York City, Chicago, Toronto, Seattle, Sacramento, Los Angeles, and Northridge, Calif., and Honolulu.

Periodicals

Journal for Anthroposophy, published semiannually by the Anthroposophical Society in America (Harlemville, N.Y.), is a substantial ninety-six-page periodical, typically featuring five to ten articles and select reviews.

Anthroposophical Review (formerly *Anthroposophical Quarterly*) is published in England.

Newsletter of The Anthroposophical Society in America, published quarterly for Society members, ordinarily offers three to five articles or translations, more than a dozen book reviews, and reports on Society activities.

The Golden Blade, featuring a large number of substantial articles, published annually in England, is available from the Anthroposophic Press.

Bio-Dynamics is a quarterly available from "Bio-Dynamics," Box 253, Wyoming, R.I. 02898.

Towards is a fifty-page, large format, semiannual magazine founded in 1977 "to explore and make better known the work of Owen Barfield, Samuel Taylor Coleridge, Wolfgang von Goethe, Rudolf Steiner, and related authors," 3948 Bannister Rd., Fair Oaks, CA. 95628.

Publishers

The Anthroposophic Press, 258 Hungry Hollow Rd., Spring Valley, N.Y. 10977. (914) 352–2295. This Press is the largest and oldest publisher and bookseller of anthroposophical books in the Western hemisphere. It is the exclusive distributor and agent in the United States for the Rudolf Steiner Press, London, and the Steiner Book Centre in North Vancouver. It also stocks a complete list of Rudolf Steiner's books in German. A catalog is available on request.

Other anthroposophically related presses include:

Rudolf Steiner Press, 38 Museum St., London, W.C.1.

St. George Publications and Book Service, Box 225, Spring Valley, N.Y. 10977, distributors of Floris Books, Edinburgh (formerly Christian Community Press), Kolisko Archive Pubications, and other anthroposophically related books and art products.

Steiner Book Centre, 151 Carisbrooke Crescent, North Vancouver, B.C., Canada.

Garber Communications, Garber Road, Blauvelt, N.Y., publisher of Rudolf Steiner Publications, Steiner Books, and Multimedia.

Floris Books, 21 Napier Road, Edinburgh, EH.

Bibliography

INTRODUCTION

Since the vast majority of books in English by and about Rudolf Steiner are published either by Rudolf Steiner Press (London), or Anthroposophic Press (New York), books with these two imprints will simply be identified by London or New York, followed by the date of publication. The second and third dates, in parentheses, indicate the year of original publication (or for lectures, the city and date of delivery) in German, indicated with a "G" and, where appropriate, the year of first publication in English, indicated by an "E." Books published by other houses are so indicated. Some of the volumes translated from German to English do not list the name of the translator. Hardback/paperback editions are indicated by "hb." or "pb." or both, after the year of publication; "op" refers to books presently out of print.

All of the books listed as in print in this bibliography are available from Anthroposophic Press, 258 Hungry Hollow Road, Spring Valley, N.Y. 10977. Almost all of the out of print books are available to members of the Anthroposophic Library, RD 2, Ghent (Harlemville) N.Y. 12075.

In addition to the works cited in this bibliography, there are many other pamphlets, articles, and slim volumes of single lectures, that have been printed, usually of a specialized interest. Most of these by Steiner can be found in the *Bibliographical Reference List of Rudolf Steiner's Work in English Translation,* 2 vols.

The numbers (1–12) in parentheses at the end of some entries refer to the appropriate sections of the Guide to Further Reading where the work is discussed.

I. WORKS BY RUDOLF STEINER

Anthroposophical Approach to Medicine. Rev. trans. Charles Davy. London, 1951 (Stuttgart, 1922; E, 1928), 79 pp., hb., op.

Agriculture. Trans. George Adams. Pref. Ehrenfried Pfeiffer. London: Bio-Dynamic Agriculture Association, 1977 (Koberwitz, Silesia, 1924; E, 1958, 1972), 175 pp., pb (10).

Ancient Myths: Their Meaning and Connection with Evolution. Trans. M. Cotterell. North Vancouver, B.C.: Steiner Book Centre, 1971 (Dornach, 1918), 119 pp., pb. (5).

Anthroposophical Approach to Medicine. Rev. trans. Charles Davy. London, 1951 (Stuttgart, 1922; E, 1928), 79 pp., hb., op. (10).

Anthroposophical Leading Thoughts: Anthroposophy as a Path of Knowledge—The Michael Mystery. Trans. George and Mary Adams. London, 1973 (G, 1924), 219 pp., hb., op. (4, 11).

The Anthroposophical Movement: Its History and Life Conditions in Relation to the Anthroposophical Society—An Occasion for Self-Recollection. Trans. E. Bowen-Wedgwood. Foreword, Marie Steiner. London, 1933 (Dornach, 1923), 206 pp., hb., op. (11).

Anthroposophy—An Introduction, rev. ed. Ed. Owen Barfield. New York, 1983 (G, 1924; E, 1931, 1961), 130 pp., hb., op. (11).

Anthroposophy and the Social Question. New York, 1958, 43 pp., pb.

The Apocalypse of St. John: Lectures on the Book of Revelation. London, 1977 (Nuremberg, 1908), 228 pp., pb., illustrations of seven seals (6).

Art in the Light of Mystery Wisdom. Trans. Shirley M. K. Gandell et al. New York, 1955, 191 pp., hb., op. (9).

The Arts and Their Mission. Trans. Lisa D. Monges and Virginia Moore. Introd. Virginia Moore. New York, 1964 (G, 1923), 116 pp., pb. (9).

At the Gates of Spiritual Science. Trans. E. H. Goddard and Charles Davy. London, 1970 (Stuttgart, 1906), 158 pp., hb., pb., op. (3).

An Autobiography. Trans. Rita Stebbing. Ed., Foreward, Notes, and Chronological Outline Paul M. Allen. Blauvelt, N.Y.: Garber Communications,* 1977 (G, 1924), 540 pp., hb. (1).

Awakening to Community. Trans. Majorie Spock. New York, 1974 (Stuttgart, 1923), 178 pp., hb. (11).

Background to the Gospel of St. Mark. Trans. E. H. Goddard and D. S. Osmond. London, 1968 (Berlin, 1910–11), 220 pp., hb. (6).

Balance in Teaching. Spring Valley, N.Y.: Mercury Press, 1982 (Stuttgart, 1920), 58 pp., pb. (8).

The Balance in the World and Man: Lucifer and Ahriman. Trans. D. S. Osmond and Mary Adams. North Vancouver, B.C.: Steiner Book Centre, 1977 (Dornach, 1914; E, 1948), 45 pp., pb. (4).

---

* As of 1983, Garber Communications is the imprint for books previously published by Rudolf Steiner Publications, Steiner Books, and Multimedia.

Between Death and Rebirth in Relation to Cosmic Facts. See *The Life Between Death and Rebirth in Relation to Cosmic Facts,* below.

The Being of Man and His Future Evolution. Trans. Pauline Wehrle. London, 1981 (G. 1908–09), 148 pp., pb. (3).

The Bhagavad Gita and the Epistles of Paul. Trans. Lisa D. Monges and Doris M. Bugbey. New York, 1971 (Cologne, 1912–13), 102 pp., pb. (5).

Boundaries of Natural Science. Trans. Frederick Amrine and Konrad Oberhuber. Introd. Saul Bellow. New York, 1983 (Dornach, 1920), 158 pp. hb., pb.

The Bridge between Universal Spirituality and the Physical Constitution of Man. New York, 1979 (Dornach, 1920; E, 1958), 64 pp., pb.

Building Stones for an Understanding of the Mystery of Golgotha. Trans. A. H. Parker. London, 1972 (Berlin, 1972), 238 pp., hb. (6).

The Calendar of the Soul (52 verses in German and English). Trans. E. Lehrs. Commentary, E. C. Merry. London, 1970, hb., op; Trans. Daisy Alden, New York, 1974, hb; Trans. Ruth and Hans Pusch. New York, 1982, hb. (3).

The Case for Anthroposophy. (*Extracts from Von Seelenrätseln,* 1917). Trans. Owen Barfield, London, 1970, 95 pp., pb., op.

Challenge of the Times. New York, 1941 (Dornach, 1918), 218 pp., pb. (originally *In the Changed Conditions of the Times* (7).

The Change in the Path to Supersensible Knowledge. North Vancouver, B.C.: Steiner Book Centre, 1982 (Dornach, 1922; E, 1959), 22 pp., pb.

Christ and the Human Soul. Rev. trans. Charles Davy. London, 1972 (Norrköping, 1914), 78 pp., pb., op. (6).

Christ and the Spiritual World; The Search for the Holy Grail. Trans. Charles Davy and D. S. Osmond. London, 1963 (Leipzig, 1913–14), 142 pp., hb., op.

The Christ Impulse and the Development of Ego Consciousness. Trans. Lisa D. Monges and Gilbert Church. New York, 1976 (Berlin, 1909–10), 156 pp., pb. (6).

Christ in the Twentieth Century. Trans. Marjorie Spock. New York, 1971 (Cologne, 1912), 20 pp., pb. (6).

The Christian Foundation Meeting at the Anthroposophical Society: Extracts from Rudolf Steiner's Addresses. Ed. R. G. Seddon. London, 1980, 37 pp., pb.

Christianity and Occult Mysteries of Antiquity. Trans. E. A. Frommer et al. Introd. Alfred Heidenrich. Blauvelt, N.Y.: Garber Communications, 1977, 231 pp., hb., pb. (also published as *Christianity as Mystical Fact,* below) (2, 5, 6).

Christianity as Mystical Fact. Rev. trans. Charles Davy and Adam Bittleston. London, 1972 (G, 1902; E, 1914), 155 pp., hb., pb. (also published as *Christianity and Occult Mysteries of Antiquity*) (2, 5, 6).

Colour. Trans. H. Salter. London, 1977 (Dornach, 1921), 100 pp., pb., originally New York, 1935 (Dornach, 1923) 176 pp., hb, op. (9).

The Constitution of the School of Spiritual Science: Its Arrangement in Sections. Trans. G. Adams and S. & J. Rudel. London, 1964 (Dornach, 1924), 84 pp., pb. (10).

Cosmic Memory: Prehistory of Earth and Man. Trans. Karl E. Zimmer. San Francisco: Harper & Row, 1981 (G, 1904; E, 1959), 262 pp., pb. (4).

The Course of My Life. 2nd ed. Rev. trans. Olin D. Wannamaker. New York, 1951, 258 pp., hb., op. (see also *An Autobiography*) (1).

Creative Speech: The Nature of Speech Formation. Trans. W. Budgett et al. London, 1978, 240 pp., hb. (9).

Curative Education: Twelve Lectures for Doctors and Curative Teachers. Trans. Mary Adams. London, 1981 (Dornach, 1924; E, 1972), 228 pp., pb. (10).

The Cycle of the Year As Breathing Process of the Earth: The Four Great Festival-Seasons of the Year. Trans. M. Cotterell. London, 1956 (Dornach, 1923), 76 pp.

The Deed of Christ and the Opposing Spiritual Powers: Lucifer, Ahriman, Mephistopheles, Asuras. North Vancouver, B.C.: Steiner Book Centre, 1976 (Berlin, 1909), 43 pp., pb. (4, 6).

Deeper Insights into Education: The Waldorf Approach. Trans. René Querido. New York, 1983, ca. 65 pp., pb.

Deeper Secrets of Human History in the Light of the Gospel of St. Matthew. London, 1957 (Berlin, 1909), 80 pp., hb., op (6).

Discussions with Teachers. Trans. Helen Fox. New York, 1983 (G, 1919; E, 1967), hb., (8).

The Driving Force of Spiritual Powers in World History. Trans. Dorothy Osmond with Johanna Collis. North Vancouver, B.C.: Steiner Book Centre, 1983 (Dornach, 1923), 96 pp., pb. (5).

Earthly and Cosmic Man. Trans. D. S. Osmond. London, 1948 (Berlin, 1911–12). 176 pp., hb., op.

Earthly Death and Cosmic Life. Trans. Charles Davy and D. S. Osmond. London, 1964, (Berlin, 1918), 160 pp., hb., op.

The East in the Light of the West. Trans. Shirley M. K. Gandell and D. S. Osmond. London and New York, 1940 (Vienna, 1922), 222 pp., hb., op (5).

The Easter Festival Considered in Relation to the Mysteries. Trans. George Adams. London, 1968 (Dornach, 1924), 79 pp., pb.

Education as a Social Problem. New York, 1969 (Dornach, 1919), 113 pp., hb., op. (8).

The Education of the Child in the Light of Anthroposophy. Trans. George and Mary Adams. London, 1965 (G, 1909; E, 1927), 48 pp., pb. (8).

The Effects of Spiritual Development. Rev. trans. A. H. Parker. London, 1978 (The Hague, 1913), 155 pp, hb., pb., op. (first edition published as *The Effect of Occult Development Upon the Self and Sheaths of Man*, 1945) (3).

Egyptian Myths and Mysteries. New York, 1971 (Leipzig, 1908), 155 pp., pb. (5).

Eleven European Mystics. Trans. Karl Zimmer. Introd. Paul M. Allen. Blauvelt, N.Y.: Garber Communications, 1971 (G, 1901; E, 1960), 242 pp., pb [also published as *Mysticism at the Dawn of the Modern Age* (below) and *Mystics of the Renaissance and their Relations to Modern Thought* (below)] (2).

An Esoteric Cosmology. Preface by René Querido. Spring Valley, N.Y.: St. George Book Service, 1978, 133 pp., pb., op.

Esoteric Development: Selected Lectures and Writings from the Work of Rudolf Steiner. Ed. Alice Woulsin. Introd. Alan Howard. New York, 1980, 185 pp., hb., pb., (3).

The Essentials of Education. Trans. Jesse Darrell. London, 1983 (Stuttgart, 1924; E, 1926, 1968), 79 pp., pb. (8).

The Etherisation of the Blood: The Entry of the Etheric Christ into the Evolution of the Earth. Trans. Arnold Freeman and D. S. Osmond. London, 1971 (Basel, 1911), 42 pp., pb. (reprinted in *The Reappearance of Christ in the Etheric*).

Eurythmy as Visible Music. Trans. V. and J. Compton-Burnett. London, 1977 (Dornach, 1924), 150 pp., hb. (previously published as *Eurythmy as Visible Song*. London, 1932, hb.) (9).

Eurythmy as Visible Speech. Trans. V. and J. Compton-Burnett and F. C. Duprovik. London, 1956 (Dornach, 1929), 128 pp., hb., op. (9).

The Evolution of Consciousness as Revealed through Initiation-Consciousness. Trans. V. E. Watkins and John Davy. London, 1979 (Penmaenmawr, Wales, 1923; E, 1966), 198 pp., pb. (previously published as *Evolution of the World and of Humanity*, 243 pp., hb., op.) (5).

Facing Karma. Trans. Dietrich V. Asten. New York, 1975 (Vienna, 1912). 20 pp., pb.

The Festivals and Their Meaning: Christmas, Easter, Ascension and Pentecost, Michaelmas. Trans. D. S. Osmond et al. London, 1981 (G, 1905–24; E, 1955–67), 399 pp., pb. (4).

Festivals of the Seasons (19 lectures). Ed. H. Collison. London, 1928. (G, 1907–1926), 198 pp., hb., op.

The Fifth Gospel. Trans. Charles Davy and D. S. Osmond. London, 1968 (Oslo and Cologne, 1913), 166 pp., hb., op. (6).

First Scientific Lecture Course: Light. 2 vols. Trans. George Adams. Foreword by Guenther Wachsmuth. Forest Row, Sussex, England: Steiner Schools Fellowship, 1949 (Stuttgart, 1919–20), 107 pp., pb.

The Foundation Stone: The Laying of the Foundation Stone of the General Anthroposophical Society. Trans. George Adams. London, 1977 (G, 1923–24), 72 pp., op.

Foundations of Esotericism. Trans. Vera and Judith Compton-Burnett, London, 1982, 286 pp., hb.

Four Mystery Dramas: The Portal of Initiation, The Soul's Probation, The Guardian of the Threshold, and The Soul's Awakening. Trans. Ruth and Hans Pusch. North Vancouver, B.C., Canada: Steiner Book Centre, 1973, 564 pp., pb. (9).

The Four Seasons and the Archangels: Experience of the Course of the Year in Four Cosmic Imaginations. Revised trans. Charles Davy and D. S. Osmond, London, 1968 (Dornach, 1923; E, 1947), 95 pp., hb., op.

The Four Temperaments. New York, 1971 (G, 1908–09; E, 1944), 59 pp., pb. (8).

Friedrich Nietzsche: Fighter for Freedom. Trans. Margaret Ingram de-Ris. Introd. Paul M. Allen. Bleuvelt, N.Y.: Garber Communications, 1960 (G, 1895), 222 pp., hb., pb., op. (2).

From Buddha to Christ. Ed., rev. trans. Gilbert Church. New York, 1978 (G, 1909–12), 103 pp., pb., (5).

From Jesus to Christ. London, 1973 (Karlsruhe, 1911), 184 pp., pb. (6).

From Symptom to Reality in Modern History. Trans. A. H. Parker. London, 1976 (G, 1918), 246 pp., hb. (5).

Fundamentals of Therapy: An Extension of the Art of Healing Through Spiritual Knowledge, with Ita Weyman. Trans. George [Kaufman] Adams. London, 1967 (G, 1925; E, 1925), 159 pp., hb., op. (10).

Genesis: Biblical Secrets of Creation—The Six Days' Work in the First Book of Moses. Foreword by Marie Steiner. London, 1983 (Munich, 1910; E, 1944), 140 pp., pb. (5).

Goethe as the Founder of a New Science of Aesthetics. Trans. G. Metaxa. London, 1922, 30 pp., hb., op. (9).

Goethe's Conception of the World. Trans. H. Collison. New York, 1928. 193 pp., hb., op. (2).

Goethe's Secret Revelation and the Riddle of Faust. London, 1933 (Berlin, 1908–1909), 135 pp., hb., op.

Goethe's Standard of the Soul as Illustrated in "Faust" and in the Fairy Story of "The Green Snake and the Beautiful Lily." Trans. D. S. Osmond. London, 1925, 53 pp., hb. (reprinted in *The Portal of Initiation,* below). (9).

Goethe the Scientist. Trans. Olin D. Wannamaker. New York, 1950 (G, 1882–97; 1926), 280 pp., hb., op. (2).

The Gospel of St. John. Trans. Maud B. Monges. Introd. Marie Steiner. New York, 1962 (Hamburg, 1908), 192 pp., pb. (6).

The Gospel of St. John and Its Relations to the Other Three Gospels. Trans. Samuel and Loni Lockwood: rev. trans., Maria St. Goar. Introd. Stewart C. Easton. New York, 1982 (Kassel, 1909), 289 pp., hb., pb. (6).

The Gospel of St. Luke. Trans. D. S. Osmond and Owen Barfield. London, 1964 (Basel, 1909), 203 pp., hb., pb. (6).

The Gospel of St. Mark. Trans. Erna McArthur. New York, 1950 (Basel, 1912), 195 pp., hb., op. (6).

The Gospel of St. Matthew. Trans. and ed. Dorothy Osmond and Mildred Kircaldy, London, 1965 (Berne, 1910), 237 pp., hb., op. (6).

Guidance in Esoteric Training. Rev. trans. Charles Davy and Owen Barfield. London, 1972, 108 pp., hb., op.

Health and Illness: Nine Lectures to the Workmen at the Goetheanum, 1922–23, Vol. 1. Trans. Maria St. Goar. New York, 1981, 155 pp., pb.; Vol 2. Trans. Maria St. Goar. New York, 1983, 165 pp., pb. (10).

Human and Cosmic Thought. Trans. Charles Davy. London, 1967 (Berlin, 1914), 70 pp., hb., op.

Human Values in Education. Trans. Vera Compton-Burnett. New York, 1969 (Arnheim, 1924), 189 pp., hb., op. (8).

In the Changed Conditions of the Times. Trans. Olin D. Wannamaker. New York, 1941, 122 pp., hb., op. (reissued as *The Challenge of the Times,* above.

The Influences of Lucifer and Ahriman: Man's Responsibility for the Earth. Trans. D. S. Osmond. North Vancouver, B.C.: Steiner Book Centre, 1976 (G, 1919; E, 1954), 83 pp., pb. (4).

The Influence of Spiritual Beings Upon Man. New York, 1982 (Berlin, 1908; E, 1961), 191 pp., pb. (3, 4).

Initiate Consciousness. See *True and False Paths in Spiritual Investigation*, below.

Initiation, Eternity and the Passing Moment. New York, 1980 (Munich, 1912), 157 pp., hb. (3).

The Inner Aspect of the Social Question. Trans. Charles Davy. London, 1974 (Zurich, 1919; E, 1950), 71 pp., pb., op. (7).

The Inner Realities of Evolution. London, 1953 (Berlin, 1911), 88 pp., hb., op. (previously published as *Evolution in the Aspect of Realities*) (4).

An Introduction to Eurythmy. Trans. Gladys Hahn. New York, 1983, 90 pp., pb.

The Karma of Vocation in Connection with the Life of Goethe. Ed. Marie Steiner. Trans. Olin D. Wannamaker. New York, 1944 (Dornach, 1916), 214 pp., hb., op. (scheduled to be reprinted in 1985) (3).

Karmic Relationships: Esoteric Studies. 8 vols. Trans. George Adams, M. Cotterell, Charles Davy, and D. S. Osmond. London, 1955–72 (G, 1923–24), hb. (2, 3).

The Kingdom of Childhood. Trans. Helen Fox. London, 1982 (Torquay, 1924; E, 1924), 155 pp., pb. (8).

Knowledge of the Higher Worlds: How Is It Achieved? Trans. D. S. Osmond and Charles Davy. London, 1976 (G, 1904; E, 1909), 222 pp., pb. (also published as *Knowledge of the Higher Worlds and Its Attainment,* below) (1, 3).

Knowledge of the Higher Worlds and Its Attainment. Trans. Henry B. and Lisa D. Monges. New York, 1947 (G, 1904; E, 1947), pp., 272, hb., pb, (also published as *Knowledge of the Higher Worlds: How Is It Achieved?* above) (1, 3).

A Lecture on Eurythmy. London, 1926 (Penmaenmawr, Wales, 1923), 36 pp., pb.

Lectures to Teachers. Trans. D. Harwood. London, 1948 (Dornach, 1921, E, 1923) 95 pp., hb., op.

Life Between Death and Rebirth: The Active Connection between the Living and the Dead. Trans. René Querido. New York, 1968 (G, 1912–13), 308 pp., pb. (3).

The Life between Death and Rebirth in Relation to Cosmic Facts. London, 1930 (Berlin, 1912–13), 129 pp., hb, op (reprinted as *Between Death and Rebirth*, London, 1975, above) (3).

The Life, Nature, and Cultivation of Anthroposophy: Letters to Members Trans. George Adams. London, 1975 (G, 1924; E, 1963), 62 pp., pb. (11).

The Lord's Prayer. New York, 1977 (Berlin, 1907), 26 pp., pb.

Love and Its Meaning in the World. Trans. D. S. Osmond and F. Gerry. London, 1972 (Zurich, 1912), 27 pp., pb., op.

Macroscosm and Microcosm. London, 1968 (Vienna, 1910), 207 pp., hb., op. (4).

Man and the World of the Stars; The Spiritual Communion of Mankind. Trans. D. S. Osmond. New York, 1982 (Dornach, 1922), 189 pp., pb. (4).

Man as a Being of Sense and Perception. Trans. Dorothy Lenn. North Vancouver, B.C.; Steiner Book Centre, 1981 (Dornach, 1921; E, 1958), 53 pp., pb.

Man as a Being of Spirit and Soul. Blauvelt, N.Y.: Garber Communications, 1964, 91 pp., hb., op.

Man as Symphony of the Creative Word. Trans. Judith Compton-Burnett. London, 1978 (Dornach, 1923; E, 1945), 224 pp., pb. (4).

Man: Hieroglyph of the Universe. Trans. George and Mary Adams. London, 1972 (Dornach, 1920), 222 pp., hb., op.

Man in the Light of Occultism, Theosophy and Philosophy. London, 1964 (Oslo, 1914; E, 1945), 212 pp., hb., op.

Man in the Past, The Present and the Future. Trans. E. Goddard. London, 1982 (Stuttgart, 1923; E, 1966), 78 pp., pb. (includes "The Sun-Initiation of the Druid Priest and His Moon-Science" on pp. 65–78.

Manifestations of Karma. London, 1976 (Hamburg, 1910; E, 1924), 220 pp., pb., op. (available in U.S. only on special order because poorly bound) (3).

Man's Being, His Destiny, and World Evolution. 2nd ed. Trans. Erna McArthur. New York, 1966 (Oslo, 1923), 122 pp., hb., op. (4).

Man's Life on Earth and in the Spiritual World. London, 1952 (London, 1922), 116 pp., hb., op. (reprinted as *Planetary Spheres and Their Influence on Man's Life on Earth and in Spiritual Worlds*, below).

Metamorphoses of the Soul. Ed. H. Collison. Trans. G. Metaxa. Preface by Marie Steiner. New York, n.d. (Berlin, 1909–10), 222 pp., hb., op.

Methods of Spiritual Research. Blauvelt, N.Y.: Garber Communications, 1973, 128 pp., pb (3).

Michaelmas and the Soul-Forces of Man. Trans. Samuel and Loni Lockwood. New York, 1982 (Vienna, 1923; E, 1946), 69 pp., pb. (previously published as *Anthroposophy and the Human Gemüt*).

The Mission of Christian Rosenkreutz: Its Character and Purpose. Trans.

Dorothy Osmond. Introd. Marie Steiner. London, 1950 (G, 1911–12), 189 pp., hb., op.; includes "Rosicrucianism and Modern Initiation." Trans. Mary Adams (Dornach 1924), pp. 91–189.

The Mission of the Archangel Michael. Trans. Lisa D. Monges. New York, 1961 (G, 1918–19), 154 pp., hb., pb. (4, 7).

The Mission of the Individual Folk Souls in Relations to Teutonic Mythology. Trans. A. H. Parker. London, 1970 (Oslo, 1910; E, 1929), 189 pp., hb., op. (5).

A Modern Art of Education. Rev. trans. Jesse Darrell. London, 1972 (Ilkley, Yorkshire, 1923), 232 pp., hb., pb. (previously published as *The New Art of Education*) (8).

Mystery Knowledge and Mystery Centers. Trans. E. H. Goddard and D. S. Osmond. London, 1973 (Dornach, 1923), 206 pp., hb. (5).

The Mystery of the Trinity. Trans. George Adams and Dorothy Osmond. London, 1947 (Dornach, 1922), 47 pp., pb., op.

The Mysteries of the East and of Christianity. Rev. trans. Charles Davy. London, 1972 (Berlin, 1913), 77 pp., pb., op. (5).

The Mysteries of Light, of Space and of the Earth. Trans. Francis E. Dawson. London, 1945 (Dornach, 1919), 70 pp., hb., op.

Mysticism at the Dawn of the Modern Age. Trans. Karl Zimmer. Intro. Paul M. Allen. Blauvelt, N.Y.: Garber Communications, 1960, 256 pp., hb. (also published as *Eleven European Mystics*, above) (2).

Mystics of the Renaissance and Their Relation to Modern Thought. Trans. Bertram Keightley New York, n.d., hb., pp. op. (see *Eleven European Mystics*, above) (2).

The Nature of Anthroposophy. Blauvelt, N.Y.: Garber Communications, 1964, 116 pp., hb., op.

Nine Lectures on Bees. (Given to the Workmen at the First Goetheanum). 2nd ed. Trans. M. Pease and C. A. Mier. Spring Valley, New York: St. George Publications, 1975, 91 pp., diagrams, pb.

Occult History: Historical Personalities and Events in the Light of Spiritual Science. Trans. D. S. Osmond and Charles Davy. London, 1982 (Stuttgart, 1910–11; E, 1957), 123 pp., pb., op.

The Occult Movement in the Nineteenth Century and Its Relations to Modern Culture. Trans. D. S. Osmond. London, 1973 (Dornach, 1915), 190 pp., hb.

An Occult Physiology. Rev. ed. London, 1951 (Prague, 1911), 208 pp., hb., op. (10).

Occult Reading and Occult Hearing. Trans. D. S. Osmond. London, 1975 (Dornach, 1914), 79 pp., pb.

Occult Science—An Outline. Trans. Maud and Henry B. Monges. Rev.

trans. Lisa D. Monges. New York, 1972 (G, 1909), 388 pp., hb., pb.; Trans. George and Mary Adams. London, 1969 (E, 1922), 350 pp., pb. (3, 4).

The Occult Significance of the Bhagavad Gita. Trans. George and Mary Adams with Doris M. Bugbey. New York, 1968 (Helsingfors, 1913), 142 pp., hb., op. (5).

Overcoming Nervousness. Trans. René Querido and Gilbert Church. New York, 1978 (Munich, 1912; E, 1969), 19 pp., pb.

Paths of Experience: On Prayer, Mysticism, Laughing and Weeping and Other Experiences of the Soul. London, 1934 (Berlin, 1909–10), 236 pp., hb., op.

Paths to Knowledge of Higher Worlds. North Vancouver, B.C., Canada: Steiner Book Centre, 1970 (Oslo, 1921), 36 pp., pb.

The Philosophy of Freedom: The Basis for a Modern World Conception. Trans. Michael Wilson. London, 1970, 230 pp., hb., pb. (also published as *Philosophy of Spiritual Activity*, below) (2, 7).

The Philosophy of Spiritual Activity. Trans. Rita Stebbing. Ed. Paul M. Allen. Blauvelt, N.Y.: Garber Communications, 1963, 302 pp., hb., pb. (2).

The Philosophy of Spiritual Activity (and *Truth and Knowledge*). Trans. Rita Stebbing. New York, 1963, (G, 1894; E, 1921), 418 pp., hb., op (also published as *The Philosophy of Freedom*, above) (2).

Planetary Spheres and Their Influence on Man's Life on Earth and in Spiritual Worlds. Trans. George and Mary Adams. London, 1982 (London, 1922) 121 pp., pb. (previously titled *Man's Life on Earth and in the Spiritual World*. London, 1952) (4).

The Portal of Initiation: A Rosicrucian Mystery. Trans. Adam Bittleston, with essays by Paul M. Allen, Hans Pusch, and Adam Bittelston. Blauvelt, N.Y.: Garber Communications, 1961, 260 pp., hb., op. (9).

Poetry and the Art of Speech. Trans. Julia Wedgwood and Andrew Welburn. London: School of Speech Formation, Rudolf Steiner House, 35 Park Road, 1981 (Dornach, 1920), 299 pp., typescript, pb. (9).

Practical Advice to Teachers. Trans. Johanna Collis. London, 1976 (Stuttgart, 1919), 205 pp., hb., pb. (previously published as *Practical Course for Teachers*. New York, 1957, op.) (8).

Practical Training in Thought. New York, 1977 (Karlsruhe, 1909; E, 1949), 25 pp., pb.

Pre-Earthly Deeds of Christ. North Vancouver, B.C., Canada: Steiner Book Centre, 1976 (Pforzheim, 1914), 16 pp., pb. (6).

Psychoanalysis in the Light of Anthroposophy. *Trans. May Laird-Brown. London, 1946 (G, 1912–21), 91 pp., hb., op.*

The Reappearance of Christ in the Etheric. Ed. Gilbert Church and Alice Wulsin. Introd. René Querido. New York, 1983, 234 pp., hb., pb. (6).

The Redemption of Thinking: A Study in the Philosophy of Thomas Aquinas. Trans. ed., introd. A. P. Shepherd and Mildred Robertson Nicoll. New York, 1983, pb. (originally, London: Hodder & Stoughton, 1956 (G, 1920), 191 pp., hb.) (5).

Reincarnation and Immortality. New York: Harper & Row, 1982, 204 pp., pb.; Blauvelt, N.Y.: Garber Communications, 1970, 204 pp., hb., pb., op. (3).

Reincarnation and Karma/How Karma Works. Trans. Lisa D. Monges. New York, 1962, 57 pp., pb., op.

Reincarnation and Karma: Their Significance in Modern Culture. North Vancouver, B.C.: Steiner Book Centre, 1977 (G, 1912; E, 1960), 94 pp., pb. (3).

The Renewal of Education through the Science of the Spirit. Trans. Roland Everett. Michael Hall, Forest Row, East Sussex, England: Kolisko Archive Publications, 1981 (G, 1920), 217 pp., pb. (8).

Results of Spiritual Investigation. Blauvelt, N.Y.: Garber Communications, 1973, 121 pp., pb., op. (3).

Riddles of Philosophy. Introd. Fritz Koelln. New York, 1973 (G, 1974), 479 pp., hb., pb. (5).

A Road to Self-Knowledge and The Threshold of the Spiritual World. Trans. H. Collison and M. Cotterell. London, 1975 (G, 1912; E, 1918), 173 pp., hb., pb. (3).

The Roots of Education. Trans. Helen Fox. London, 1983 (Bern, 1924; E, 1968), 94 pp., pb. (8).

Rosicrucian Esotericism. Trans. D. S. Osmond. New York, 1978 (Budapest, 1909), 122 pp., hb.

Rosicrucianism and Modern Initiation: Mystery Centres of the Middle Ages. Trans. Mary Adams. London, 1965, 1982 (Dornach, 1924; E, 1950), 93 pp., pb.

Schiller and Our Times. Ed. H. Collison. London, 1938 (Berlin, 1905) 104 pp., hb., op.

The Secrets of the Threshold. New York, 1928 (Munich, 1913), 109 pp., hb., op. (4).

The Significance of Spiritual Research for Moral Action. Trans. Alan P. Cottrell. New York, 1981 (Bielefeld, 1911), 17 pp., pb.

Social and Anti-Social Forces in the Human Being. Rev. trans. Christopher Schaefer. Spring Valley, N.Y.: Mercury Press, 1982, 29 pp., pb.

A Social Basis for Primary and Secondary Education. New York: Waldorf Institute, Adelphi University, 1975, 43 pp., pb. (8).

The Social Future. 3rd ed. Trans. Henry B. Monges. New York, 1972 (Zurich, 1919; E, 1935), 151 pp., pb. (7).

Speech and Drama. Trans. Mary Adams. Foreword by Marie Steiner. London, 1960 (Dornach, 1924), 419 pp., hb., op.

The Spirit of Fichte Present in Our Midst. Trans. Beresford Kemmis. London, n.d., 75 pp., hb., op.

The Spiritual Beings in the Heavenly Bodies and in the Kingdoms of Nature. North Vancouver, B.C., Canada: Steiner Book Centre, 1981 (G, 1912; E, 1951), 210 pp., pb. (4).

The Spiritual Foundation of Morality: Francis of Assisi and the Mission of Love. North Vancouver, B.C.: Steiner Book Centre, n.d. (G, 1912), 90 pp., pb. (previously published as *Anthroposophical Ethics*. London, 1955 (3).

The Spiritual Ground of Education. Trans. D. Harwood. London, 1947 (Oxford, 1922), 136 pp., hb., op.

The Spiritual Guidance of Man. Ed. Henry B. Monges. New York, 1983, 85 pp., pb. (previously published as *The Spiritual Guidance of Man and Humanity*, 1950) (3, 5).

The Spiritual Hierarchies and Their Reflection in the Physical World: Zodiac, Planets, Cosmos. Trans. René Querido. New York, 1983 (G, 1909), 144 pp., pb. (4).

Spiritual Research: Methods and Results. Trans. Paul M. Allen, Adam B. Aleston, Michael and Elisabeth Tapp. Ed. Paul M. Allen. Blauvelt, N.Y.: Garber Communications, 1981, 271 pp., hb., pb., op.

Spiritual Science and Medicine. London, 1975 (Dornach, 1920; E, 1948), 273 pp., pb., op. (10).

Spiritual Science and the Art of Healing. London, 1950 (Arnheim, 1924), 83 pp., pb., op.

The Stages of Higher Knowledge. Rev. trans. Lisa D. Monges and Floyd McKnight. Preface by Marie Steiner. New York, 1981 (G, 1906; E, 1961), 58 pp., pb. (originally translated as *The Gates of Knowledge*, 1916) (3).

The Study of Man: General Education Course. Trans. Daphne Harwood, Helen Fox, and A. C. Harwood. London, 1966, 190 pp., hb., pb. (8).

Structure of the Lord's Prayer. Trans. A. H. Parker. London, 1971 (Karlsruhe, 1907), 29 pp., pb.

Supersensible Influences in the History of Mankind with Special Reference to Cult in later Egypt and in Later Times). Trans. D. S. Osmond. London, 1956 (Dornach, 1922), 83 pp., hb., op.

Supersensible Knowledge: Anthroposophy as a Demand of the Age/Anthroposophy and the Ethical-Religious Conduct of Life. Trans. Olin D. Wannamaker. London and New York, 1943 (Vienna, 1923), 58 pp., hb., op.

Supersensible Man. Trans. Mary Adams. London, 1961 (The Hague, 1923), 102 pp., hb. (3).

The Tension between East and West. Trans. B. A. Rowley. Introd. Owen Barfield. London: Hodder & Stoughton, 1963, 183 pp., hb. (previously published as *West and East: Contrasting Worlds*, below) (5).

A Theory of Knowledge Based on Goethe's World Conception. 2nd ed. Trans. Olin D. Wannamaker. New York, 1968 (G, 1886), 131 pp., hb. (previously published as *The Theory of Knowledge Implicit in Goethe's World Conception*).

Theosophy: An Introduction to the Supersensible Knowledge of the World and the Destination of Man. 4th ed. Trans. M. Cotterell and A. P. Shepherd. London, 1970 (G, 1904; E, 1922), 158 pp., hb., pb.; Trans. Henry B. Monges. Rev. trans. Gilbert Church. New York, 1971, 195 pp., hb., pb. (1, 3).

Theosophy of the Rosicrucian. Trans. M. Cotterell and D. S. Osmond. London 1981 (Munich 1907; E, 1954), 168 pp., hb., pb. (3).

Theosophie-Theosophy (German-English edition). Trans. A. P. Shepherd. London and Dornach: Rudolf Steiner Verlag, 1975, 311 pp., pb.

The Threefold Social Order. Rev. trans. Frederick C. Heckel. New York, 1972 (G, 1919; E, 1966), 82 pp., pb.; see *Towards Social Renewal* (7).

Threefolding: A Social Alternative. Preface, trans. Rudolf Lissau. London, 1980 (Oxford, 1922), 54 pp., pb. (7).

Three Lectures on the Mystery Dramas. Trans. Ruth and Hans Pusch. New York, 1983, 99 pp., pb.

Three Streams in the Evolution of Mankind: The Connection of the Luciferic-Ahrimanic Impulses with the Christ-Jahve Impulse. Rev. trans. Charles Davy. London, 1965 (Dornach, 1918), 124 pp., hb., op. (4).

Towards Social Renewal: Basic Issues of the Social Question. Trans. Frank Thomas Smith. London, 1977 (G, 1919; E, 1923), 150 pp., pb. (7).

True and False Paths in Spiritual Investigation. Trans. A. H. Parker. London, 1969 (G, 1924), 222 pp., hb. (previously published as *Initiate Consciousness: Truth and Error in Spiritual Research*. Trans. Olin D. Wannamaker. Foreword and Notes by Marie Steiner. New York, 1928, 180 pp., hb., op.) (4).

Truth and Knowledge: An Introduction to Philosophy of Freedom. Trans. Rita Stebbing. Ed. and Notes Paul M. Allen. Blauvelt, N.Y.: Garber Communications, 1981, 110 pp., hb. (2).

Turning Points in Spiritual History. Trans. Walter F. Knox. Introd. Marie Steiner. London, 1934 (Berlin, 1911–12), 301 pp., hb., op. (5).

Universe, Earth and Man in Their Relationship to Egyptian Myths and Modern Civilization. Introd. Marie Steiner. Rev. trans. M. Cotterell. London, 1955 (G, 1908; E, 1941), 251 pp., hb., op.

Verses and Meditations. Trans. George and Mary Adams. Introd. and Notes, George Adams. London, 1979 (1961), 250 pp., hb. (11).

Waldorf Education for Adolescence: Supplementary Course—The Upper School. Michael Hall, Forest Row, East Sussex, England: Kolisko Archive Publications, 1980 (G, 1921), 107 pp., pb. (8).

Warmth Course. Spring Valley, N.Y.: Mercury Press, 1980 (Stuttgart, 1920), 115 pp., pb.

Ways to a New Style of Architecture. Ed. H. Collison. Foreword by Marie Steiner. London, 1927, 60 pp., hb., op.

West and East: Contrasting Worlds. Trans. Olin Wannamaker. Ed., Foreword, Final Comment by Marie Steiner. Includes "Vienna Days" (pp. 243–50) and "West-East Aphorisms" (pp. 263–72). New York, n.d., hb., op. (see *The Tension between East and West*, above).

The Wisdom of Man, of the Soul, and of the Spirit: Anthroposophy, Psychosophy, Pneumatosophy. New York, 1971 (Berlin, 1909–11), 104 pp., hb.

Wonders of the World, Ordeals of the Soul, Revelations of the Spirit. Trans. Dorothy Lenn and Owen Barfield. New York, 1983 (Munich, 1911; E, 1963) 191 pp., hb., (5).

The Work of the Angels in Man's Astral Body. Trans. D. S. Osmond and Owen Barfield. London, 1972 (Zurich, 1918), 38 pp., pb.

World Economy: The Formation of a Science of World Economics. Trans. Owen Barfield and T. Gordon-Jones. London, 1972 (Dornach, 1922; E, 1936, 1949), 186 pp., hb. (7).

World History in the Light of Anthroposophy as a Foundation for Knowledge of the Human Spirit. Trans. George and Mary Adams with Dorothy Osmond. London, 1977 (G, 1923–24; E, 1950), 157 pp., pb. (5).

The World of the Senses and the World of the Spirit. North Vancouver, B.C.: Steiner Book Centre, 1979 (Hanover, 1912; E, 1947), 88 pp., pb. (4).

The Younger Generation: Educational and Spiritual Impulses for Life in the Twentieth Century. Trans. René Querido. New York, 1967 (Stuttgart 1922), 179 pp., pb. (7).

II. BOOKS BY OTHER AUTHORS

Adams (Kaufman), George. *Fruits of Anthroposophy: An Introduction to the Work of Dr. Rudolf Steiner*. London, 1922, 151 pp., hb., pb., op. (1).

———. *George Adams—Interpreter of Rudolf Steiner: His Life and a Selection of His Essays*. Ed. Olive Whicher. Foreword by Owen Barfield. East Grinstead, Sussex, England: Henry Goulden, Ltd., 1977, 180 pp. hb.

———. *Physical and Ethereal Spaces*. London, 1978 (1965), 71 pp., pb., (10).

——— and Olive Whicher. *The Plant between Sun and Earth and the Sciences of Physical and Ethereal Spaces*. London, 1980 (1952), 71 pb. (10).

Adey, Lionel. *C. S. Lewis's "Great War" with Owen Barfield*. British Columbia: University of Victoria (English Literary Studies Monograph #14), 1978, 136 pp. (5).

Alden, Daisy. *The Art and Craft of Poetry*. N.p.: North River Press, 1981, 120 pp., hb. (9).

Allen, Paul M., ed., with Carlo Pietzner, *A Christian Rosenkreutz Anthology*. Blauvelt, N.Y.: Garber Communications, 1981 (E, 1968), 646 pp., large format, hb.

———, Ed. *Education as an Art* (by Rudolf Steiner and other writers). Blauvelt, N.Y.: Garber Communications, 1970, 126 pp., pb. (8).

———. *Vladimir Soloviev: Russian Mystic*. Blauvelt, N.Y.: Garber Communications, 1978, 544 pp., pb.

———. *The Writings and Lectures of Rudolf Steiner: A Chronological Bibliography*. New York: Whittier Books, 1956, 140 pp., hb., op.

Babbel, Ulrich and Craig Giddens. *Bibliographical Reference List of the Published Works of Rudolf Steiner in English Translation*, Vol. I. London, 1977, 51 pp., pb.; Craig Giddens, Vol. 2, 1979, 131 pp., pb.

Barfield, Owen, ed., trans., introd. *The Case for Anthroposophy* (Selections from *Von Seelensrätseln* by Rudolf Steiner). London, 1970, 91 pp., pb. (5).

_____. *History, Guilt and Habit*. Foreword by G. B. Tennyson. Middletown, Conn.: Wesleyan University Press, 1979, 97 pp., hb. (5).

_____. *History in English Words*. Grand Rapids, Mich.: William B. Eerdmans Publishing Co., 1967, 246 pp., pb.

_____. *Orpheus: A Poetic Drama*. Ed., Afterword, John Ulreich, Jr. West Stockbridge, Mass.: Lindisfarne Press, 1983, 143 pp., pb.

_____. *Poetic Diction: A Study in Meaning*. 3rd ed. Afterword by Author. Middletown, Conn.: Wesleyan University Press, 1973 (1928; 1952), 225 pp., pb. (5) (9).

_____. *The Rediscovery of Meaning, and Other Essays*. Middletown, Conn.: Wesleyan University Press, 1977, 260 pp., hb. (5).

_____. *Romanticism Comes of Age*. London, 1966 (1944), 254 pp., pb. (5).

_____. *Saving the Appearances: A Study in Idolatry*. New York: Harcourt, Brace & World (Harbinger), n.d., 186 pp., pb. (5).

_____. *Speaker's Meaning*. London, 1967, 118 pp., pb. (5).

_____. *Unancestral Voice*. Midletown, Conn.: Wesleyan University Press, 1965, 163 pp., hb. op. (5).

_____. *What Coleridge Thought*. Middletown, Conn.: Wesleyan University Press, 1971, 267 pp., hb. (5).

_____. *Worlds Apart: A Dialogue of the 1960s*. Middletown, Conn.: Wesleyan University Press, 1963, 211 pp., pb. (5).

Benesch, Friedrich. *Ascension*. Trans. Christian von Arnim. Edinburgh, Scotland: Floris Books, 1979 (G, 1974), 47 pp., pb. (6).

_____. *Easter*. Trans. Christian von Arnim. Edinburgh, Scotland: Floris Books, 1981 (G, 1978), 79 pp., pb. (6).

_____. *Whitsun: Community in the Age of Individualism*. Trans. Christian von Arnim. Edinburgh, Scotland: Floris Books, 1979 (G, 1976), 45 pp., pb. (6).

Biezantz, Hagen, et al. *The Goetheanum: Rudolf Steiner's Architectural Impulse*. Trans. Jean Schmid. London, 1979, 130 pp., pb. (9).

Bittleston, Adam. *Our Spiritual Companions; From Angels and Archangels to Cherubim and Seraphim*. Edinburgh, Scotland: Floris Books, 1980, 128 pp. hb. (6).

_____. *The Spirit of the Circling Stars: Human Needs and Cosmic Answers*. Edinburgh, Scotland: Floris Books, 1975, 192 pp. hb.

Blankerburg, Wolfgang, M.D., Karl Ernst Schaefer, M.D., Uwe Stave, M.D., eds. *Individuation Process and Biographical Aspects of Disease*. Vol. 3 Mt. Kisco, N.Y.: Futura Publishing Company, 1979, 233 pp., hb. (10).

Blattman, George. *Radiant Matter: Decay and Consecration*. Edinburgh, Scotland: Floris Books, 1983, 40 pp., pb.

Bock, Emil. *The Apocalypse of St. John*. Trans. Alfred Heidenrich. Edinburgh, Scotland: Floris Books, 1980 (G, 1951; E, 1957), 190 pp., pb. (6).

――――. *Genesis: Creation and the Patriarchs*. Trans. Maria St. Goar. Edinburgh, Scotland: Floris Books, 1983 (G, 1934), 188 pp., hb. pb.(5, 6).

――――. *The Three Years: The Life of Christ between Baptism and Ascension*. Edinburgh, Scotland: Floris Books, 1980 (G, 1948; E, 1955), 285 pp., pb. (6).

Boos-Hamburger, Hilde. *Creative Power of Colour*. London: The Michael Press, 1973 (G, 1941; E, 1961), 61 pp., 8 color plates, pb. (distributed by New Knowledge Books, East Grinstead, Sussex, England) (9).

Bott, Victor. *Anthroposophical Medicine: An Extension of the Art of Healing*. London, 1978 (French 1972), 200 pp., pb. (10).

Budd, Christopher J. *Prelude in Economics: A New Approach to Economics*. West Hoathly, England: Johannus Academy of Sociology and Economics, 1979, 78 pp., pb. (7).

Buhler, Walther. *How to Overcome Sleeplessness*. East Grinstead, Sussex, England: New Knowledge Books, 1971, 56 pp., pb. (10).

――――. *Living With Your Body*. Trans. L. Maloney. London, 1979 (G, 1978), 116 pp., pb.

Capel, Evelyn Frances. *The Making of Christianity and the Greek Spirit*. Edinburgh, Scotland: Floris Books, 1980, 128 pp., pb.

Carlgren, Frans. *Education Towards Freedom*. Ed. Joan and Sigfried Rudel. Prefaces by Rudolf Grosse and Alan Howard. Layout by Arne Klingborg. East Grinstead, Sussex, England: Lanthorn Press, 1976, 208 pp., illustrations (most in color), large format, hb. (8).

――――. *Rudolf Steiner: 1861–1925*. Trans. Joan and Sigfried Rudel. Dornach, Switzerland: The Goetheanum School of Spiritual Science, 1972, 32 illustrations, 80 pp., pb. (1).

――――. *Rudolf Steiner and Anthroposophy*. Trans. Joan and Sigfried Rudel. London, 1979 Reprint, 32 illustrations, 80 pp., pb. (1).

Castelliz, Katherine. *Life to the Land: Guidelines to Bio-Dynamic Husbandry*. East Grinstead, Sussex, England: Lanthorn Press, 1980, 72 pp. pb.

Cloos, Walter. *The Living Earth: The Organic Origin of Rocks and Minerals*. Trans. K. Castelliz and B. Saunders-Davies. Peredur, England: Lanthorn Press, 1977, 160 pp., pb. (10).

Cottrell, Alan P. *Goethe's Faust: Seven Essays*. Chapel Hill, N.C.: The University of North Carolina Press, 1976, 140 pp., hb.

_____. *Goethe's View of Evil and the Search of a New Image of Man in our Time*. Edinburgh, Scotland: Floris Books, 1982, 338 pp., hb.

Creese, Robb. "Anthroposophical Performance." *The Drama Review* (New York University School of the Arts) 22:2 (June 1978): 45–79 (9).

Davenport, Russell. *The Divinity of Man*. Westport, Conn.: Greenwood Press, 1973 (E. 1955), 338 pp., hb.

Davy, Charles. *Towards a Third Culture*. Edinburgh, Scotland: Floris Books, 1978 (E. 1961), 178 pp., pb. (see Charles Waterman, pseudonym for Charles Davy) (7).

Davy, John. "The Movement That Everyone Tries to Forget." *The (London) Times*, Educational Supplement (23 March 1973) (8).

_____. Ed. *Work Arising: From the Life of Rudolf Steiner*. London, 1975, 232 pp., pb. (1, 6, 9, 10).

D'herbois, Collot. *Colour, Part One: A Textbook for the Painting Group "Magenta."* Driebergen: The Netherland's Stichting Magenta, 1979, 100 pp., pb.; Part Two, 1981, 78 pp., pp. (9).

Easton, Stewart C. *And Another Strong Angel: A Study of the Cosmic Mission of the Archangel Michael in Antiquity and Now According to the Teachings of Anthroposophy*. Phoenixville, Penn.: Rudolf Steiner Institute Press, 1979, 78 pp., pb. (4).

_____. *Man and World in the Light of Anthroposophy*. New York, 1983 (1975), 517 pp., hb., pb. (1, 3, 5, 6, 9, 10, 11).

_____. *Rudolf Steiner: Herald of a New Epoch*. New York, 1980, 368 pp., pb. (1, 11).

Edmunds, Francis. *Anthroposophy—A Way of Life*. Hartfield, East Sussex, England: Carnant Books, 1982, 170 pp., pb. (1, 3).

Edwards, Lawrence. *The Field of Form: Research Concerning the Outer World of Living Forms and the Inner World of Geometric Imagination*. Edinburgh, Scotland: Floris Books, 1982, 223 pp., pb. (10).

Ege, Arvia. *The Christmas Foundation Meeting, 1923*. Hillsdale, N.Y.: Adonis Press, 1981, 14 pp., pb. (11).

_____. *The Secret Iron of the Heart: Songs at the Forge of Awakening Man*. Hawthorne Valley-Ghent, N.Y.: Adonis Press, 1982, 182 pp., hb.

Ege, Karl. *An Evident Need of Our Times: Goals of Education at the Close of the Century*. Hillsdale, N.Y.: Adonis Press, 1979, 65 pp., pb.

Fant, Ake, Arne Klingborg, and A. John Wilkes. Introd. Hagen Biesantz. Trans. Erik Westerberg and A. John Wilkes. *Rudolf Steiner's Sculpture in Dornach*. London, 1975 (G. 1969), 85 pp., hb. (9).

_____ with Arne Klingborg, and Rex Raab., *Eloquent Concrete*. London 1979, 180 pp., hb. (9).

Fill, Herbert, M.D. *The Mental Breakdown of a Nation*. New York: Franklin Watts, 1974, 136 pp., hb.

Fisher, Bernhard. *Healing Education Based on Anthroposophy's Image of Man: Living, Learning, Working with Children and Adults in Need of Special Care*. Essays, photographs and guide to healing communities. Trans. C. A. and G. F. Meir. North Vancouver, B.C.: Steiner Book Center, 1974. 227 pp., hb.

Frieling, Rudolf. *Christianity and Islam: A Battle for the True Image of Man*. Edinburgh, Scotland: Floris Books, 1978, 144 pp., hb., pb. (6).

————. *Christianity and Reincarnation*. Trans. Rudolf and Margaret Koehler. Edinburgh, Scotland: Floris Books, 1977 (G, 1974), 117 pp., pb. (3, 6).

————. *Hidden Treasures in the Psalms*. 2nd ed. Trans. M. Cottrell, A. Heidenreich, and E. Hersey. London: Christian Community Press, 1967 (G, 1954), 191 pp., hb.

————. *The Essence of Christianity*. London: Christian Community Press, 1971, 31 pp., pb.

Gardner, John Fentress. *The Experience of Knowledge: Essays on American Education*. Garden City, N.Y.: Waldorf Press, 1975, 222 pp., pb., op.

Giddens, Craig. *Biographical Reference List of Rudolf Steiner's Work in English Translation*. Vol. 2. London, 1979, 131 pp., pb., op.

Glas, Norbert. *Conception, Birth and Early Childhood*. New York, 1972. 142 pp., pb., op. (planned reprint 1984) (10).

————. *The Fulfillment of Old Age*. New York, 1970, 141 pp., hb. (10).

Glas, Werner. *The Waldorf School Approach to History*. New York, 1963, 102 pp., pb.

Goethe, Johann Wolfgang von. *The Metamorphosis of Plants*. Introd. Rudolf Steiner. Illustrations, Dennis Klocek. Wyoming, R.I.: Bio-Dynamic Literature, 1983, SC pp.

Grohmann, Gerbert. *The Plant: A Guide to Understanding its Nature*. Trans. K. Castelliz. London, 1974, 209 pp., hb. (10).

Harwood, A. C., ed. *The Faithful Thinker: Centenary Essays on the Work and Thought of Rudolf Steiner, 1861–1925*. London: Hodder & Stoughton, 1961, 249 pp., hb., op. (1, 10).

————. *The Recovery of Man in Childhood—A Study in the Educational Work of Rudolf Steiner*. New York, 1981, 211 pp., pb.; London: Hodder & Stoughton, 1958, 208 pp., pb. (8).

————. *The Way of a Child: An Introduction to the Work of Rudolf Steiner for Children*. London, 1967 (A, 1940), 144 pp., pb. (8).

Harwood, A. C., Marguerite Lundgren, and Marjorie Raffe. *Eurythmy and the Impulse of Dance*. London, 1974, 63 pp., 34 illustrations, pb. 34 (9).

Hauschka, Rudolf. *Nutrition*. Trans. Marjorie Spock and Mary T. Richards. London: Vincent Stuart and John M. Watkins, 1967 (G, 1951), 212 pp., hb., op.

Heckel, Alice, ed. *The Pfeiffer Garden Book: Bio-Dynamics in the Home Garden*. Intro. Herbert Koepf. Springfield, Ill.: Bio-Dynamic Farming and Gardening Association, 1976 (1967), 190 pp., pb. (10).

Heidenreich, Alfred. *The Book of Revelation*. Ed. Margaret Roberts. Edinburgh, Scotland: Floris Books, 1977, 192 pp., pb.

_____. *Growing Point: The Story of the Foundation of the Movement for Religious Renewal—The Christian Community*. London: Christian Community Press, 1965, 126 pp., hb. (6).

_____. *Healings in the Gospels*. Edinburgh, Scotland: Floris Books, 1980 (G, 1936–1968), 88 pp., pb. (6).

_____. *The Unknown in the Gospel*. London: Christian Community Press, 1972, 150 pp., hb. (6).

Hemleben, Johannes. *Rudolf Steiner: A Documentary Biography*. Trans. Leo Twyman. East Grinstead,, Sussex: Henry Goulden, 1975 (G, 1963), 176 pp., hb., pb.

Hiebel, Frederick. *The Epistles of Paul and Rudolf Steiner's Philosophy of Freedom*. Trans. Alan and Mary Howard. Spring Valley, N.Y.: St. George Publications, 1980 (G, 1955), 98 pp., pb. (6).

_____. *The Gospel of Hellas: The Mission of Ancient Greece and the Advent of Christ*. New York, 1949, 290 pp., hb., op. (5, 6).

Hildebrandt, Gunther, M.D., Norman Macbeth L.L.D., and Karl Ernst Schaefer, M.D., eds. *Basis of an Individual Physiology*. Mt. Kisco, N.Y.: Futura Publishing Company, 1979, 215 pp., hb. (10).

Howard, Alan. *Sex in the Light of Reincarnation and Freedom*. Spring Valley, N.Y.: St. George Publications, 1980, 65 pp., pb.

Huseman, Friedrich, M.D. *Goethe and The Art of Healing: A Commentary on the Crisis in Medicine*. Trans. R. K. MacKaye and A. Goudschaal. New York, n.d., 165 pp., hb., op. (10).

_____. *The Image of Man as the Basis of the Art of Healing*. Trans. Madge Childs. Spring Valley, N.Y.: Mercury Press, 1982 (G, 1950), 235 pp., hb., pb. (10).

_____, and Otto Wolff, M.D. *The Anthroposophical Approach to Medicine: An Outline of a Spiritual-Scientifically Oriented Medicine*. Vol. 1. Trans. Peter Luborsky with Lisa Davisson, New York, 1982, 401 pp., hb. (10).

Jocelyn, Beredene. *Citizens of the Cosmos: Life's Unfolding from Conception through Death to Rebirth*. New York: Continuum, 1981, 186 pp., hb.

Jones, O. E. Faulkner. *The English Spirit*. Introd. Owen Barfield. London, 1982 (E, 1935), 217 pp., hb., pb.

Jones, Michael. *Nuclear Energy: A Spiritual Perspective*. Edinburgh, Scotland: Floris Books, 1983, 40 pp., pb.

Kaufman, George. *See* George Adams.

The Kimnberton Hills Agricultural Calendar for Farmers and Gardeners: A Beginner's Aid for Understanding the Influence of Cosmic Rhythms on the Land. Kimberton, Penn., Kimberton Hills Publications, (1983), 41 pp., published annually, pb. (10).

Kirchner-Bockholdt, Margareta. *Fundamentals of Curative Eurythmy*. Trans. Janet Wood. London, 1977, 200 pp., pb., op.

Knottenbelt. *The Art of Poetry in Light of Anthroposophy*. Trans. Ineka Wiersma. London, 1973, 142 pp., pb., op.

Koch, Elizabeth, and Gerard Wagner. *The Individuality of Colour: Contributions to a Methodical Schooling in the Experience of Colour*. Trans. Peter Stebbing. London, 1980, 107 pp., hb. (9).

Koepf, Herbert H. *What Is Bio-Dynamic Agriculture?* Wyoming, R.I.: Bio-Dynamic Literature, 1976, 44 pp., pb.

————, and L. Jolly, eds. *Readings in Goethean Science*. Wyoming, R.I.: Bio-Dynamic literature, 1978, 62 pp., pb.

————, B. D. Pettersson, and Wolfgang Schaumann. *Bio-Dynamic Agriculture: An Introduction*. New York, 1976, 429 pp., hb. (10).

Kolisko, Eugen, M.D. *Reincarnation and Other Essays*. Introd. N. V. Dagg. Bournemouth, England: Kolisko Archive Publications, 1978 (1940) 195 pp., hb (3).

————, and Lily. *Agriculture of Tomorrow*. Buornemouth, England: Kolisko Archive Publications, 1978, 321 pp., hb.

König, Karl. *Brothers and Sisters: A Study in Child Psychology*. Edinburgh, Scotland: Floris Books, 1980 (E, 1958), 91 pp., pb.

————. *Rudolf Steiner's Calendar of the Soul—A Commentary*. Trans. E. H. Goddard and A. C. Harwood. London, 1977, 101 pp., pb.

————. *The Human Soul*. New York, 1973, 118 pp., pb. (3).

Lauenstein, Deither. *Biblical Rhythms in Biography*. Trans. James H. Hindes. Edinburgh, Scotland: Floris Books, 1983, 40 pp., pb.

Lauer, Hans Erhard. *Aggression and Repression*. London, 1981, 109 pp. hb.

Lehrs, Ernst. *Man or Matter: Introduction to a Spiritual Understanding of Nature on the Basis of Goethe's Method of Training Observation and Thought.* Rev. ed. New York: Harper & Row, 1958, 447 pp., hb., op. (10).

_____. *The Rosicrucian Foundations of the Age of Natural Science.* Spring Valley, N.Y.: St. George Publications, 1976 (E, 1934), 42 pp., pb., op.

Lievegoed, Bernard C. J. *Developing Organizations.* Trans. J. Collis. London: Tavistock Publishing Co., 1973 (Dutch 1970), 258 pp., hb. (distributed by Harper & Row).

_____. *Forming Curative Communities: Lectures to Teachers and Staff in Anthroposophical Curative Schools and Homes.* Trans. S. Briault. London: 1978 (G, 1970), 148 pp., typescript, pb. (7).

_____. *Phases: Crisis and Development in the Individual.* London, 1979, 250 pp., pb.

_____. *Towards the Twenty-first Century.* Ed. R. Goodwin. North Vancouver, B.C., Canada: Steiner Book Centre, 1972, 82 pp., pb.

Linden, Wilhelm zur, M.D. *A Child is Born: Pregnancy, Birth, Early Childhood.* 2nd ed. Trans. J. Collis. London, 1980, 209 pp., pb. (10).

Lytton, Bulwer. *Zanoni.* Blauvelt, N.Y.: Garber Communications, 1971 (1842), 410 pp., pb.

Mayer, Gladys. *Colour and Healing.* East Grinstead, Sussex, England: New Knowledge Books, 1976 (G, 1960), 38 pp., pb. (9).

_____, *Colour and the Human Soul.* East Grinstead, Sussex, England: New Knowledge Books, 1978 (1961), 25 pp., pb. (9).

_____. *The Mystery Wisdom of Colour: Its Creative and and Healing Powers.* East Grinstead, Sussex, England: New Knowledge Books, 1975 (G, 1961), 110 pp., typescript, 29 color illustrations, pb. (9).

Mees, F. C. *Blessed by Illness.* New York, 1983, 242 pp., hb.

Merry, Eleanor C. *Art: Its Occult Basis and Healing Value.* London, 1961, 190 pp., pb.

_____. *Living Metals: Relationship between Man and Metals.* New York: Regency Press, 1974, 125 pp., pb.

Nesfield-Cookson, Bernard. *Rudolf Steiner's Vision of Love.* Wellingborough, Northants, England: Aquarian Press, 1983, 370 pp., pb.

Ogletree, Earl J. *Introduction to Waldorf Education: Curriculum and Methods.* Washington, D.C.: Universities Press of America, 1979, 464 pp., hb.

Palmer, Otto. ed., *Rudolf Steiner on His Book "The Philosophy of Freedom."* Trans. Marjorie Spock. New York, 1975, 123 pp., pb. (2).

Pank, C. J. *Dirt Farmers' Catalogue: Full Discussions About Bio-dynamic Farming*. Sprakus, N.Y.: Bio-dynamic Press, 1976, 133 pp., pb.

Pelikan, Wilhelm. *The Secrets of Metals*. Trans., Charlotte Levensart. New York, 1973, 179 pp., pb.

Pfeiffer, Ehrenfried E. *Bio-Dynamic Farming and Gardening*. Vol. 1. Spring Valley, N.Y.: Mercury Press, 1983, 199 pp., pb.

―――. *Life's Resources and Esoteric Streams of Christianity*. (Two series of lectures at Spring Valley, N.Y.). New York, 1963, 86 pp., pb.

―――. *The Pfeiffer Garden Book: Bio-Dynamics in the Home Garden*. Wyoming, R.I.: Bio-Dynamic Literature, 1976, 204 pp., pb.

―――, and Erika Riese. *Grow a Garden and be Self-sufficient*. Trans. Alice Heckel. Spring Valley, N.Y.: Mercury Press, 1981, 118 pp., pb. (10).

Philbrick, John and Helen. *Gardening for Health and Nutrition: An Introduction to the Method of Bio-Dynamic Gardening Inaugurated by Rudolf Steiner*. Blauvelt, N.Y.: Garber Communications, 1971, 93 pp., pb. (10).

Piening, Ekkehard, and Nick Lyons. eds. *Educating as an Art: Essays on the Rudolf Steiner Method—Waldorf Education*. Introd. Henry Barnes. New York: The Rudolf Steiner School Press, 1979, 183 pp., pb. (8).

Pietzner, Carlo. ed. *Aspects of Curative Education*. Kimberton Hills, PA: The Camphill Movement, 1966, 308 pp., pb.

Poppelbaum, Hermann. *Man and Animal: Their Essential Difference*. London, n.d., 182 pp., hb., op.

―――. *New Light on Heredity and Evolution*. Trans. Norman Macbeth. Spring Valley, N.Y.: St. George Publications, 1977, 84 pp., pb.

―――. *A New Zoology*. Dornach: Philosophisch-Anthroposophischer Verlag, 1961, 192 pp., hb.

Pusch, Hans. *Working Together on Rudolf Steiner's Mystery Dramas*. New York, 1980, 141 pp., pb.

Querido, René. *Creativity in Education: The Waldorf Approach*. San Francisco: H. S. Dakin, 1982, 77 pp., pb. (8).

―――. *Questions and Answers on Reincarnation and Karma*. Spring Valley, N.Y.: St. George Publications, 1977, 31 pp., pb.

Raffe, Marjorie, Cecil Harwood, and Marguerite Lundgren. *Eurythmy and the Impulse of Dance*. London, 1974, 63 pp., 32 illustrations, pb. (9).

Richards, Mary Caroline. *Centering—In Pottery, Poetry and the Person*. Middletown, Conn.: Wesleyan University Press, 1962, 159 pp., hb., pb. (8, 9).

_____. *The Crossing Point: Selected Talks and Writings*. Middletown, Conn.: Wesleyan Univesity Press, 1966, 245 pp., hb., pb. (8, 9).

_____. *Toward Wholeness: Rudolf Steiner Education in America*. Middletown, Conn.: Wesleyan University Press, 1980, 210 pp., hb., pb. (8, 9, 12).

Rittelmeyer, Friedrich. *Meditation: Letters on the Guidance of the Inner Life, According to the Gospel of St. John*. Trans. M. L. Mitchell. Edinburgh, Scotland: Floris Books, 1983 (1960) (G, 1932), 226 pp., hb. (6).

_____. *Reincarnation in the Light of Thought, Religion and Ethics*. Trans. M. L. Mitchell. London: The Christian Community Bookshop, n.d., 144 pp., hb. (6).

_____. *Rudolf Steiner Enters My Life*. Edinburgh, Scotland: Floris Books, 1982 (G, 1963), 150 pp., pb. (6).

Schad, Wolfgang. *Man and Mammals: Toward a Biology of Form*. Trans. Carroll Scherer. Garden City, N.Y.: Waldorf Press, 1977, 309 pp., 183 plates, hb. (10).

Schiller, Paul Eugens. *Rudolf Steiner and Initiation: The Anthroposophical Path of Inner Schooling—A Survey*. Trans. Henry Barnes. New York, 1981, 143 pp., pb. (3).

Schindler, Maria. *Goethe's Theory of Colour*. East Grinstead, Sussex, England: New Knowledge Books, 1964, 210 pp., hb. (9).

Schmidt, Gerhard, M.D. *The Dynamics of Nutrition: The Impulse of Rudolf Steiner's Spiritual Science for a New Nutritional Hygiene*. Vol. I. Wyoming, R.I.: Bio-Dynamic Literature, 1980 (G, 1975), 243 pp., pb. (10).

_____. *Nutrition and Education*. Trans. Mel Belenson. Spring Valley, N.Y.: St. George Publications, 1983, 50 pp., pb.

Schuré, Edouard. *From Sphinx to Christ: An Occult History*. Blauvelt, N.Y.: Garber Communications, 1970, 248 pp., pb. (5).

_____. *The Great Initiates: A Study of the Secret History of Religions*. Trans. Gloria Rasberry. Introd. Paul M. Allen. Blauvelt, N.Y.: Garber Communications, 1977 (French, 1889), 522 pp., pb. (5).

Schwenk, Theodor. *Sensitive Chaos: The Creation of Flowing Forms in Water and Air*. Trans. Olive Whicher and Johanna Wrigley with illustrations by Walter Roggenkamp and preface by Commandant Jacques Y. Cousteau. London, 1965, 144 pp., 88 pp. illustrations, hb.; New York: Schocken Books, 1976, 144 pp., 88 prints, pb. (10).

Seddon, R. G., ed. *The Christmas Foundation Meeting of the Anthroposophical Society: Extracts from Rudolf Steiner's Addresses*. London, 1980, 37 pp., pb.

Shepherd, A. O. *A Scientist of the Invisible: An Introduction to the Life and Work of Rudolf Steiner*. New York: Inner Traditions, 1983 (E. 1954), 218 pp., pb. (1).

Sloan, Douglas. *Insight-Imagination: The Emancipation of Thought and the Modern World*. Westport, Conn.: Greenwood Press, 1983, 272 pp., hb.

Spock, Marjorie. *Eurythmy*. New York, 1980, 137 pp., hb., pb. (8).

————. *Teaching as a Lively Art*. New York, 1978, 137 pp., pb.

Stegman, Carl. *The Other America: The Western World in the Light of Spiritual Science*. Typescript distributed by The Anthroposophic Press, n.d.: I. "The Abilities and Task of America" (69 pp.); II. "Battle and Future" (69 pp.).

Steiner, Rudolf, and Marie Steiner. *Creative Speech: The Nature of Speech Formation*. Trans. Winifred Budgett, Nancy Hummel, and Maisie Jones. London, 1978, 240 pp., hb. (9).

Steiner, Rudolf, and Ita Wegman. *Fundamentals of Therapy: An Extension of the Art of Healing through Spiritual Knowledge*. Trans. George (Kaufman) Adams. New York, 1967 (1928), hb.

Stockmeyer, Karl E. A. *Rudolf Steiner's Curriculum for Waldorf Schools*. Trans. E. Everett-Zade. Forest Row, England: Steiner Schools Fellowship, 1982, 240 pp., pb.

Storl, Wolf D. *Culture and Horticulture: A Philosophy of Gardening*. Wyoming, R.I.; Bio-Dynamic Literature, 1979, 435 pp., pb.

Sugarman, Shirley, ed. *The Evolution of Consciousness: Essays in Honor of Owen Barfield*. Middletown, Conn.: Wesleyan University Press, 1978, 240 pp., hb. (5).

Teachers College Record. "Special Section: Waldorf Education—An Introduction." Ed. Douglas Sloan. New York: Columbia University, Spring 1980, pp. 322–70 (8).

Tomberg, Valentin. *Anthroposophical Studies of the Apocalypse*. Trans. R. H. Bruce. Spring Valley, N.Y.: Candeur Manuscripts, 1980, 50 pp., pb.

————. *Anthroposophical Studies of the New Testament*. Trans. R. H. Bruce. Spring Valley, N.Y.: Candeur Manuscripts, 1981, 188 pp., pb.

————. *Anthroposophical Studies of the Old Testament*. Trans. R. H. Bruce. Spring Valley, N.Y.: Candeur Manuscripts, 1980, 13 sections, wrapped, pb. (5).

————. *The Four Sacrifices of Christ and the Appearance of Christ in the Etheric*. Spring Valley, N.Y.: Candeur Manuscripts, 1983, 89 pp., pb.

————. *Inner Development*. Spring Valley, N.Y.: Candeur Manuscripts, 1983, 103 pp., pb.

Unger, Carl. *The Language of the Consciousness Soul as a Basis for the Study of Rudolf Steiner's "Leading Thoughts."* Ed. Alan and Mary Howard. Spring Valley, New York; St. George Publications, 1983 (G, 1925), 379 pp., large format, boards.

————. *Principles of Spiritual Science*. Introd. Alan Howard. New York, 1976, 80 pp., pb.

————. *Steiner's Theosophy: Notes on the Book "Theosophy."* Spring Valley, N.Y.: St. George Publications, n.d., 79 pp., hb., op. (3).

Ungar, George. *On Nuclear Energy and the Occult Atom*. New York, 1982, 41 pp., pb.

Wachsmuth, Guenther. *Etheric Formative Forces in Cosmos, Earth and Man: A Path of Investigation into the World of the Living*. Trans. Olin D. Wannamaker. London, 1932, 245 pp., hb., op.

————. *The Evolution of Mankind*. Trans. Norman Macbeth. Dornach, Switzerland: Philosophic-Anthroposophic Press, 1961, 208 pp., hb., op. (10).

————. *The Life of Rudolf Steiner from the Turn of the Century to His Death*. 2nd ed. Trans. Olin D. Wannamaker and Reginald E. Raab. New York: Whittier Books, 1955, 594 pp., hb., op. (1).

————. *Reincarnation as a Phenomenon of Metamorphosis*. Trans. Olin D. Wannamaker. New York, 1937, 307 pp., hb., op. (30.

Wannamaker, Olin D. *Rudolf Steiner's Philosophy of Spiritual Activity (Philosophy of Freedom): Man's Freedom of Will—A Student's Introduction and Analysis*. New York, 1963, 93 pp., pb., op. (2).

Waterman, Charles (Charles Davy). *The Three Spheres of Society*. London: Faber and Faber, n.d., 294 pp., hb., op.

Weihs, Thomas. *Children in Need of Special Care*. New York: Schocken Books, 1979, 184 pp., hb. (10).

Werbeck-Svardstrom, Valborg. *Uncovering the Voice: A Path Towards Catharsis in the Act of Singing*. Trans. P. Luborsky. London, 1980, 205 pp., pb., op.

————, ed., *George Adams—Interpreter of Rudolf Steiner: His Life and a Selection of His Essays*. Foreword by Owen Barfield. East Grinstead, Sussex, England: Henry Goulden, Ltd., 1977, 180 pp., pb.

————. *Projective Geometry: Creative Polarities in Space and Time*. London, 1971, 292 pp., hb. (10).

Wilken, Folkart. *The Liberation of Capital*. Trans. David Green. Introd. Alistair Clayre. London: George Allen & Unwin, 1982, 294 pp., hb. (7).

————. *The Liberation of Work: The Elimination of Strikes and Strife in Industry through Associative Organisations of Enterprise.* Intro. E. F. Schumacher. London: Routledge, Kegan Paul, 1969 (G, 1965), 109 pp. (7).

Wilson, Michael. *Goethe's Colour Experiments.* London: The Physical Society, 1958, 111 pp., pb., op.

Winkler, Franz E. *For Freedom Destined: Mysteries of Man's Evolution in the Mythology of Wagner's Ring Operas and Parsifal.* New York: Myrin Institute Books, 1974, 174 pp., pb., hb.

————. *Man: The Bridge Between Two Worlds.* New York: Myrin Institute Books; New York: Harper & Row, 1960, 268 pp., pb.

Witzenmann, Herbert. *Beppe Assenza: Introduction and Aphorisms.* London, 1979, 122 pp., hb. (9).

Wolff, Otto. *Anthroposophically Oriented Medicine and Its Remedies.* Arlesheim, Switzerland: Weleda, 1977 51 pp., pb. (distributed by Mercury Press (10).

Zeylmans van Emmichoven, F. W. *The Anthroposophical Understanding of the Soul.* Trans. Friedmann Schwarzkopf et al. New York, 1983, 170 pp., pb.

————. *The Foundation Stone.* Trans. John Davy. London, 1963, 118 pp., hb., op. (11).

————. *The Reality in Which We Live.* Trans. René Querido. East Grinstead, Sussex, England: New Knowledge Books, 1964, 306 pp., pb.